D1397750

MACMILLAN
PROFILES

Asian American Portraits

Macmillan Reference USA
an imprint of the Gale Group
New York • Detroit • San Francisco • London • Boston • Woodbridge, CT

Macmillan Reference USA
1633 Broadway
New York, NY 10019

Gale Group
27500 Drake Road
Farmington Hills, MI 48331-3535

Printed in Canada

10 9 8 7 6 5 4 3 2 1

Cover design by Mike Logusz

Library of Congress Cataloging - Publication Data
Asian American portraits.
    p.cm – (Macmillan profiles)
    Includes bibliographical references and index.
    ISBN 0-02-865636-9 (hc. : alk.paper)
    1. Asian Americans—Biography. I. Macmillan Reference USA. II. Series.
    E184.O6 A8415 2002
    920'.0092—dc21

                        2001034525

Front cover: clockwise from top: Sarah Chang, David Ho, Kristi Yamaguchi, Benjamin Cayetano. Photo of Chang courtesy of Christian Steiner Photography; photo of Cayetano courtesy of Benjamin Cayetano; photo of Ho courtesy of David Ho; photo of Yamaguchi courtesy of AP/Wide World.

Contents

Macmillan Profiles: *Asian American Portraits* is a unique reference featuring 125 biographies describing notable Americans who were born in, or whose ancestors came from, the countries of the Far East, Southeast Asia, or the Indian subcontinent. Macmillan Reference recognizes the need for reliable, accurate, and accessible biographies of notable figures in American history, science, and culture. The Macmillan Profiles series can help meet that need by providing new collections of biographies that were carefully selected to appeal to young readers and to compliment the middle and high school curriculum.

The 2000 United States census reveals that more than 10 million people of Asian descent live in America. *Asian American Portraits* brings the heritage of this multifaceted community to life by presenting an introduction to the life and times of its artists, entertainers, scientists, writers, politicians, activists, educators, journalists, businesspeople, and athletes. We hope that the remarkable men and women described in this volume can provide role models for intelligent and ambitious young readers, and can instill in them a desire to learn about the history and culture of Asians in America. The article list was based on the following criteria: relevance to the curriculum, importance to history, name recognition for students, and representation of as broad a cultural and occupational range as possible. For the purposes of this book, our definition of "Asian-American" does not include men and women of primarily Middle-Eastern or Pacific Islander descent. Notables from those parts of the world may fill a future volume.

FEATURES

Asian American Portraits is part of Macmillan's **Profiles Series.** To add visual appeal and enhance the usefulness of the volume, the page format was designed to include the following helpful features:

- ■ Timelines: Found throughout the text in the margins, timelines provide a quick reference source for dates and important events in the life and times of these important men and women.

- ■ Notable Quotations: Found throughout the text in the margins, these thought-provoking quotations are drawn from interviews, speeches, and writings of the person covered in the article. Such quotations give readers a special insight into the distinctive personalities of these great men and women.

- Definitions and Glossary: Brief definitions of important terms in the main text can be found in the margin. A glossary at the end of the book provides students with an even broader list of definitions.
- Sidebars: Appearing in shaded boxes throughout the volume, these provocative asides relate to and amplify topics.
- Pull Quotes: Found throughout the text in the margin, pull quotes highlight essential facts.
- Suggested Reading: An extensive list of books and articles about the men and women covered in the volume will help students who want to do further research.
- Index: A thorough index provides thousands of additional points of entry into the work.

Macmillan Profiles: *Asian American Portraits* would not have been possible without the hard-work and creativity of our staff. We offer our sincere thanks to all who helped create this work.

Macmillan Library Reference

Abiko, Kyutaro

1865–1936 ● Newspaper Publisher

Kyutaro Abiko was born in 1865 in the town of Suibara, Japan. He never knew his mother, as she died shortly after he was born. After his mother's death, he was taken in by her parents, who raised him as if he was their own child. Abiko had a strong work ethic from an early age, and worked selling candles and paper to help make money for the family business.

While he did not mind the work, Abiko had bigger dreams than selling candles in a small Japanese town. When he was 17, he joined several friends leaving Suibara and heading for Tokyo, one of the biggest—and busiest—cities in the world. He hoped to stow away on a ship as soon as he arrived in Tokyo and sail to America, but he remained in Tokyo for several years, taking advantage of his time there by taking English classes.

In 1885, Abiko's dream of reaching the United States came true, but because he had waited, he did not have to sail as a stow away. Instead, his journey was sponsored by Fukuinkai, or Gospel Society, of San Francisco. Most Japanese citizens are **Buddhist,** which Abiko had been when he was a young child, but he had converted to **Christianity** in 1883, and became affiliated with a Christian gospel center. Fukuinkai was the first organization of its kind in America; California, especially San Francisco, was a popular destination for Japanese.

When he reached San Francisco, Abiko made living arrangements in an English-speaking home. Despite the fact that he was 20 years old, Abiko enrolled in the Lincoln Grammar

Buddhist individual practicing the religion of Buddhism, a religion of central and eastern Asia derived from the teachings of Gautama Buddha; the central tenent is that suffering is inherent in life, and that one is relieved from suffering by moral and mental self-purification.

Christianity the religion derived from the teachings of Jesus Christ, based on the Holy Bible of scriptures.

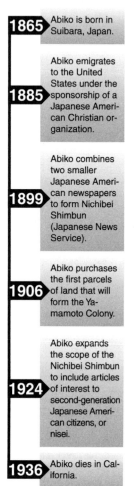

1865 Abiko is born in Suibara, Japan.

1885 Abiko emigrates to the United States under the sponsorship of a Japanese American Christian organization.

1899 Abiko combines two smaller Japanese American newspapers to form Nichibei Shimbun (Japanese News Service).

1906 Abiko purchases the first parcels of land that will form the Yamamoto Colony.

1924 Abiko expands the scope of the Nichibei Shimbun to include articles of interest to second-generation Japanese American citizens, or nisei.

1936 Abiko dies in California.

issei first generation Japanese immigrant to the United States.

School, from which he moved on to the Boys' High School. Upon graduation from high school, Abiko began attending the University of California at Berkeley and became active in the Japanese community. He showed early signs of leadership that would make him a cornerstone of Japanese American society in the years to come, as he quietly became one of the primary leaders of the Methodist wing of Fukuinkai.

Abiko graduated from Berkeley and immediately went into business for himself, first purchasing a laundry business and then opening a restaurant. In 1897, not satisfied with the profits his other endeavors were earning, Abiko purchased a small newspaper, and added a second newspaper in 1899. He decided to combine the two papers and form one, larger newspaper that would serve the Japanese community. Called the *Nichibei Shimbun (Japanese American News)*, the Japanese-language daily would be a force in Japanese-American society for nearly four decades.

As publisher of *Nichibei Shimbun*, Abiko was most concerned with making life in America easier for the first-generation Japanese immigrants, who were known as **issei.** He provided news from Japan and America, and printed information on American social skills and etiquette that the immigrants might not otherwise know. He helped Japanese-American males find brides back in Japan through the system known as "picture brides" because the only contact the men had with the women before they were married was through letters and pictures exchanged in advance of the wedding. Abiko also strongly advocated the importance of getting an education, and he regularly shared his fervent belief that Japanese-Americans would not get ahead in their new country unless they stopped working as migrant laborers and took more permanent jobs or started their own businesses.

Abiko's position as a newspaper publisher earned him a certain degree of political power, which he used when necessary. He persuaded President Theodore Roosevelt to pressure the San Francisco school board to rescind a ruling that forced Japanese students to attend "Oriental School" in the Chinatown section of the city by the bay. In addition, Abiko used his power and wealth in an attempt to found a permanent community for Japanese Christians. To reach that goal, he founded the Nichibei Kangyosha (Japanese American Industrial Company) in 1902 in order to acquire farmland in central California and to create permanent jobs for his followers. Through the company, Abiko provided skilled laborers to many of the developing industries around San Francisco and to agricultural endeavors, including the railroads, sugar refineries, farms, and mining companies.

With the Industrial Company taking care of the economic aspects of his planned community, Abiko formed another company to procure land where his supporters could live. The Bikoku Shikusan Kaisha (American Land and Produce Company) purchased land, primarily in Merced County, outside San Francisco. Abiko founded an agricultural community known as the Yamamoto Colony. He believed that if the Japanese in the Central Valley area of California were going to survive, it would be through farming. He saw this as a much better alternative to the gambling and drinking that was destroying the Japanese immigrants in his area. To launch the colony, Abiko purchased 3,000 acres of land in near the town of Livingston and divided it into 40-acre parcels. He then advertised in his own newspaper and in other local Japanese-language newspapers, offering the land at reasonable terms to any Japanese immigrant who wanted to use it for farming.

At just $35 an acre, the offer was too good for many to turn down. Within two years, there were 30 families farming on the land. By 1940, that number had grown to 69. Money was hard to come by in the early years, as it took time to develop the land and harvest the first crops, but residents looked out for each other and helped out where they could. When one farmer discovered that eggplant grew quickly and earned a decent selling price in San Francisco, she shared her knowledge with the other farmers. Other crops included sweet potatoes, asparagus, tomatoes, and melons.

As more and more people came to the colony, other enterprises arose, although the Land and Produce Company closed due to financial difficulties in 1913. In 1910, farmers formed a food buying cooperative, which was followed four years later by a marketing cooperative. While most Japanese in the United States were Buddhist, those in the Yamamoto Colony were mostly Christian, so a Christian church was built. Later, a Methodist church was built on land that Abiko donated. When the Japanese land owners were interned in detainment camps during World War II, they hired an overseer to take care of their farms so that they would still be there when the war ended. By the 1970s, the Livingston Farmer's Association, the cooperative that oversaw farm production, owned more than 8,500 acres of prime farmland. Primary crops included almonds and peaches. The colony was still in existence as of 2001.

With his dream of founding a Japanese Christian community realized, Abiko turned his attention back to his newspaper. In 1924, he added a section specifically aimed at the group known as **nisei,** which is the term used for the Japanese American children of the issei. Much as he had done for the issei, Abiko published articles on the how American society worked and what etiquette the nisei should use to get ahead in the United States. In 1926, Abiko used his power and wealth to begin sponsoring immigrants to move to San Francisco.

nisei children of the issei.

Abiko continued his **philanthropic** and business endeavors during the final years of his life. He was well-liked and respected in the Japanese-American community, and many people were indebted to him for the assistance he had provided. When Abiko died in 1936, he was survived by his wife, Yona Tsuda Suto, who ran the Nichibei Shimbun until it folded in 1942 after nearly all Japanese Americans living in California were interned in detention camps at the outbreak of World War II. ◆

philanthropic generous; charitable.

Akaka, Daniel

SEPTEMBER 11, 1924– ● POLITICIAN

The first elected United States senator of native Hawaiian ancestry, Daniel Akaka played a prominent role in the political life of Hawaii as the director of the Hawaii Office of Economic Opportunity (1971-1974), the head of the Progressive Neighborhoods Program (1975-1976), the United States Congressmen from the Second Congressional District of Hawaii (1977-1990), and as a U.S. Senator since 1990.

Daniel Kahikina Akaka was born on September 11, 1924, in Honolulu, Hawaii, to parents of Chinese and Hawaiian descent. He attended high school at the Kamehameha School for Boys. After graduating in 1942, he worked briefly as a welder before joining the U.S. Army, serving as a welder in 1943 and 1944 and a mechanic in the Army Corps of Engineers on Saipan and Tinian from 1945-47. He served as a first mate on the schooner *Morning Star* in 1948 and then enrolled in the

University of Hawaii, graduating with a Bachelor of Education degree in 1952. After receiving his Professional Certificate in Secondary Education in 1953, Akaka spent the next seven years as an elementary school teacher.

Seeking to enter school administration, Akaka received his Professional Certificate in School Administration in 1961 and worked as a vice-principal from 1960 to 1963 and as a principal from 1963 to 1968. Akaka crowned his academic studies in 1966 with a master's degree in Education. His distinguished record as a school administrator led Akaka to his first government post in 1969, when he became the chief program planner for the Department of Education for the state of Hawaii. After two years in that position, Akaka became the director of Hawaii's Office of Economic Opportunity for three years.

Daniel Akaka

In 1975 Akaka was elevated in the state **bureaucracy** when the governor appointed him special assistant for human resources and, later that year, director of the state's Progressive Neighborhoods Program. Now firmly dedicated to a career in government service, Akaka felt ready to make the leap from appointive to elective service and ran successfully for the U.S. Congress from Hawaii's Second Congressional District in 1976. After winning seven consecutive elections by wide margins, Akaka was appointed to the U.S. Senate in 1990 to fill the vacancy created by the death of Spark M. Matsunaga. After serving out the remaining four years of Matsunaga's term, Akaka was re-elected in 1994 and again in 2000, the second time with more than 70 percent of the popular vote.

Akaka became one of the most versatile and effective legislators in the Senate, serving with distinction on several key committees: Armed Services, Energy and Natural Resources, Governmental Affairs, Veterans' Affairs, Indian Affairs, and the Select Committee on Ethics. Representing a state richly endowed with natural beauty, he was a tireless proponent of key

bureaucracy the organization of non-elected government workers and officials.

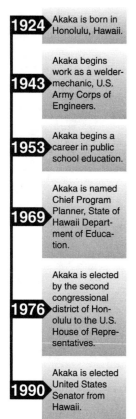

1924 Akaka is born in Honolulu, Hawaii.

1943 Akaka begins work as a welder-mechanic, U.S. Army Corps of Engineers.

1953 Akaka begins a career in public school education.

1969 Akaka is named Chief Program Planner, State of Hawaii Department of Education.

1976 Akaka is elected by the second congressional district of Honolulu to the U.S. House of Representatives.

1990 Akaka is elected United States Senator from Hawaii.

purview the range or limit of one's authority to act.

environmental legislation, including renewable energy research and development, park and wildlife preservation, tropical agriculture and coral reef conservation, subsidies for ocean sciences and technology, aquaculture research, and marine protection.

Senator Akaka's **purview** extended to critical matters of national security in his role as ranking member of the Governmental Affairs Committee International Security, Proliferation, and Federal Services Subcommittee, on which he championed a workable and cost-effective national missile defense system, better controls on technologically sensitive dual-use exports, and improved supervision of the handling of classified materials at the nation's nuclear weapons research laboratories. He was one of the staunchest supporters of the Comprehensive Nuclear Test Ban Treaty and strove to curb the spread of nuclear weapons to other nations. Akaka recently joined the Armed Services Committee, where he played a key role in representing Hawaii's robust defense industries. He also was a persistent advocate of improved services and employment opportunities for veterans of the armed forces.

Senator Akaka worked forcefully for the rights of indigenous peoples, especially through his efforts to promote communication between native Hawaiians and the federal government, and in his role as chairman of the Hawaii Congressional Task Force on Native Hawaiian Issues. He initiated the General Accounting Office's investigation of immigration policy in the Northern Mariana Islands and supported the State Department's efforts to curb the traffic in sex slaves throughout the globe.

Daniel Akaka married Mildred Chong in 1948. They had four children, fourteen grandchildren, and one great-grandson. ◆

Akiyoshi, Toshiko

DECEMBER 18, 1929– ● JAZZ BANDLEADER AND MUSICIAN

Toshiko Akiyoshi was born on December 18, 1929, to a wealthy Japanese family living in Manchuria, China. She was the fourth of four daughters. Her father, who was involved with Japanese Noh drama, encouraged his daughters to become involved in the arts. They took lessons in ballet, traditional Japanese dancing, and piano. Akiyoshi began piano lessons at age six and was soon playing classical music.

The family moved to Beppu, Japan, in 1947, because the conditions in Manchuria had become less hospitable to Japanese families. During World War II, there were many U.S. soldiers in the area, and Akiyoshi soon had her first exposure to **jazz** music. The song that reportedly inspired her love of jazz was "Sweet Lorraine" by Teddy Wilson. Akiyoshi decided that she would like to play jazz herself. Even though her father had previously encouraged her to play music, he was unhappy about her new love of jazz, feeling that it was not appropriate for a traditional Japanese woman to play jazz music. It was the first time Akiyoshi would come up against this kind of attitude, but it would not be the last.

Toshiko Akiyoshi at the piano.

Akiyoshi defied her father and pursued her love anyway. One day she was walking by one of the many dance halls set up in their resort town for the occupying soldiers and Akiyoshi saw a sign up that said, "Pianist wanted." Even though Akiyoshi's background was in classical music, she got the job, and justified the job to her father by saying that she would just work at the club until the school year started. But when the school year started, she kept on working.

Akiyoshi soon outgrew her small town and moved to Tokyo. By 1952, she had formed her own group. In those days, jazz musicians who were touring would stop by the club in which she was playing and sit down to **jam** together. Akiyoshi met many of the great musicians of the day, including the pianist Oscar Peterson. Peterson immediately recognized Akiyoshi's talent and told his colleague Norman Granz about her. Granz signed her up for a record deal and she recorded her first album for him. On the record, she was backed by Peterson's rhythm section.

jam improvisational playing by musicians who may not be familiar with one another.

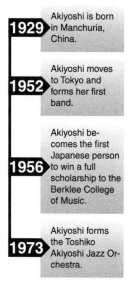

1929 Akiyoshi is born in Manchuria, China.

1952 Akiyoshi moves to Tokyo and forms her first band.

1956 Akiyoshi becomes the first Japanese person to win a full scholarship to the Berklee College of Music.

1973 Akiyoshi forms the Toshiko Akiyoshi Jazz Orchestra.

"That's my mission: to integrate Japanese musical culture with jazz—and do it in a way that sounds natural, even if it sounds different." Toshiko Akiyoshi, Electronic Mail & Guardian, September 11, 1997

kimono a traditional Japanese long robe with wide sleeves and worn with a broad sash.

The record led to Akiyoshi's acceptance to the prestigious Berklee College of Music, in Boston, Massachusetts, in 1956. She was the first Japanese person, male or female to get a scholarship to study there. She graduated in 1959 and began playing shows by herself or with small bands. She played with many of the great musicians of the day, including Miles Davis, Oscar Pettiford and Max Roach, in the local Boston clubs. Also in 1959, she married a saxophonist named Charlie Mariano and had a daughter, Michiru. The two later divorced.

In the 1960s Toshiko continued to gain renown. She played in New York and Tokyo with musicians like Charles Mingus. In 1969, she married a saxophone player and flutist named Lew Tabackin. The couple moved to Los Angeles in 1972 when Tabackin got a job on "The Tonight Show." There, Akiyoshi began to develop her talents in composing and arranging music. The two formed a "rehearsal" band, which eventually became the Toshiko Akiyoshi Jazz Orchestra.

The marriage was a great success both professionally and personally. Their first record with the group, *Kogun* became a top selling big band jazz album and the band continued to gain a good reputation worldwide. Akiyoshi became known as an arranger in the style of Duke Ellington because she changed the music to conform with the particular talents of each musician. Her band has received 14 Grammy nominations and Akiyoshi became the first woman to win *Downbeat* magazine's Best Arranger/Composer award. She was the subject of a documentary called "Jazz in My Native Language," in 1982. In 1996, she finished her autobiography, *Life With Jazz*. The book has been extremely popular in Japan.

During Akiyoshi's life, she repeatedly felt the effects of racism and sexism. Akiyoshi found that some of the musicians she hired were uncomfortable taking directions from a woman, especially a barely five-foot tall Japanese woman. Instead of feeling inferior, Akiyoshi realized that the musicians who were most uncooperative tended to be the less talented ones who felt most threatened by her. When she first arrived in the United States, people could not seem to believe that a Japanese woman could play jazz. Akiyoshi played with their expectations by playing wearing a **kimono.** Despite suffering because of her background, Akiyoshi never turned her back on her heritage and instead embraced it. Her songs often dealt with Japanese topics, like the song "Minimata," which is about mercury poisoning in a small Japanese fishing village. She incorporated Japanese sounds like the susumi drums into her work and sought to make a kind of music that was a hybrid between traditional jazz and Japanese musical ideas. ◆

Ariyoshi, George R.

MARCH 12, 1926– ● POLITICIAN

George Ariyoshi was born March 12, 1926, in Honolulu, Hawaii. His father, Ryozo, and his mother, Mitsue, were recent immigrants from Japan. In Japan, his father had been a sumo wrestler. Once the couple moved to Hawaii, the father worked at a shipyard and then later bought a dry cleaning business.

George Ariyoshi

Ariyoshi was a conscientious and popular student. When he was a senior at McKinley High School, he was the president of his class. Even when he was young, he wanted to be a lawyer, but his plans were put on hold when he graduated in 1944. It was wartime, so Ariyoshi joined the army and was shipped off to Japan. In Japan, which was occupied at the time, he was an interpreter for the U.S. Military Intelligence Service.

After his service in the military, Ariyoshi got on track again to pursue his goal of being a lawyer. He went to the University of Hawaii for a short time then transferred to Michigan State University in East Lansing, Michigan, taking a pre-law curriculum, majoring in political science and history. Later both Michigan State and the University of Hawaii awarded him Distinguished Alumni Awards. At the

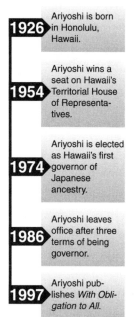

1926 Ariyoshi is born in Honolulu, Hawaii.

1954 Ariyoshi wins a seat on Hawaii's Territorial House of Representatives.

1974 Ariyoshi is elected as Hawaii's first governor of Japanese ancestry.

1986 Ariyoshi leaves office after three terms of being governor.

1997 Ariyoshi publishes *With Obligation to All*.

veto official rejection of a law passed by a legislature by the executive in a representative democracy.

majority leader individual elected by colleagues as the leader of the party with the most members among a group of elected representatives of a legislative body.

time, Hawaii was not yet a state and many people Ariyoshi met in Michigan could not imagine what the area was like. Some even asked him if people on the island really lived in grass huts.

In 1952, Ariyoshi earned a degree from the University of Michigan Law School. The next year, he went back to Hawaii to start working as an attorney. His first job was in Honolulu, working as a criminal lawyer. Even though he was a new lawyer, he caught the attention of John Burns, who was the head of the Democratic Party in Hawaii. Burns asked Ariyoshi to run for a seat in the Territorial House of Representatives and Ariyoshi agreed. Ariyoshi won; in fact, in his long political career, he never lost an election. The 1954 election showcased Ariyoshi's dedication to his positions. Party forces wanted him to campaign with other candidates as a team member in his race, but Ariyoshi refused. Sticking to his own position was a trait that would be a mark of Ariyoshi's political style.

In 1955, he married Jean Miya Hayashi. The two had three children, one daughter and two sons.

In 1958 he won his bid for a Territorial Senate seat. Ariyoshi went against party forces again. In one session, the Democrats were voting against the appointment of a judge because the man's father, during his term as governor had **vetoed** many Democratic bills. Ariyoshi considered the man to be qualified and voted for him. In the Senate, Ariyoshi served as the Ways and Means chairman. In a session on an education budget, several members of the committee walked out when Ariyoshi refused to budge on the budget. It marked the beginning of another hallmark of Ariyoshi's career—paying extreme attention to sticking with a budget.

In 1959, Hawaii became a state. Ariyoshi considered this to be a good thing. "It gave us our political voice," he said later in an interview with *U.S. News and World Report*. "Economically, Hawaii became known to everyone."

In the Senate, Ariyoshi served as **majority leader** and the majority floor leader. Ariyoshi got another political boost from his old friend John Burns when Burns became Hawaii's governor. Burns asked Ariyoshi to run as his lieutenant governor in the 1970 race. Burns believed that Hawaii would be better under governors of revolving ethnicity. Ariyoshi's Japanese ancestry made him an appealing choice and the two won the race.

In 1973, Burns was diagnosed with cancer and handed over his governor chores to Ariyoshi, making Ariyoshi the Acting

Governor. When the next election came around in 1974, Ariyoshi ran himself and won, making him the first Hawaiian governor of Japanese ancestry. He would win three terms as governor, which is the limit in Hawaii.

In office, Ariyoshi was not afraid to speak his mind and try new things. He wanted to bolster Hawaii's economic growth, but he was very against growth with a cost of environmental problems and out of control development. Ariyoshi was strict about keeping the budget in line and earned the **moniker** "The Governor Who Says No." Ariyoshi likened the budget situation to being in a family where each member wants to use the money for their own purposes. He saw himself as the voice of reason who needed to balance various interests.

moniker label; name given by others.

Another mark of Ariyoshi's governorship was the influx of young people into the capital. Ariyoshi believed in getting young people involved with government and went out of his way to populate his staff with bright newcomers.

Ariyoshi left office in 1986 and became a private citizen for the first time in over 30 years. He juggled his time between many activities, including serving as President of Prince Resorts Hawaii, chairing the Board of Governors of the East-West Center and practicing law.

In 1997, Ariyoshi wrote a book *With Obligation To All*, detailing his political career from 1954 to his election as governor in 1974. Proceeds from the book were donated to a foundation to send young Hawaiians to Asia to study the business practices of the Far East. The publication of the book brought a renewed wave of fondness for this governor who was willing to make unpopular decisions and stand by them. ◆

Barry, Lynda

JANUARY 2, 1956– ● CARTOONIST AND AUTHOR

Lynda Barry was born January 2, 1956, in a small town in Wisconsin. Her mother was Filipino and her father was Norweigan-Irish. When she was young, her family moved to Seattle, Washington, so that her mother could be closer to her Filipino relatives. Barry grew up poor. Her mother was a night janitor at a hospital and her father was a butcher. Barry's childhood was a difficult one. Besides the financial troubles and living in a rough neighborhood, Barry's parents were not very nurturing. She has claimed that her mother called her "ugly" and said that Barry should not make direct eye contact with her. Barry's life got even worse when she was 13 when her father left the family. To help earn money for the family, the young girl had to help her mother on the custodial job.

Barry's childhood difficulties were eased by her teacher in first and second grade. She let Barry come into school early so she could draw and was one of the few adults to show affection to the young girl.

Lynda Barry

1956 Barry is born in Wisconsin.

1977 Barry creates "Ernie Pook's Comeek."

1988 Barry publishes *The Good Times Are Killing Me.*

1999 Barry publishes *Cruddy.*

clique a group of people with particular commonalities who regularly associate with one another.

refuge a safe escape or retreat.

Racial issues came into play in Barry's young life, but she considered them minor when compared to her emotional struggles. "On the street where I lived, there were so many kinds of people in so many situations that it wasn't logical to group into a category as general as race," she told the web magazine *Salon.com*. As she got older, school grew worse. It was a dangerous place where kids were always beating each other up and, by junior high, Barry felt like she could take it no longer. But Barry got another good break. Because she was a quarter Filipino, she was allowed to switch to a better public school. She then went to college at the liberal Evergreen State in Olympia, Washington. Here she studied painting and became part of an artist's **clique** which included future Simpsons creator, Matt Groening.

After breaking up with a serious boyfriend, Barry found a **refuge** in her art. Instead of working on the fine art that she had been doing for school, Barry began drawing a comic strip about the relations between men and women. In "Spinal Comics," the men were drawn as cacti who tried to seduce women. Groening, who was the editor of the school paper, ran Barry's cartoon.

After graduation, Barry tried to make a living from her comics but was not successful. To earn extra money, she had to work in a movie theater. Once, after a boss was irrationally mean to her, she vowed that she would never work for anyone else again. So serious was she about it that she wrote a contract with herself, saying as much, and signed it.

Barry's next stroke of luck came after Groening wrote an article describing his group of Seattle artist friends. An editor at the alternative paper, *The Chicago Reader*, took an interest in Barry's work and offered her a weekly strip. Barry was overjoyed. Although the pay was meager, to her it was a fortune and meant that she could make a living as a cartoonist. Within a short time, the strip was syndicated to papers around the nation and Barry got other work with publications like the *Village Voice* and a monthly strip in *Esquire*. In 1977, she named her strip "Ernie Pook's Comeek," in tribute to her younger brother who, when he was a boy, had named all his pets and toys Ernie Pook, Ernie Pook the 2nd, etc. (Ironically, her brother did not remember this habit.) The strip, drawn in a crude, primitive style, detailed the adventures of a group of kids growing up in the 1960s. Even though the strip was about kids, its subject matter was not childish. Barry wrote funny strips, but was unafraid to tackle darker subject matter.

"Ernie Pook's Comeek" became a hit, or as much of a hit as an "alternative" comic can be. But Barry, who was true to her own artistic voice, was not content doing the same old thing. Throughout her career, she has balanced cartooning with whatever other projects she feels like taking on. In the 1980s, she decided to paint portraits of some of her favorite musicians, such as Ma Rainey. When she was ready to publish a book of the paintings, Barry started working on a foreward to accompany them. While she was trying to write this foreward, she found herself being compelled by a story in her head about the doomed friendship between a black girl and a white girl in the 1960s. Barry focused her energies on the story and ended up with a novel, *The Good Times Are Killing Me*, which was published in 1988. Barry later adapted the book into a play which featured music that ranged from "Volare" to the song from the Rice-A-Roni ad.

In her career, Barry has always been brave about tackling forbidden subjects. One of Barry's projects was entitled *Naked Ladies! Naked Ladies! Naked Ladies!* It was a coloring book filled with drawings of a wide range of normal women's bodies. Barry did it as a reaction to the way that women's magazines present only one kind of body as acceptable.

Barry's most recent project was a novel called *Cruddy*. The book was about Roberta Rohbeson, a teen drug addict recalling a wild road trip she took with her father when she was 11. Some called the novel dark, even for Barry, but saw her stories as following in the tradition of fairy tales.

After a failed marriage that began in 1986 and ended a year and a half later, Barry seemed to have found success in her personal life, too. In 1993, while at a artists' retreat, she met a prairie restorer and artist named Kevin Kawula. The two fell in love and moved into a house in Evanston, Illinois, with their dogs and art. Barry was happy having no job description and following her artistic visions. "I guess I like to think of myself as being whatever Dr. Seuss would have said he was." ◆

Bhatia, Sabeer

DECEMBER 30, 1968– ● INTERNET ENTREPRENEUR

Sabeer Bhatia was born December 30, 1968, in Bangalore, a southern city in India. Both of his parents were highly successful in their respective fields. Bhatia's father, Balev,

1968 Bhatia is born in Bangalore, India.

1988 Bhatia leaves India for Cal Tech.

1996 Bhatia debuts Hotmail.

Bhatia sells Hotmail to Microsoft for over two and a half million shares of Microsoft.

1997

1999 Bhatia founds Arzoo.com.

entreprenuer individual who manages, organizes, and assumes the risk of a business or enterprise venture.

was a captain in the Indian Ministry of Defense and his mother, Daman, was a senior official at the Central Bank of India. Both parents stressed the value of an education to their son and Bhatia took their words to heart.

Bhatia studied at Bishop Cotton's School in Pune and attended St. Joseph's College in Bangalore. He did very well in school and his teachers often asked him to show the rest of the class how to solve a problem. Even as a boy, Bhatia considered himself to be an **entrepreneur.** When a college opened near his home, Bhatia decided that he would open a sandwich shop and even drew up a business plan. It was only his mother's admonishments to concentrate on his schoolwork that persuaded him to abandon the plan.

Bhatia worked hard in school and became interested in technology. He decided to attend the Birla Institute of Technology at Pilani. Bhatia did well there and decided he would try to get a transfer scholarship to the California Institute of Technology in Pasadena. The scholarship was extremely difficult to win because applicants must pass a famously difficult exam. Bhatia was the only person in the world in 1988 who actually passed the exam, scoring a 62, a full 20 points better than the next highest mark.

As articles about Bhatia were fond of pointing out, the 19-year old arrived in the United States with less than $300 in his pocket. At that point, it was hard to imagine that less than 10 years later, he would join the ranks of the richest people in the country.

When he arrived in the United States, Bhatia felt isolated because of his heritage. "I felt I had made a big mistake. I knew nobody, people looked different, it was hard for them to understand my accent and me to understand theirs. I felt pretty lonely," he told *Asiaweek.* Later, after he became successful, Bhatia became a champion for India, trying to mentor computer students from his homeland and working to set up the country with widespread Internet access.

Bhatia earned his Bachelor of Science with honors and then a master's from Stanford University in electrical engineering. He was working on his doctorate in 1992, when he suddenly decided to leave school to begin working. He had been inspired by lectures given by computer wizards like Steve Jobs of Apple and Scott McNealy and Vinod Khosia of Sun Microsystems. Bhatia was struck by how ordinary these people seemed and it gave him confidence. If they could create such large companies, then surely he could, too. Bhatia also began attending meetings of TIE, The IndUS Entrepreneurs, where he met many other successful Indian men.

Bhatia went to work at Apple as a hardware engineer. His parents were overjoyed, thinking that their son had found nice, long term, steady employment. Yet Bhatia had other ideas and still yearned to start his own company. He tried to convince one of his co-workers, Jack Smith, to work on ideas with him. Smith was initially reluctant—he was a family man who was comfortable in his job—but Bhatia's legendary enthusiasm finally got the better of Smith.

Bhatia left to work at a startup, Firepower Systems, Inc., but kept developing ideas. Bhatia wanted to discuss plans with Smith via E-mail but did not want his supervisors to see what he was working on. In trying to solve this problem, Smith and Bhatia stumbled upon their big idea—E-mail accounts that could be accessed by anyone with any kind of Internet connection. The result was something they called Hotmail. Hotmail was to be free to users; the cost would by borne by advertisers. On each piece of E-mail a user sent, there would be a brief ad, "Get your free, private E-mail at Hotmail," thus spreading the word each time it was used.

Bhatia knew they had a great idea but had trouble convincing others of its viability. He was rejected 19 times by potential investors before he walked into the offices of Draper-Fisher-Jurvetson. Steve Jurvetson knew Bhatia's idea would work and offered him a generous investment. Bhatia, who said that he learned to bargain for everything growing up in India, refused the deal. The bold, possibly unwise bargaining technique was typical for Bhatia. Luckily for him, his bluff worked. The firm offered Bhatia a better deal and Hotmail was ready to go.

Hotmail debuted on July 4, 1996, and was an immediate success. In the first hour, they signed on 100 subscribers. And it kept on growing, faster than CNN or America Online. By the end of their year, they had a million customers; a year after that, they had 10 million.

When they hit the 10 million mark, Bill Gates and Microsoft became interested. Again, Bhatia was a shrewd bargainer and purposefully asked for an unreasonably high amount for his company. He and Smith had carefully studied Microsoft's negotiating tactics and were prepared when the Microsoft team walked out on a meeting. Bhatia knew it was a ploy. Bhatia kept turning down Microsoft's offers until they came up with a deal he wanted—about $400 million in Microsoft stock. Bhatia took the offer and was suddenly a rich man.

> *"The greatest risk in life is not to take one at all!"* Sabeer Bhatia on "Sabeer Bhatia on the Internet Revolution," CNN.com, July 3, 2000

Bhatia was working at Microsoft, overseeing his company but soon grew bored. He had always been excited by new challenges and needed something new to work on. He left the company and in 1999 launched a new start-up, Arzoo.com (arzoo is the Indian Word for desire). The idea was initially that the site would be for consumers looking for information about shopping on the Internet. But as the technology economy faltered, Bhatia abandoned that idea and shifted the focus of the company entirely. Now Arzoo.com is a site where large companies can get expert computer advice in real time. The success of the site remained to be seen. Whether or not it works or not, Bhatia was happy to go on to the next thing. ◆

Bulosan, Carlos

NOVEMBER 2, 1911–SEPTEMBER 11, 1956 ● AUTHOR AND POET

Carlos Bulosan

Carlos Bulosan was born on November 2, 1911, in a small rural village in the Philippines called Binalonan. Bulosan had three brothers and two sisters, and his family was poor. The Philippines was a colony of the United States, and American influence was strong. The education system had recently changed to reflect American culture; Filipino children learned about George Washington and the American style of government. Bulosan took particular interest in learning about Abraham Lincoln and became intrigued by how Lincoln rose from being a poor boy to president of the United States.

Bulosan became fascinated by the United States and saw it as a land of opportunity. Two of his brothers had moved there and Bulosan was determined to follow in their footsteps. His resolve was furthered because the economy in the Philippines was not favorable, and Bulosan was eking out a living selling vegetables for his family. In

1930, he paid $75 for an ocean liner trip to Seattle, Washington, and later in life recalled his happiness at seeing the beauty of this new land of promise.

But Bulosan was in for a rude shock. The United States was in the midst of the Great Depression and jobs were scarce. Immigrants were seen as competition for jobs and, as such, treated poorly. Bulosan, who was small, not very strong, and generally sickly, was not in demand for any of the manual labor jobs that were available, but eventually found work at an Alaskan fish cannery. He worked hard the whole season yet ended up earning only $13. His corrupt bosses had been making questionable deductions from his paycheck for things like bedding.

Bulosan was unprepared for the racism he would face. It was common at the time to see signs outside of businesses like "No Dogs or Filipinos." Filipinos were often stopped by police for no reason and Filipino men were prohibited from dating white women. There was also violence against the Filipinos, including an incident where Bulosan and his bunkmates were driven out of their bunk by a fire-wielding mob of white men. "I feel like a criminal running away from a crime I did not commit. And this crime is that I am a Filipino in America," wrote Bulosan later in his autobiographical work *America Is In The Heart*.

The way that Filipino migrant workers were treated radicalized Bulosan. In the late 1930s, Bulosan began working to unionize his fellow migrant workers. Bulosan continued to make his living traveling up and down the west coast, picking crops. The hard work was too harsh for Bulosan's weak body. When he was too weak to work, he read and began to write. In 1934, he published a literary magazine, *The New Tide*. The magazine was filled with radical writings and caught the attention of several noted writers such as William Carlos Williams and William Saroyan.

In 1936, Bulosan contracted **tuberculosis** and had to be hospitalized in Los Angeles for two years. In a way, the forced bed rest turned out be a blessing. Bulosan spent his time reading authors like Pablo Neruda and John Steinbeck and working on his writing.

In 1942, his book of poems, *Letter from America*, was published. It helped make Bulosan more known and marked the beginning of the best period in Bulosan's literary life. He would become a respected writer and be considered a peer by the nation's top writers. In 1943, President Franklin Roosevelt

1911 Bulosan is born in Binalonan, Philippines.

1930 Bulosan arrives in the United States.

1943 Bulosan writes "Freedom From Want" for the Saturday Evening Post.

1944 Bulosan publishes *Laughter of My Father.*

1946 Bulosan publishes *America Is In The Heart.*

1956 Bulosan dies in Seattle, Washington.

tuberculosis a communicable disease in humans and some vertebrates caused by the tubercle bacillus and characterized by toxic symptoms or allergies in the lungs.

communist an advocate or supporter of communism, a system in theory in which property and goods are owned collectively and distributed equally.

McCarthyism period of time during the 1950s when U.S. senator Joseph McCarthy of Wisconsin sought to identify and eliminate suspected communists from the United States government, as well as the entertainment industry, and other facets of life.

selected Bulosan to write an essay for the *Saturday Evening Post* on "Freedom from Want," as part of a series on the "Four Freedoms." *Laughter of My Father* in 1944 was Bulosan's first major breakthrough. The book, a collection of variations on Philippines folk tales, brought Bulosan critical acclaim.

Bulosan's biggest hit came in 1946, when he published *America Is In The Heart*. The book was semi-autobiographical and described the rough treatment given to Filipino immigrants.

In 1948, Bulosan met Josephine Patrick at a party of union activists. The two began dating, even though other people were against the relationship. Patrick was a **communist** and her communist friends thought that Bulosan could not be trusted. Others disapproved of the relationship because Patrick was a French-Indian woman. Though their relationship was sometimes difficult, the two stayed together for the rest of Bulosan's life.

The 1950s saw Bulosan's downfall. After the war, the country had turned conservative and **McCarthyism** was at its strongest. Bulosan was blacklisted because of his communist associations. Bulosan was shocked when some of his friends in the literary elite shunned him, too.

Bulosan's health suffered and his drinking became a problem. He spent time in hospitals and had finanacial troubles. At the end of his life, Bulosan was trying to make a comeback. He was working on several projects and showing an enthusiasm that had been dormant for years. On September 11, 1956, Bulosan died of pneumonia. He was only 44 and penniless. Bulosan's grave remained unmarked until 1982, when a group of his admirers raised money and purchased a proper headstone.

In recent years, Bulosan's work underwent a resurgence. His books were a mainstay in Asian-American studies classes and he was considered to be one of the major figures in Philippines literature. ◆

Bunker, Chang and Eng

MAY 11, 1811–JANUARY 17, 1874 ● PERFORMERS, FARMERS

conjoined brought together so as to meet, touch, or overlap.

Chang and Eng Bunker, the **conjoined** twins who gave the world the term **"Siamese twins,"** were born on a houseboat on May 11, 1811, in the village of Meklong.

The town was near Bangkok in the kingdom of Siam (which became Thailand in 1939). They were the fifth and sixth children of Nok and Ti-eye, who were Chinese. Eventually their parents would have nine children.

It was immediately apparent that there was something unusual about the twins. They were joined together by a piece of ligament-like material, and they shared a liver and a navel. Their birth caused quite a stir. The midwives refused to touch them, thinking their condition to be somehow contagious. Several medical doctors wanted to separate the twins, even though the considered options were as primitive as using a saw to cut them apart. Even the King of Siam was superstitious about the joined twins. He thought they were a symbol of bad things to come and put out a death threat on them.

Despite what the boys were up against, their mother was determined that they live as normal a life as possible. Chang and Eng learned to walk and could soon run and play. Their activity stretched the joined ligament which gave them even more freedom. When they were eight, an epidemic of **cholera** struck the family, killing five of their brothers and sisters as well as their father. The boys were forced to start working as fishermen. They were industrious and soon became successful enough to acquire their own boat. They also worked as merchants and would sell items such as duck eggs and ducks.

When Chang and Eng were sixteen, a British trader, Robert Hunter, met the boys and decided that they should tour the world. He offered money to the twins' mother in exchange for the boys. Perhaps she was mollified that part of the deal was that the twins would have their freedom when they were 21. Hunter was also required to ask the King's permission to take the twins out of the country. The King, who had removed the death threat after meeting and being charmed by Chang and Eng, gave his permission.

The twins went on the road with Hunter and his partner, Captain Abel Coffin. They toured all over the United States and England as medical curiosities. Coffin and Hunter were savvy at attracting publicity for the show. In each town, they would enlist a local doctor to examine the boys, which bought their show credibility as well as publicity. During the early shows, the boys would just stand on the stage while people stared at them and asked questions. Later the boys started showing off their athletic prowess. They would do flips, lift audience members, and even played a badminton-like game called

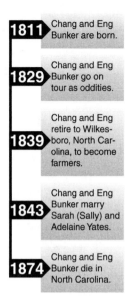

1811 Chang and Eng Bunker are born.

1829 Chang and Eng Bunker go on tour as oddities.

1839 Chang and Eng retire to Wilkesboro, North Carolina, to become farmers.

1843 Chang and Eng Bunker marry Sarah (Sally) and Adelaine Yates.

1874 Chang and Eng Bunker die in North Carolina.

Siamese twins congenitally joined twins among man or lower animals.

cholera any of a range of diseases in humans and domestic animals usually characterized by severe gastrointestinal problems.

Conjoined Twins

Conjoined twins begin life just like regular identical twins, as a single fertilized egg. However, the egg that forms normal identical twins undergoes a complete split, resulting in two individual embryos whereas, in conjoined twins, this split occurs only incompletely. As a result, the two individual fetuses share organs and, in some cases, limbs. This incomplete splitting happens very rarely: only one in 200,000 births are conjoined twins. Very few survive the difficult birth process, and most who do rarely survive the first 24 hours after birth.

Because conjoined twins originate from a single egg they are always identical. There are approximately three dozen types of conjoined twins, defined according to where their bodies are joined and the degree to which they share internal organs. The most common form is called *thoracopagus* twinning, from the Greek words *thorax*, meaning chest, and *pagus*, meaning fastened. About 35-40 percent of all conjoined twins are of this type. The degree of joining can vary widely; Chang and Eng Bunker simply shared a thick band of flesh that linked their separate livers, but some *thoracopagus* twins share a single heart. Other types of conjoined twins include *omphalopagus* twins, joined at the waist; and *ischiopagus* twins, joined at the lower portion of the spine. An extremely rare form is the type known as *parasitic* twins, in which a relatively normally formed individual is born with a much smaller, primitively developed twin attached.

Some conjoined twins can be separated surgically, because each twin's internal organs are complete enough to permit them both to survive independently. Chang and Eng, for example, could have easily survived such surgery. Others, however, share too many important organs, and to separate them means that one of the twins must die. In these cases, even when the surgery is successful, the surviving twin is unlikely to live a year beyond the date of separation.

battledore and shuttlecock. In France, the boys were barred from touring because of a belief that their appearance might cause a similar effect on the unborn children of pregnant women.

Hunter and Coffin were adequate as managers and promoters, but they were not especially kind. They made Chang and Eng work long hours and refused to pay them a fair wage. When they were traveling, the boys had lower-class accommodations, while their managers traveled in style. However, when the boys turned 21, the managers did honor their contract. The Bunkers set out and toured on their own. They continued to be successful and soon had amassed a respectable amount of money.

In 1839, Chang and Eng decided to settle in Wilkesboro, North Carolina, on the advice of a friend, Dr. James Calloway. North Carolina was a rural and lightly populated area and the time. The Bunkers suffered prejudice but it was a result of their medical situation rather than the fact that they were Chinese. Since the men had traveled so extensively, they had learned to speak perfect English and were well accustomed to the ways of the Western world. The twins bought land in North Carolina and embarked on a farming career. They became United States citizens and took the last name of Bunker.

The Bunkers became respectable local citizens and Chang Bunker soon took an interest in Adelaine Yates, the daughter of a neighbor. The two fell in love. Eng Bunker, perhaps out of convenience rather than a rush of emotion, started dating Adelaine's sister Sarah (Sally) Yates. Eventually, they all married, which caused an outcry among the citizens, including the girls' father, David Yates. Their father agreed to the marriage only after they threatened to **elope.**

The Bunkers were married in 1843 and soon were living with their wives in a house at Trap Hill, near Wilkesboro. They slept in a specially built four-person bed. A little over nine months later, Sally gave birth to a girl and, six days later, Adelaine also had a girl. The two couples would go on to have 21 (or 22, depending on the source) children between them. At first, the families got along well, but soon the wives began arguing and then Chang and Eng were arguing about various matters. Chang Bunker reportedly became fond of drinking and Eng Bunker was prone to gambling. The situation got so bad that the brothers set up their families in separate houses. They would live at one house for three days, then the other for the next three.

In their final years, the Bunkers spent most of their days in North Carolina but would go back out on tour whenever they needed money. They educated themselves and were smart men who read **voraciously,** especially poetry and Shakespeare. As farmers, they were among the first in North Carolina to raise "bright leaf" tobacco.

The Bunkers' medical situation was extensively documented. Doctors found that when Chang Bunker drank alcohol, Eng Bunker could not feel the effects. However, if one of the twins was secretly tickled, the other twin could feel it as well. Chang Bunker had more bad habits and was much less healthy than his brother. A few times during the twins' lives, they considered being separated, but the medical technology of the time made the operation a very dangerous prospect.

"(We) have endeavored to live soberly, honestly and in peace with all the good citizens of the county."
Chang and Eng Bunker in response to an unflattering letter printed in the *Greensboro Patriot*, The People's Press, December 11, 1852, vol. II, No. 44

elope to secretly run away with the intention of marrying, usually without parental consent.

voracious enthusiastic; intense.

In 1870, Chang Bunker had a stroke. Chang was partially paralyzed and Eng Bunker had to carry Chang's leg so the two could be mobile. In 1874, Eng awoke and discovered that his brother was dead. Eng died a few hours later. Later, doctors discovered a blood clot in Chang's brain, but could not find a cause for Eng's death. Some speculated that he died of fright. ◆

Carrere, Tia

JANUARY 2, 1967– ● ACTRESS AND SINGER

Tia Carrere

Tia Carrere was born in Honolulu, Hawaii, on January 2, 1967. She describes her ethnic heritage as Filipino, Chinese and Spanish. She and her sisters Alesaundra and Audra grew up surrounded by music. Her grandmother sent her to her first vocal lessons when Carrere was 11. The love of singing would stay with her. As an adult, after Carrere became a successful actress, she still considered herself to be more of a singer than an actress.

When Carrere was 12, her family moved to Samoa where her father took a job. Her parents and sister went to Samoa, but Carrere stayed in Hawaii with her grandmother so that she could stay in the Hawaii's better school system. Being separated from her parents was difficult for her, especially during adolescence. Her family situation became more complicated three years later when her mother and sister returned without her father. She learned that her parents had divorced and her father had married his secretary in Samoa. Today, her

25

The Asian American Arts Foundation

Based in northern California, The Asian American Arts Foundation (AAAF) is a non-profit organization dedicated to providing financial support to, and public recognition of artistic excellence within the Asian American community. A group of Asian American community and business leaders, sharing a belief in that "art is a unifying force that celebrates culture and history," pooled their resources to create the foundation in 1995. They were prompted to do so upon learning that budget of the National Endowment of the Arts (NEA), the primary institutional supporter of arts in America, was slated to be cut in 1996; the group felt that Asian American artists and organizations who were dependent on NEA funding would be left without resources. Working together, this group of businesses and individuals determined to guarantee that support would be there for the members of their community whose artistic endeavors merited assistance and recognition.

AAAF's principle means of accomplishing its goals is through providing several annual grants. The organization particularly favors artists and organizations whose work reflects important aspects of the Asian American experience, and gives preference to projects designed to give newer artists a chance for public recognition.

In addition to providing financial support, the AAAF sponsors the Golden Ring Awards; each year the organization honors ten artists who have made significant achievements in Asian American art. The AAAF selects its award winners from all artistic venues, and recipients have included actors Lou Diamond Phillips (1999) and Tia Carrere (1997) as well as comedian Margaret Cho (1995) and film director John Woo (1997). In addition, the AAAF grants one lifetime achievement award each year, honoring an Asian American artist who has been shown to have produced excellent work over a long career. Both the Golden Ring awards and the financial support packages are funded through the contributions of corporate and individual sponsors, and through fundraising events sponsored by the AAAF each year.

father still lives in Samoa and works for a refrigeration company. Her mother lives in Hawaii and works for American Savings.

When Carrere was 17, she had a chance encounter that changed her life. She was shopping at the local Safeway supermarket when an older couple approached her and exclaimed, "Darling, you're gorgeous! You should meet our son who's producing a movie." Carrere agreed to meet their son, Mike Greco, and ended up with a part in a low-budget film called *Aloha Summer*.

Carrere was excited by working in films and, even though she was only 17, moved straight to Los Angeles, California, eager to begin her career. She changed her name from her given name of Althea Janairo to the sleeker-sounding Tia Carrere. It wasn't long before she landed several jobs as a model as well as jobs on several commercials for fast food restaurants, soft drinks and hair care products. But her first plum role was Jade Soong on the television soap opera *General Hospital*. While playing that character, Carrere was also offered a part on *The A-Team* but was unable to take the job because of her exclusive contract with *General Hospital*. Carrere, at the suggestion of her boyfriend and manager who was sixteen years older than she, decided to sue the show. She not only lost the suit, but created a feeling of ill will between her and her coworkers. The incident also garnered her some bad press. The episode helped Carrere realize that she wanted to change her life so that she was in more control of her career. Carrere decided her manager/boyfriend was too manipulative and broke with him personally and professionally.

The biggest break for Carrere was landing a role in *Wayne's World*, as Wayne's love interest, Cassandra. This role took her from relative obscurity to worldwide renown as a result of the popular film. She then acted in a variety of different roles in a variety of different kinds of films. She was a disabled computer scientist in the Sean Connery and Wesley Snipes film *Rising Sun*, a hardboiled international art smuggler in the Arnold Schwarzenegger film *True Lies*, and a witch-queen in *Kull the Conqueror*. Carrere has said that because she doesn't have typical girl-next-door looks, it has been more difficult for producers to pigeonhole her.

Carrere has applied a vigorous work ethic to her singing career but as of yet that road has not been as successful as her acting. Her most famous appearance on a soundtrack was for the *Wayne's World* films, but she has also been on soundtracks for *Batman–Mask of the Phantasm* and *Angel City*. She released a solo record called "Dream" with Warner/Reprise and is currently working on a follow-up album for Interscope Records.

In her personal life, Carrere began a steady relationship in the early 1990s with a Lebanese-Italian man named Elie Samaha. The two were married on November 22, 1992. Samaha served as Carrere's business manager and pushed her career in new directions, including starting their own production company, Phoenician Films. The two even bought a bar together, Dublin's on Sunset Blvd. in West Hollywood. However, the marriage did not work out and the couple was divorced in 1999.

In recent years, Carrere kept busy with many different aspects of show business. Besides working on her music, she con-

1967 Carrere is born in Honolulu, Hawaii.

1984 Carrere is "discovered" at a grocery store.

1985 Carrere moves to Los Angeles.

1992 Carrere appears in *Wayne's World*.

lowbrow not highly
cultivated or cultured.

tinued to take on acting roles. She was in the **lowbrow** comedy *High School High*, played a housewife in the film *Five Acres* and made her primetime television debut on the adventure series, "Relic Hunter." Carrere also joined the business side of things, most notably as the executive producer for the independent film *20 Dates*. ◆

Cayetano, Benjamin J.

NOVEMBER 14, 1939– ● POLITICIAN

Benjamin J. Cayetano, Hawaii's fifth governor and first of Filipino ancestry, was born November 14, 1939, in Honolulu, Hawaii. His father, Bonifacio, was a Filipino immigrant who earned money waiting tables. His mother, Eleanor, was often left alone to raise Cayetano and his younger brother, Kenneth. The family lived in a rough neighborhood called Kalihi where careers in politics were not considered to be an option.

Benjamin Cayetano

When Cayetano was only six, his parents separated and the boys went to live with their father. Money was tight and Benjamin's father worked extra hours, leaving the boys without care for long periods of time. Cayetano began fighting at school and gained a reputation as a troublemaker. He was sent to live with his mother to get straightened out, but it didn't work. After another fight, he was thrown in jail and had to be bailed out.

Cayetano attended Farrington High School and nearly flunked out. He did manage to graduate in 1958, but found that the employment opportunities for a boy like him were limited. He married Lorraine Gueco and the two had three children.

Cayetano took his responsibilities as a wage earner seriously and got jobs working at a junkyard, driving a truck and working with an electrician. He took an exam to become a draftsman and scored well, but was unable to find any jobs. Cayetano began to suspect that he was the victim of racial discrimination. He thought that certain ethnic groups were only hiring members of their own group despite his qualifications.

Discouraged, Cayetano left for Los Angeles, determined to make something of himself. At this point, it seemed unlikely that he would return to Hawaii and, of course, unthinkable that he would be governor. But Cayetano was a determined, hard-working young man. When he was a boy, he had read a book about the famous attorney Clarence Darrow and had become interested in law. In Hawaii, pursuing such a dream had seemed impossible, but in Los Angeles, Cayetano felt like he could do what he wanted if he applied himself, despite his background.

The next years were filled with hard work. He went to a junior college and worked when he was not attending school. His wife helped out by working as a waitress at night. Cayetano did well enough in school to be admitted to UCLA then Loyola Law School in Los Angeles. The sacrifices and suffering paid off. In 1968, he earned a B.A. in Political Science and in 1971, Cayetano was the proud owner of a degree in law.

Cayetano returned to Honolulu and got a job at a law firm. His first break into politics happened quickly, the very next year. The governor, John A. Burns, asked Cayetano to work on the Hawaiian Housing Authority and Cayetano accepted. By 1974, when he was only 34 years old, he had won a race for the state House of Representatives, where he served for two terms. From 1978-1986, he was a member of Hawaii's Senate. During his time in the legislature, he worked hard to make a mark. He headed the Transportation Committee, helped establish the first Hula Mae loan program to provide low interest loans and helped enact laws providing for auto insurance premium rollbacks. He drafted laws to begin a program in Hawaii designed to test veterans of the Vietnam War for exposure to the toxic chemical **Agent Orange,** and he chaired the Senate investigative committee that discovered the heptachlor milk contamination scandal.

In 1986, Cayetano became Lieutenant Governor. His biggest success in office was his development of the A+ program, an afterschool program for underprivileged children. In

1939 Cayetano is born in Honolulu, Hawaii.

1971 Cayetano graduates from Loyola Law School.

1974 Cayetano is elected to the Hawaii state House.

1986 Cayetano becomes Lieutenant Governor.

1994 Cayetano becomes the first Hawaiian governor of Filipino heritage.

Agent Orange an herbicide used widely in the Vietnam War to clear foiliage; contains dioxin as a contaminant.

1994, he looked like a good candidate for Governor on the Democratic ticket, and entered a difficult race. It was a three-way contest between strong candidates, but Cayetano managed to win with a plurality of 37% of the votes. As Governor, Cayetano's first big problem was a budget that was difficult to tame. His solution was to make severe cutbacks in the government's payroll. This move, of course, initially made him very unpopular with government workers. Cayetano planned to bolster the economy by increasing Hawaii's most lucrative money-maker, tourism. One of the ways he tried to promote Hawaii was by personally asking producers of the globally popular television show *Baywatch* to come film in Hawaii, which it did. Despite Cayetano's efforts, however, Hawaii's economy still languished.

In 1996, while in office, Cayetano divorced his wife after 37 years of marriage. The next year he married Vicky Liu, who served as president of United Laundry Services. The two went on to have a son and a daughter.

When Cayetano was up for re-election in 1998, he was not a shoo-in for the job. Polls showed him to be trailing badly to Republican opponent Linda Lingle, the popular longtime mayor of Maui. It was a surprise to everyone when Cayetano ended up winning the race. Cayetano's success was attributed to his "friend to friend" campaigning. In the last days of the campaign close to 80,000 to 100,000 people got phone calls from Cayetano supporters. Cayetano ran a very emotional campaign. At a speech asking the Hawaii State Teachers Association for their endorsement, Cayetano broke down in tears. Cayetano's wife was also instrumental in getting her husband re-elected. She campaigned tirelessly for him and even sang, with her two sisters, the Cayetano re-election song "Don't Give Your Vote To Anyone Else But Ben" at a state function.

Despite winning, Cayetano was shaken by the tough race. "We have to get back into touch with what the people are really concerned about: education and the economy," he said after the race. Lingle said that she would run again in the next election.

During his career, Cayetano was given many awards and honors, including the UCLA Alumni of the Year Award in 1998, the Harvard Foundation Leadership Award in 1996 and an Honorary Doctorate of Public Service from Loyola Marymount University in California. ◆

Chandrasekhar, Subrahmanyan

OCTOBER 19, 1910–AUGUST 21, 1995 ● ASTROPHYSICIST

Subrahmanyan Chandrasekhar (known to the world as Chandra) was born on October 19, 1910, in Lahore, India, which is now part of Pakistan. His family valued education and knowledge. His uncle, Sir C. V. Raman, was an Indian physicist who won a Nobel Prize for his work on the quantum effects in the scattering of light from molecules. Chandra was the first son and the third child of a family of four sons and six daughters. His father, Chandrasekhara Subrahmanyan Ayyar, was an officer in Government Service in the Indian Audits and Accounts Department. His father taught the children math and English before leaving for work in the morning and after arriving back home in the evening. Although Chandra's mother, Sita only had a few years of formal education, as was the custom of the time, she was as influential as—if not even more so—than the uncle and father on Chandra's intellectual development. Despite her lack of official education, his mother had wide ranging interests and had translated Ibsen's work into **Tamil.** She taught the children Tamil and English and was very interested in her children's development and ambitions. For his first 12 years, Chandra did not attend school and was taught at home.

In 1918, the family moved to Madras. In 1922, Chandra went to the local high school, Hindu High School, Triplicane. At school, Chandra became so interested in math that he read all the textbooks before the school year even began. When he was 15, he enrolled in

Tamil Dravidian language of Tamil Nadu state in eastern Ceylon.

Subrahmanyan Chandrasekhar

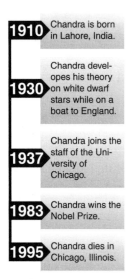

1910 Chandra is born in Lahore, India.

1930 Chandra developes his theory on white dwarf stars while on a boat to England.

1937 Chandra joins the staff of the University of Chicago.

1983 Chandra wins the Nobel Prize.

1995 Chandra dies in Chicago, Illinois.

Sanskrit an ancient language that is the classic language of India and Hinduism.

vivacious lively in spirit, conduct, and temper.

Presidency College, the best in the area. He took **Sanskrit,** English and Chemistry but it was his mathematics classes that excited him most. Chandra wished to take the honors mathematics course, but his father thought that was impractical. He believed Chandra should be in the Indian Civil Service. But Chandra's mother thought that Chandra should follow his passion. Chandra compromised and took the honors physics classes instead. (His professors, noticing that Chandra was a gifted mathematician let him sit in on the math classes anyway.) Though physics was not his first choice, he loved the subject and read anything he could find on physics, whether or not it was part of the courses. He graduated in 1930 at the top of his class, but what made him stand out to university officials was a paper he had written. During school, Chandra had become excited by some readings he had done on white dwarf stars. He wrote a scientific paper about them called "Compton Scattering and the New Statistics." The paper helped him attain a scholarship from the Indian Government to attend Trinity College in Cambridge.

While he was traveling by boat to the school in 1930, Chandra had one of his greatest insights. He was trying to overcome his seasickness and thinking about Ralph H. Fowler's work on white dwarf stars. Chandra worked out some calculations and realized that these stars could only exist up to a certain mass. This went against all the prevailing wisdom of the day and suggested the existence of black holes. This work would later become his greatest legacy.

Chandra earned his doctorate from Cambridge in 1933. He then won a highly regarded fellowship to be a fellow at Trinity College. Chandra was spending time working on his white dwarf problem again and in 1934 submitted his findings to the Royal Astronomical Society. He gave his presentation in January, 1935. After his speech, a prominent astrophysicist, Sir Arthur Stanley Eddington, stood up and declared Chandra's findings nonsense. Eddington's refusal to see the logic of Chandra's research was probably out of frustration since Chandra's findings refuted Eddington's own work. Although Chandra's work was correct, Eddington's power and influence were so great that it was not accepted until years later. (Oddly, the two would remain friends for years after this.) Chandra would eventually win the Nobel Prize for his work, though not until 1983.

In 1936, Chandra married an old friend from India, Lalitha Doraiswamy. She was a **vivacious** woman who was a good balance for Chandra's focused intensity.

In 1937, Chandra took at position at Yerkes Observatory in Wisconsin, which was a part of the University of Chicago. Chandra would stay affiliated with the university for the rest of his academic career. He later worked in Fermi's Research Institute on the main campus. He was a good teacher who was known for his lectures, given in his crisp, British accent and his devotion to his students. He helped over 50 students through their doctorate programs.

Chandra took over the editor's position of the *Astrophysical Journal* in 1952. At the time, it was a small publication of the University of Chicago. Chandra made the magazine into a national journal and one of the most influential in the world.

Throughout his life, Chandra dealt with difficulties concerning his background. These problems stemmed from people he met in the Western world, as well as those he left behind in Indian. When he received a scholarship to study in England, his fellow Indians felt that he was turning his back on India. Their feeling was heightened when Chandra and his wife decided to become citizens of the United States. But Chandra was not wholly accepted in the U.S. either. A dean of physical sciences at the University of Chicago once asked that Chandra not teach a course in astronomy. The dean's only justification was skin color. When World War II was raging, Chandra wanted to help the Allies fight the Axis powers, but was unable to obtain a security clearance, most likely because of his ethnicity. Chandra, however, was not one to dwell on such matters and instead kept his attention on his work.

Chandra kept busy until the end of his life. In his final days, he was busy working on various projects, such as a book on Newton's Principia. Along with the Nobel Prize, he was given many other honors, including the Dr. Tomalla Prize from the ETH of Zurich and the Copley Prize from the Royal Society of London. He died of heart failure in 1995. He was 82. ◆

> *"The simple is the seal of truth. And beauty is the splendor of truth."* Subrahmanyan Chandrasekhar, upon accepting the Nobel Prize in 1983, University of Chicago Magazine, October, 1995.

Chang, Iris

MARCH 28, 1968– ● AUTHOR

Iris Chang was born in Princeton, New Jersey, March 28, 1968. Her father, Shau-jin Chang, was a physics professor, and her mother, Ying-Ying Chang, was a microbiology

1968 Chang is born in Princeton, New Jersey, on March 28.

1991 Chang receives her degree from Johns Hopkins University, in Baltimore, Maryland.

1997 Chang publishes *The Rape of Nanking: The Forgotten Holocaust of World War II.*

professor. The Changs had fled China for Taiwan before immigrating to the United States. Chang earned a Bachelor of Science degree from the University of Illinois at Urbana-Champaign in 1989. She then worked in the Chicago bureau of The Associated Press and at the *Chicago Tribune*. From there she earned a scholarship from the Asian American Journalists Association, taking her to the master's program in writing at Johns Hopkins University, in Baltimore, Maryland, where she received a degree in 1991.

Working as a freelance writer, Chang soon became famous for her book *The Rape of Nanking: The Forgotten Holocaust of World War II*, published in 1997. The book grew from an interest Chang developed as a child when her parents told her stories of her grandparents' escape from Nanking (Nanjing), China, when the Japanese invaded. In November 1937, the Japanese Imperial Army overpowered Nanking, China's capital and home to 1.3 million people, and began a massive attack of murder, rape, and looting. By the time order was restored two months later, hundreds of thousands of Chinese had died, and hundreds of thousands more were left homeless, starving, and in shock. "The Rape of Nanking", as it became known, continued to cause international controversy at the end of the 1900s. Japanese politicians refused to apologize completely to China and Chang argued that Japanese school textbooks continued to distort the events. Chang's book drew criticism from some Japanese people.

Chang's book was the first full account of the "Rape of Nanking" written in English. While many books and investigations had been done on the horrors of the Holocaust in Europe, few Westerners—or even Asians—knew of the carnage of Nanking until Chang wrote her book. People did not know that the Japanese troops behaved so brutally towards the people of Nanking. Chang's book details how, on orders from the Imperial family of Japan, the soldiers tortured and killed more than 300,000 Chinese civilians over eight weeks. Japanese invaders raped 80,000 women, killed babies with bayonets, skinned living people, and beheaded civilians with swords.

Chang's research took her to several sources. Finding little that was not obscure and scholarly she attended a convention in 1994 called the Global Alliance for Preserving the Truth of the Sino-Japanese War. ("Sino" means Chinese.) There she saw her first photographs of the brutalities of the battle. She also researched sources at the Yale Divinity School and the United

States National Archives in Washington, D.C., Chang was able to use many untapped sources, including the diaries of foreign missionaries who lived in China when the Japanese attacked. A very ironic source was a German Nazi businessman, John Rabe, who lived in Nanking. Rabe worked tirelessly to help many Chinese people, and became known as "the living Buddha of Nanking." Ironically, as a committed Nazi, Rabe wore a swastika armband. Rabe's diaries were later published in several languages, including *The Good Man of Nanking: The Diaries of John Rabe* (2000) in English. Rabe had been head of the Nanjing branch of Siemens, the German electronics firm, and had lived and worked in China for almost 30 years. When the Japanese invaded, Rabe organized a safety zone as a refuge for Chinese civilians. His diaries describe the terrible events and his saving of nearly 250,000 lives. Rabe even pleaded with Adolf Hitler to intervene and stop the slaughter, though Hitler did not do so.

Another person profiled in Chang's book was Minnie Vautrin, a **missionary** educator who became remembered as the legendary "Living Goddess of Mercy" for her courage during the Japanese invasion. Vautrin was among a handful of foreigners who helped shield civilians from Japanese troops. "She could have easily left Nanking when embassy personnel fled, but she stayed in the city. That she stayed with the Nanking women and acted as their champion was stunning," said Chang.

The Rape of Nanking became an immediate best seller, being the first complete narrative on the topic. It came out at a time when Americans were memorializing World War II at its 50th anniversary. The *Rape of Nanking* remained on *The New York Times* best seller list for 10 months.

Chang experienced intense emotions writing the book. She learned about the terrible things that ordinary people can do to others, and she concluded from her research that "almost all people have this potential for evil." Most of the Japanese who committed the atrocities, she said, "were model citizens from Japan" and after they returned home from China, they again "became respectable members of the community." Chang's book suggested that the Japanese government pay reparations to the Chinese and apologize for their army's horrific acts of 60 years ago.

Chang's work helped many second-generation Japanese and Chinese Americans to become more aware of their history. In 1996, Chang helped host a three-day conference on the

The Rape of Nanking became an immediate best seller, being the first complete narrative on the topic.

missionaries representatives of a particular religion in a foreign land, seeking to win converts.

Nanking massacre at Stanford University. Professors also began teaching the story of Nanking in history classes attended by Asian Americans. Chang applauded the growth of activism among young Chinese Americans as they entered fields of filmmaking and literature.

Chang's first book also gained a great deal of respect. The book, *Thread of the Silkworm* (1996), told the story of Tsian Hsue-shen, a Chinese-born aeronautics scientist who was deported from the United States on false charges during a period of American paranoia about Communism called McCarthyism. Senator Joseph McCarthy headed the frenzy during the 1950s. In China, Tsian Hsue-shen directed the development of the Silkworm missiles, the Chinese missile that was sold to enemy countries of the United States, including Iraq.

Chang married Bretton Lee Douglas, an electrical engineer, in 1991. She lived in Sunnyvale, California, and worked on a third book she called *The Chinese in America: A Narrative History.* ◆

Chang, Michael

FEBRUARY 22, 1972– ● TENNIS PLAYER

Only seventeen when he became the youngest man in history to win the French Open tennis championship, the American racquet whiz Michael Chang has gone on to maintain his stature as one of the top dozen or so tennis players in the world, accumulating 34 tournament championships. At five feet nine inches, Chang is one of the smaller players in today's power game, but his catlike speed, agility, and tenacity have made him one of the past decade's most successful—as recently as 1997, he ranked number three in the world although he had dropped to number fifty by 1999.

Michael Te Pei Chang was born on February 22, 1972, in Hoboken, New Jersey, the second of two sons of Joe and Betty Chang. Joe, a research chemist who emigrated from China in 1948, made a scientific project of his sons' tennis training almost as soon as they could walk. Young Michael started at two with table tennis and then moved on to the tennis court with his older brother, Carl, now his coach. By the late 1970s the

Changs had moved to St. Paul, Minnesota, where the Chang brothers were the class of the junior tennis circuit, often facing each other in tournament finals. As Michael later told an interviewer, "I've spent my life playing guys who are bigger and stronger than I am. My introduction to that came against my older brother, Carl. When we were younger, our matches were absolute battles, and he was always taller, bigger, and stronger. Playing him made me stronger."

By the time Michael was ten, Joe and Betty Chang had moved the family to southern California in search of more challenging tennis opponents for their sons. They found plenty—including Peter Sampras, Jim Courier, and Andre Agassi, who joined Michael in dominating U.S. tennis throughout the 1990s. By his midteens, Michael had begun to pull away from that illustrious pack of **prodigies,** capturing the U.S. junior championship at the age of fifteen and, a year later, becoming the youngest player in nearly 60 years to qualify for play on Wimbledon's center court. Having dropped out of high school at the age of fifteen to concentrate on his training, young Michael was betting everything on tennis.

Michael Chang after winning the 1989 French Open.

prodigies unusually precocious and gifted children or young people.

The wager paid off handsomely only two years later when Chang catapulted to international stardom with his stunning victory at the 1989 French Open. After overcoming severe cramps to prevail in a punishing five-set clash with number-one-ranked Ivan Lendl in the round of sixteen world (the match Chang considers his greatest achievement), Chang rolled over the opposition in the next two rounds to face Sweden's Stefan Edberg in the finals. Falling behind two sets to one, Chang won the next two sets to become the youngest player ever to win a major tournament and the first American victor in the French Open since 1955. Standing on center court in his moment of triumph, the 17-year-old champion told a worldwide television audience, "I

1972 Chang is born in Hoboken, New Jersey.

1984 Chang wins first national title, the USTA Junior Hardcourt Singles.

1987 Chang wins USTA Boys 18's Hardcourts.

1989 Chang upsets top-seeded Ivan Lendl to win the French Open.

1997 Chang is ranked as the number three tennis player in the world.

thank the Lord Jesus Christ," eliciting a sprinkling of boos from the famously anticlerical Parisian sophisticates in the crowd.

In the dizzying rush of media attention and commercial endorsements over the next year, Chang seemed to lose the razor edge of concentration that had catapulted him to the top of the tennis heap. After zooming to number five in the world after the French Open, Chang slid to number fifteen over the next two years as Agassi, Sampras, and Courier surpassed him in victories and renown. A number of tennis analysts began to write Chang off as a one-hit wonder. Determined to reenter the circle of the tennis elite, Chang fired his coach Phil Dent in 1991 and brought on his brother, Carl, to oversee his game.

Despite the skepticism of some observers, who thought that Michael was trading competence for family loyalty, the change wrought a marked improvement within one year—by 1992 Chang was back in the top ten and remained there for the next five years despite his failure to capture any more Grand Slam titles. To compete in what was increasingly becoming a power game, the Changs worked at adding velocity to Michael's underwhelming first serve. Advancing from his sedate baseline style of play, Michael Chang evolved into a serve-and-volley aggressor and saw his rankings rise accordingly. Reflecting on his oscillating fortunes, Chang told a reporter, "I certainly would not compare what I've endured with Job. But I see the point. One thing I can relate to is the patience and perseverance of Job. In many ways I think I need to be more patient. It's easy to get caught up in wondering, 'When's my turn?' But that only creates unnecessary pressure."

The unmarried Chang resided in Henderson, Nevada, where he devoted himself to his off-court hobbies, catching and breeding fish. ◆

Chang, Sarah

1981– ● CONCERT VIOLINIST

Sarah Chang was born in Philadelphia, Pennsylvania, in 1981 to Korean parents who immigrated to the United States in 1979. Chang's father, Dr. Min Soo Chang, was a violinist, and her mother, Myoung, was a pianist and composer. Clearly a child prodigy, Chang began to study violin with her father at age four. Although she longed to play her father's violin, he bought her a more suitable one that was a 1/16 size. Within a year, Chang had performed with several orchestras in the Philadelphia area. At the age of eight, famous conductor Zubin Mehta invited Chang to appear as a soloist with the New York Philharmonic at Avery Fisher Hall. The audience gave her a standing ovation for her rendition of Paganini's Violin Concerto No. 1. She then auditioned for Riccardo Muti at the Philadelphia Orchestra, leading to another engagement that year.

By age 18, violinist Chang had gained worldwide recognition as one of classical music's most captivating and gifted artists. Appearing in the music capitals of Asia, Europe, and the Americas, she collaborated with nearly every major orchestra, including the New York Philharmonic, the Philadelphia Orchestra, the Chicago Symphony, the Boston Symphony, the Cleveland Orchestra, the Los Angeles Philharmonic, the San Francisco Symphony, and the Pittsburgh Symphony. After her Pittsburgh performance, a critic with the *Washington Post* wrote, "Nine-year-old Sarah Chang mixed supple phrasing and mind-boggling technique in virtually tossing off Paganini's fiendish First Concerto. Chang plays with controlled abandon, never distorting her gorgeous tone or the music's structure and leaving plenty of room for her maturing lyric sense to shine."

Her other North American engagements included appearances with the Saint Paul Chamber Orchestra and the symphony orchestras of Baltimore, Milwaukee, Montreal, Seattle, and Vancouver. Internationally, Chang appeared with the Berlin Philharmonic, the Vienna Philharmonic, the Royal Concertgebouw Orchestra of Amsterdam, the Leipzig Gewandhaus Orchestra, the Orchestre National de France and the principal London orchestras.

Among the distinguished conductors with whom Chang has worked are Daniel Barenboim, Sir Colin Davis, Charles Dutoit, Bernard Haitink, James Levine, Lorin Maazel, Kurt Masur, Zubin Mehta, Riccardo Muti, Andre Previn, Wolfgang Sawallisch and Leonard Slatkin.

During the 1998-99 season, Chang had an especially active season in Europe, appearing with Valery Gergiev and the London Philharmonic, Sir Colin Davis and the London Symphony Orchestra and Wolfgang Sawallisch and the Vienna Symphony, as well as with the Bamberg Symphony, the Bilbao Symphony, the Gulbenkian Orchestra of Lisbon, the Prague Chamber Orchestra and the Warsaw Philharmonic.

1981 Chang is born in Philadelphia, Pennsylvania.

1992 Chang becomes the youngest artist to receive the highly desired Avery Fisher Career Grant.

1992 Chang's performance at the Concert for Planet Earth is broadcast worldwide, airing on PBS's *Great Performances in the United States*.

Chang gave a series of concerts in Israel with the Israel Philharmonic Orchestra under Zubin Mehta and joined Charles Dutoit and the NHK Symphony on their United States tour in 1999.

Chang reached an even wider audience through her many television appearances, including several concert broadcasts. Chang's 1992 performance at the Concert for Planet Earth was broadcast worldwide, airing on PBS's *Great Performances in the United States*. The concert was later released on a Sony compact disc.

She also produced best-selling recordings for EMI Classics, releasing two albums of **virtuoso** encore pieces, *Debut* and *Simply Sarah*. She recorded the Tchaikovsky Concerto with Sir Colin Davis and the London Symphony; the Paganini Concerto No. 1 and works of Saint-Saens with Wolfgang Sawallisch and the Philadelphia Orchestra; and a coupling of the Lalo "Symphonie espangole" and the Vieuxtemps Violin Concerto No. 5 with the Concertgebouw and Philharmonia orchestras led by Charles Dutoit.

Chang also recorded Vaughan Williams' "The Lark Ascending" with Bernard Haitink and the London Philharmonic. She released the Mendelssohn and Sibelius Concertos with Mariss Jansons and the Berlin Philharmonic.

In 1992, Chang became the youngest artist to receive the coveted Avery Fisher Career Grant. She also earned a special Gramophone award as "Young Artist of the Year" (1993) and "Newcomer of the Year" honors at the International Classical Music Awards in London for 1994.

Critics often compared Chang to Korean prodigy Midori because both were Asian and both studied under the same teacher at Juilliard, DeLay. Chang's style, though, could be contrasted to Midori's style in that Chang was known for her brilliant technical skill and a boldness that contrasted to Midori's more elegant style.

Chang continued to attend the Germantown Friends High School in Cherry Hill, New Jersey. Her favorite school topics were social studies and French. Chang continued violin studies with famed Dorothy DeLay at the Juilliard School for performing arts in New York City, which she had begun at age six. She faxed her homework back to school while traveling for concerts. Chang practiced violin four hours a day and attended Juilliard all day Saturday, studying such subjects as music theory and chamber music. In her free time, Chang enjoyed roller-skating and favorite television shows, including Saturday morning cartoons. Chang avoided such sports as gymnastics in which she could injure her fingers. Her parents and teachers made sure she only performed two times a month so she could have a relatively normal life.

As she entered the 21st century and young adulthood, Chang continued to shine. In *Strings* magazine, Feb/Mar 2001, music critic Robert Moon reviewed the fall violin concerts in the San Francisco Bay Area. Of Chang's performance he wrote, "Chang, at 20, enters the post-prodigy period of her life as a musician striving to replace the pristine wonder of youth with maturity and substance. Her Dvorak was serenely beautiful, while the lengthy solo introduction of the Ravel was brilliant if not flawlessly executed." ◆

Chang, Sun-Young Alice

MARCH 24, 1948– ● MATHEMATICIAN

Sun-Young Alice Chang was born March 24, 1948, in Ci-an, China. She studied at the National University of Taiwan, receiving her bachelor's of science degree in 1970. She then traveled to the United States to study for her doctorate. In 1974, Chang was awarded a Ph.D. from the University of California, Berkeley.

Chang was appointed assistant professor at the State University of New York at Buffalo, where she taught from 1974 to 1975. She then became the Hedrick Assistant Professor at the University of California at Los Angeles until 1977, when she moved to the University of Maryland to serve as an assistant professor. She became a Sloan Fellow at the university from 1979 to 1980. Chang returned in 1980 to the University of California at Los Angeles as an associate professor, and was later promoted to full professor.

Sun-Young Alice Chang

1948 Chang is born in Ci-an, China.

1974 Chang earns a doctorate in mathematics from the University of California at Berkeley.

1974 Chang is appointed assistant professor at the State University of New York at Buffalo.

1988 Chang is appointed full professor at Berkeley.

1995 Chang wins the Ruth Lyttle Satter Prize in mathematics.

In 1986, Chang was invited to be the speaker at the International Congress of Mathematicians at Berkeley. During the 1988-1989 taught as a full professor at the University of California, Berkeley.

Chang's work involved a very complex level of mathematics. Her research interests included the study of certain geometric types of nonlinear partial differential equations. She also researched the related extremal inequalities and problems in isospectral geometry.

Perhaps Chang's greatest honor came when she received the Ruth Lyttle Satter Prize in Mathematics. This prize is awarded every two years to a woman who has made an outstanding contribution to mathematics research in the previous five years. Chang won the award in 1995. The monetary award is valued at $4,000.

Chang won the award for a study she conducted involving partial differential equations as they related to Riemannian manifolds, and for particular work on extremal problems in spectral geometry and the compact nature of isospectral metrics. The studies were conducted with the assistance of her co-authors Paul Yan, Tom Branson, and Matt Gursky.

At the awards ceremony for the Satter Prize, Chang reflected on the status of women in the profession of mathematics. She said that since her days as a student, the opportunities and avenues for advancement in the profession had increased, and that her success was due primarily to not only hard work, but to role models and the reassurance provided by other women striving to succeed in that particular field. Chang added that even in light of all that has changed, "I think we need even more women mathematicians to prove good theorems and to contribute to the profession." ◆

Chao, Elaine

MARCH 26, 1953– ● POLITICIAN

When President George W. Bush chose Elaine Chao as his Secretary of Labor, she became the first Asian-American woman to occupy a cabinet post. As President Bush said in announcing her nomination, "Elaine Chao believes deeply in the American dream because she has lived it.

She came to the United States at the age of eight, not speaking a word of English."

Chao's rise to eminence is indeed a classic American saga of hard work and ambition rewarded. Elaine Lan Chao was born on March 26, 1953, in Taiwan, where her father, James, arrived in 1949 as a merchant seaman from mainland China in 1949, then in the throes of Mao Ze Dong's communist uprising. Settling in Taiwan, James met and married Ruth, another transplant from the mainland. Seven years after his marriage, James moved to Queens, New York, and later to Nassau County, where struggled at three jobs while putting himself through college. By 1961, having launched his shipping business, James felt secure enough to send for his wife and children.

The eight-year-old Elaine faced the intimidating task of beginning school without knowing any English. Heeding her father's instruction to bow to the teacher, she heard **derisive** laughter from her classmates. As she later told a reporter, "I know what discrimination is." Undaunted, she set feverishly to work mastering her new language and her coursework, aided by her father's firm oversight. Within two years her remarkable progress changed her classmates' ridicule into the ultimate gesture of peer respect: she was elected class president.

After graduating from high school in Syosset, New York, in 1971, Chao set about exploring future careers with characteristic diligence, taking two successive summer jobs. She later recalled, "I had to beg my father. I had to convince him that to be American, I had to get a summer job." To acquaint herself with law, she worked as a librarian's assistant at a Manhattan law firm, and then explored medicine during a stint at the Rusk Institute of Rehabilitation Medicine in New York City. As she later said, "I had an early start at being a workaholic."

Chao went on to attend the prestigious Mount Holyoke College in South Hadley, Massachusetts, from which she graduated with a degree in economics in 1975. She then moved on to Harvard Business School, which awarded her an MBA in 1979. Chao spent the next four years in New York City as a specialist in transportation finance at Citibank before accepting a one-year fellowship at the Reagan White House in 1983.

In 1984 Chao moved to San Francisco to accept a vice presidency at BankAmerica Capital Markets Group. Two years later Chao returned to government as the deputy administrator of the Maritime Administration of the U.S. Department of Transportation. Chao became chairman of the Federal Maritime

1953 Chao is born in Taiwan.

1975 Chao graduates from Mount Holyoke College with a degree in economics.

1979 Chao receives her MBA from Harvard University.

1979 Chao works in the private sector.

1988 Chao begins service as chairman of the Federal Maritime Administration.

1989 Chao begins her service as deputy secretary of transportation.

1992 Chao is named head of the United Way.

1996 Chao begins as a fellow of the Heritage Foundation, a conservative think tank in Washington, D.C.

2001 Chao is appointed and confirmed United States Secretary of Labor.

derisive mocking; taunting.

The Heritage Foundation Asian Studies Center

The Heritage Foundation, founded in 1973, is a politically conservative think tank dedicated to promoting "public policies based on the principles of free enterprise, limited government, individual freedom, traditional American values, and a strong national defense." It supports scholarly research on these issues and presents its findings to members of Congress. The goal is to influence federal legislation on policy issues. The foundation maintains a high public profile through the news media, and Heritage scholars frequently present their findings at academic conferences and in on-campus college lectures as well. It funds its activities through corporate and private donations.

Within the foundation there are a number of divisions and study centers, each dedicated to particular aspects of policy and to the major regions of the world. Among these is the Asian Studies Center (ASC), established in 1983. The ASC, led by Dr. Larry Wortzel (director) and Elaine Chao (advisory council chairperson) is particularly interested in fostering research on how best to spread democracy throughout the nations of the Pacific and in China. Of particular interest to the center is the question of trade between the United States and the nations of Asia and Southeast Asia. A further important area of study is regional security, particularly the proliferation of nuclear arms in Asian countries like North Korea. In times of crisis, as during the 2001 confrontation between the United States and China over a downed American spy plane, ASC scholars are among the select groups of outside experts consulted by the White House for advice.

Administration in 1988, leaving after a year to serve as a deputy secretary in the Department of Transportation, where her effective responses to a series of major disasters—the bombing of Pan Am Flight 103, the Exxon *Valdez* oil spill, the San Francisco earthquake, and Hurricane Hugo—helped to establish her reputation as a first-rate administrator.

From 1991-1992 Chao headed the Peace Corps, where she initiated programs in many of the Eastern European countries that had recently spun out of the orbit of the collapsing Soviet Union. In 1992 Chao accepted the directorship of the country's largest charity, United Way of America, where she burnished the organization's tarnished image with streamlined management techniques and expanded outreach programs. As a reward for her services, the board of the charity offered Chao a bonus of $292,500 when she announced her resignation in 1996, but public indignation obliged her to refuse the money. Betty Beene, the United Way's current president, said of Chao, "She restored the financial stability of the organization and, probably more importantly, the public trust."

think tank organization of intellectuals who write and propose policy for consideration by lawmakers.

In 1996 Chao joined a **think tank,** the Heritage Foundation, in Washington, D.C. There she served as a distinguished fellow for two years before assuming the chairmanship of the foundation's Asian Studies Center Advisory Council. Chao's opportunity to serve as George W. Bush's labor secretary came on the heels of misfortune for the president-elect's first choice, Lynda Chavez, who withdrew from consideration in the face of public outcry over her past retention of the services of an illegal immigrant.

By contrast, Chao's nomination met with warm approval from members of both parties as well as her prospective participants in the labor community. Senator Edward M. Kennedy of Massachusetts, at the time the ranking Democrat on the Senate's Education, Health Labor, and Pensions Committee, said of Chao, "She is an accomplished manager, graceful leader, and she has distinguished herself and her family by her strong commitment to public service." Morton Bahr, president of the Communications Workers of America, praised Chao for "her leadership skills, her integrity, and her ability to bring together diverse interests. Her proven administrative experience and stature are the qualities needed for this important cabinet position, and I believe she will be responsive to the needs of working families. We look forward to working with her."

Upon being nominated as secretary of labor, Chao, a lifelong Republican and the wife of Senator Mitch McConnell of Kentucky, was enthusiastically received by conservative groups and leaders, thus affording her a unique opportunity to foster enhanced cooperation between both sides of the management-labor divide. ◆

> *"I know what discrimination is."*
> Elaine Chao quoted in *The New York Times*, February 26, 2001

Chawla, Kalpana

APRIL 19, 1970– ● ASTRONAUT

Kalpana Chawla was born in Karnal, India, in April 19, 1970. She graduated from Tagore School in Karnal in 1976 and then earned a bachelor of science degree in aeronautical engineering from Punjab Engineering College, India, 1982. Chawla went to the United States to attend the University of Texas, where she earned her master of science degree in aerospace engineering from 1984. Chawla earned her doctorate of philosophy in aerospace engineering from the University of Colorado in 1988.

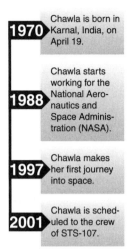

1970 Chawla is born in Karnal, India, on April 19.

1988 Chawla starts working for the National Aeronautics and Space Administration (NASA).

1997 Chawla makes her first journey into space.

2001 Chawla is scheduled to the crew of STS-107.

In 1988, Chawla started working for the National Aeronautics and Space Administration (NASA), the United States government agency that conducts and coordinates research of flight within and beyond the Earth's atmosphere. Chawla worked at the NASA Ames Research Center, which is located at Moffett Field, California, in the heart of "Silicon Valley." Ames specializes in research geared toward creating new knowledge and new technologies that span the spectrum of NASA interests.

At Ames, Chawla worked in the area of powered-lift computational fluid dynamics. Fluid dynamics is a branch of engineering that includes aerodynamics, the study of the forces acting on an object as it moves through air or some other fluid. Aerodynamic forces act on airplanes, sailboats, and any other object moving through the air. Engineers study aerodynamic forces because these forces affect the motion of objects.

Chawla's research concentrated on simulation (imitation) of complex airflows encountered around aircraft such as the Harrier. The Harrier is one of a type of aircraft called V/STOL, which can take off and land vertically or on a very short runway. (V/STOL stands for Vertical/Short Take-Off and Landing.) V/STOLs have great military value because they can land on small airfields near battles. The Harrier is used by the armed forces of the United Kingdom and the United States as a combat plane. It can fly faster than 700 miles per hour. Chawla studied such dynamics as "ground-effect," the cushioning airflow around such craft as the Harrier. Chawla then went on to conduct supporting research in mapping of flow solvers to parallel computers, and tested these solvers by carrying out powered lift computations.

In 1993, Chawla joined the private company of Overset Methods Inc., in Los Altos, California, as Vice President and Research Scientist. She formed a team with other researchers specializing in simulation of moving multiple body problems. Chawla became responsible for developing and implementing efficient techniques involving aerodynamics. Chawla and her colleagues published the results of various projects in technical conference papers and professional journals.

In December 1994, NASA hired Chawla. She reported to the Johnson Space Center in Houston, Texas, in March 1995 as an astronaut candidate in the 15th Group of Astronauts. After completing a year of training and evaluation, she was assigned as a crew representative to work on technical issues for the Astronaut Office EVA/Robotics and Computer Branches. Chawla's assignments included working on development of Robotic Situational Awareness Displays and testing space shuttle control software in the Shuttle Avionics Integration Laboratory.

Chawla made her first journey into space in 1997, when the space shuttle *Columbia* lifted off. She was part of a six-person crew sent to study the sun's outer atmosphere during *Columbia's* 16-day mission. The crew would deploy and retrieve a satellite that will gather information about the sun and conduct several **microgravity** experiments.

microgravity the condition in outer space; also called zero gravity of weightlessness.

Chawla's adventure actually began in November 1996, when she received her assignment as mission specialist and prime robotic arm operator on the STS-87, a position she held from November 19 to December 5, 1997. Mission specialists are astronauts who work with pilot astronauts to maintain the spacecraft and its equipment. They also conduct experiments, launch satellites, and perform space walks. STS-87 was the fourth microgravity flight of its kind. Microgravity is the condition that every space vehicle in orbit experiences. The vehicle and its contents fall freely, resulting in a seemingly weightless floating aboard the spacecraft. Microgravity is often called "zero gravity" or "weightlessness."

Chawla's STS-87 mission focused on experiments designed to study how the weightless environment of space affects various physical processes, and on observations of the sun's outer atmospheric layers. Two members of the crew performed an **extravehicular activity** (EVA), which is when astronauts work outside their vehicle in space, often called a spacewalk. This spacewalk featured the manual capture of a Spartan satellite, in addition to testing EVA tools and procedures for future Space Station assembly.

extravehicular activity work space shuttle astronauts perform in space outside of the shuttle, such as a spacewalk.

In this first mission, Chawla traveled 6.5 million miles in 252 orbits of the Earth and logged 376 hours and 34 minutes in space—more than 15 days. In January 1998, Chawla was assigned as crew representative for shuttle and station flight crew equipment. Later, she was assigned as the lead for Astronaut Office's Crew Systems and Habitability section. She then was assigned to the crew of STS-107 scheduled for launch in 2001.

Chawla enjoyed flying, hiking, backpacking, and reading. She held a certified flight instructor's license with airplane and glider ratings. She also held commercial pilot's licenses for single- and multi-engine land and seaplanes and Gliders. She enjoyed flying aerobatics and tail-wheel airplanes. ◆

Chen, Joan

<small>APRIL 26, 1961– ● ACTRESS</small>

bourgeois relating to or characterization of the middle social class.

ethos the moral sentiment or characteristics that set a group or individual apart.

egalitarianism belief in human equality with respect to social, economic, and political rights.

Joan Chen

By the time she was 26, Joan Chen had managed to vault to film stardom not once, but twice, in two vastly different cultures—first in China, and then in the United States—and each time in a manner that would strain the credulity of the most indulgent movie audience: in China she was plucked from a rifle team by Mao Zedong's wife, then a film producer, and designated for film stardom; and in the United States, a decade later, she was espied in a Hollywood parking lot by the high-powered producer Dino DeLaurentis. But Chen's rise to fame was no mere stroke of dumb luck: a history of family hardship, diligent training, and dogged determination combined with her native beauty and talent to prepare her for her improbable brushes with fate.

Chen Chong was born on April, 26, 1961, in Shanghai, China. Her childhood was disrupted by the convulsions of Mao Zedong's Cultural Revolution, in which a far-left authoritarian faction of the Communist Party sought to rid the country of all vestiges of "**bourgeois**" culture and privilege. Her parents, both distinguished physicians and politically engaged intellectuals, were exiled to the countryside to be cleansed of their corrupting urban cosmopolitanism through "re-education" in the Maoist **ethos** of primitive **egalitarianism.** Unlike millions of other Chinese children, Chen and her younger brother were spared the trauma of being "sent down" to the countryside to "build socialism"; they remained in Shanghai with their grandparents during their long stretches of separation from their parents.

In her first year of high school, while performing with her school's rifle squad, the fourteen-year-old Chen caught the eye of Mao Zedong's wife, then producing a vast, multipart film epic about Mao's legendary Long March during the 1930s. Although the movie in which Chen appeared was never released, she was inspired to lend her talents to China's mostly **propagandistic** film industry. As she later recalled, "I was proud to be doing propaganda, to be of use to the Communist cause." Chen's next major project was *Youth* (1977), in which she played a virtuous young women whose deafness is cured by acupuncture. The hugely popular film made her an instant star in China, prompting talk of Chen becoming a "Chinese Elizabeth Taylor." In her numerous public appearances throughout China, Chen did her best to replicate her cinematic image of purity and virtue for her adoring public. As she later recalled, "I was very young and pure, and I didn't enjoy fame. I would be on a street in any city, and there would be thousands of people falling down hurting themselves, crowding me, their bicycles all trampled, and I wouldn't be able to get out. That scared me."

While attending acting school at the Shanghai Film Studio, Chen made two more notable films: *The Little Flower* (1981), for which she was received The Golden Rooster Award (China's version of the Oscar) for best actress, and *Awakening* (1981). She also won the Hundred Flowers award, bestowed annually on the movie performer who won a nationwide popularity poll.

But Chen soon wearied of the demands of fame and the attendant straitjacket of unwavering virtue that she was obliged to don on and off the screen. As she told a reporter, "In a sense, everything came too easily for me. I was happy to walk away from it all." And that is exactly what she did in 1981, when the 20-year-old Chen decided to join her parents in the United States, where they had been living since the late 1970s on a government-sponsored research grant. After a brief sampling of pre-med courses at the State University of New York at New Paltz, Chen decided to pursue a degree in film at California Sate University at Northridge, which she had discovered as the school's guest at its festival of her films.

While studying at Northridge, Chen, having adopted the English name Joan, began making the rounds of acting auditions while working as a restaurant hostess to pay the bills. As she later recalled, "I started part-time during my summer vacations. But a very surprising thing happened to me. I got rejections. I was highly in demand in China. If I wanted to act [in China], of course people wanted me. I had to realize that [in the United

1961 Chen is born in Singapore, China.

1977 Chen stars in Chinese film *Youth*, which makes her a major star in China.

1981 Chen emigrates to the United States to attend college.

1986 Chen is discovered in a Hollywood parking lot by producer Dino DeLaurentis and lands a role in his television miniseries *Tai-pan*.

1987 Chen stars in *The Last Emperor* to critical acclaim.

1990 Chen stars in David Lynch's innovative television series *Twin Peaks*.

1998 Chen goes to China to direct her first feature film, *Xiu Xiu: The Sent-Down Girl*.

propagandistic description of government-sponsored opinion-shaping methods.

concubine a woman living with a man to whom she is not legally married.

States] nobody had seen Chinese movies. . . . I learned that what [American casting directors] wanted was different. So I changed myself. I felt it was a challenge." What they wanted was the vampish siren stereotype to which so many Asian actresses were consigned in TV and feature-film dramas.

It was a chance encounter in a Hollywood parking lot that lifted Chen's career from the doldrums. When she passed the influential Italian producer Dino DeLaurentis in the lot, he asked her, "Did you know that Lana Turner was discovered in a drugstore?" The flustered Chen had never even heard of Lana Turner, but she sensed the hand of fate on her shoulder. In short order De Laurentis had cast her as the **concubine** May-May in his sweeping TV miniseries *Tai-Pan* (1986), an evocation of the British conquest of Hong Kong. A major ratings success, the series proved a huge career boost for Chen despite the show's critical savaging in the United States and its disrepute among her fans in China, who were appalled to hear about their young icon's descent into the Western decadence of steamy seminude love scenes.

Chen's next major project was a featured role in Bernardo Bertolucci's *The Last Emperor* (1987), an epic feature film about the decline of the Chinese imperial dynasty. Chen's public visibility rose even further with her role as Josie Packard, the eerily menacing widow in *Twin Peaks* (1990), the celebrated, offbeat television miniseries in which producer-director David Lynch explored the surreal depths of a small town's collective unconscious.

Throughout the 1990s Chen sustained the momentum of her feature-film acting career; although Chen was confined to exotic femme-fatale stereotypes in such projects as *Where Sleeping Dogs Lie* (1991), *Steel Justice* (1992), *Shadow of a Stranger* (1992), and *Killing Beach* (1993), her acting talents were afforded more serious material in films such as Oliver Stone's *Heaven and Earth* (1993) and *On Deadly Ground* (1994). She continued to perform in her native tongue in several Hong Kong productions, including *Red Rose, White Rose* (1994).

Chen's longstanding ambition to direct a feature film was realized in her 1998 project *Xiu Xiu: The Sent-Down Girl.* Filmed on location in China, it is the poignant tale of a young Chinese woman who is psychologically ravaged by her deportation to a rural reeducation camp. Because Chinese government officials had insisted on an unacceptable softening of the film's harsh view of the Cultural Revolution, Chen proceeded to shoot surreptitiously, smuggling footage out of the country each day and ultimately incurring a $50,000 fine from the Chinese government. The second film Chen directed, *Autumn in New York* (2000), a romance starring Richard Gere and Winona Ryder, was popular with audiences, but widely panned by critics.

Despite occasional homesickness for Shanghai, Chen happily settled in San Francisco, where she lived with her second husband (a cardiologist) and their daughter. ◆

Chen, Joie

AUGUST 28, 1961– ● NEWSCASTER

Joie Chen, long a familiar face on CNN newscasts, is now the anchor of the network's hour-long weekday program *News-Site*. The CableACE Award-winning newscaster—previously the co-anchor of *The World Today, World News,* and *Prime News*—is one of the few Asian Americans to have earned a top anchor position in a national network news division.

Joie Chen was born on August 28, 1961, in Evanston, Illinois, where her father was a professor of biochemistry at Northwestern University. Chen's father had traveled from his native China in the 1930s to study in Germany and Switzerland. Chen's mother was a forensic physician in her native Japan; she came to the United States in 1958 to refine her command of English and pursue advanced graduate work in medicine. When Joie was three, the couple moved to Evanston, where Mr. Chen joined the Northwestern faculty while Mrs. Chen became a medical researcher specializing in **immunology.**

While growing up in the prosperous suburb of Evanston, where she attended the local public schools, Joie was influenced by her parents' serious attention to current events. One of her earliest memories as a child is watching her father sitting at the kitchen table carefully perusing the day's newspaper while she sat by his side and demanded, "Tell me this story."

Joie's **precocious** affinity for the news never left her. When she was a 12-year-old student at Haven Middle School in Evanston, the school sponsored a career day during which students could go to an Evanston high school to spend a day seeing what life was like in the higher grades. When she was told that high school juniors could take a year of journalism instead of

immunology the science of the causes of immunity and immunity repsonses.

precocious extremely intelligent or talented at a young age.

standard English, her ears pricked up and she returned home and announced to her parents, "I'm going to become a newspaper reporter."

Chen never wavered from that youthful resolution. At Evanston Township High School she was news editor of the school newspaper in her senior year. After graduating in 1978, she enrolled at Northwestern, from which she graduated with a B.S. degree in journalism in 1983. She then went on to study at Northwestern's presitgious Medill School of journalism, which awarded her an M.S. degree in 1983.

Despite her father's pleas that she turn her attention to a more secure career in law, Chen was adamant in pursuing her journalistic dreams. Concerned about the rapid retrenchment in daily newspapers throughout the United States, Chen heeded the advice of a Northwestern professor who urged her to apply for a job in broadcast journalism. The shy and makeup-averse Chen was reluctant to trade newsprint for a microphone, but when she received a job offer from WCIV-TV in Charleston, South Carolina, she grabbed it. Chen initially envisioned herself working behind the camera as a producer and at first divided her time between production work and local on-camera reporting. But Chen proved a natural in front of the camera, and she quickly established herself as one of the market's top local TV journalists. In December 1985 Chen moved on to WXIA-TV in Atlanta, Georgia, where she spent six years chiefly as a beat reporter but also served as a weekend anchor and did a brief stint as the anchor of USA *Today's* syndicated daily new program.

Chen's next major career opening resulted from CNN's decision to expand its interantional division after the Gulf War, when Ted Turner decided to invest in a serious international news division. When she found out through a friend that the Japanese anchor for CNN's international newscast bailed out at the last minute, Chen applied for the spot and in 1991 was hired to anchor the network's morning *World News* program. Three years later Chen became a weekend anchor for CNN's domestic news division. In 1996, after two years in that slot, she teamed up with Leon Harris to anchor CNN's 8:00 P.M. *Prime News*, a stint that earned the pair that year's CableACE award. In the four ensuing years Chen's co-anchors on the evening news have included Jim Moret and Wolf Blitzer. During her stint on Prime News, Chen led the way on numerous breaking stories, including the Timothy McVeigh verdict in May 1997, and the Olympic Park bombing in July 1996.

When CNN revamped its prime-time schedule in November 2000, Chen was reassigned to the network's 4:00 P.M. anchor slot, from which she presides over *NewsSite*, an hour-long survey of the day's major national and internatonal news stories. The word "site" betokens a serious effort to blend news coverage with Internet resources; at each day's production meeting, Chen and her colleagues engage in on-line chats with audience members to elicit their opinions on that day's topics in the news, and the newscast is shaped in accordance with their concerns. Chen then writes a good portion of the script for the newscast. No mere passive newsreader, Chen is actively involved in all major aspects of production of her daily broadcast.

Married since 1991, Chen lived in Atlanta with her husband and their son. ◆

Chiao, Leroy

AUGUST 28, 1960– ● ASTRONAUT

Leroy Chiao was born on August 28, 1960, in Milwaukee, Wisconsin, but grew up in Danville, California. He graduated from Monte Vista High School in 1978 and went on to earn a bachelor of science degree in chemical engineering from the University of California, Berkeley, in 1983. Chiao earned a master of science degree in 1985 and a doctorate in chemical engineering in 1987, both from the University of California, Santa Barbara.

Dr. Chiao joined the Hexcel Corporation in Dublin, California, in 1987. He worked for Hexcel until 1989, during which time he was involved in process, manufacturing, and engineering research on advanced aerospace materials. He worked on a joint project with the National Aeronautics and Space Administration (NASA) and the Jet Propulsion Laboratory (JPL) and Hexcel.

The Jet Propulsion Laboratory is a center for the design of unmanned spacecraft and their control in space. The California Institute of Technology operates the laboratory, located in Pasadena, California, for the National Aeronautics and Space Administration (NASA). NASA is a United States government agency that conducts and coordinates research of flight within and beyond the Earth's atmosphere.

Leroy Chiao

polymer a mixture of chemical compounds formed by a reaction and consisting of competing structural units.

The project Chiao worked on was to develop a practical, optically correct reflector, made entirely of advanced **polymer** composite materials, for future space telescopes. He also worked on cure modeling and finite element analysis.

In January 1989, Chiao joined the Lawrence Livermore National Laboratory in Livermore, California. The Lawrence Livermore Laboratory is a research facility involved primarily in developing national security systems for the United States. The laboratory has produced nuclear warheads for land and air strategic missiles. There Chiao became involved in processing research for fabrication of filament-wound and thick-section aerospace composites. Chiao also developed and demonstrated a mechanistic cure model for graphite fiber/epoxy composite material.

After Chiao had became an instrument-rated pilot, logging over 2,000 flight hours in a variety of aircraft, NASA selected him in January 1990. Dr. Chiao became an astronaut in July 1991. He became qualified for flight assignment as a mission specialist. Mission specialist astronauts work with pilot astronauts to maintain the spacecraft and its equipment. They also conduct experiments, launch satellites, and perform space walks.

Chiao's technical assignments included Space Shuttle flight software verification in the Shuttle Avionics Integration Laboratory (SAIL). He worked for the Astronaut Office Mission Development Branch on crew equipment, the Spacelab, Spacehab, and payloads. Chiao worked on Training and Flight Data File issues. Chiao worked on EVA issues for the EVA Branch of NASA. EVA stands for extravehicular activity and refers to the work that astronauts do outside their vehicle while in space, often called a space walk.

Chiao flew on three space flights. He flew as a mission specialist on STS-65 in 1994, STS-72 in 1996, and STS-92 in 2000. Chiao logged a total of 36 days, 12 hours, 36 minutes and 5 seconds in space—over one month—including over 26 EVA hours in four space walks.

1960 ▶ Chiao is born in Milwaukee, Wisconsin.

1994 ▶ Chiao flies as a mission specialist on STS-65.

1996 ▶ Chiao flies as a mission specialist on STS-72.

2000 ▶ Chiao flies as a mission specialist on STS-92.

The STS-65 Columbia took place from July 8-23, 1994, and was launched from and returned to land at the Kennedy Space Center, Florida, setting a new flight duration record for the Space Shuttle program at that time. The STS-65 mission flew the second International Microgravity Laboratory (IML-2). During the 15-day flight, the seven-member crew conducted more than 80 experiments focusing on materials and life sciences research in microgravity. Microgravity is the condition that every space vehicle in orbit experiences. The vehicle and its contents fall freely, resulting in seemingly weightless floating aboard the spacecraft. Microgravity is also referred to as "zero gravity" or "weightlessness." The STS-65 mission was accomplished in 236 orbits of the Earth, traveling 6.1 million miles in 353 hours and 55 minutes.

The STS-72 *Endeavour* was a nine-day mission, from January 11 to 20, 1996, during which the crew retrieved the Space Flyer Unit (launched from Japan 10 months earlier), and deployed and retrieved the OAST-Flyer. Chiao performed two space walks designed to demonstrate tools and hardware, and evaluate techniques to be used in the assembly of the International Space Station. In completing this mission, Chiao logged a total of 214 hours and 41 seconds in space, including just over 13 EVA hours, and traveled 3.7 million miles in 142 orbits of the Earth.

The STS-92 Discovery, traveling from October 11 to 24, 2000, was launched from the Kennedy Space Center, Florida, and returned to land at Edwards Air Force Base, California. During the 13-day flight, the seven-member crew attached the Z1 Truss and Pressurized Mating Adapter 3 to the International

Space Station using Discovery's robotic arm and performed four space walks to configure these elements. This expansion of the ISS opened the door for future assembly missions and prepared the station for its first resident crew. Chiao totaled 13 hours and 16 minutes of EVA time in two space walks. The STS-92 mission was accomplished in 202 orbits, traveling 5.3 million miles in 12 days, 21 hours, 40 minutes and 25 seconds.

Chaio's expertise earned him a number of professional honors. He was invited to give technical seminars on honeycomb material and bonded panels, and cure modeling of aerospace composite materials, at the Beijing [China] Institute of Aeronautical Materials, and at the Changsha [China] Institute of Technology. He has written for the *International Encyclopedia of Composite Materials*, and was listed in the *Who's Who in Science and Engineering*. Chaio received the Distinguished Alumni Award from University of California, Santa Barbara. He was the Keynote Commencement Speaker for the Departments of Engineering at the University of California at Berkeley, and at Santa Barbara, in 1996.

As of 2001, Chaio remained single and enjoyed flying, basketball, racquetball, and skiing. ◆

Cho, Margaret

DECEMBER 5, 1968– ● COMEDIAN

salvos spirited verbal attacks.

milieu setting.

In a field traditionally dominated by male performers, the stand-up comedian Margaret Cho has won a loyal following with her caustic **salvos** about the hypocrisies and banalities of American culture, especially the ethnic and racial stereotyping that she has had to battle in forging her uncompromisingly impudent style of humor.

Cho attributes her skewed sensibility to the raffish **milieu** of the Haight-Ashbury district of San Francisco in which she was raised. As Cho later told a reporter, "I grew up and went to grammar school on Haight Street during the '70s. There were old hippies, ex-druggies, burnouts from the '60s, drag queens, and Chinese people. To me it was a melting pot—that's the least of it. It was a really confusing, enlightening, wonderful time." It was also the source of Cho's fascination with and affection for gay subculture; as she once, "Gay men are my true audience."

Cho's parents emigrated to the United States in 1963, settling in San Francisco, where her mother, Young-Hie, worked as a teacher and her father, Seung-Hoon, as a janitor and later as an auditor. Her parents eventually opened a bookstore in the Haight District, where Margaret helped out and assimilated the rebellious attitudes of shop's **bohemian** customers. As Cho later commented, "[My parents] couldn't afford charm school for me, so this was the next best thing."

Cho attended the San Francisco High School of the Performing Arts, where she began assembling material for a stand-up comedy act, regularly honing her material before audiences at the Rose and Thistle, a club located right above her parents' bookstore. As she branched out to other local clubs, she enrolled as a theater arts major at San Francisco State University. While there she placed first in the West Coast division championship of the U.S. College Comedy Competition. After a second-place finish at the competition finals later that year in Daytona Beach, Florida, the contest's emcee, Jerry Seinfeld, was impressed enough to offer her personal encouragement.

That important vote of confidence emboldened Cho to drop out of college in 1991 and try her luck in Los Angeles, from which she fanned out across the country on the college and club comedy circuit, attracting a growing following among audiences and talent scouts alike. She made her national TV debut on *The Arsenio Hall Show,* which was followed shortly by a guest appearance on a Bob Hope prime-time comedy special on NBC. She soon became a familiar face on the late-night talk shows while maintaining an increasingly hectic and lucrative schedule of bookings on the road, a period Cho recalls with mixed emotions. "I had kind of a hard time," she said of her touring life, "because it was one of the first times I ever really experienced racism. Really weird things would happen, like people staring at me or curious about me or whatever. When I was out there, I would think that if we had some kind of material out here to show these people Asians aren't so different, they could see Asians as being Americans, too."

After Cho was voted the nation's top female comedian at the 1994 American Comedy Awards, she was offered the opportunity to develop a sitcom for ABC. The show's premise—the trials of a mercurial, rebellious young women contending with her traditionalist bookstore-owner parents—was obviously a loose re-creation of Cho's upbringing in San Francisco. Cho characterized the show's main character as another aspect of

1968 Cho is born in the Haight-Ashbury district of San Francisco.

1991 Cho drops out of college and moves to Los Angeles to try to make it as a stand-up comic; she wins the West Coast division championship of the U.S. College Comedy competition.

1994 Cho becomes the first Asian American of Korean descent to star in a TV sitcom, *All-American Girl.*

1995 *All-American Girl* is canceled because of poor ratings.

1999 Cho stars in Off-Broadway and film version of her one-woman show, *I'm the One That I Want.*

bohemian person living an unconventional lifestyle, usually in a community of like-minded people.

> *"I think that I get a lot of humor and jokes and stories from painful experience, uncomfortable experience; but I can alter my perspective and really enjoy what's happened to me and enjoy it again and again in the storytelling."*
> Margaret Cho during an interview with Scott Simon on National Public Radio's *Morning Edition*, August 12, 2000

timorous fearful or timid; reluctant to change.

herself. As the first network series to feature an Asian American star, the show raised equal measures of hope and anxiety in the community it sought to depict. The results were disappointing both to critics, who found the show labored and trite, and to Asian Americans, many of whom found the premise patronizing and caricatured. The show fared only slightly better among the audience—after a strong debut, *All-American Girl* sagged among nationally ranked shows and was canceled after only one troubled season.

Cho was devastated by the show's abrupt demise, which she believed was a result of the undermining of **timorous** network executives in unfamiliar ethnic territory. "[They were] used to seeing a certain kind of woman; meek, quiet and slim. I was none of that." The cancelation and its aftermath, which Cho called "my journey to hell," led the troubled star to seek solace in a prolonged bout of drugs and alcohol that took a temporary toll on her stand-up career. The normally self-revelatory Cho is still reluctant to discuss those trying years. "I really haven't talked about it, and I certainly haven't been able to laugh about it," she told an interviewer.

Fully recovered from those debilitating indulgences, Cho rebounded in 1999 with a rousingly successful one-woman Off-Broadway show in New York, *I'm the One That I Want*. The production earned her *New York* magazine's Performance of the Year award along with Entertainment Weekly's rating as one of the great performances of the year. Filmed for limited release in movie theaters, the show proved equally successful among movie critics and audiences, becoming one of three films to gross at least $1 million from the distribution of ten or fewer prints.

Cho began writing material for her next one-woman show, *Notorious C.H.O.*, scheduled to begin touring in the fall of 2001. ◆

Chopra, Deepak

1947– ● AUTHOR

Time magazine has called Deepak Chopra "the poet-prophet of alternative medicine"; since the publication of his first book in 1987, the Indian-born Chopra has emerged as America's leading **apostle** of New Age spirituality and **holistic** healing through a series of best-selling books and popular PBS television specials. A founder of the American Association of **Ayurvedic Medicine** in Colorado Springs, Colorado, he has championed Eastern notions of the interaction of mind and body in achieving mental and physical health.

Deepak Chopra

apostle believer and advocate.

holistic concerned with wholes or complete systems instead of analysis of parts.

Ayurvedic medicine the ancient Indian doctrine of physical and mental well-being are interrelated; ayurvedic is a Sanskrit word meaning "life science."

Chopra claims to have forgotten his exact age, although he has acknowledged having been born in 1947 in New Delhi, India. His father, Kishnan, was an Indian Army doctor during World War II who later trained as a cardiologist in London. Raised in middle-class comfort in New Delhi, Deepak and his younger brother Sanjiv, who also became a doctor, attended Christian missionary schools. By the time he reached high school, Deepak was writing short stories, several of which were published and won awards. He was intent on becoming a writer until his encounter with medical heroes in various novels inspired him to study medicine. As Chopra later told a reporter, "My father really wanted me to go into medicine, and I had told him I wasn't interested, that I was, in fact, going to graduate in English literature in college and them seek a career in England as a journalist. I had it all planned out. And then I read these books. I was fascinated by these doctors, and so I took my father by surprise and informed that I wanted to go to medical school."

Chopra completed a combined undergraduate/medical course at the All-India Institute of Medical Sciences in six years. He then spent six months working with impoverished patients in the Indian countryside, where he felt unprepared by his training for the dire suffering he confronted. It was there that Chopra first encountered Ayurvedic medicine, the ancient Indian doctrine that sees mental and physical well-being as intertwined. Although he later became a major proponent of this doctrine in the West, at first he was skeptical: "I viewed it the

1947 Chopra is born in New Delhi, India.

1960s Chopra works as a village doctor in rural India.

1970s Chopra practices endocrinology in New Jersey and Massachusetts.

1985 Chopra meets Maharishi Mahesh Yogi and with him helps to found TM Ayurvedic foundation; resigns from his medical position and becomes the director of the TM Ayurvedic Clinic in Lancaster, Massachusetts.

1993 Chopra moves to La Jolla, California to assume the directorship of the Sharp Institute for Human Potential and Mind-Body Medicine in La Jolla, California.

1996 Chopra founds the Chopra Center for Well Being in La Jolla.

endocrinology the science dealing with the endocrine glands.

transcend to go beyond the limits or rise above something.

way most people do now: as some traditional folklore, with maybe a little relevance. I had no idea it was so profound."

Chopra and his wife, Rita, moved to the United States in 1970. After completing a one-year internship at Muhlenberg Hospital in Plainfield, New Jersey, Chopra moved to Boston, where he served as a resident for two years at a private clinic and noted that the patients who most earnestly sought healing were those who proved most responsive to treatment. This experience proved decisive in shaping Chopra's conviction that "what a patient believes can be the deciding factor in his disease."

Remaining in Boston, Chopra established a successful practice in **endocrinology** while also teaching at various medical schools: Tufts University, Harvard University, and Boston University. Despite his outstanding success—he eventually became chief of staff at New England Memorial Hospital in Stoneham, Massachusetts—Chopra was beset by doubts and anxieties about the direction of his career. He could meet his demanding schedule only with the aid of coffee and cigarettes all day and could relax at night only with a glass of whiskey. Seeking to escape the tightening coil of his unhealthy career demands, Chopra took up **Transcendental** Meditation (TM) and within just a few weeks had relinquished caffeine, tobacco, and alcohol.

The success of his TM regimen prompted Chopra to rediscover the Hindu tradition of Ayurveda (a Sanskrit word meaning "life science"), which seeks health and inner peace through a balance of mental and physical energies through meditation and herbal supplements. Chopra met with TM's leader and founder, the Maharishi Mahesh Yogi, in 1985 and agreed to help in establishing a TM Ayurvedic foundation. Chopra resigned from his medical position and became the director of the TM Ayurvedic Clinic in Lancaster, Massachusetts. He also co-founded the Maharishi's herbal supplement supplier, Ayur-Veda Products, Inc.

The Lancaster Clinic became a favorite alternative healing resource of the rich and famous—fees ranged as high as $4,000 per week—submitting to regimens that included daily enemas, sesame-oil massages, baths, special diets, and various herbal treatments. While working at the clinic, Chopra began writing books on his alternative therapies, the first of which, *Creating Health: The Psychophysiological Connection*, was self-published in 1985. Chopra's second book, *Return of the Rishi* (1987), disappointed many reviewers, who expected to find in it a detailed explanation of Ayurvedic medicine but found instead an anecdotal, mostly autobiographical account of Chopra's path to alternative healing.

Chopra and two coauthors wrote an article on Ayurvedic medicine for the *Journal of the American Medical Association* (JAMA) in May 1991. Five months later a rebuttal appeared in which two doctors castigated Chopra and his collaborators for having failed to divulge their affiliation with the TM movement and its allied companies, thus using the **auspices** of JAMA to promote their line of herbal supplements. The ensuing controversy, in which Chopra unsuccessfully sued JAMA for damage to his professional reputation, led him to sever his ties with the Maharishi's TM movement in 1993.

In June 1993 Chopra moved to La Jolla, California to assume the directorship of the Sharp Institute for Human Potential and Mind-Body Medicine in La Jolla, California. In 1996 he founded the Chopra Center for Well Being in La Jolla, where clients are offered a variety of Ayurvedic treatments, both preventive and curative. During his time in La Jolla Chopra's renown has flourished, thanks to his series of best-selling books and his appearances on PBS, in which he offers counsel not only on bodily health but also on overall spiritual enlightenment. Among his most popular works in recent years have been *Ageless Body, Timeless Mind* (1993); *The Seven Spiritual Laws of Success: A Practical Guide to the Fulfillment of Your Dreams* (1994); *The Return of Merlin* (1995); *How to Know God: The Soul's Journey into the Mystery of Mysteries* (2000); and *The Soul in Love: Poems of Prayer and Ecstasy* (2001).

Chopra lived in La Jolla with his wife, Rita. ◆

> *"Understand that the physical world is just a mirror of a deeper intelligence."*
> Ageless Body, Timeless Mind by Deepak Chopra (1993)

auspices kindly patronage and support.

Chow, Amy

MAY 15, 1978– ● OLYMPIC GYMNAST

Amy Chow, a six-year member of the U.S. National Gymnastics Team, became the first Asian American on that team. At the 1996 Olympics, she helped her team win the first American women's gymnastics gold medal. Chow also earned an individual silver medal on the uneven bars in the apparatus finals at the 1996 Olympics.

Amy Chow was born in San Jose, California, on May 15, 1978 to Nelson and Susan Chow. Nelson was born in Canton,

Amy Chow (right) and Shannon Miller with their gold medals at the 1995 Pan American Games.

China, and Susan was born in Hong Kong. They met in the United States, where both had come to attend university. Amy had one brother, Kevin, born in 1979. The Chows wanted their children to have the best advantages that America had to offer. Although they spoke their native language together, they raised their children to speak only English. Susan Chow cooked the traditional dishes of her native country, though, and Amy especially loved her mother's broccoli beef.

Susan Chow, who had once had dreams of being a ballerina, took Amy to a ballet class, but the teacher said she was too young. Amy was three. So Mrs. Chow took her to the West Valley Gymnastics School for a tumbling class. Little did she know that Amy would remain there for over 15 years and that her coaches—Mark Young and Diane Amos—would lead her to be an Olympic gymnast.

Chow began gymnastics in 1981 with weekly sessions that soon increased to more sessions when her talent showed. At age six, Amy became enamoured—as did the nation—of gymnast Mary Lou Retton, winner in the 1984 Olympics. Amy's brother also studied gymnastics and dreamed of the Olympics.

Amy's favorite apparatus/event became the uneven parallel bars, for which she often created new moves. She was fortunate in having the same coaches for the whole of her young training years, receiving gentle but strong guidance from them. Amy also received training from choreographer Geza Pozsar, who helped her with floor exercises and routines.

Chow began winning in national competitions in 1990, winning more than 15 major competitions all over the United States by 1996. In 1992, she won her first international competition, and went on to win 10 major international events by 1996. At the 1995 Pan American Games, she won the vault, placed second on bars, and came in third in the all-around, helping her team clinch the gold medal. She was a member of the U.S. team that won the 1994 World Championship silver medal.

Chow graduated from Castilleja High School with honors and a grade point average over 4.0. Her coaches then cranked up her training schedule for the Olympic trials. Amy would spend all day in the gym, training from 9:30 A.M. to 12:30, then going from 4 P.M. to 7:30 P.M. She did well enough at the trials in Boston to make the U.S. team.

Chow joined a team that was to become famous by the end of the 1996 Summer Olympics in Atlanta. The U.S. women's gymnastics team, which was to earn the nickname, "Magnificent Seven," included Shannon Miller, Amanda Borden, Dominique Dawes, Dominique Moceanu, Jaycie Phelps, and Kerri Strug. Chow enjoyed sharing housing in Atlanta with her new set of girlfriends.

Delivering one of the Olympics' most impressive performances and thrilling world viewers with their flawless routines, the team won the gold medal. This was the first gold medal ever for a U.S. women's gymnastics team and Chow was the first Asian American on a U.S. women's gymnastics team. She also distinguished herself by winning the individual silver Olympic medal for her performance on the parallel bars.

After the 1996 Olympics, America's new darlings went on a 30-city tour. On a gymnastics scholarship, Chow enrolled at Stanford University in Palo Alto, California, that fall. She chose Stanford partly to remain close to home, and majored in biology. She planned to go to medical school to become a pediatrician.

Continuing in gymnastic competitions, Chow took a year off from her studies to train for the 2000 Olympic Games in Sydney, Australia. In July 2000, she competed at U.S. Gymnastics

1978 Chow is born in San Jose, California.

1981 Chow begins gymnastics at age three.

1996 Chow and her teammates win the first ever gold medal for a U.S. women's gymnastics team.

1996 Chow wins the individual silver Olympic medal for her performance on the parallel bars.

2000 Chow competes in the Olympic Games in Sydney, Australia.

Championships for the first time since 1996, placing sixth in the all-around and earning a spot at the Olympic Trials. She also won the balance beam national title.

At Sydney, the U.S. women's gymnastics team showed great spirit under the guidance of world-famous coach Bela Karolyi. But the team did not have what it needed to defeat world champion Romania, which won its second gold medal, or Russia, which won the silver, or China, which took the bronze. Four years after the great triumph in Atlanta, the American team finished fourth in the women's team final competition.

In spite of not achieving top place, the American team impressed Olympic watchers with their spirit on the floor and their exuberance off of it. They pranced and played and charmed, winning the affections of a world audience. At age 22, Chow was old for a gymnast, but commentators suggested she may try again for the 2004 Olympic games.

Chow was an accomplished pianist, having taken lessons since age five. Her favorite book was *The Joy Luck Club* by Amy Tan and she listened to pop singer Celine Dion and classical music. She enjoyed old *I Love Lucy* television shows and collected dolphin mementos. Her family encouraged her to have fun, and she enjoyed movies, swimming, and friends. Chow's brother, Kevin, also attended Stanford, where he competed for the men's gymnastics team. ◆

Chu, David

1955– ● CLOTHING DESIGNER; CEO

David Chu turned an interesting summer class into a road that led to becoming the founder and designer for Nautica, a popular American clothing manufacturing company.

David Chu was born in Taiwan in 1955. As a child, he liked to draw and enjoyed making sketches of his family and friends. Chu came to America in 1968 as a teenager to pursue his dream of being an architect, landing in New York City. But he ended up taking summer drawing classes at New York's Fashion Institute of Technology, which changed his career path. "The fundamentals of architecture and fashion are the same," Chu later declared. "Always start with a good base and never regret it."

The drawing course sparked Chu's interest in apparel. He suddenly became inspired to turn his considerable design talents to clothing. Chu perceived a lack of excitement in men's outerwear designs at the time and saw an opportunity to create a line that was fashionable, bold, and fun—but also highly functional. He gained experience by designing for Catalina Sportswear.

Chu launched his own business in 1983 with six original designs for men's outerwear. He named his company Nautica—from the Latin word for ship, *nauticus*. As the company's symbol, Chu used a spinnaker, a large triangular sail set on a long pole used when running before the wind. Spinnakers are often made in red, blue, and other bright colors. Chu liked the imagery of a spinnaker in full sail as a symbol of adventure, action, and classicism that his company would represent. Chu said, "The image of a boat in full sail is an image of bold adventure around the world."

Chu took advantage of Americans' increased interest in physical health to create high quality designer athletic wear. His designs were applauded as clean cut, non–fussy styles. Nautica did not break fashion frontiers, but rather held a classic line.

Chu built Nautica into a multimillion dollar retailing force and a household name. By the late 1990s, men's sportswear remained the signature component of the Nautica collection. However, the company also featured men's tailored clothing, furnishings, eyewear, shoes, swimwear, fragrances, gloves, hats, and watches. Nautica had a women's line of clothing and collections for boys, girls, and infants. Nautica also had its imprint on a Lincoln-Mercury Villager minivan.

Before long, Nautica had opened more than 76 stores internationally. Chu's international marketing aimed to cater to the different needs of each country. By 2000, Nautica had a flagship store in New York and over 100 retail stores worldwide. Nautica stock was publicly traded on the NASDAQ stock exchange under the symbol NAUT.

In 1996, Chu and Nautica sponsored the yacht *Falconer 2000* for the America's Cup "Young America" team. America's Cup is the world's most famous sailing competition.

Employees found Chu to be down to earth. He took his work seriously, but did not make it his only priority. Chu often wore Nautica clothes, such as an ensemble of yellow polo top, khakis, navy blazer, and loafers, without socks. Chu's love for Asian art and history, traveling, and the pursuit of his business around the globe gave him the opportunity to explore his roots.

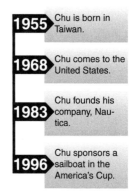

1955 Chu is born in Taiwan.

1968 Chu comes to the United States.

1983 Chu founds his company, Nautica.

1996 Chu sponsors a sailboat in the America's Cup.

He revisited China and Taiwan, expanding his business to include shops in Beijing and Shanghai. Chu always searched for better solutions, and constantly tried to improve on what he had already done. Despite his many successes, he remained modest about his accomplishments and tried to maintain an even temperament.

True to his childhood dream of creating architecture, Chu remained fascinated with houses. As the founder, designer, and CEO of Nautica International, he launched "Nautica Home." This line of products aimed to fill every room with Nautica furniture, bedding, accessories, window treatments, table linens, china, and wall coverings.

The oldest of three sons, Chu maintained a close relationship with his family. His mother remained in Taiwan, but his father traveled back and forth between the designer's native country and Manhattan. Chu often played golf with one brother, an interior designer, who helped with the layout of freestanding Nautica stores, both in the U.S. and abroad. Chu offered advice to aspiring designers, "Understand the business side, or work with someone who does; know the audience you're talking to; and always love what you do." ◆

Chu, Steven

1948– ● PHYSICIST

Steven Chu was an American physicist who won the 1997 Nobel Prize for physics for working on the technique of trapping atoms.

Steven Chu was born in St. Louis, Missouri, in 1948. His father, Ju Chin Chu, came to the United States in 1943 to continue his education at the Massachusetts Institute of Technology in chemical engineering. Two years later, Ju Chin Chu's wife, Ching Chen Li Chu, joined him to study economics. Her own grandfather had earned advanced degrees in civil engineering at Cornell University in New York while his brother studied physics at the Sorbonne in Paris. When Chu's parents married in 1945, China was in turmoil, so they remained in the United States. Chu's older brother was born in 1946, and Chu was born during the time his father taught at Washington University in St. Louis. His younger brother completed the family in Queens,

Steven Chu at work.

New York City, after his father took a position as a professor at the Brooklyn Polytechnic Institute.

In 1950, the family settled in Garden City, New York, within commuting distance of Brooklyn Polytechnic. There were only two other Chinese families in their town of 25,000, but the Chus appreciated the quality of the public school system. Education was their top family value. Nearly all of Chu's aunts and uncles had doctorates in science or engineering.

Chu's older bother outshone him in high school, while Chu's performance was "decidedly mediocre," he would later say. He found schoolwork more a chore than an intellectual adventure. However, Chu loved building model airplanes and warships, and spent many happy hours constructing with an erector set. His interests expanded to chemistry, and he and a friend experimented with homemade rockets, which Chu bought partly with school lunch money. One summer, the boys turned their hobby into a business by testing their neighbors' soil for **acidity** and missing nutrients.

In Chu's senior year, he took advanced physics and calculus classes, and two talented and dedicated teachers fired his interest

acidity amount of acid in a particular object or thing.

1948 Chu is born in St. Louis, Missouri.

1970 Chu enters Berkeley.

1978 Chu begins working at Bell Laboratories.

1997 Chu earns the Nobel prize in physics.

in those topics. Chu applied to a number of colleges in the fall of his senior year. Although he had a good grade average, he was rejected by the Ivy League schools, but was accepted at the University of Rochester in New York. By comparison, his older brother was attending Princeton, two cousins were in Harvard, and a third was at Bryn Mawr.

At Rochester, Chu became mesmerized and inspired by *The Feynman Lectures in Physics,* used as a textbook. As Chu's love of physics grew, he declared a major in both mathematics and physics. Several math professors befriended him and invited him to social events.

Hoping to become a theoretical physicist, Chu applied to the University of California at Berkeley and entered in the fall of 1970. The number of available jobs in physics was shrinking, and his professors had admonished him that he would be better off in experimental physics. Nevertheless, Chu received his doctorate at the University of California at Berkeley in 1976.

Berkeley offered Chu a job as assistant professor in the spring of 1978. However, he took a leave of absence before starting the position. During that leave, Chu joined Bell Laboratories (now part of Lucent Technologies) in New Jersey and never returned to Berkeley. It was at Bell that Chu was to do the work that would win him the Nobel prize.

When Chu joined Bell Labs in the fall of 1978, he was one of about two dozen newly hired young scientists. These lucky scientists had no obligation other than to do the research they loved. As Bell gave them a blank slate to work with, the young workers shared the excitement of doing raw science together. Their lively discussions filled the halls, labs, and office cubicles, often continuing over lunch, tennis games, and at parties.

Bell Labs supplied them with funding and urged them to do their best. Chu was told to spend his first six months in the library and to talk to people before deciding what to do. He was encouraged to "start a new field." In the fall of 1983, Chu became head of the Quantum Electronics Research Department and moved to another branch of Bell Labs at Holmdel, New Jersey.

It was there that Chu began the work in laser cooling and trapping of atoms that would earn him the Nobel prize. The technique of trapping atoms involved slowing them down until they are almost stationary, so that they can be studied without being constantly barraged by other atoms. This allowed scientists to study these atoms and molecules more easily.

The work began in 1985, when Chu and his colleagues began to investigate the possibility of slowing down atoms with laser beams. Chu's technique was to shine laser beams onto a cloud of sodium atoms in a vacuum chamber. The laser light consisted of three pairs of oppositely directed laser beams—for example, one pair from above and below, and two pairs horizontally, at right angles to each other. The frequency of the laser light must be chosen carefully. When an atom moves against the direction of any of the beams, it feels a push that slows it down. When it moves in the same direction as any beam, it feels no force from that beam.

The atoms are slowed down by this arrangement, which Chu called optical molasses. A glowing, pea-sized cloud of about a million sodium atoms was formed, cooled to 240 millionths of a Celsius degree above absolute zero, the lowest possible temperature. However, even these slow-moving atoms lingered for no more than half a second. To keep them for a longer time, the researchers trapped them with optical tweezers—another intense beam of laser light. Atoms feel a slight electrical attraction to a region where there is intense light or other electromagnetic radiation, because electromagnetic radiation.

Chu won the 1997 Nobel Prize for physics for this work. He shared the award with Claude Cohen-Tannoudji of France and William D. Phillips of the United States.

Although life at Bell Labs was nearly perfect for Chu, in 1987 he decided to leave his comfortable niche. He was recruited by Stanford, turning down offers by Berkeley and Harvard. In 1987, Chu became professor of physics and applied physics at Stanford University in Palo Alto, California, and held the chair of the physics department there from 1990 to 1993.

Chu continued at Stanford, embracing teaching for the chance it gave him to help launch new, young scientists. While continuing work on laser cooling and trapping of atoms, Chu moved on to work with polymer physics and biology. ◆

Chung, Connie

AUGUST 20, 1946– ● TELEVISION NEWSCASTER

Connie Chung has occupied anchor chairs in the news divisions of all three major broadcast networks, but her rise to eminence has been anything but smooth. Her initially soaring trajectory at CBS in the 1990s went into a

Connie Chung (right) with her husband Maury Povich.

nosedive after several troubling episodes: incurring the ire of her co-anchor Dan Rather, raising a storm of controversy over journalistic ethics, and stumbling badly in the ratings in her own marquee primetime show. With her career temporarily at bay, Chung's fortunes were revived in 1997 when she was hired by ABC to coanchor the primetime magazine series *20/20*.

Constance Yuhwa Chung was born in Washington, D.C., on August 20, 1946. With desperate shortages in adequate medical care in China during the Second World War, five of Chung's older siblings died before the family managed to migrate to the United States in 1944. The Chungs finally settled in Maryland, where Connie attended local schools, excelling in school theater and student government in high school. In 1965 Chung enrolled in the University of Maryland, beginning as a biology major but switching to journalism after serving a summer internship with Congressman Seymour Halpern in 1967. During the school year she gained some hands-on experience working as a part-time copy clerk in the news department of the Washington television station WTTG, where she was hired as a secretary in the news department after her graduation from college in 1969.

Chung quickly ascended the rungs at the station, advancing to news writer, assignment editor, and then reporter, earning her journalistic spurs amid the turbulent political and cultural swirl of the late 1960s and early 1970s. With all the major networks facing increasing pressures to hire more women and people of color, in 1971 Chung was invited to join the Washington bureau of CBS news, where zeal and thoroughness soon won her the plum assignment of covering George McGovern's 1972 presidential campaign. After covering President Richard Nixon's diplomatic missions to the Middle East and the Soviet Union later that year, she returned to Washington to report on the gathering Watergate scandal.

In 1976 Chung headed west to become the chief news anchor at KNXT, the Los Angeles CBS affiliate. Chung proved a major ratings success during her seven years in Los Angeles, where she became the highest-paid female anchor in local news. But by 1983 the lure of national politics led her to take a pay cut in accepting NBC's offer to anchor its early-morning news program, *NBC News at Sunrise*. As she later recalled, "I could see 1984 coming at me, and I just didn't want to sit out another presidential election." She also served as a political reporter for the *NBC Nightly News*, which she anchored on Saturday evenings.

Chung's favorable audience response led to an accelerating pace of assignments, including occasional substitute hosting duties on the *Today* show and the chief correspondent slot on NBC's worthy but ultimately ill-fated primetime newsmagazine, *American Almanac*. She also hosted a series of special primetime documentaries, most notably *Life in the Fat Lane* (1987), *Scared Sexless* (1987), *Stressed to Kill* (1988), *Guns, Guns, Guns* (1988), and a five-part report from China that included interviews with long-lost relatives and a visit to the graves of her grandparents.

After playing a prominent role in NBC's coverage of the 1988 presidential campaign, Chung announced, in March 1989, that she would rejoin CBS News, where her duties initially included hosting *West 57th Street* and serving as Dan Rather's substitute during his absences from the anchor's chair of the *CBS Evening News*. In 1989 CBS sought to rescue the faltering *West 57th Street* by revamping it under the title *Saturday Night with Connie Chung*, an exercise in "infotainment" that affronted many critics with its staged recreations of many of the stories it reported on.

1946 Chung is born in Washington, D.C.

1971 Chung becomes a reporter for the CBS News Washington bureau.

1976 Chung is the country's highest paid local news anchor at KNXT-TV in Los Angeles.

1983 Chung joins NBC News.

1989 Chung returns to CBS News.

1993 Chung briefly co-hosts the *CBS Evening News* with Dan Rather.

1997 Chung joins ABC News.

In 1993 CBS sought to jolt the sagging ratings of its nightly newscast by pairing Chung with Dan Rather, who had been the sole anchor for more than a decade. The uneasy pairing, which Rather resented from the start, came to a merciful end in 1995, by which time Chung found herself embroiled in another journalistic controversy. On her latest primetime magazine show, *Eye to Eye with Connie Chung*, Chung coaxed Newt Gingrich's mother into confiding, on the air, that Gingrich regarded Hillary Clinton as a "bitch." Because the coaxing involved Chung's intervening reassurance "just between you and me," many viewers and colleagues were outraged that Chung would broadcast what she seemingly had implied would be off the record. The insistent questioning of Chung's judgment, combined with her show's poor ratings, led to her departure from CBS later that year.

Chung was absent from the national airwaves during the presidential campaign of 1996, and her future as a national correspondent seemed uncertain until ABC News hired her in November 1997, after Chung had completed a year-long stint as a fellow at the Joan Shorenstein Center on the press Politics and Public Policy at the John F. Kennedy School of Government at Harvard University. Chung now serves as coanchor of ABC's popular primetime newsmagazine, *20/20*.

Chung's professional accolades include three Emmy Awards and a George Foster Peabody award. She lived in Manhattan with her husband, Maury Povich, and their son, Matthew. ◆

Chung, Eugene

JUNE 14, 1969– ● PROFESSIONAL FOOTBALL PLAYER

Eugene Chung was born on June 14, 1969, in Prince George's County, Maryland, and grew up in nearby northern Virginia. Chung's father, Choon, moved to the United States from Korea in 1956, arriving with nothing but the clothes on his back and the desire to start a new life in America. He studied public administration at City College in New York and later continued his studies at Columbia University and Yale University, eventually earning his law degree. Using his own life as an example, the elder Chung told his three sons that there was no limit to how successful they could be in the United States. "I told them then can do whatever they want to do," said Choon Chung. "America is free."

The younger Chung realized at an early age that he was blessed with excellent athletic ability. He displayed enormous size at an early age, eventually growing to be 6 feet, 5 inches tall and 295 pounds. In high school, he excelled at football and also competed in track and **judo**. In football, he earned All-District and All-Region honors, while in judo, he won his weight class at the Virginia State Judo Championship in 1990. Thanks to his football prowess, he was awarded a full scholarship to Virginia Tech University in Blacksburg, Virginia.

At Virginia Tech, Chung wasted no time in making his mark on the football field, earning a starting job just seven games into his freshman season. He quickly became the team's best **offensive lineman,** and his senior season, he was named All-Big East Conference and All-America. Blacksburg was a small town, but racism was never a problem for Chung. Instead, he felt more pressure as an athlete, as many students thought he received special treatment and was nothing more than a dumb jock.

Upon graduating from Tech in 1992, Chung was ready to pursue his dream—playing professional football in the National Football League (NFL). He was ready to break down any stereotypes people might have about Asian athletes: "I think by having a chance to play in the NFL, it's going to do a lot for the Korean community. I'd like to be somewhat of a spokesperson for that . . . I think by doing this it will let the people know back in Korea and in the United States to be aware that we are able to do this. We're not a meek people. The Korean American kids should know that Asians can do more than play ping-pong."

Chung was selected by the New England Patriots as the 13th pick overall in the first round of the NFL's collegiate draft, becoming the first Asian American to be selected in that round. Chung was expected to be an important part of the Patriots' offense in his first year, but his career got off to a slow start. Unhappy with the team's contract offer, Chung did not report to training camp, electing to hold out. When he eventually agreed to terms, he was far behind all the other players in terms of conditioning and learning the playbook. When he finally did report to camp, he experienced a personal tragedy when his father died unexpectedly.

Chung never really recovered that first year. Minor injuries bothered him all year, and the Patriots asked him to play four different positions on the offensive line when other lineman

1969 Chung is born in Prince George's County, Maryland.

1990 Chung wins the Virginia State Judo Championship in his weight class.

1992 Chung is named All-America at Virginia Tech in football and becomes the first Asian-American selected in the first round of the NFL draft.

1993 Chung starts at right guard for the New England Patriots.

1995 Chung is married and his son Kyle is born.

judo a marital art developed from jujitsu that emphasizes quick movement and leverage against an opponent.

offensive line line of blockers in American football who help advance the ball by blocking for the quarterback and running backs.

were hurt as well. For a rookie just trying to learn his way around the league, having to learn four different positions was a nearly impossible task. The Patriots struggled even more than Chung did, as they finished with a 2-14 record.

The next year went better for Chung, as he settled in as the starting right guard. He played well on a young team, but in 1995, the Patriots were forced to leave him unprotected in a draft that was held to stock the newly formed Jacksonville Jaguars with players. The Jaguars were looking for young players to build around, so they selected Chung.

After playing for Jacksonville for a year, Chung's career took a series of twists and turns. He was let go by the Jaguars at the end of the 1995 season, and he signed with the San Francisco 49ers. However, the 49ers had several other young lineman on their roster and chose to cut Chung before the start of the 1996 season. Chung then sat out a season before signing with the Indianapolis Colts in 1997, playing 10 games for that team. He was again the victim of a youth movement as the Colts let him go after only one season on their roster.

For the second time, Chung sat out an entire season, as he failed to sign with a team for the 1998 campaign. In 1999, he was back in the NFL, as the Kansas City Chiefs signed him to compete for a role as a reserve center. Chung was familiar with the Chiefs because he had briefly participated in their training camp before he sat out the 1998 season. As the 2001 season approached, it was unclear if Chung would retire or would catch on with another team.

Off the football field, Chung liked to ride motorcycles, especially his Harley-Davidson. He was active with the Rise-and-Shine Foundation, a charitable organization in Florida, and also owned a health club in Bethesda, Maryland. He married his wife Lisa in 1995 and had a son, Kyle, who was born in 1995. The Chungs lived in Oakton, Virginia. ◆

Curry, Ann

NOVEMBER 19, 1956– ● NEWSCASTER

The news anchor NBC's *Today* show since 1997 and a correspondent for *Dateline*, Ann Curry rivals Connie Chung as the most visible and important Asian Ameri-

can in television network news. Of
mixed racial heritage—her mother
was a Japanese immigrant and her
father is a mixture of French,
Scotch-Irish, and American Indian—Curry has had to surmount
ethnic prejudice and financial exi-
gency on her path to the top of the
news business. Addressing a convention of Asian American journalists
in 1997, Curry said, "My message for
you tonight is that it is good to remember that my mother and your
mothers and your fathers, and our
grandparents paved the way for our
dreams."

Ann Curry

The oldest of five children—and
the only one to attend college—
Curry grew up in Ashland, Oregon, but her roots extend back to
the Far East. Her father, who grew up in a poor family from
Pueblo, Colorado, joined the navy when he was eighteen and
was an occupying soldier in postwar Japan in 1948 when he was
taken by the sight of a woman conductor on a trolley in Yoka-
hama. The next day he summoned the courage to ask her out,
and they married several months later. While he was stationed
in Agana, Guam, Ann Curry was born on November 19, 1956.

As a child Ann endured the constant displacements of a
Navy family, attending schools in Japan, Hawaii, San Diego,
and Virginia. Curry still recalls with bitterness the day a sixth-
grade classmate called her a Jap, an incident that instilled in her
an unwavering commitment to racial tolerance. She also recalls
watching network news shows, including *Today*, and feeling
subtly cowed by the all-white faces on her TV screen. As she
later told a reporter, "When you're a child and you don't see
people like you doing something, it doesn't enter your mind
that you could do it. It's like looking through a shut glass door
into a room that seems so tantalizing, but the door isn't open
to you."

By the time Ann entered high school, the family had settled
in Ashland, Oregon, where she attended Ashland Senior High
School. Curry was an excellent student who threw herself into
a variety of extracurricular activities: acting, debating, junior
business projects, but her real love was writing and words. Curry

1956 Curry is born in Agana, Guam.

1978 Curry graduates from the University of Oregon with a degree in journalism.

1979 Curry is hired as on-air reporter at KGW in Portland, Oregon.

1984 Curry becomes a reporter for KCBS in Los Angeles.

1985 Curry becomes midwest correspondent for NBC News.

1986 Curry becomes anchor for NBC's "Sunrise."

1987 Curry becomes anchor of NBC's "Today" show.

Bard nickname for William Shakespeare; a writer of heroic, epic verse.

dragooned to force or attempt to force; to coerce.

fondly recalls her eager attendance at the annual Ashland Shakespeare festival, where the **Bard's** eloquence sparked a germinal literary ambition. That love of words began to take a journalistic turn during her senior year, when lively dinner-table arguments about the Vietnam War and Watergate imbued her with a passion for politics and international affairs. Curry vividly remembers the impact of the nightly family ritual of gathering around the television to take in Walter Cronkite's national newscast: "Cronkite's newscasts had an enormous influence on me" she later recalled. "I was really struck by how much world events could affect the lives and minds of people in a small town like Ashland."

After graduating from high school in 1974, Curry accepted a scholarship to the University of Oregon, where she majored in journalism, devoting herself to her studies in the intervals of the round robin of jobs that kept her afloat during those financially perilous years: cashier jobs during the school year, two summers as a bookstore clerk in Ashland, one summer as a food ship clerk, and a summer as a maid in Lake Tahoe. "I was scrubbing bathtubs, dreaming about one day becoming the anchor of NBC," Curry recalled.

Although Curry was originally intent on becoming a print journalist, one of her professors encouraged her to apply her talents to the burgeoing field of broadcast news. "I was so shy," Curry later recalled. "I couldn't imagine myself in front of a camera." Nevertheless, upon taking her B.A. in 1978, Curry took a job as an intern at a local television station while supporting herself as a cocktail waitress. Shortly thereafter she landed a job at a small as a mail clerk and camera operator at a TV station, KTVL in Medford, Oregon. A year into Curry's very modest beginning in the business, the station's chief newsreader became pregnant and began training Ann to fill in for her during her anticipated absence, schooling Ann in the basics of writing and back-timing news stories. When a permanent replacement was brought in, Curry served as the newscast's producer, a slot she was content to fill until the anchor walked out abruptly over a salary dispute with management. Ann was **dragooned** into on-air duty, and, as she candidly stated, "I was awful." But management saw her potential and stuck with her, and she soon found herself as the station's noon news anchor.

After acquiring the requisite smoothness and polish in front of the camera, Curry began to send out tapes to larger stations, and in 1981 she was hired as a reporter by KGW in Portland,

Oregon. Three years later she headed to Los Angeles to work as a local reporter for KCBS, a position she held until 1990, when the NBC network hired her to cover the middle section of the nation out of its Chicago bureau.

During Curry's tenure in Chicago, the network called on her to fill in periodically as the *Today* show news anchor, and the executives noticed a bump in the viewers each time she appeared. Don Brown, then the vice president of the network's news division, called Curry in to offer her the anchor spot on the network's *Sunrise* program. Curry was initially reluctant, viewing herself as a hands-on serious journalist who would bridle at the constraint of sitting in the same chair each day, reading from a **TelePrompter.** But Brown was insistent. "You are the next generation, part of the new face of network television news." Curry finally relented and served as the *Sunrise* anchor until 1996, when she helped to launch MSNBC, where she found she could combine her reporting and anchoring talents.

TelePrompter a machine used by television personalities and speechmakers; the device unrolls a magnetic script in front of the speaker.

In April 1997 Curry ascended to the news anchor's chair at NBC prestigious, venerable morning talk-news franchise, *Today*, where she has remained ever since while also serving as a correspondent for the network's evening news magazine, *Dateline*. Curry reports many of her own stories on *Today* and diligently edits everything she reads on the air. Her repertorial energy and dedication have brought her a trove of coveted awards, including Emmys for her live coverage of the 1987 Los Angeles earthquake and her report on the 1989 San Bernardino pipeline explosion. A four-time winner of the "Golden Mike" award, she has received several Associated Press Certificates of Excellence and an NAACP Award for excellence in reporting.

Curry lived in Manhattan with her husband, Brian, an Internet company manager. Despite her hectic schedule, Curry managed to make ample time for their two children, McKenzie and Walker. "I'm able to pick up the kids from school everyday, have dinner with them every evening, and put them to bed at night," Curry says. "That's very important to me."

Reflecting on her ability to combine professional renown with a rewarding family life, Curry commented, "I've achieved most of what I've wanted and far more than I ever expected." ◆

D'Souza, Dinesh

APRIL 25, 1961– ● AUTHOR, POLITICAL COMMENTATOR

So swift was Dinesh D'Souza's ascent to the elite ranks of America's intellectuals that in 1990 a reporter said of him, "At the tender age of 28, Dinesh D'Souza has the dubious distinction of being a has-been." A mere half year later, that appraisal was disproved by the stunning success of D'Souza's book *Illiberal Education: The Politics of Race and Sex on Campus*, which remained a top-ten bestseller for more than three months. Now widely acknowledged as one of the nation's most influential conservative commentators, D'Souza has welcomed the often bitter controversy his edgy critiques have engendered. He once told an interviewer, "I seem to have gotten under the skin of every aging hippie, every depressed post-Marxist kook, every radical feminist who has hung out in academic enclaves. I've gotten used to the phenomenon of being heckled by people twice my age."

Dinesh D'Souza was born on April 25, 1961, in India, where his father worked as an executive for the giant pharmaceutical company Johnson and Johnson. As part of his strict Catholic upbringing, D'Souza was educated at a **Jesuit** school until the last year of high school, which he spent in Patagonia, Arizona, as an exchange student. Fascinated with American culture, D'Souza chose to attend college in the United States, enrolling in Dartmouth College in Hanover, New Hampshire. It was there that he felt the first stirrings of literary ambition. As he later wrote, "It was only when I came to America and attended Dartmouth College in the early 1980s that I became interested in politics and journalism. . . . During my college years I became

Jesuit member of a Roman Catholic society founded by St. Ignatius Loyola in 1534; devoted to educational and missionary work.

1961 D'Souza is born in Bombay, India.

1983 D'Souza graduates from Dartmouth College; becomes editor of *Prospect*, an independent magazine for Princeton alumni.

1987 D'Souza is hired to work on domestic-policy proposals at the Reagan White House.

1988 D'Souza is named a fellow at the American Enterprise Institute.

satire literary work holding human folly to humorous irony or ridicule.

japes mocking or humorous statements.

sorties missions, usually associated with military affairs.

excited by the prospect of engaging these issues, and applying them to contemporary political and cultural dilemmas, through the medium of writing." D'Souza served his undergraduate journalistic apprenticeship on the college newspaper and as a founder of the *Dartmouth Review*, an acidly **satirical** journal of decidedly right-wing bent whose **japes** often aroused the ire of more sedate conservatives; when D'Souza penned an article ridiculing African American dialect, then-Congressman Jack Kemp, one of the magazines patrons, resigned in protest.

After graduating from Dartmouth in 1983, D'Souza became the editor of *Prospect*, an independent magazine for Princeton alumni that was founded and subsidized by wealthy conservatives who opposed the admission of women to the prestigious Ivy League school. D'Souza obliged their expectations with suitably caustic attacks on Princeton's prevailing liberal ethos, most notably its women studies program, which was characterized as "the pock-marked face of feminism." While at *Prospect*, D'Souza published his first book, a defense of Jerry Falwell entitled *Falwell, Before the Millennium: A Critical Biography* (1984), which aroused mixed reviews, typically skewed by the political sympathies of the critics, a pattern that has recurred with each of D'Souza's subsequent books.

D'Souza's take-no-prisoners **sorties** against the liberal establishment won the admiration of Gary Bauer, President Reagan's domestic policy chief, who invited D'Souza to join the White House Staff in 1987. D'Souza later recalled, "My department was policy development, which had the utopian mission of coming up with new policies." With less than a year left in the administration, however, few of his initiatives saw the light of day. His next book, *My Dear Alex: Letters from the KGB* (1987), was a work of fiction that he coauthored with his Dartmouth classmate Gregory A. Fossedal.

In 1988 D'Souza moved on to the American Enterprise Institute (AEI), a conservative think tank that has been his base of operations for the past twelve years under annual fellowships sponsored by the John M. Olin Foundation, a philanthropy that promotes conservative causes. While also taking on editorial duties at the Catholic magazine *Crisis* and *Policy Review*, D'Souza began to contribute articles to the *National Review*, the nation's leading conservative magazine.

D'Souza's first major impact on the national political debate came in 1991 with the publication of *Illiberal Education: The*

Politics of Race and Sex on Campus, a relentless broadside against the growing influence of "politically correct" identity politics on the nation's college campuses. While arousing the ire of much of the academic and journalistic left, the book nevertheless struck a chord of sympathy among many prominent liberals such as Morton Halperin, William Banks, and C. Vann Woodward.

His next book was even more controversial. *The End of Racism: Principles for a Multiracial Society* (1995) argued that the United States had overcome the burden of racism, attributing urban poverty to what he called "black pathology." He even claimed that segregation was less "a system established by white racists for the purpose of oppressing blacks" than a means of protecting them, "to assure that [they], the handicapped, would be . . . permitted to perform to the capacity of their arrested development." He argued that racial segregation would end when "blacks as a group can show that they are capable of performing competitively in schools and the work force." The ensuing firestorm of controversy was not confined to the pages of magazines and journals; two of the American Enterprise Institute's most prominent black intellectuals, Glenn C. Loury and Robert Woodson, resigned from the AEI in protest over its sponsorship of the book, which a *Time* reviewer called "one of the creepiest books to appear in recent years." The eminent philosopher Richard Rorty, writing in *The New York Times Book Review,* wrote that the book "is bloated with quotations and anecdotes, but has virtually no argumentative structure."

The reviews of D'Souza's next book—*Ronald Reagan: How an Ordinary Man Became an Extraordinary Leader*—were less contentious although still divided along partisan lines. D'Souza's latest book is *The Virtue of Prosperity: Finding Values in an Age of Techno-Affluence* (2001), in which he argues that poverty, "understood as the absence of food, clothing, and shelter, is no longer a significant problem in America." One critic, leftist Eric Alterman of *The Nation* magazine, has written, "his evidence for this breathtaking claim is that even poor people have refrigerators these days, and many of them are fat. That 30 million Americans still struggle beneath the poverty line and 42 million lack other benefit of health insurance represent, to D'Souza, mere speed bumps on our highway to capitalist utopia."

D'Souza became an American citizen on October 15, 1990. He and his wife, Dixie Brubaker, had a daughter, Danielle. ◆

> *"The agenda of the PC [politically correct] movement is to delegitimatize the idea of the West, the idea of America, and to taint those ideas as being irretrievably linked with imperialism, sexism, and a host of other evils."*
> Dinesh D'Souza, interview with *Investor's Business Daily,* December 9, 1991

Fong, Hiram Leong

1906– ● UNITED STATES SENATOR

H iram Leong Fong, a Republican from Hawaii, became the first Asian American to serve in the United States Senate.

Hiram Fong was born in the Kalihi district of Honolulu, Hawaii, in 1906. His given first name was Yau, but in college he changed it to Hiram after Hiram Bingham, a **Congregationalist** missionary who went to Hawaii in 1819. Fong's parents—his father, Lum Fong, and his mother Lum Fong Shee—were Chinese immigrants from the Kwangtung Province of China. They had come in 1872 to work as **indentured** laborers. Working on a sugar plantation, Lum Fong earned $12 a month. Fong, the seventh of ten children, went to work at an early age shining shoes, selling newspapers, and caddying at golf courses to help support the family. He grew up in the Kalihi slum section of Honolulu and attended Kalihi Waena Grammar School. Later he went to St. Louis College, a private school in Honolulu, and McKinley High School, one of Honolulu's largest public high schools.

Fong worked for three years as a clerk at the Pearl Harbor Naval Shipyard, and also held jobs as a bill collector and tour guide. When he had saved enough, Fong enrolled in the University of Hawaii. He became editor of the school newspaper, associate editor of the school annual, **adjutant** of the ROTC, and a member of the debating, volleyball, and rifle teams. Fong graduated from the University of Hawaii with honors in 1930, after only three years.

Fong then went to work with the Suburban Water System. Within two years he had saved $2,000 and borrowed $3,000 so

Congregationalist member of a body of Protestant churches deriving from the 17th century English Independents, supporting local autonomy of churches.

indentured bound to perform a particular service for a fixed amount of time.

adjutant staff officer in the military who assists a commanding officer.

Hiram Leong Fong

he could enter Harvard Law School. He earned a juris doctorate from Harvard Law School in 1935. He came home to Honolulu, where he was admitted to the bar and began the practice of law. First he worked as a municipal clerk then served as deputy attorney for the city and county of Honolulu from 1935-1938.

In 1942, Fong founded the law firm of Fong, Miho, Choy & Robinson, the first law office in Honolulu to become deliberately multiracial (Chinese, Japanese, Korean, and Caucasian). Fong's firm was so successful that he invested in real estate, insurance, shopping centers, finance, and a banana plantation. He became the president or served on boards of Finance Factors, Grand Pacific Life Insurance Company, Finance Realty, Finance Investment Company, and Market City, Ltd. Fong became very wealthy.

In 1942, Fong joined the Army Air Forces, where he served as a major until 1944. During World War II, Fong served as judge advocate of the 7th Fighter Command of the Seventh Air Force with the rank of major to 1945. For 19 years, Fong remained an officer of the United States Army Reserve.

Senator Fong's Plantation and Gardens

Spread across 725 acres on the island of Oahu is a spectacular, privately owned estate, dedicated to preserving the native wildlife and plants of the Hawaiian Islands. With 20 miles of shoreline, lush valleys and majestic plateaus, the estate is the product of United States Senator Hiram Fong's great love of his heritage. It began humbly; in 1950 Fong purchased a few acres of land on which to stable his children's horses. Struck by the beauty of the area, he began buying more and more of the neighboring property, and soon became fascinated by the land's rich history, flora, and fauna.

By the late 1950s, the property had grown substantially, and Fong began his gardens, planting indigenous Hawaiian plants on the grounds of the estate, including the flowering species from which traditional leis are made. By the late 1960s he began adding Hawaii's native bird and animal species. By the time Fong retired in 1977, the property had grown to its present size.

The gardens are divided into five separate areas, each named for one of the presidents with whom Fong served: Eisenhower, Kennedy, Johnson, Nixon, and Ford. The bird sanctuary and nature preserve within the gardens are Fong's gift to present and future generations, and the public is welcome to take one of the daily tours or to attend events such as lessons in making leis. Senator Fong always insisted that the gardens are a work in progress, needing several more generations of continued tending and expansion. He has made arrangements to leave the property to his children, stipulating that the land may never be sold or diverted from its current use.

Interest in politics and a commitment to public service led Fong to serve in Hawaii's territorial House of Representatives from 1938 to 1954, including three terms as speaker and two as vice-speaker. In 1954, when the Democrats gained control of the legislature for the first time, Fong was one of the Republicans who were unseated. He lost by only 31 votes. Fong served as a delegate to the Republican National Conventions of 1952 and 1956 and vice-president of the Territorial Constitutional Convention in 1950.

Fong was a longtime supporter of statehood for Hawaii. Native kings and queens had ruled Hawaii until sugar cane and pineapple plantation owners developed the power to overturn the government. In 1898, sugar cane planters succeeded in getting the United States to annex Hawaii as a possession. The island group then became a U.S. territory on June 14, 1900, and all Hawaiian citizens became American citizens. A move for the state to become a full state of the union began in 1919.

When Hawaiians went to the polls in June 1959 to accept statehood, they also voted in a primary election in which Fong

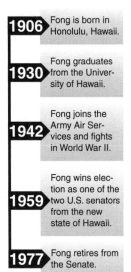

1906 Fong is born in Honolulu, Hawaii.

1930 Fong graduates from the University of Hawaii.

1942 Fong joins the Army Air Services and fights in World War II.

1959 Fong wins election as one of the two U.S. senators from the new state of Hawaii.

1977 Fong retires from the Senate.

ran unopposed as a Republican candidate for the United States Senate. Hawaii was officially proclaimed the 50th state of the union on August 21, 1959. Hiram L. Fong, a self-made millionaire lawyer and businessman, became one of the two new senators from Hawaii. Three days later Fong and his colleagues, Oren E. Long in the Senate and Daniel K. Inouye in the House of Representatives, were sworn in as members of Congress. Fong was re-elected in 1964 and again in 1970, serving until January 3, 1977. He was not a candidate for re-election in 1976.

As the first person of Chinese descent to serve in the United States Senate, Fong took advantage of his unique opportunity to increase understanding between the United States and the nations of Asia.

In the 86th Congress, Fong was assigned to the Senate's Interior and Insular Affairs Committee and the Public Works Committee. During the last weeks of the 1959 session he voted on a number of legislative proposals, supporting appropriations for the Mutual Security Program and opposing the housing bill of 1959 and a measure to give the President of the United States authority to approve economic aid for Communist-dominated countries (other than the Soviet Union or those in the Far East) when it was deemed important for national security.

Soon after Congress adjourned in 1959, Fong undertook an extended voyage through Asia at his own expense. In October, Senator and Mrs. Fong embarked on a 45-day tour of fourteen Asian countries to increase his understanding of Asia and its problems and to show Asians an example of Hawaii's interracial equality.

During his brief stay in the Philippines, Singapore, and elsewhere, Fong received a warm welcome from both government officials and the local Chinese populations. He expressed his conviction that both the Far East nations and their resident Chinese populations would benefit if the Chinese were integrated into the nations in which they live instead of remaining loyal to China.

Fong was considered a liberal Republican early in his Senate career, though he supported the policies of the Nixon Administration in the late 1960s and early 1970s. As a political leader, he worked to promote harmony among Hawaii's various ethnic groups.

In 1953 the University of Hawaii awarded Fong an honorary law degree and made him a foundation member of Phi

Beta Kappa. He was a member of the Chinese American Club, Warriors of the Pacific, Commercial Associates, University of Hawaii Alumni Association, Harvard Club of Hawaii, Chinese Civic Club, Chamber of Commerce of Honolulu, and the Chinese Chamber of Commerce.

Fong was married to Ellyn Lo, also of Chinese ancestry, in Honolulu on June 25, 1938, soon after she graduated from the University of Hawaii. The couple had four children: Hiram, Jr., who studied at Lafayette College in Pennsylvania; Rodney, who went to Western Military Academy in Illinois; and twins, Merie-Ellen and Marvin-Allan. Besides their banana plantation, the Fongs had two homes in Hawaii—one on the heights in Honolulu and another on the beach. Fong was a member of the Congregational First Chinese Church of Christ. ◆

Hattori, James

● TELEVISION JOURNALIST

James Hattori was born and raised in Los Angeles, California. The Hattori family lived among a community of Japanese Americans in the inner-city neighborhood of Crenshaw. Hattori was the youngest of three children. While Hattori was in junior high school, his family moved to an area near the Los Angeles suburb of Torrance. Hattori finished high school in Torrance, then he went on to the University of Southern California School of Journalism. While he was in college, Hattori decided that he would like to work as a reporter. He was 20 when he made his decision, and from that point on, Hattori followed a very successful career path. In 1977, Hattori graduated cum laude (with distinction) from the university.

Hattori's first job out of journalism school was as a weekend assignment editor and writer at KGTV-TV in San Diego. He soon joined KFMB-TV in Spokane, Washington, as a reporter and midday anchor. He spent the next four years at Spokane's KREM-TV. This was to be one of his longest gigs. In 1982, Hattori joined KING-TV in Seattle, Washington, as a reporter, legislative correspondent, and weekend anchor. After five years in Seattle, Hattori joined KPRC-TV in Houston, Texas, as a reporter in the special projects unit.

While in Houston, Hattori received an invitation to join CBS News as their Dallas correspondent. Hattori accepted the job and went on to work for CBS News for eight years as a correspondent based in New York, Tokyo, and Dallas. While at CBS, he reported on a wide range of stories for *60 Minutes, 48 Hours, CBS Evening News with Dan Rather, CBS Morning News, CBS*

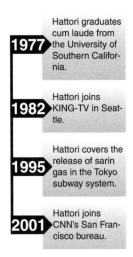

1977 Hattori graduates cum laude from the University of Southern California.

1982 Hattori joins KING-TV in Seattle.

1995 Hattori covers the release of sarin gas in the Tokyo subway system.

2001 Hattori joins CNN's San Francisco bureau.

sarin an extremely toxic chemical warfare agent.

indicted state of standing formally accused of an offense by a judicial process known as a grand jury.

This Morning, and CBS *Sunday Morning.* The show *48 Hours* premiered in 1988 as an innovative primetime news series similar to *60 Minutes.* In a unique approach, *48 Hours* explores a single subject, examining it from multiple angles with saturation coverage and action-driven style.

During his career, Hattori covered a variety of breaking news stories, including the subway poisoning attack in Tokyo. On March 20, 1995, religious terrorists released **sarin**, a nerve gas at several points in the Tokyo subway system, killing 11 and injuring more than 5,500 people.

Hattori also covered the Exxon *Valdez* oil spill in Alaska. In March 1989, one of Exxon's oil tankers, the Exxon *Valdez,* struck a reef in Prince William Sound in southeastern Alaska. The tanker spilled nearly 11 million gallons of crude oil, the largest oil spill in United States history. The accident killed thousands of marine animals and sea birds and polluted over 1,200 miles of shoreline.

Hattori also covered the American invasion of Panama. In 1983, General Manuel Antonio Noriega had become head of Panama's military and the nation's most powerful leader. In 1988, after Noriega was **indicted** on charges of drug trafficking and racketeering, Panamanian President Eric Arturo Delvalle dismissed Noriega from his military command, but Noriega supporters forced President Delvalle from office. In 1989, after Panamanian soldiers killed a United States Marine lieutenant, U.S. President George Bush ordered troops into Panama to overthrow Noriega.

In 1992, Hattori covered the beginning of Ross Perot's bid as an independent candidate for the presidency. Perot, an American billionaire businessman, gained widespread support even though he had little political experience. Hattori also reported on the 1992 Republican National Convention in Houston.

At the end of 1999, Hattori received a National Headliner Award for his breaking news coverage of Hurricane Floyd. The National Headliner Awards were founded in 1934 by the Press Club of Atlantic City, making them one of the oldest and largest annual contests recognizing journalistic excellence.

Following his work for CBS, Hattori served as a weekend anchor and reporter for KRON-TV, the NBC affiliate in San Francisco. Hattori then went on to co-anchor CNN.com, the interactive online service operated by Cable News Network (CNN) on the World Wide Web of the Internet. CNN.com consists of information services and content provided by CNN, affiliates of CNN and other third parties.

Hattori became a correspondent for CNN's San Francisco bureau in January 2001, and remained based in CNN's San Francisco bureau. In March 2001, Hattori reported from the federal court in San Francisco on the hearing regarding the terms of the **injunction** that would block Napster from posting copyrighted material on its song-swapping service. The Ninth Circuit Court of Appeals ruled that Napster must police its more than 50 million users and stop them from sharing copyrighted material. Napster was an Internet site from which users could download music for free. ◆

injunction official court order commanding an individual or entity to cease a particular act.

Hayakawa, Sessue

JUNE 10, 1889–NOVEMBER 23, 1973 ● ACTOR, PRODUCER

The talent, skill, and desire of Sessue Hayakawa enabled him to become a major Hollywood star during a time in which minority performers were seldom—if ever—accorded leading roles in front of and behind the camera.

Hayakawa was born on June 10, 1889, in Naaura, Japan. His family was quite affluent and he enjoyed the priveleges of an upper-class lifestyle, which included access to the finest education. Growing up, Hayakawa wished to enlist in the Japanese military and embark on a career in the Japanese naval forces; however, Hayakawa suffered from partial hearing loss, which prevented him from a career in the armed forces. Hayakawa was extremely disappointed, but with the help of an uncle, began acting on stage in various plays. Giving in to the **wanderlust** that characterized his dream to be in the Japanese navy, Hayakawa immigrated to the United States to attend the University of Chicago. Following graduation, he returned to Japan and formed his own stage company.

wanderlust urge to travel frequently without settling in one place for any significant length of time.

Hayakawa's company began touring around Japan, and eventually made it to the United States, where his group performed in California and other western states in 1913. They put on a production called *The Typhoon*, which Hayakawa had written. While in California, *The Typhoon* came to the attention of a young Japanese actress named Tsuru Aoki, who was a member of her own stage performance group in Los Angeles. Aoki urged

1889 Hayakawa is born in Naaura, Japan.

1913 Hayakawa leads a stage play group in the United States and is noticed by a Hollywood producer.

1918 Hayakawa forms his own production company and produces feature films.

1949 Hayakawa returns to the United States after World War II to resume his acting career.

1957 Hayakawa is nominated for an Academy Award for his work in *The Bridge On the River Kwai.*

1973 Hayakawa dies in Tokyo, Japan.

Zen a Japanese sect of Buddhism aiming at enlightenment through meditation.

samurai Japanese warrior aristocracy.

producer Thomas Ince to watch the play and to pay particular attention to Hayakawa.

Ince was suitably impressed and decided to bring *The Typhoon* to the movie screen. The motion picture version starred Hayakawa and actress Gladys Brockwell; Aoki appeared in the film as an extra and Hayakawa and Aoki were married by the spring of 1914. *The Typhoon* was critically acclaimed as was Hayakawa's abilities as an actor. Hayakawa and Ince worked together on films for Ince's Domino production company such as *The Last of the Line*, and *The Courtship of O San*. In 1915, Hayakawa signed on with Paramount Pictures and starred in *Each to his Kind* and *Forbidden Paths*.

In 1918, Hayakawa founded his own production company, the Haworth Film Corporation, and immediately produced *His Birthright* starring Marin Sais and Aoki. In 1919 alone, Hayakawa produced six feature films. Movies such as *The Tong Man* and *The Courageous Coward* did quite well at the box office, and Hayakawa and Aoki began to enjoy a very affluent lifestyle. They built a mansion in Hollywood called Greystone Castle, which still stands today. There they regularly hosted luncheons for 500 people and opulent ballroom dances for 900. Unlike many who are distracted by the lifestyle and money of Hollywood, Hayakawa continued to focus on his work and his art, and insisted on maintaining the highest standards and practices for his production company.

Hayakawa flourished in Hollywood during a time of considerable challenge for Asian-Americans. Newspaper publisher William Randolph Hearst was conducting a newspaper campaign trying to drum up a feeling of American paranoia regarding citizens of Asian descent, focusing on the "yellow peril" that "afflicted" the United States. And in Hollywood, minorities were rarely given important roles, and usually focused on stereotypes and myths. Yet Hayakawa seemed unaffected by all of this, and was continually recognized and respected by his peers. One leading lady—Florence Vidor—indicated that everything she knew about the craft of acting had been learned simply by watching Hayakawa at work.

Hayakawa took great pride in his heritage. He practiced **Zen** and Buddhism, and took on the disciplinary methods of the **Samurai** warriors, even incorporating them into his acting. Hayakawa once explained why he rarely showed emotion on his face during a scene where one might expect an emotional response. "I was always taught that it was disgraceful to show emotion . . . I purposely tried to show nothing by my face and of course it got over to the audience with far greater force than any facial expression could."

Hayakawa's career continued to blossom and in 1921 he began producing films under the Hayakawa Feature Play Company. During the late 1920s and early 1930s, however, Hayakawa and Aoki could see a mounting anti-Japanese sentiment in the United States, and they left for France. During World War II, Hayakawa turned to painting for a living.

Once World War II ended, Hayakawa decided to return to Hollywood to resume his film career, and appeared mostly as a character actor in World War II films. His first film back in the United States was *Tokyo Joe* with Humphrey Bogart. In 1957, Hayakawa was nominated for an Academy Award for his portrayal of a brutish commandant of a prisoner camp in *The Bride On the River Kwai*. Hayakawa appeared in popular movies such as *The Geisha Boy*, *The Swiss Family Robinson*, and *The Day Dreamer*, his final feature film.

Hayakawa, who had lived alone following the death of Aoki five years before *The Day Dreamer* was released, returned to Japan to teach acting and become a Zen Buddhist priest. He wrote an autobiography entitled *Zen Showed Me the Way to Peace, Happiness and Tranquility* in 1960. Hayakawa died on November 23, 1973, in Tokyo, Japan, from a blood clot to the brain complicated by pneumonia. ◆

Hayslip, Le Ly

1949– ● AUTHOR, ACTIVIST

L e Ly Hayslip was born in 1949 in Ky La, a village near Da Nang, Vietnam. She was the seventh child in a farming family. Because war ripped her country apart, Hayslip only received a third grade education. The Vietnam War lasted from 1957 to 1975, pitting the communist-ruled North Vietnam against South Vietnam. However, the country had already been at war, beginning in 1946 when Vietnam struggled to become free of France. The United States became deeply embroiled on the side of South Vietnam in the 1960s, and the war became the longest of any U.S. military conflict.

1949 Hayslip is born near Da Nang, Vietnam.

1970 Hayslip escapes to the United States.

1988 Hayslip founds the East Meets West Foundation.

1989 Hayslip publishes *When Heaven and Earth Changed Places: A Vietnamese Woman's Journey from War to Peace.*

1993 Hayslip publishes *Child of War, Woman of Peace.*

1999 Hayslip founds the Global Village Foundation.

Viet Cong soldiers in the North Vietnamese armed forces during the Vietnam War.

Hayslip's brothers fought in both the Republican (South Vietnamese) and **Viet Cong** (North Vietnamese communist) armies. By the time she was 14, she had been tortured in a South Vietnamese government prison for "revolutionary sympathies." She fell under suspicion for being a government spy, and received a sentence of death by the Viet Cong (communist soldiers). Instead of killing her, her executors raped her. She managed to flee to Da Nang and then Saigon where she worked as a maid, black market vendor, waitress, and hospital attendant.

When Hayslip was 21, she married an American civilian working in Vietnam. In 1970, they escaped to the United States. After her husband's death, she began writing her childhood memories. Her oldest son James helped her with English and typed the manuscript. Hayslip worked as a housekeeper, factory assembly line worker, and restaurant host and manager, supporting the three sons she had through two husbands.

Hayslip wrote her first memoir, *When Heaven and Earth Changed Places: A Vietnamese Woman's Journey from War to Peace*, with the help of Jay Wurts and published it in 1989. The memoir covers Hayslip's survival through her misfortunes during the Vietnam War. It also recounts her return to her mother and her homeland after 16 years in the United States. Hayslip tells her story in a lively, honest style, recalling her turbulent childhood in rural Vietnam and her eventual escape to America. Her story unfolds in a journal-like style, complete with detailed dates and locations.

Hayslip's work earned great attention due to its unique viewpoint of a woman in a war that devastated many people. Her eyewitness account of Vietnam's history over 40 years gave voice to the experiences of many, though clearly she had an extraordinary life. Some critics found a bias in Hayslip's writing against the South Vietnamese government and against nearly all Vietnamese males except her father. Other reviewers mentioned the "preachy" tone in the second half of the book. But most agreed that Hayslip's emphasis on hope and forgiveness balanced the negative aspects of her writing.

Hayslip's second memoir, written in collaboration with her son James, was published in 1993. *Child of War, Woman of Peace* focuses on her life after her emigration to the United States in 1970. Shortly after Hayslip settled in California with her first husband, Ed Munro, he died. She remarried, but her second,

Vietnamese Boat Refugees

When the United States Armed Forces pulled out of the Vietnam War in 1975, its South Vietnamese allies were left behind to face political persecution at the hands of the victorious North Vietnamese army. Desperate and in fear for their lives, many chose to flee the country. Some fled on foot through the jungles into Cambodia, but many took to the sea, hoping to make it to South Thailand, the nearest landfall.

They set sail in anything they could find, trusting their lives to vessels that were often little more than crude rafts. Many never made it to safety; thousands drowned when storms broke up their fragile boats, others fell prey to pirates who prowled the Gulf of Thailand in search of victims. Tales of rape and torture by the pirates soon filtered back to Vietnam, and by 1977 later waves of refugees looked for alternative destinations, and many elected to try the longer voyage to Malaysia, across the South China Sea.

Throughout the 1970s and 1980s, hundreds of thousands took to the sea. Many of the later refugees fled not for political reasons but in hopes of finding better economic opportunity. The seemingly endless flood of refugees threatened to overwhelm the destination countries: Hong Kong, Japan, and the Philippines in particular. In the 1980s a backlash against the "boat people" began, as groups in the asylum nations began threatening to push the boats back out to sea, refusing the refugees safe harbor.

Through the work of concerned activists, including notables such as Le Ly Hayslip, the United Nations High Commission on Refugees was induced to intervene, ultimately establishing procedures according to which some of the refugees could return to Vietnam safely, and in 1990 the first wave of repatriations began. Political refugees, however, were granted permanent asylum in several Western nations, notably in the United States, Britain, Australia.

abusive husband also quickly died. Hayslip's second book did not receive the great praise from reviewers that her first did, but they did appreciate her blending Eastern and Western values. Hayslip's book made a notable contribution to the American tradition of immigrant literature.

Oliver Stone, a highly accomplished Hollywood filmmaker and a Vietnam veteran, made a movie based on Hayslip's two memoirs. Released in 1993 and called *Heaven and Earth*, it was filmed on location in Thailand and starred Hiep Thi Le, Tommy Lee Jones, and Joan Chen. The movie received only moderate reviews.

In 1986, Hayslip returned to Vietnam after a 16-year absence. She was stunned by the devastation, poverty, and illness

> "I would always be in-between – south-north, east-west, peace-war, Vietnam-America. It is my fate to be in-between heaven and earth. Lasting victories are won in the heart, not on this land or that."
>
> Le Ly Hayslip,
> When Heaven and
> Earth Changed
> Places

left by the war. She felt moved to help provide housing, educational, and medical care for the thousands of needy Vietnamese children. In 1988, Hayslip founded the East Meets West Foundation, a humanitarian relief organization that worked to help rebuild lives physically and emotionally on both sides of the Vietnamese conflict. Filmmaker Stone funded the building of the Mother's Love Clinic for homeless children in Hayslip's village in Da Nang. With help from actor-comedian, Robert Kline and U.S. Senator John Kerry, the foundation raised money to build Peace Village, a medical center for children.

Hayslip sought to help heal the emotional wounds of many American soldiers who fought in Vietnam. She encouraged many of these men to return to Vietnam to build schools and medical facilities for children, women, and the disabled. She believed that positive action could heal old wounds. As a result, the foundation saw many new buildings constructed by returning Americans.

In 1999, Hayslip expanded her work when she founded the Global Village Foundation to empower Vietnam's rural population by building self-sustaining model villages. The Foundation is a non-profit, humanitarian organization serving as a bridge of healing between the two worlds of Vietnam and the United States. The mission of the foundation was to preserve and promote the unique heritage of Vietnamese villages by breaking generational cycles of poverty, illiteracy, and hopelessness. They accomplished this goal by implementing humanitarian programs that provide housing and basic infrastructure for poor villages, improving health and educational facilities, and developing vocational opportunities.

Nevertheless, Vietnam remained one of the poorest countries in the world. Eighty percent of the nation's 80 million people lived in rural areas that missed out on economic growth enjoyed in the nation's cities. Over 16,000 villages in Vietnam fall below the poverty level. Many of those villages lacked basic necessities. ◆

Ho, David

NOVEMBER 3, 1952– ● MEDICAL RESEARCHER

David Ho was born in Taichung, Taiwan, on November 3, 1952. At birth, he was named Da-i, which means "great one." Ho's father, Paul, an engineer, traveled 18 days on a freighter to the United States in 1956 to obtain an advanced degree. For nine years, Ho, his mother Sonia, and his younger brother would know his father only through the mail.

Ho learned early the importance of scholarship and education. His father's sacrifice inspired Ho to excel academically. Other relatives were also scientists or engineers, leading Ho to become interested in science at an early age. In 1964, Ho left Taiwan with his mother and brother to join his father in Los Angeles. His father renamed him David and renamed his brother Philip. A third son, Sidney, was born after the family's reunion. The move was a shock for Ho. His inadequate English caused classmates to tease him, but Ho worked very hard to achieve academic success. He soon earned A's in English and other subjects.

David Ho

After high school, Ho attended the Massachusetts Institute of Technology, in Cambridge, for one year before transferring to the California Institute of Technology, in Pasadena. After graduating from college with a bachelor of science degree **summa cum laude,** in 1974, Ho moved back to Cambridge and entered Harvard Medical School, from which he earned a medical degree in 1978. Ho completed his residency in internal medicine at the Cedars-Sinai Medical Center in Los Angeles in 1981. He then served there for a year as chief medical resident.

summa cum laude graduating from an educational institution with high distinction.

It was at Cedars-Sinai that Ho first encountered some of the earliest known cases of AIDS, though he did not know that then. Medical personnel at Cedars-Sinai began seeing homosexual men who had been healthy but became very sick from infections that were normally not seen in people with healthy immune systems.

In addition to gay men, other patients with similar infections began coming in. These patients included intravenous drug users, **hemophiliacs,** and others who had received blood

hemophiliacs an individual afflicted with hemophilia, a blood defect in males marked by delayed blood clotting and difficulty controlling hemorrhages.

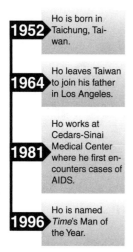

1952 Ho is born in Taichung, Taiwan.

1964 Ho leaves Taiwan to join his father in Los Angeles.

1981 Ho works at Cedars-Sinai Medical Center where he first encounters cases of AIDS.

1996 Ho is named *Time*'s Man of the Year.

virologist a scientist who studies viruses.

white blood cells blood cells without hemoglobin.

transfusions—even some babies. Ho could see that this was a growing epidemic, and he suspected that the cause was a virus.

In 1982, Ho left Los Angeles to become a clinical and research fellow in the Infectious Diseases Unit of Massachusetts General Hospital, in Boston. Along with **virologist** Martin Hirsch, Ho pursued his intense interest in the mysterious virus. Ho's labors finally bore fruit when he isolated the HIV virus, becoming the world's fourth person (in 1983 and 1984) to discover HIV as the cause of the disease they called AIDS. AIDS stands for acquired immunodeficiency syndrome and is the final stage of infection with human immunodeficiency virus (HIV). HIV severely damages the immune system, creating a life-threatening vulnerability to many diseases.

Working in the lab, Ho went on to became the first to show that HIV grows in cells called macrophages, normal cells that absorb harmful matter and dead tissue. He also found HIV in the nervous system and semen, and showed that saliva did not transmit HIV.

During his three years with Hirsch, Ho also served as a research fellow in medicine at Harvard University. In 1985, he also served as a clinical assistant in medicine at Massachusetts General Hospital and as an instructor in medicine at Harvard University. In 1986, Ho returned to Los Angeles to become a physician and research scientist in the Division of Infectious Diseases of the Department of Medicine at Cedars-Sinai Medical Center. He also joined the faculty of the University of California, Los Angeles, School of Medicine as an assistant professor of medicine in residence. In 1989, he was promoted to associate professor.

By 1986, scientists had determined that HIV destroys the body's immune system by attacking T cells, which play an important role in warding off disease. HIV makes its victims susceptible to infections that are not typical, or if they do occur, are usually serious. These infections are called opportunistic because they take advantage of a damaged immune system.

An HIV-infected person is considered to have AIDS if they have contracted an opportunistic infection or one of several other severe illnesses, or if they show a marked decline in the number of CD4 cells. CD4 cells are **white blood cells** that are infected by HIV. Most people with AIDS have fewer than 200 CD4 cells per microliter of blood, with most deaths occurring in patients with CD4-cell counts below 50.

Scientists discovered that the HIV virus entered T cells (a disease-fighting cell called a lymphocyte) via CD4 receptor proteins, which lie on the surface of the cells. Some test-tube experiments showed that flooding the bloodstream of AIDS patients with CD4 molecules could stop the HIV virus by preventing it from attaching to the CD4 receptors.

With Dr. Robert Schooley of Colorado, Ho tested this theory on two dozen patients. The CD4 infusion did not work, but the experiment reinforced Ho's determination to find out more about the virus's life cycle. He recalled that between 1982 and 1985, while moonlighting at the of Massachusetts General Hospital, he had cared for gay men suffering from what seemed to be a severe flu. But their blood did not contain any influenza viruses. After recovering from the flu-like illness, the men remained healthy for the next three to 10 years, at which point they developed symptoms of full-blown AIDS. This suggested to doctors that after the initial infection, the virus simply lay dormant somewhere in the body until something triggered a second outbreak of an AIDS-like illness. It was also believed that HIV did not directly cause the collapse of the immune system but instead the body had an autoimmune reaction. An autoimmune response occurs when the immune system attacks the body's own healthy tissues.

Ho measured the number of virus particles (called the viral load) in blood taken from several young homosexual men with the flu-like illness that signals HIV infection. He discovered that the particle numbers were huge—equal to that of people with AIDS. As he explained in the December 14, 1989, issue of the *New England Journal of Medicine*, he found large amounts of the virus in individuals in the early stages of HIV infection. His work demonstrated that, even when HIV-positive people felt fine and showed no signs of illness, the virus was actively reproducing itself.

In 1990, the philanthropist Irene Diamond named Ho the scientific director and chief executive officer of the newly established Aaron Diamond AIDS Research Center. Ho was also named co-director of the Center for AIDS Research and professor of medicine and microbiology at the New York University School of Medicine. In 1996, the Diamond Center became affiliated with the Rockefeller University, and Ho became a professor there, too.

Ho began to focus on the changes that occur following the initial HIV infection and before the appearance of any symptoms of AIDS. He realized that, during that period, the daily reproduction of the virus might be much greater than the viral

"For helping lift a death sentence—for a few years at least, and perhaps longer—on tens of thousands of AIDS sufferers, and for pioneering the treatment that might, just might, lead to a cure, David Da-i Ho, M.D., in TIME's Man of the Year for 1996."

Time magazine, December 30, 1996/January 6, 1997 issue

Ho concluded that treatment of HIV with a combination of drugs in the weeks immediately after infection might prevent the disease from progressing.

load indicates, because the body's disease-fighting cells might be killing many of the viral particles each day. Ho theorized that the body could defeat the viral load at a steady level until it finally succumbed and the virus would dominate. Working independently, Dr. George Shaw also developed the same theory as Ho.

AIDS researchers soon learned that HIV uses a certain **enzyme** to reproduce, and they created a drug called AZT to block that action. The drug AZT could slow HIV reproduction, but it could not bring it to a halt.

In 1994, drug researchers developed protease inhibitors, which could arrest reproduction of HIV temporarily. This temporary halt gave Ho and Shaw time to conduct certain experiments. They showed that billions of virus particles were created daily in HIV-positive volunteer subjects. They also saw that each day the body responded by producing billions of disease-fighting white blood cells.

enzyme any of numerous complex proteins produced by living cells and catalyze specific biochemical reactions at body temperatures.

Ho described the results of his experiment in the January 12, 1995, issue of *Nature*. In light of his surprising findings, Ho concluded that treatment of HIV with a combination of drugs in the weeks immediately after infection might prevent the disease from progressing. He concluded that if HIV is bombarded with several drugs, each of which cripples the HIV reproductive process at a different point, the chance of its changing into forms resistant to all of them at once becomes tiny.

In 1995, Ho and his co-workers launched several treatment programs in which a combination of three drugs was administered to patients. Most of the patients responded extremely well. After just a few weeks, the number of viral particles in each subject's blood dropped a hundredfold, and as of late 1996, no virus was detectable in any patient's blood.

Although he was greatly pleased with these developments in the fight against what had become the world's most feared disease, Ho emphasized that these drugs still could not cure AIDS. He stressed that much work remains, pointing to the importance of developing a vaccine. By the end of the 1990s, more than 33 million people had HIV/AIDS worldwide, and over 12 million had died since the epidemic began. Nearly 70 percent of those cases were in Africa, making that one of the world's most challenging health crises.

Ho had written or co-written more than 110 scientific articles and has served on a number of AIDS-related organizations and committees, including the National Task Force on AIDS

Drug Development. His honors included the Ernst Jung Prize in Medicine, the New York City Mayor's Award for Excellence in Science and Technology, and the Scientific Award of the Chinese-American Medical Society.

Ho was named *Time* magazine's Man of the Year for 1996. He was overwhelmed by the honor and said, "I do want to emphasize that this honor should be shared with a lot of people in AIDS research: my colleagues, my collaborators, and many other researchers who laid the foundation for the success of the last couple of years."

Ho and his wife, Susan Kuo, an artist whom he married in 1976, lived in a suburb of New York City with their two daughters, Kathryn and Jaclyn, and their son, Jonathan. ◆

Howe, James Wong

AUGUST 29, 1899–JULY 12, 1976 ● CINEMATOGRAPHER

James Wong Howe was born Wong Tung Jim in Kwantung (then Canton), China, on August 29, 1899. In 1904, Howe, his stepmother, and the rest of the family moved to the United States, rejoining his father, who had emigrated shortly after Howe's birth in order to make more money and to make a better life for his family. For almost five years, Howe's father, Wong How, lived alone in Pasco, Washington, until he could make enough money to move his family. When Wong Jung Jim's teacher had trouble remembering his Chinese name, she simply changed it to James Wong Howe by combining his surname "Jim" with his father's full name, Wong How. She told the young boy that this would be his American name.

Howe's father purchased and operated a general store in Pasco and later owned a restaurant in the same town. The Howe family was the only Chinese family in town, so Howe had an unhappy childhood that was filled with racial taunts from the other children. He managed to stay in school until he was 15, at which time he dropped out. At the same time, he moved out of the family home after he had a falling out with his stepmother after his father's death. The stepmother wanted Howe to take over the family business, as was customary in Chinese families, but Howe wanted no part of the business or of the small town that he disliked so much. After living with a friend

James Wong Howe

of his father's for a brief time, Howe set out on his own, traveling up and down the West Coast, surviving by taking odd jobs. One of Howe's jobs included professional boxing, as he had learned to be a skilled fighter while defending himself from the racial jabs he had received as a student.

In 1917, Howe was living in Los Angeles. He tried working as a hotel bellhop, but that only lasted two weeks. As he was walking the streets looking for work, he had a chance encounter that changed his life. He came upon a crowd of people gathered in the street and realized that they were watching the making of a Mack Sennett movie. Intrigued, he asked about getting a job on the set. Told he was too small to move the large movie cameras, he instead was given a job as a janitor, with the responsibility for sweeping up the film editing rooms. Howe was in the world of show business for the first time, and he never left.

Over the course of the next eight years, Howe would make a meteoric rise through the film ranks. When Howe worked as a janitor, it was common knowledge among the directors and producers that he was interested in the photography side of filmmaking. He took an entry-level position working for noted director Cecil B. DeMille so he could be closer to the production process, and that job led to part-time stints as a cameraman and still photographer. When he came up with an important innovation that changed the way actresses' still portraits were taken in 1922, he was given a large promotion and made chief cameraman on the film *Drums of Fate*. Within three years, his amazing technical skills had lifted him to the position of director of photography at Paramount Studios.

A few years after the start of his photography career, Hollywood underwent a period of rapid change when sound pictures replaced the old silent films. Howe, who went by Jimmie in Hollywood, decided to take some time off, and he returned to his native China to visit with his natural mother. When he returned to Hollywood in 1930, he initially had difficulty landing a job because he did not understand the new processes used to create sound films. Finally, Howard Hawkes gave him a two-year contract at William Fox Studio, during which time Howe established himself as a master of the new type of motion pictures.

For the next four decades, Howe would hold a number of positions working for Hollywood studios, and he also spent time working on films in England, where he was a celebrity thanks to his photographic skills. He worked for MGM Studios from 1933 to 1936, where he worked on such notable films as *The Thin Man*. He then left for England, where he spent two years freelancing. Upon his return in 1938, he was hired by David O. Selznick, and that same year, he received his first Academy Award nomination for his photography work on the film *Algiers*. He did not win the award that year. Also in 1938, Howe signed a seven-year contract to work at Warner Brothers Studios, where he remained for nine years, making 36 films.

After leaving Warner in 1947, Howe again took a break and returned to China. This time, he intended to direct his first film, which would be based on the novel *Rickshaw Boy*. Howe never got to finish his film, however, as the rise of communism throughout China forced him to flee the country. When he returned to the United States, he found that his stay in China had hurt his career. Senator Joseph McCarthy and his House Un-American Activities Committee was in full swing, seeking to eradicate communists from all aspects of American society. Because of his Chinese roots and the time he had just spent in that country, Howe was labeled a possible communist and was

1899 — Howe is born in Kwantung, China.

1904 — Howe is brought to live in the United States.

1917 — Howe obtains his first job in the movie industry.

1925 — Howe is named director of photography at Paramount Studios.

1955 — Howe receives his first Academy Award for cinematography for *The Rose Tattoo*.

1963 — Howe receives his second Academy Award for cinematography for *Hud*.

1974 — Howe works on his last film, *Funny Lady*.

1976 — Howe dies of cancer.

My husband loved his work. . . . He was critical of poor quality in any area of film, but quick to see and appreciate the good. His mature style was realistic, never naturalistic. . . . If the story allowed, his style was poetic realism, for he was a poet of the camera.

Sanora Babb Howe on her husband's career, quoted in *James Howe: A Relative's Perspective*, by Richard Francia James Lee

freelancer an independent agent available for hire and not affiliated with or bound by a single entity.

"graylisted," by the committee, which meant that most studios would not hire him to work on their films. Howe survived the next few years by working on low-budget independent films, which were far below the quality level to which he was accustomed.

Finally, in the mid-1950s, he found that he was able to work on large-budget films again. However, Howe spent the rest of his career working as a **freelancer**, refusing to be tied down to any one studio. He tried his hand at directing when he helmed a documentary about the founder of the Harlem Globetrotters called *Go, Man, Go* (1954), but his most notable accomplishments were still behind the camera. In 1955, he won his first Academy Award for the film *The Rose Tattoo*, which fully resurrected his career at the major studio level.

Ten years after his first Oscar, Howe won his second, for the Paul Newman classic, *Hud* (1963). In the decade between the awards, Howe directed television commercials and documentaries and tried teaching for the first time, working at the University of California, Los Angeles campus. He became ill after receiving his Oscar for *Hud*, and for the next nine years, Howe did very little work. In 1974 he made a triumphant return when he took over the struggling production of the Barbra Streisand film *Funny Lady* and turned it into a winner, earning yet another Academy Award nomination. After filming, his illness returned and worsened, and on July 12, 1976, Howe passed away from the effects of cancer. He was survived by his widow Sanora, whom he married in 1949.

Howe was a perfectionist who was sometimes difficult to work with. However, he was also a technical genius who changed the way films were made. In 1931, he invented a technique called "deep focus" that he used for the first time on the film *Transatlantic*. The new approach used lighting so that every element of a camera shot, whether in the front or the back of the frame, appeared in focus. Gregg Toland was given credit for creating deep focus when he shot *Citizen Kane* in 1941, but records show that Howe was the first to use the technique. Howe is also remembered for daring to use creative camera work to obtain the shot he wanted, such as riding backward in a roller coaster car to shoot the reaction of the people riding in the next car (*The King on Main Street*, 1925); roller-skating around a boxing ring with a camera to obtain a boxer's point of view (*Body and Soul*, 1947); and using wide-angle, wildly distorted shots in John Frankenheimer's *Seconds* (1966). ◆

Hwang, David Henry

AUGUST 11, 1957– ● AUTHOR

David Henry Hwang was born in Los Angeles, California, on August 11, 1957. His Chinese immigrant parents were Henry Yuan Hwang, a banker, and Dorothy Yu Hwang, a piano professor whose maiden name was Huang.

Hwang, whose name is pronounced "Wong," attended Stanford University in Palo Alto, California, earning a bachelor of arts degree in 1979, and Yale School of Drama from 1980 to 1981.

Hwang began writing plays as a young adult and his success was nearly immediate. At age 21, just graduating from Stanford, the prestigious National Playwright's Conference accepted Hwang's play *F.O.B.* to produce at the O'Neill Theater Center in Connecticut in 1979. The next year, the play debuted off-Broadway in New York City and won an Obie Award as the best new play of the season.

First staged at Stanford, *F.O.B.*, an acronym for "fresh off the boat," tells the story of Steve, a young Chinese immigrant in Los Angeles. Steve meets several students who either accept or reject him as a foreigner. Although the story of immigrants assimilating into the American mainstream is a common theme, Hwang earned praise for his fresh approach to the topic. For example, Hwang used techniques of traditional Chinese theater in one act. Critics also noted Hwang's humorous spirit in the story.

Hwang followed this success with two more plays that focused on the Chinese-American experience. *The Dance and the Railroad* (1981) portrayed Chinese men working on the American transcontinental railroad in the 1800s. This play also mixed humor and Chinese theater technique with themes of immigrant concerns. The character Lone has been in America two years after his parents pulled him from the study of Chinese opera to sell him into servitude. He is a cynical loner who dances each day outside the labor camp. The second lead character, Ma, is a newcomer who persuades Lone to teach him to dance. As they dance, the men share their thoughts and feelings.

Critics called *Family Devotions* (1981) Hwang's funniest play. The farce portrays a clash between a wealthy Chinese-American family, who are fanatical Christians, and their **atheist**

atheist individual who does not believe in the existence of God.

David Henry Hwang

novella a story with a pointed and compact plot.

uncle visiting from communist China. Another play by Hwang that explored similar themes, *Rich Relations*, was produced in 1986 but did not fare well with critics.

In 1983, Hwang produced *Sound and Beauty*, which consisted of two one-act dramas set in Japan. Hwang modeled one of them, "The House of Sleeping Beauties," on a **novella** that depicted a brothel of comatose virgins in which elderly men slept beside the drugged women to learn to accept their own mortality. The other drama, "The Sound of a Voice," reaches into the realm of folk tales to examine the psychology of men and women. In the story, a samurai warrior meets a bewitching female hermit in a forest. The warrior thinks the woman has the power to destroy men, so he plans to kill her. But he changes his mind after spending several weeks with her.

Hwang achieved his greatest success in 1988 with *M. Butterfly*, a play that he based on the famous opera by Italian composer Giacomo Puccini, *Madama Butterfly*. The opera tells of a Japanese woman who falls in love with a Western man and commits suicide after he rejects her. In Hwang's play, the Western man is a diplomat and the female character is a Chinese opera star who is actually a male pretending to be in love with the Westerner. Hwang drew part of his inspiration from a 1986 newspaper story, in which a French diplomat on trial for espionage had a relationship with a woman who turned out to be a man.

The beautiful set of M. *Butterfly* worked to inform the viewer of the conflicting elements in the story. The set contained two worlds: a world of fantasy on butterfly-shaped platforms, and a world of reality in the off-white area surrounding the butterfly platforms. The play's events that happen in Chinese locations were played on the butterfly platform. Action taking place in other than Chinese locations, such as the French embassy, played on the off-white area.

While M. *Butterfly* drew mixed and lively reviews, the play moved from Washington, D.C., to Broadway and earned a Pulitzer Prize nomination and a Tony Award.

Switching into a very different **genre,** Hwang collaborated with famous **avant-garde** composer Philip Glass in 1988 to produce *One Thousand Airplanes on the Roof*. The multimedia performance involved a female character who believes she has been kidnapped by aliens. She is afraid to tell anyone, but she is also afraid of going crazy if she doesn't. The play was produced in Vienna, Austria, and New York City.

In *Bondage* (1992), two actors in leather gear and masks assume various racial roles in what Hwang described as a "romantic comedy about two people trying to connect and being vulnerable."

Hwang wrote screenplays for the movies M. *Butterfly*, which starred Jeremy Irons and John Lone, and *Golden Gate*, starring Matt Dillon and Joan Chen. Both were released in 1993, but neither earned critical praise or great box office success.

Hwang's play *Golden Child* (1996) takes place mainly in a small Chinese village at the turn of the century, but the play begins in the back seat of a taxi. There a young Chinese-American man is visited by the ghost of his grandmother, who urges him to honor his ancestors and his origins. Magically, the young man becomes his grandfather, Eng Tieng-Bin, who returns to his village after traveling abroad. The domestic life of his three wives is disrupted when Tieng-Bin shares his new ideas about marriage and education. He has become a Christian and sees religion as the path to the modern world. Although *Golden Child* did not reach the heights of M. *Butterfly*, it was considered a thoughtful examination of the meeting of Western values with Chinese culture.

1957 Hwang is born in Los Angeles, California.

1980 Hwang's play *F.O.B.* debuts off-Broadway in New York City and wins an Obie Award as the best new play of the season.

1988 Hwang achieves his greatest success with M. *Butterfly*, based on the famous opera *Madama Butterfly*.

1993 Hwang's two screenplays are made into the movies M. *Butterfly* and *Golden Gate*.

genre style or category of form and content.
avant garde a group of intelligentsia that develops new concepts in art or literature.

Other works by Hwang include *The Sound of a Voice* (1984); *As the Crow Flies* (1986); *My American Son* (television drama, 1987); *The Voyage* (opera, with music by Philip Glass, 1992); *Face Values* (1993); and *The Silver River* (musical, 1997).

Hwang made his home in Los Angeles. He married artist Ophelia Y. M. Chong in 1985 and then actress Kathryn A. Layng in 1993, after divorcing Chong in 1989. Hwang had one son, Noah, through his second marriage. ◆

Iha, James

MARCH 26, 1968– ● MUSICIAN

James Iha was a guitar player and songwriter for the alternative rock band the Smashing Pumpkins. Selling more than 16 million records in the United States and over 22 million worldwide, the Pumpkins became one of the most popular bands of the 1990s.

James Iha was born March 26, 1968, in Chicago, Illinois. He was Japanese-American and attended Elk Grove Village High School in a Chicago suburb.

In 1988, guitarist Iha met singer-guitarist Billy Corgan in a Polish bar on Chicago's northwest side. The duo hit it off musically and formed a band that they called the Smashing Pumpkins. In addition to Corgan and Iha, the band included bassist D'Arcy Wretzky and drummer Jimmy Chamberlin. The group played their first concert as a four-piece rock band at Chicago's Metro on October 5, 1988. In 1989, the quartet's debut single, "I Am One," was released.

In 1991, the Pumpkins released their debut album, "Gish". Rock critics hailed their sound as giving new color to the emerging alternative-rock movement. The album was widely acclaimed, and sold a surprising 300,000 copies on the independent label Caroline.

In 1993, the Pumpkins released the album "Siamese Dream". The recording was an astonishing success. It debuted in the Top 10 and went on to sell more than 4 million copies in the United States. The record's dense, multitracked guitars and Corgan's introspective lyrics made it an alternative-rock milestone.

1968 James Iha is born in Chicago.

1988 The Smashing Pumpkins play their first show at the Metro in Chicago.

1993 *Siamese Dream* is released.

1995 *Mellon Collie and the Infinite Sadness* is released.

2000 The Smashing Pumpkins disband.

Iha wrote two of the songs on "Siamese Dream", "Soma" and "Mayonnaise." "Soma" speaks of a man tormented by the ups and downs of love. In the first verse he says, "Nothing left to say/And all I've left to do/Is run away/From you." Later verses declare, "Wrap my hurt in you/And took my shelter in that pain/The opiate of blame/Is your broken heart, your heart/So now I'm all by myself/As I've always felt/I'll betray my tears/To anyone caught in our ruse of fools//One last kiss for me . . . yeah/One last kiss good night."

In "Mayonnaise," Iha seems to draw upon his experience of being an ethnic minority in a middle-class environment, declaring, "Fool enough to almost be it/Cool enough to not quite see it/Doomed/Pick your pockets full of sorrow/And run away with me tomorrow/June." The song closes with, "No more promise no more sorrow/No longer will I follow/Can anybody hear me/I just want to be me/When I can, I will/Try to understand/That when I can, I will."

In 1994, the Pumpkins headlined the Lollapalooza tour, a traveling rock festival that included a number of bands. Other groups on the tour were Jane's Addiction, the Red Hot Chili Peppers, and Alice in Chains. After wrapping up Lollapalooza that summer, the band came to a crossroads. They were exhausted and still feeling the effects of their amazing success from "Siamese Dream."

Only weeks after the tour ended, though, Corgan submerged himself in writing songs and soon the band was laying down rough rhythm tracks at its rehearsal space on the north side of Chicago. The Pumpkins spent the summer of 1995 working 12- to 16-hour days for weeks on end to finish the most highly anticipated rock release of the season. In late 1995, the album "Mellon Collie and the Infinite Sadness" was released on Virgin records. A double album containing 28 songs and spanning more than two hours, it became one of the defining albums of the 1990s. *Time*, *Rolling Stone*, and *Spin* magazines honored it as the album of the year, and it went on to sell 11 million copies worldwide.

In 1996, the band fired Chamberlin for drug abuse, and soon after touring, their keyboard player Jonathan Melvoin died of a heroin overdose in a New York City hotel room. Later, the band released "The Aeroplane Flies High," a boxed set, containing more tracks recorded during the "Mellon Collie" sessions.

In 1997, the Pumpkins' song "Bullet With Butterfly Wings" received a Grammy Award for best hard-rock performance.

Although the Pumpkins were primarily an outlet for Corgan's tunes, Iha's music, mostly confined to B-sides, shone with promise in such songs as "Blew Away" and "Said Sadly."

Iha's songwriting talent finally had a forum to itself on "Let It Come Down", Iha's first solo album, which came out in February 1998 on Virgin Records. Although Iha was famous for playing guitar like a man in a cyclone, with blazing guitar solos in Pumpkin's concerts, "Let It Come Down" surprised many with its gentleness.

In 1998, the Pumpkins released "Adore." Critics praised the album's low-key introspection and spiritual bent, representing their creative growth. However, sales went slowly compared to the Pumpkins' earlier releases.

For their 1998 tour, the Pumpkins were expected to make a huge profit on the concert circuit after consistently selling out arenas on their 1995-96 tour. Instead, the Pumpkins did something completely unexpected. They gave every dollar of profit—more than $2 million—to charity. In explaining why his band would willingly forfeit so much money, Corgan simply said, "We've all made more money than we'll ever need. It's time to take responsibility for our generation and subsequent generations." Also in 1998, the band won a second hard-rock **Grammy** for "The End is the Beginning is the End."

In 1999, Chamberlin came back on drums for a brief Pumpkins tour of North American clubs. However, Wretzky later departed and was replaced on bass by Melissa Auf Der Maur, formerly of the female rock band Hole.

In 2000, "Machina/The Machines of God" was released, the band's final album for Virgin Records. They followed it with "Machina II: The Friends and Enemies of Modern Music." The Pumpkins shocked the music world again by releasing Machina II on the Internet free of charge as a gift to fans.

Though critically acclaimed, "Machina" quickly slipped down the charts, dropping out of the *Billboard* Top 100 after a month. Even though the record sold 500,000 copies—a success by most standards—its performance was disappointing.

In May 2000, Corgan pulled the plug on one of the era's most commercially successful and artistically accomplished rock bands when he announced that the Smashing Pumpkins would disband. Friends said that the pressure on the group had been immense and the band had hit some snags. They had suffered the sudden departure of bassist Wretzky and a volatile three-month

In 1998, the band won a second hard-rock Grammy for "The End is the Beginning is the End."

Grammy annual award given in various categories for excellence in the music recording industry.

relationship with manager Sharon Osbourne, which resulted in the Pumpkins suing her for breach of contract.

After Corgan's announcement, the band decided it would play its final show on December 2, 2000, at the Metro on Chicago's north side, where their journey had begun.

Returning to the same small venue where they debuted 13 years before, the Smashing Pumpkins bid farewell to their fans with a blazing four-hour survey of their songs. The finale at the 1,100-person capacity Metro was one of the hottest tickets of the year. It sold out in 20 minutes on October 21 with almost as many tickets bought outside the United States as within.

The Pumpkins opened the concert with the powerful "Rocket." The second set featured more introspective work, opening with the beautifully mournful "Muzzle" from "Mellon Collie and the Infinite Sadness." After a driving third set that again put the crowd in motion, the band followed with three encores.

The three remaining founders of Chicago's star rock band did not grandstand. Iha wore a sequined Grand Ole Opry suit but exited quietly into the shadows as the show ended. Jimmy Chamberlin, in a black muscle shirt, blew kisses before hastening off. Corgan, in an androgynous silver outfit and commando boots, smiled, waved, and then finally put his shaven head in his hands and sobbed.

Iha had long been the Pumpkins' "other guitarist," playing in the shadow of singer-songwriter Corgan. Following the band's breakup, the slender, self-effacing Iha faded out of the shared limelight.

Sometimes referred to as "the cute one" by female Pumpkins fans, Iha wore his straight black hair to his shoulders and streaked with white at the front. Known for his intelligence and sarcasm, he also wore makeup and fingernail polish. Iha had eyes that were called veiled, seductive, and sullen.

Iha's other interests included graphic design and runway modeling. He sleekly modeled the fashions of designer Anna Sui in one show. ◆

Inouye, Daniel K.

SEPTEMBER 7, 1924– ● POLITICIAN

By the time Daniel Inouye first came to national prominence through the nationally televised hearings of the Senate Watergate Committee, he had already been an

influential member of the U.S. Senate for more than a decade after having served earlier as Hawaii's first United States congressman.

The oldest son of Japanese immigrants to Hawaii, Daniel Ken Inouye was born on September 7, 1924, in Honolulu, where he grew up in the secure if modest circumstance afforded by his father's salary as a jewelry salesman in a large department store. While attending McKinley High School in Honolulu, he parked cars and gave haircuts to fellow students to earn extra money.

Inouye was pressed into war service as a 17-year-old when his medical aid training led to his appointment as head of a first-aid team attending to the wounded at Pearl Harbor in December 1941. While Inouye was enrolled as a pre-med student at the University of Hawaii, the U.S. Army reversed its initial policy of banning all Japanese-Americans from military service, and in March 1943 the 18-year-old Inouye enlisted in the 442nd Regimental Combat team. After completing his training at Camp Shelby, Mississippi, Inouye and his regiment joined another all-Japanese-American unit, the 100th Infantry Battalion, in a punishing three-month campaign in Italy. Inouye

Senator Daniel Inouye shakes hands with President Gerald Ford before Ford's 1976 void of the executive order creating the Japanese internment camps during World War II.

Civil Liberties Act of 1988

On August 10, 1988, Senator Daniel Inouye watched with pride as President Ronald Reagan signed into law an extraordinary civil rights act. With the stroke of his pen, Reagan committed the United States government to formally apologize to the nation's Japanese-American citizens for injustices committed against them during World War II. In addition, the act obligated the government to provide token compensation to some 80,000 individuals who had lost property and savings during those years.

After the Japanese attack on Pearl Harbor, on December 7, 1941, anti-Asian fears ran rampant throughout the American West. Amid public hysteria that Japanese-American citizens would somehow betray the country, on February 19, 1942, President Franklin D. Roosevelt signed an executive order prohibiting people of Japanese ancestry from living freely on the West Coast. Approximately 120,000 Japanese Americans were forced to leave their homes, farms and businesses in California, Washington, Oregon, and Arizona. Some were shipped east for relocation, but most were rounded up and forced to live in internment camps.

A few had friends who would care for their property during the war years, but most were forced to sell everything they owned, usually for a small fraction of its worth. At war's end they were released from the camps, but most had no resources and nowhere to go. A few prominent Japanese Americans spoke out passionately against this injustice, and President Harry S. Truman finally agreed to allow former internees to file claims for restitution of their lost property. The claims process was cumbersome, however, and few claimants were successful.

The Japanese-American community never gave up in its quest for justice. In 1980 Inouye and others succeeded in getting Congress to create the Commission on Wartime Relocation and Internment of Civilians to investigate the claims of former internees. It was not until 1985, however, that Congress began to draft truly meaningful legislation, finally drafting the Civil Rights Act of 1988. With the passage of this law, the government finally took at least a symbolic step toward taking responsibly for the profoundly racist policies of the World War II era.

valorous courageous; brave.

Bronze Star a United States military medal awarded for heroic or meritorious service to the nation not involving aerial flights.

quickly distinguished himself as a **valorous** leader under fire, rallying his "Go for Broke" regiment through heavy fire for two weeks in France to rescue the famous "lost battalion" in one of the most celebrated episodes of the war.

Awarded the **Bronze Star** and promoted to second lieutenant, Inouye soon found himself back in Italy, where he was wounded in the abdomen by a bullet that barely missed his spine. Despite his wound Inouye pressed his platoon forward toward their objective, a German machine-gun nest. After tossing two grenades into the nest, another enemy bullet ravaged his right arm; the unstoppable Inouye continued his grenade assault with his left hand until he was finally felled by a leg wound. Elevated to the rank of captain, Inouye was decorated with the **Distinguished Service Cross**, the Bronze Star, the **Purple Heart**, and a dozen more honors.

After more than a year and a half **convalescing** in army hospitals, Inouye, returned to Honolulu and resumed his studies at the University of Hawaii. His dream of becoming a surgeon having been shattered by the loss of his right arm, Inouye enrolled in a prelaw program. After graduating in 1950, Inouye entered George Washington University Law School in Washington, D.C., where his studies were supported in part by his schoolteacher wife, Maggie.

Inouye graduated from law school in 1952 and returned to Honolulu, where, the following year, he launched his career in public service as the deputy public prosecutor for the City and County of Honolulu. A year later he entered electoral politics, winning the Hawaiian seat in the Territorial House of Representatives, in which he served for the following four years before his election to the Territorial Senate, from which he resigned after one year to run for Congress after Hawaii won statehood on August 21, 1959. After winning easily and serving a one-year term, Inouye was reelected by a landslide to his first full term in 1960.

In 1962 Inouye won the Democratic nomination for that year's Senatorial race in Hawaii and he again triumphed easily in the general election.

Inouye carried the fight against prejudice to the floor of the Senate as a vigorous champion of civil rights legislation and as an eloquent spokesman for racial understanding as the keynote speaker at the turbulent 1968 Democratic Convention in Chicago.

The national spotlight next fell on Inouye during the 1973-74 Watergate hearings, during which Inouye's sharp and penetrating questioning of witnesses was a highlight of the daily drama unfolding before a rapt national television audience. Shortly thereafter Inouye served a two year term as the first chairman of the Senate Select Committee on Intelligence; was the secretary of the Democratic Conference for (1979-88); chaired the Senate Democratic Central America Study group; chaired the Senate Select Committee on Secret Military Assistance to Iran during the widely publicized hearings on the Iran-contra scandal; and chaired the Committee on Indian Affairs. ◆

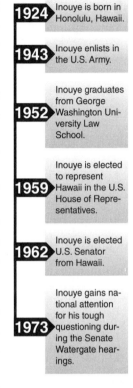

1924 Inouye is born in Honolulu, Hawaii.

1943 Inouye enlists in the U.S. Army.

1952 Inouye graduates from George Washington University Law School.

1959 Inouye is elected to represent Hawaii in the U.S. House of Representatives.

1962 Inouye is elected U.S. Senator from Hawaii.

1973 Inouye gains national attention for his tough questioning during the Senate Watergate hearings.

Distinguished Service Cross U.S. Army medal awarded for extraordinary heroism during action against an armed enemy.

Purple Heart United States military medal awarded to individuals wounded or killed in combat during the service of the nation.

convalescing recuperating; recovering from an injury or illness.

Ito, Lance

AUGUST 2, 1950– ● JUDGE

Long before *Survivor* spawned the "reality-programming" rage among television executives, there was a *real* reality TV series that held the nation glued tighter to their screens—day after day, week after week, for a full year—than had any other event of the television era: the 1994-95 double-murder trial of the glamorous football star, television commentator, and B-movie actor O. J. Simpson. And, like any reality television program, the Simpson trial had its host/moderator: Judge Lance Ito, whose pensive face and occasionally rowdy courtroom became as famous as any in American history.

Like the other **dramatis personae** of those often lurid proceedings, Ito has now retreated into the modest eminence from which destiny plucked him in 1994 for his year in the glare of the spotlight. From his behavior during the trial, it is difficult to tell whether Ito's preferred image in posterity is that of competent, admired, popular judge of the Los Angeles Superior Court or as ringmaster of a circus: despite his strenuous protestations against the media's instrusions on the solemn workings of justice in the Simpson case, Ito himself succumbed to the siren song of the cameras, agreeing to a five-part series of ten-minute interviews broadcast in November 1994 on the CBS affiliate station in Los Angeles, KCBS-TV. Although the interviews were broadcast before the trial began and were restricted to personal issues, Ito was roundly castigated for taking this healthy bite out of the media apple. One Los Angeles-area lawyer told *The New York Times*, "Granted, he did not talk directly about the case. Judges, however, must avoid the appearance of impro-

dramatis personae characters in a play or production.

Lance Ito

priety . . . Putting everything else aside, it exhibits extraordinarily poor judgment."

Few people had ever questioned Ito's judgment up until then. He had acquitted himself admirably in his only previous stewardship of a high-profile case: the 1991 securities-fraud prosecution of Charles Keating, the former owner of the notorious Lincoln Saving and Loan Association, through which he was alleged to have bilked thousands of investors of their life savings. Ito did manage to stir considerable controversy by dismissing half of the government's charges against Keating, but he handed down the maximum allowable sentence.

Ito's mastery of detail and dogged work ethic lifted him from his modest if comfortable origins to his current judicial eminence. The son of two schoolteachers, Lance Allan Ito was born on August 2, 1950. Ito always ascribed a good measure of his passion for justice to his parents' confinement in detention camps for Japanese-Americans during World War II. After graduating from John Marshall High School in 1968, he enrolled in the University of California at Los Angeles, from which he graduated cum laude in 1972 with a degree in political science. Ito then moved on to the Boalt Hall School of Law at the University of California at Berkeley.

In 1975 Ito graduated from law school and shortly thereafter was admitted to the bar. His first job was in the firm of Irsfield, Irsfield, and Yournger, where he remained for two years before leaving private practice to join the district attorney's office, where he spent four years tackling challenging gang violence and homicide cases. While working on homicide he met Margaret York, then a detective in the Los Angeles Police Department, at the scene of the murder. They were married not long after.

After a decade of distinguished service as a prosecutor, Ito, a Democrat, was appointed to the the Los Angeles County Superior Court by a Republican governor, George Deukmajian. During the early 1990s Ito worked on the court as an assistent supervising judge, a job that entailed assigning judges and courtroom to upcoming cases—"air traffic control for the criminal system," in the words of one journalist. It was in this role that Ito presided over the Keating fraud trial in 1991, for which he was voted Trial Judge of the Year by the Los Angeles County Bar Association in 1992.

Ito's days of competent toil in modest semiobscurity came to an end in the fall of 1994, when he as appointed to preside over

1950 Ito is born in Los Angeles, California.

1975 Ito graduates from Boalt Hall School of Law at the University of California at Berkeley.

1977 Ito leaves private law practice to become a prosecutor in Los Angeles.

1978 Ito is appointed to the Superior Court of Los Angeles.

1979 Ito presides over the savings and loan fraud trial of Charles Keating.

1980 Ito presides over the double-murder trial of football star and actor O. J. Simpson.

Ito was targeted for withering criticism for his seeming inability to contain the food-fight atmosphere of the trial.

the full-time media extravaganza that became known as "the trial of the century": the O. J. Simpson double-murder case. Ito was at first appalled by the pre-trial leaks of evidence that spiced the marathon coverage of the case. In September 1994, he told a reporter, "I'm so saturated by the irresponsibility of the media that I'm beyond being outraged. I'm almost numb to this point." After threatening to bar live television coverage of the trial, Ito relented and agreed to allow cameras into the courtroom as the proceedings got underway in January 1995.

By turns tedious and tawdry, the daily soap opera commanded the daytime airwaves for more than a year, during which time the contending lawyers periodically made a shambles of the trial with their objections, tirades, and histrionics. Ito was targeted for withering criticism for his seeming inability to contain the food-fight atmosphere of the trial. *Newsweek* featured Ito on its cover with the headline, "What a Mess!" In the words of Ronald Allen, a law professor at Northwestern University, "Ito has let the process run amok. He is just not controlling this the way he should." But Ito also earned praise for his **equipoise** under difficult circumstances. Commenting on Ito's conduct of the trial on a live television interview, President Bill Clinton said, "He strikes me as someone who has been firm and fair. He's trying very hard. And he has an enormously difficult task."

equipoise state of balance; equilibrium.

After the Simpson trial, Ito still presided over cases for the Los Angeles Superior Court. He lived with his wife, Margaret, in Pasadena, where he indulged in hobbies of marathon running and photography. Judging by his absence from the television screens, newspapers, and magazines over the past five years, he seemed happy to have retreated from the pitiless gaze of public scrutiny that made his name a household word. ◆

Jen, Gish

AUGUST 12, 1955– ● AUTHOR

The novels and short stories of Gish Jen have won wide admiration for their emotionally gripping portrayals of Asian-Americans negotiating the tension of ethnic and the uprooting pull of modern American life. Although she grew up in middle-class comfort in Scarsdale, an affluent suburb of New York City, Jen's path to literary eminence was anything but smooth, requiring a steadfast force of will and vocation to overcome the countervailing pressures of family expectation and her own **trepidation** about the uncertainties of a writing career.

The second of five children, Lillian Jen (she later changed her name to Gish) was born on August 12, 1955, in Queens, New York City, to Chinese immigrant parents. Although she grew up in a household steeped in learning—her father worked as a professor of civil engineering and her mother as a teacher—Lillian was the only Jen with a passion for reading fiction. When the family moved from Queens to Scarsdale during her childhood, the impressive public library there opened up vast new worlds to her. As she later told an interviewer, "I felt like a kid in a chocolate factory. I must have read every book. I read indiscriminately, whether it was Albert Camus or Walter Farley. They all made me say, 'wow.'" Growing up in a neighborhood where hers was the only Asian family also sharpened her awareness of the plight of nonwhites in America. "People threw things at us and called us names," she later recalled. We thought it was normal—it was only later that I realized it had been hard."

In the throes of her teenage infatuation with great literature, Jen decided to adopt the first name "Gish," taken from her

trepidation fears or concerns.

119

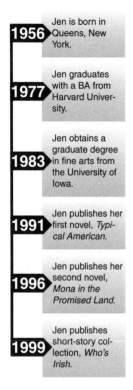

1956 Jen is born in Queens, New York.

1977 Jen graduates with a BA from Harvard University.

1983 Jen obtains a graduate degree in fine arts from the University of Iowa.

1991 Jen publishes her first novel, *Typical American*.

1996 Jen publishes her second novel, *Mona in the Promised Land*.

1999 Jen publishes short-story collection, *Who's Irish*.

prosody the study of versification.

favorite silent-film star, Lillian Gish. As she later recalled, "It was part of becoming a writer, not becoming the person I was supposed to be." Jen's absorption in fiction did not divert her from her outstanding work in math and science, however, which helped to land her at Harvard College in 1972. Once there she promptly relegated her literary ambitions to the shelf of adolescent fantasy and embarked on studies geared for medical school. "I was pre-med, pre-law, in business school, thought about being an architect, a contractor, an antiques dealer," she later told a reporter.

In fact, Gen did not write a single creative sentence until her junior year, when she took a course in **prosody** with the renowned classicist and translator Robert Fitzgerald. That course rekindled her passion for words, but even after switching her major to literature, she could not conceive of writing as a career. "But I'm the daughter of immigrants," she later commented, "and I'd completely internalized all their practical ideas, so I didn't even consider for a moment becoming a poet."

After she took her degree in literature, Jen took a job as an assistant editor at Doubleday, a major book publisher, but felt directionless and impoverished in her high-prestige, low-paying job. She then enrolled in an MBA program at Stanford, where she knew she could avail herself of excellent writing courses on the side. Her first year at Stanford was a continual battle to subordinate writing to commerce; during her second year her business school class-cutting gradually ballooned into a total exit from the program.

After dropping out of business school, Jen was estranged from her parents for a year, during which time she traveled to China to work as an English teacher. She later recalled, "Not only was it a discovery of my roots, it was also the first time that I really felt I was contributing to something larger than myself. . . . I couldn't have written *Typical American* without that trip." Upon returning to the United States, Jen entered the graduate writing program at the University of Iowa. After obtaining a degree in fine arts there in 1983, Jen returned to San Francisco to marry David O'Connor, a computer-software specialist she had known at Stanford.

But Jen soon wearied of her wifely routine in Silicon Valley, and with her husband's encouragement, renewed her determination to make a go of a serious literature career. Once David managed to find a job at the Massachusetts Institute of Technology, the couple moved to the more artistically stimulating environs of Cambridge, Massachusetts. With the help of a one-year fellowship from Radcliffe's Bunting Institute, Jen began work in earnest on her first novel while publishing short stories in leading publications such as the *Atlantic Monthly, Iowa Review, The New Yorker, Southern Review,* and *Yale Review.*

Jen's first novel, *Typical American* (1991), told the tale of the Changs, an immigrant family that unravels under the relentless pressures of American rootlessness and commercialism. The work was generally lauded by critics, who greeted her as a burgeoning talent on a par with Amy Tan and Maxine Hong Kingston. As one critic wrote, "*Typical American* is a rich addition to the ever-growing body of immigrant literature, a lovingly imagined, thoroughly satisfying account of one Chinese family picking its way through the hazards of the American Dream."

In Jen's second novel, *Mona in the Promised Land* (1996), the Chang saga continues in the coming-of-age adventures of Mona Changowitz, a second-generation Chinese-American suburbanite whose identification with the surrounding Jewish culture is reflected in the hybrid last name she adopts. One critic described the book as a pop-culture potpourri: "Imagine P. G. Wodehouse reincarnated as an American-born Chinese person writing the novelization of the screenplay for a movie codirected by Woody Allen and Wayne Wang."

Who's Irish (1999), Jen's collection of short stories, also elicited plaudits from the critics. In the words of David Gates of *Newsweek*, "Jen uses her ever-ready wit to provide ironic distance from genuinely dark places."

Jen lived in Massachusetts with her husband, her son, Luke, and daughter, Paloma. ◆

> "*Until recently, it did not occur to most of us that the absence of Asian and Asian-American images was symptomatic of a more pround invisibility.*"
> Jen quoted in "Challenging the Asian Illusion," *The New York Times,* August 11, 1991.

Jin, Ha

FEBRUARY 21, 1956– ● AUTHOR

Xuefei Jin, who later wrote under the name Ha Jin, was born on February 21, 1956, in Liaoning, China. His father was Danlin, an officer, and his mother was Yuanfen, a worker whose maiden name was Zhao. The Jin family lived under the newly established communist government of Mao Zedong in a small rural town in Liaoning Province. At the

Ha Jin (right) with Ernest Hemingway's son Patrick at the 1997 Hemingway Foundation/Penn Awards.

age of 14, Jin volunteered to serve in the People's Army and was stationed on the northeastern border between China and the Soviet Union. He began studying on his own and, after six years, left the army to attend college. But the Cultural Revolution closed the colleges, so he put in three years as a railroad telegrapher in another remote area. In 1977, when the colleges finally reopened, he enrolled at Heilongjiang University in Harbin, where the study of English was assigned to him. There he earned his bachelor of arts degree in 1981. At Shangdong University, he earned a master of fine arts degree in American literature in 1984.

In 1986, at age 30 Jin emigrated from China to work on his doctorate in English at Brandeis University in Waltham, Massachusetts. He also studied fiction writing at Boston University. After the 1989 government massacre of student protesters in Beijing's Tiananmen Square in China, Jin realized it would be impossible for him to write honestly in China, so he decided to remain in the Unites States. Since he had not established an audience in Chinese, he decided that the only way to become a writer was to write in English. Jin published his first book of poems, *Between Silences*, in 1990, mixing autobiography with other voices to look at the history of China in the second half of the twentieth century.

In 1993, Jin became an assistant professor of creative writing at Emory University, in Atlanta, Georgia, where he remained. Jin told an interviewer, "Since I teach full time, my writing process has been adapted to my teaching. When I have a large piece of time, I write drafts of stories, or a draft of a novel, which I revise and edit when I teach. Each draft is revised thirty times before it is finished." In 1996, Jin published a book of poems called *Facing Shadows*.

Jin's first book of short stories, *Ocean of Words: Army Stories* (1998), is set on China's northern border in the 1970s, when Russia and China were close to war. The stories describe the lives of soldiers living in constant close contact, who have even less privacy than normal in China. Attitudes about privacy show a fundamental difference between Chinese and Western societies. The book probes the Chinese psyche, touching on such topics as food, family, attitudes toward women, hunger, fear, sexual embarrassment, and curiosity about the world. The title refers to a treasured dictionary in a story that brings together a maladjusted young man and an elderly officer.

For his collection of 12 short stories in *Under the Red Flag* (1997), Jin won the prestigious Flannery O'Connor Award. The stories look into the lives of citizens of modern communist state of China. Jin's stories all contain a tone of cynicism in the face of authority, but are not tales of outright **dissidence**. In one of the most powerful stories, a dutiful Party official is torn by his dying mother's wish for a traditional burial, because Party rules demand cremation. In the story "In Broad Daylight," a prostitute is scheduled to be degraded publicly, and a young boy looks forward to the event.

In one story in *Under the Red Flag*, an arrogant and miserly communist man finds that a minor event such as an accidentally smashed Mao button can lead to his downfall. In another, a widow kills the nephew of a party boss in the course of a rape. She faces serious consequences until her actions can be showed to seem patriotic. A soldier in "A Man-to-Be" refrains from taking part in a gang rape and then has to defend his manliness to his fiancé's family, who doubt his ability to father children. Meanwhile, bullies who terrorize their fellow classmates in "Emperor" become more popular with each brutal act they commit.

1956 Jin is born on in Liaoning, China.

1986 Jin emigrates from China to attend Brandeis University in Waltham, Massachusetts.

1998 Jin's first book of short stories, *Ocean of Words: Army Stories*, is published.

1999 Jin wins the National Book Award for *Waiting*.

dissidence disagreement; dissent.

Jin reached a pinnacle in his career when he won the National Book Award for *Waiting* (1999).

In the Pond (1998), Jin's first novel, was about power, vanity, art, injustice, and politics. Set in Communist China, its hero is a small man named Shao Bin, a maintenance employee at the Harvest Fertilizer Plant and also a self-taught artist. Together with his wife and two-year-old daughter, Bin lives in a tiny 12x20-foot room. Bin is desperate to move into the newly built workers' compound, and he places his name on the waiting list with high hopes. When the plant managers pass him over, despite the fact that he has been working there for years, Bin finally cracks. He publishes a satirical cartoon protesting official corruption. As Bin gets into deeper and deeper trouble, he aims higher and higher with his **satire**. The book is a character study, political allegory, and satire.

Jin reached a pinnacle in his career when he won the National Book Award for *Waiting* (1999). The lead character, Lin, is a Chinese physician who serves as an officer in the Revolutionary Army. While a medical student in the early 1960s, Lin is pressured into an arranged marriage by his elderly parents, who choose Shuyu, an illiterate village girl. Shuyu is plain but good-natured and devotes herself to serving Lin and his parents. Lin's heart is never in the marriage, and after the birth of their only child, Lin and Shuyu sleep apart.

furlough limited release from an organized institution or group.

The situation is helped somewhat by Lin's army career, which keeps him posted at great distances from home and allows him only 12 days **furlough** a year. Eventually, though, Lin falls in love with Manna Wu, a nurse at his hospital, and the two wish to marry. However, Shuyu does not want to grant her husband a divorce. The court probably would not allow it anyway, because Party officials view divorce with deep suspicion. Lin and Manna have one chance at happiness: a clause in the marriage code that permits divorce without spousal consent after 18 years of separation. The years tick on, bringing Lin and Manna gradually closer to their happiness. However, the story has an ironic ending.

China is the setting for Jin's 12 stories in *The Bridegroom* (2000). Each of the stories takes place in Muji City, China, the setting of *Waiting*. In the title story, "The Bridegroom," a seemingly model husband joins a secret men's literary club and finds himself arrested for the "crime" of homosexuality. The story "Alive" centers on an official who loses his memory in an earthquake and lives happily for months as a simple worker. When he suddenly remembers who he is, his return to his old life proves inconvenient for everyone. In "A Tiger-

Fighter Is Hard to Find," a television crew's inept attempt to film a fight scene with a live Siberian tiger lands their lead actor in a mental hospital, convinced that he is the mythical tiger—fighter Wu Song.

Jin told an interviewer, "Because I failed to do something else, writing in English became my means of survival, of spending or wasting my life, of retrieving losses, mine and those of others. Because my life has been a constant struggle, I feel close in my heart to the great Russian masters, including Chekhov, Gogol, and Babel."

Jin married Lisah Bian in 1982 and the couple had one child, Wen. ◆

Kashiwahara, Ken

TELEVISION JOURNALIST

In his quarter century as San Francisco bureau chief of ABC News, Ken Kashiwahara covered some of the most important stories of the past two decades, including the O.J. Simpson trial, the bloody suppression of the Tiananmen Square protests in China, and the massive earthquake that ravaged San Francisco in 1989.

Ken Kashiwara

A native of California, Kashiwahara attended San Francisco State College, from which he graduated with a degree in broadcasting. He then joined the U.S. Air Force, for which he worked as an information officer during tours of duty in Europe, Vietnam, and Europe. His many reports for civilian and military periodicals included an acclaimed article on the effort to resupply besieged allied troops at Khe Sanh.

After leaving the service, Kashiwahara became a radio reporter in California, first at KCBS and later at KHUM. Kashiwahara then moved to Honolulu, Hawaii, to take a job as a reporter for KHVH-TV. From there he moved on to Honolulu's KGMB-TV, first as

The Asian American Journalists Association

The Asian American Journalists Association (AAJA) was founded in 1980 as a way for established journalists to share their experience and to give voice to matters of special concern to Asian Americans. Initially based in Los Angeles, today it boasts 1600 members with 18 chapters scattered throughout the United States and the Pacific Rim.

AAJA's three principle goals are to increase the representation of Asian Americans in the field of journalism, to monitor the fairness and accuracy of major stories relevant to the Asian American experience, and to encourage young people to explore journalism as a career. Influential members include Bill Sing, business editor for the Los Angeles Times, and Tritia Toyota, popular anchorwoman for KCBS news.

AAJA seeks to educate journalists about the dangers of prejudice and stereotypes that can be triggered by such front-page stories as the Los Alamos espionage case and former Vice President Al Gore's visit to the Buddhist temple in Los Angeles. It is AAJA's belief that journalists have a duty to avoid playing to public fears by maintaining a professional level of fairness and balance, and by remaining watchful for language and coverage that oversimplifies or misrepresents the Asian American community.

AAJA offers leadership training, scholarships, mentoring and internship programs. It is well-represented in major media centers such as New York City, San Francisco, Washington, and Chicago. Its success is demonstrated by the impressive presence of Asian Americans in broadcast journalism, from highly visible national figures such as Ken Kashiwahara (ABC News Bureau Chief and winner of the AAJA Lifetime Achievement Award) to local anchorpersons and behind-the-scenes management.

a political reporter and then as evening news anchor. He then moved on to KABC-TV in Los Angeles, where he coanchored the weekend broadcasts of *Eyewitness News* while doing general reporting during the week.

By the mid-1970s, Kashiwahara's work for ABC's local affiliate led to a job with the network, for which he covered major stories in Southeast Asia, including the collapse of the South Vietnamese regime and the evacuation of the last Americans in 1975. Kashiwahara's indefatigable reporting kept him at the chaotic scene of flight until nearly the last flight out of Saigon. Soon afterward, Kashiwahara won the plum job as ABC's Hong Kong Bureau chief, traveling from there to report on the bloody civil war in Lebanon in 1977. In 1978 Kashiwahara was named the bureau chief of the ABC News bureau in San Francisco.

The year 1980 proved to be a busy one for Kashiwahara. During the presidential contest he was assigned to the campaign of Ronald Reagan, from the early primaries through Reagan's nomination at the Republican National Convention in

Detroit. He also covered that year's epic eruption of Mt. St. Helen's in Washington State and the first space shuttle flight from his vantage points at Edwards Air Force Base. He also covered the shuttle's landing from Weed Patch, California.

In 1984 Kashiwahara reported on the Democratic National Convention in San Francisco and the Summer Olympic Games in Los Angeles, which were boycotted by the Soviet Union and most of the **eastern bloc nations.** In 1986 he won his first Emmy for "In the Fire's Path," a special report for ABC's primetime magazine *20/20.* Kashiwahara was awarded another Emmy two years later for his reporting on the ABC News special, "Burning Questions—The Poisoning of America." In each of the next two years, Kashiwahara traveled with American veterans who returned to Vietnam to reunite with children they had fathered there during the war. His ensuing special series of reports on *World News Tonight* won wide acclaim, as did his one-hour special *Nightline* report on U.S. veterans of Vietnam still suffering from **post-traumatic stress syndrome.** His other major projects in 1988 were his highly regarded segments for two ABC primetime specials on the drug crisis in America and his coverage of the America's Cup yacht race.

In 1989 Kashiwahara covered the major earthquake that rocked San Francisco during that year's World Series in the Bay Area. In 1991 he filed a special report on the fiftieth anniversary of the Japanese attack on Pearl Harbor. Kashiwahara won two major awards in 1993: the "Lifetime Achievement" award from the Asian American Journalists Association and special career honors from the Society of Professional Journalists. From 1994 through 1996 Kashiwahara's face became a familiar presence on World News Tonight during the prolonged ordeal of the O. J. Simpson murder trial and its aftermath.

After retiring, Ken Kashiwahara lived in San Francisco. ◆

1975 Kashiwahara reports on the removal of United States troops from Vietnam.

1978 Kashiwahara is named bureau chief for ABC News in San Francisco.

1986 Kashiwahara wins his first Emmy for a piece airing on ABC's newsmagazine program *20/20.*

1993 Kashiwahara wins a Lifetime Achievement award from the Asian American Journalists Association.

eastern bloc nations group of eastern European nations under Soviet rule during the Cold War such as East Germany, Poland, and Czechoslovakia.

post traumatic stress syndrome a condition common among veterans of war; recurring nightmares, images, and memories of the brutality and horror of combat.

Khorana, Har Gobind

1922– ● BIOCHEMIST

Har Gobind Khorana is an Indian-born American biochemist who made major contributions to the interpretation of the genetic code and its function in

Har Gobind Khorana

protein synthesis. In 1968, he shared the Nobel Prize in Physiology or Medicine with American biochemists Robert Holley and Marshall W. Nirenberg.

Har Gobind Khorana was born in 1922 of Hindu parents at Raipur, India, a little village in Punjab, which is now part of West Pakistan. He was the youngest in a family of one daughter and four sons. His father was a village agricultural taxation clerk in the British Indian system of government. Khorana's father was poor but committed to educating his children, thus the family was practically the only literate family in their village of 100 people. Khorana attended D.A.V. High School in Multan (now West Punjab). One of his teachers, Ratan Lal, influenced him greatly during that period.

Khorana studied at the Punjab University in Lahore, Pakistan, where he obtained a master of science degree. A great teacher and accurate experimentalist, Mahan Singh, was his supervisor.

Khorana lived in India until 1945, when the award of a Government of India Fellowship made it possible for him to go to England. There he studied for a doctorate at the University of Liverpool. Roger J. S. Beer supervised his research and helped Khorana in his new life, which was his introduction to Western civilization and culture.

Khorana spent a postdoctoral year (1948-1949) at the Eidgenössische Technische Hochschule in Zurich, Switzerland, with Professor Vladimir Prelog. This association with Prelog greatly shaped Khorana's philosophy towards science and his work.

After a brief period in India in the fall of 1949, Khorana returned to England, where he obtained a fellowship to work with Dr. G. W. Kenner and Professor A. R. Todd. Khorana remained in Cambridge as a research fellow from 1950 till 1952. Khorana's interest in both proteins and **nucleic acids** took hold during this time.

In 1952, Khorana moved to Vancouver, Canada, to work for the British Columbia Research Council in response to a job offer from Dr. Gordon M. Shrum. The Research Council offered little in the way of facilities, but they did offer "all the freedom in the world," in Shrum's words, to do research. With Shrum's inspiration and encouragement and frequent help and scientific counsel from Dr. Jack Campbell, a group formed to work in the field of phosphate esters and nucleic acids.

In 1960, Khorana began working at the Institute for Enzyme Research at the University of Wisconsin, Madison, and he became a naturalized United States citizen. It was in his affiliation with the University of Wisconsin that Khorana earned the Nobel Prize.

When Khorana, Holley, and Nirenberg won the Nobel prize in 1968, it topped off years of independent research that each man had done. Together, they had helped explain how certain units of genetic material within a cell control the synthesis of proteins. This information led to a better understanding of genetic coding.

Interest in genetic coding had begun 100 years earlier, when Swiss physician Friedrich Miescher isolated a new type of compound from cell nuclei. He called this compound nuclein. Later it became known as nucleic acid. Meanwhile, Czech monk Gregor Mendel finished a series of experiments with peas, showing that inheritance is packaged into genes.

Nucleic acids and genes came together in Holley's, Khorana's, and Nirenberg's investigations on the genetic code, sometimes called "the code of life." For a long time no connection between genes and nucleic acids could be seen. Nucleic acids are complicated molecules, but their structure shows

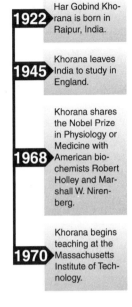

1922 Har Gobind Khorana is born in Raipur, India.

1945 Khorana leaves India to study in England.

1968 Khorana shares the Nobel Prize in Physiology or Medicine with American biochemists Robert Holley and Marshall W. Nirenberg.

1970 Khorana begins teaching at the Massachusetts Institute of Technology.

nucleic acids any of various acids composed of a sugar or derivative of a sugar.

certain regularities. They are constructed from a limited amount of smaller building blocks. Comparing a nucleic acid with a language, the building blocks can be said to be the letters of the alphabet. The language of nucleic acids in the cell describes inherited traits.

There also exists a second language in cells: the language of proteins, written in the alphabet of proteins. A single cell contains many thousands of proteins that perform all the chemical reactions required for the normal life of the organism. The synthesis of each protein is directed by a particular nucleic acid. A brown-eyed child, for example, receives nucleic acids from its parents. Those nucleic acids have the ability to direct the formation of proteins required for dark pigment of the eye. It is the chemical structure of the nucleic acid that determines the chemical structure of the protein. It can be said that the alphabet of nucleic acids dictates the alphabet of proteins. The genetic code is the dictionary that gives us the translation of one alphabet into the other.

Nirenberg synthesized a very simple nucleic acid, composed of a chain of only a single repeating letter. Using this nucleic acid, the system produced a protein that also contained a single letter, now written in the protein alphabet. In this way, Nirenberg had both deciphered the first **hieroglyph** and shown how the machinery of the cell can be used for the translation of the genetic code in general. After that, the field moved extremely rapidly. Nirenberg reported his first results in August 1961. Less than five years later, all the details of the genetic code were established, mainly from the work of Nirenberg and Khorana.

Khorana did much of the final work. Over many years, he had systematically devised methods that led to the synthesis of well-defined nucleic acids, giant molecules with every building block in its exact position. Khorana's synthetic nucleic acids were a prerequisite for the final solution of the genetic code.

Holley successfully attacked this question of what is the mechanism for the translation of the code within the cell. He was one of the discoverers of a special type of nucleic acid called transfer RNA. This nucleic acid has the capacity to read off the genetic code and to transform it to the protein alphabet. After many years' work, Holley succeeded in preparing a transfer RNA in pure form and, finally, in 1965, established its exact chemical structure. Holley's work represents the first determination of the complete chemical structure of a biologically active nucleic acid.

hieroglyph character in a system of writing depicted in pictures or codes.

The interpretation of the genetic code was the highlight of the revolution of molecular biology in the 1900s. This revolution led to an understanding of the details of the mechanism of inheritance. Through this work, researchers began to understand the causes of many diseases in which heredity plays an important role.

Khorana's key contribution was to investigate the part of the nucleic acids that produce proteins. As it is impossible to match up proteins with the nucleic acids that form them in a living cell, Khorana artificially synthesized small nucleic acids, similar to those in a living cell, and observed which proteins were formed by them.

Beginning in 1970, Khorana has been Alfred P. Sloan Professor of Biology and Chemistry at the Massachusetts Institute of Technology. Khorana married in 1952 to Esther Elizabeth Sibler, who is of Swiss origin. She brought a sense of stability to his life at a time when he had been away from his native country for six years. They had three children together: Julia Elizabeth, Emily Anne, and Dave Roy. ◆

Khosla, Vinod

1955– ● VENTURE CAPITALIST

Vinod Khosla has been called in *Fortune* magazine one of the most successful venture capitalists of all time. Venture capital is money available for investment in business enterprises, and a venture capitalist is someone who invests that money in such new businesses. Khosla has also been called one of the world's most astounding technological visionaries. Major business commentators credit him with revolutionizing electronic communications in the late 1990s.

Vinod Khosla was born in 1955 in India. His father, who had been orphaned at three weeks of age, became a conservative career military officer. Khosla began dreaming of starting companies based on new technologies when he was only 15 years old. He rejected his father's advice that he join the military, and instead he enrolled at the prestigious Indian Institute of Technology. He then came to the United States to study at Carnegie-Mellon University in Pittsburgh, Pennsylvania. He went on to earn a master's degree in business administration at

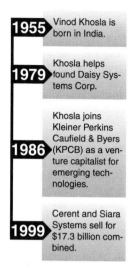

1955 Vinod Khosla is born in India.

1979 Khosla helps found Daisy Systems Corp.

1986 Khosla joins Kleiner Perkins Caufield & Byers (KPCB) as a venture capitalist for emerging technologies.

1999 Cerent and Siara Systems sell for $17.3 billion combined.

fiber optics a branch of physics based on the transfer of light through transparent fibers of glass or plastic.

routers powerful computers responsible for traffic on the Internet.

Stanford University in Palo Alto, California, in the heart of the high-tech Silicon Valley.

In 1979, Khosla helped found Daisy Systems Corp., a maker of computers and software for computer-assisted engineering. In the early 1980s, at the age of 27, Khosla cofounded Sun Microsystems Inc., whose workstations drove down prices and shook up the computing industry. In his early days at Sun Microsystems, Khosla participated in creating the first and most successful RISC-based platform. Of the two basic types of microprocessors, one is complex instruction set computer (CISC), and the other is reduced instruction set computer (RISC). Most personal computers use CISC chips, but many powerful workstations and some personal computers have RISC chips. A RISC chip uses instructions that are always the same length and can be executed in one clock cycle. By using its special circuits, a RISC chip can execute many times more instructions per second than can a comparable CISC chip. Sun became one of the ten largest computer manufacturers in the United States.

In 1986, Khosla joined up with Kleiner Perkins Caufield & Byers (KPCB) as a venture capitalist for emerging technologies. Working with KPCB, Khosla played a key role in starting companies involved in semiconductors, multimedia video games, Internet software, and computer networking. Khosla was among the first to understand that Internet technology and **fiber optics** could make communications so fast, cheap, and easy to install that it would unleash a tidal wave of productivity and growth. Fiber optics is a branch of physics based on the transmission of light through transparent fibers of glass or plastic. These optical fibers can carry light distances up to more than 100 miles. The fibers can be bundled into cables that can carry coded light signals, making it possible to send more messages faster than can be done with electricity or radio waves. Khosla studied the physics of fiber optics while lying on a beach in Hawaii and realized that investing in this technology "made a lot of sense."

In 1992, Khosla moved his family to India, working half time for Kleiner Perkins from India. But when the World Wide Web, the organized faction of the Internet, began to grow quickly, Khosla moved back to the United States in 1995 to rejoin Kleiner Perkins.

One of Khosla's most successful ventures was Juniper Networks. This winning venture began with Juniper's founder, Pradeep Sindhu, approaching Khosla in 1996 to sell him on some interesting ideas for new Internet **routers**. Routers are the powerful computers that are responsible for the flow of Internet traffic. Khosla gave Sindhu, an engineer, a few hundred thousand dollars to work with, and then he gave him $4 million more, taking on 23% of Juniper for KPCB. Kleiner soon held shares in Juniper worth more than $8 billion, and Juniper eventually became worth $62 billion.

Speaking with *Fortune* magazine in October 2000, Khosla said he was not interesting in talking about the money. "I'm more interested in helping entrepreneurs build great companies than in rates of return," he said.

It was Khosla's recognition of the importance of the communications infrastructure early on that allowed him to lay the cornerstones upon which many companies were built. He lent his support, both financial and intellectual to some of the industry's biggest success stories. Khosla was capable of combining ingenious business sense with remarkable technological insight. He wisely placed his money on a handful of companies, and his savvy paid off well. Two of his projects, for example, equipment makers Cerent and Siara Systems, sold in 1999 for $17.3 billion combined. Khosla conceived Cerent in late 1996, recruiting its first engineers and serving as its chief executive and chairman for a time. Siara Systems produced high-speed metropolitan-area and broadband fiber optic network equipment.

Khosla credited the people he worked with for his ability to stay abreast of the constant changes in the computer industry. "I have the smartest people in the world educating me every day," Khosla told the *Wall Street Journal* in 1999. "The only thing I really do is filter and modify to arrive at my own opinions." His coworkers found it challenging, though, to keep up with the steady stream of suggestions coming from Khosla.

Khosla served on the boards of Asera, Cerent Corp., Concentric Network Corp., Corio, Corvis Corp., Excite@Home, Juniper Networks, Quest Communications, U.S. West, and Siara. ◆

Kim, Jay

MARCH 27, 1939– ● POLITICIAN

Until 1997, Jay Kim led a charmed life—first as a successful businessman, and later as the first Korean-American elected to the U.S. Congress. But that fateful year Kim was convicted of violations of campaign finance laws and ended up in prison. Despite an attempt to regain his seat in 1998, he was defeated in the Republican primary that year and again in a second comeback attempt in 2000.

Jay Kim was born in Seoul, Korea, on March 27, 1939. After serving two years in the South Korean army, Kim emigrated to the United States and settled in California. Kim attended the University of Southern California, where he obtained a bachelor's degree in civil engineering in 1967. After working as a civil engineer for the ensuing decade, Kim earned his master's in the field in 1979. Soon thereafter, he founded JAYKIM Engineers. Within several years the company was rated as one of the top 500 design firms in the country.

While building his business, Kim began to take an interest in local politics, gaining election in 1990 to the city council of Diamond Bar, California, east of Los Angeles. After a year on the council, Kim won the mayoralty of Diamond Bar, serving a year in that post before deciding to run for the U.S. House seat from the 41st congressional district. Kim coasted to an easy victory in the Republican primary and went on to squeak by in a razor-thin general election. When he was sworn into office in January 1992, Kim became the first Korean-American to be elected to the United States Congress.

Kim proved a capable and popular member of Congress, winning easy re-election in 1994 and 1996. He served as chairman of the Public Buildings and Economic Development Subcommittee and was a member of the House International Relations Committee. In 1993 he was named one of the recipients of the 1993 Ellis Island Medal of Honor Award, given in recognition of those immigrants who have made an outstanding contribution to the United States.

Kim's rapid political ascent stalled abruptly in 1997, when the congressman was charged with several counts of accepting illegal campaign contributions totaling $230,000 dating back to his first campaign for Congress. On March 10, 1998, Kim was sentenced to two months of home confinement, a year of probation, mandatory community service, and a $5,000 fine after pleading guilty to misdemeanor counts of accepting illegal campaign contributions. Kim's wife was sentenced to one year of probation and a $5,000 fine. The judge also levied a $170,000 fine against Kim's campaign committee.

"Persona non grata" in his own party, Kim defied party leaders by declaring his intention to run for re-election de-

persona non grata
Spanish phrase characterizing the least desireable person in a group.

spite a growing House probe into his fundraising malfeasances. The unkindest cut of all came in May 1998, when his recently estranged wife announced her opposition to his re-election bid and called on him to resign from office. She further announced her intention to cooperate with House ethics investigators.

During the spring of 1998, Kim found himself in the awkward circumstance of a two-month confinement to the halls of Congress and his apartment in Fairfax, Virginia, wearing an electronic ankle bracelet under his trousers to allow federal probation officers to monitor his whereabouts. Kim became the third House member in the previous 200 years to remain in office while serving a prison term, but he was the first to so serve since the creation of the House ethics committee in 1968.

The gravity of Kim's offense was put into perspective by the U.S. attorney's office in Los Angeles, which asserted that Kim's illegal campaign cash flow was the largest in the history of the House of Representatives. More than a third of the funds raised during his initial 1992 race—which he won by only 889 votes—proved to be illegal. In 1998 Gary Ruskin, the director of the Congressional Accountability Project, told a reporter, "Jay Kim probably stole a congressional election in 1992 by this fraudulent campaign financing scheme. If the House is serious about the meaning of elections and democracy, they'll expel him, and soon. In my view, Jay Kim's presence cheapens the moral authority of every other member here."

That withering verdict was echoed by Kim's estranged wife, June, who told the same reporter, "He is a congressman. He should be clean. He should be a role model. In fact, he is the most crime-committing person I know."

The House was spared any disciplinary action by the voters in Kim's district, who turned back his re-election bid in the June 2, 1998, primary, which Kim lost by a wide margin. At the end of his term in 1998, Kim lectured at several universities in Korea. Kim, ever the resilient campaigner, hatched a plan to revive his congressional career in 2000 by seeking the seat in the county next to his old district. He told an interviewer that he planed to "ask for forgiveness and explain everything," claiming that in 1992 "I was a little arrogant and naïve." But the 42nd District wanted no more of Kim than the 41st did, and Kim lost the June 2000 Republican primary. His political career appeared to be at an end. ◆

> *"I've been treated like I've commited the crime of the century. The American people are very forgiving. They forgave Clinton."*
> Jay Kim, interview in *AsianWeek*, December 19, 1999

Kingman, Dong

1911– ● ARTIST

Dong Kingman, named Moy-Sui Dong at birth, was born in 1911 in Oakland, California, where his Chinese parents had settled after migrating to the United States in 1900. Kingman was the second of eight children.

Kingman moved to China in 1916 with his family when his father feared the United States might become involved in the war in Europe. During the 35-day voyage to Hong Kong, the five-year-old budding artist made sketches of fellow travelers to break the monotony of life aboard ship. In Hong Kong, where his mother painted for pleasure, Dong attracted customers outside his father's dry goods store by drawing chalk pictures on the sidewalk.

At age 10, Kingman began attending painting classes at a school in Hong Kong. He studied under Chinese artist Szetu Wei in Lingnan, China, from 1926 to 1929. The young artist earned the name of King-man, meaning scenic composition, from his teacher.

Kingman later said: "The first and only art teacher who had a true influence on me was Szetu Wei, a devout Christian and the kindest, most friendly person you would ever wish to meet. Szetu had studied art in Paris in the early twenties and returned to become headmaster and art teacher of the Lingnan Branch School in Hong Kong. In 1926, I went to Lingnan not only to study Chinese and English, but specifically to study art under Szetu. When he found out how anxious I was to study art, he took me under his wing and became my personal tutor. He took me sketching outdoors during the summer holidays. He taught me how to simplify details as well as many basic theories of composition, brush techniques, rhythm, the use of color, etc."

In 1929, at age eighteen, Kingman returned to the United States. He supported himself by working as a dishwasher, waiter, and houseboy. By 1931, he had saved enough money to buy part ownership of a restaurant for $75, allowing him a little time to paint in the afternoons and to study at a Chinatown art school for four years, from 1931 to 1935. When the headmaster saw some of Kingman's landscape paintings in oil, he told him, "You will never make it as a painter. You might as well quit painting and go back to your chop-suey house." Kingman was disappointed, but he did not quit. Instead, he switched from oils to watercolors, a medium that became his specialty thereafter.

Kingman had his first one-man exhibit in 1935. His work was hailed by the critics for its skillfulness and vision. At about this time, he also received a First Purchase prize from the San Francisco Art Association Annual Exhibition. Still, he was not able to earn a living from his art until he was assigned to the Watercolor Division of the Works Progress Administration (WPA), a Depression-era New Deal program. This allowed him to have a studio of his own, concentrate on improving his technique, and develop his own style.

During this time, Kingman's paintings were added to the permanent collections of several important museums, and when the WPA project came to an end with American involvement in World War II, the artist won a Guggenheim Fellowship. This was followed by a successful exhibition in New York that received critical acclaim in prominent news and art magazines. In 1940, the Metropolitan Museum of Art purchased the first of several of Kingman's works. Kingman said, "I felt I had found my place at long last."

After the war, Kingman moved to New York, set up a studio, and started teaching watercolor classes at Columbia University and Hunter College.

Kingman ultimately became known as one of the world's greatest watercolorists. He became famous for his storytelling watercolors depicting scenes from around the world. His energetic style, vibrant use of color, and warm sense of humor earned him the respect and admiration of the art community and the public. In such watercolors as *New Dawn*, Kingman reveals a gentle landscape with Chinese peasant farmers planting rice in a field alongside cattle reclining among pretty wildflowers—all taking place beneath festive flying kites.

Kingman's work embodied a distinct Asian-American look, with a great mixing of East and West in his art. His watercolors show a great deal of influence from his schooling in China that he applied to his cityscapes, magazine covers, and other works done in America. This artwork gained him national prestige and recognition. Kingman was also unique in being a Chinese-American who gained national recognition in a time where Asian-Americans were rarely prominent.

1911 Kingman is born in Oakland, California.

1916 Kingman moves back to China with his family.

1929 Kingman returns to the United States to seek his fortune.

1935 Kingman has his first one-man exhibit.

1981 The Ministry of Culture of the People's Republic of China invites Kingman to exhibit in China.

Kingman also distinguished himself in filmmaking producing, directing, and animating the award-winning film, *Hong Kong Dong*. His watercolors were also used in the films *Flower Drum Song* and *55 Days at Peking*.

Kingman's talents were so impressive that he was invited to hold exhibitions in numerous foreign countries, including one in China, which became one of Kingman's most important experiences. The Ministry of Culture of the People's Republic of China invited Kingman to exhibit in that country in 1981, and he became the first American artist to be accorded a one-man show since diplomatic relations between the U.S. and China resumed. Over 5,000 people filled Beijing's China Art Gallery for the opening, and over 100,000 viewers attended his exhibitions in Beijing, Hangshou, and Guangzhou.

Kingman received an extraordinary number of awards and honors throughout his long career, including two Guggenheim Fellowships and virtually every significant watercolor prize in the United States. He received the American Watercolor Society's highest award, the Dolphin Medal Award, an award that has only been given out three times in the society's 120-year history. He also earned the Oakland Art Gallery Award, 1944; Philadelphia Watercolor Club Award, 1968; National Academy of Design Award, 1977; and the San Diego Watercolor Society Prize, 1984.

By the late 1980s, Kingman's work had been acquired by over 50 museums, as well as a prominent list of private collections. His work is represented in the permanent collections of such major museums as the Metropolitan Museum of Art, the Museum of Modern Art, and the Whitney Museum in New York City; Art Institute of Chicago; Boston Museum of Art; Boston Hirshhorn Museum; Los Angeles County Fair Association; San Francisco Museum of Art; San Francisco Whitney Museum of Art; and dozens of other noted museums, public buildings, and private collections.

The artwork of Kingman can also be seen on such online websites as those of the Fine Arts Museums of San Francisco, Fred Jones Jr. Museum of Art at the University of Oklahoma, and the Sheldon Memorial Art Gallery at the University of Nebraska.

Kingman continued to paint in his home city of New York. ◆

Kingston, Maxine Hong

OCTOBER 27, 1940– ● AUTHOR

axine Hong was born October 27, 1940, in Stockton, California, of Tom and Ying Lan Hong (whose maiden name was Chew). The couple had married in China before Tom migrated to New York City. For 15 years, he worked in a laundry and sent money back to his wife, allowing her to study medicine and **midwifery.** Her ability to earn an income was an exception in the impoverished China where families often treated girls as a hindrance. Finally, Tom was able to send for Ying Lan. She came to the United States and the couple settled in California. Their first two children had died in China, but at the age of 45, Ying Lan gave birth to Maxine. They named her after a lucky blonde American woman who gambled at the gambling house where Tom worked. Ying Lan and Tom had five more children after Maxine.

midwifery the art of assisting in childbirth.

Hong's parents held a variety of jobs to support the family. Tom managed a gambling house, worked in a laundry, and was also a scholar. Ying Lan practiced medicine and midwifery. She also worked as a field hand and in a laundry. Maxine grew up surrounded by the ghostly presence of ancestors she would never know. The Americans around her who were aliens to her parents also seemed ghostly to her. This mix of worlds would surface in Kingston's writing.

Maxine Hong Kingston

In 1962, Hong married an actor named Earll Kingston. The couple later had one son, Joseph Lawrence Chung Mei. The same year as her marriage, Kingston graduated from the University of California, Berkeley. She also earned a teaching certificate from there in 1965.

Kingston taught in California before moving on to teaching high school in Hawaii. After holding several teaching positions there, she moved up to become an associate

1940 Kingston is born in Stockton, California.

1962 Kingston graduates from the University of California Berkeley.

1976 Kingston's book *The Woman Warrior* is published.

1979 *The Woman Warrior* is named one of the ten best nonfiction works of the decade by *TIME* magazine.

1988 Kingston publishes *Tripmaster Monkey: His Fake Book*, her first pure novel.

alma mater a school, college, or university which one has attended or graduated.

professor at the University of Hawaii, Honolulu. In 1990, Kingston returned to her **alma mater,** becoming a professor at the University of California, Berkeley.

Through her years as a teacher, Kingston also worked as a writer. In 1976, she published *The Woman Warrior: Memoirs of a Girlhood Among Ghosts* and then *China Men* in 1980. Both of these books tapped into Kingston's childhood experience of listening to the Chinese-American "story-talkers" of Stockton as well as members of her family. These people told historical and mythical tales. Kingston's stories are a kind of magical realism. In magic realism, writers experiment with language and structure, often injecting fantasy and fragmenting time and space. These writers blend dreams and magic with everyday reality. Kingston wrote the two books more or less simultaneously.

The *Woman Warrior* is a memoir of Kingston's childhood and dealt with the lives of the women in her family. *Washington Post* critic Henry Allen called it "a wild mix of myth, memory, history and a lucidity which verges on the eerie." Kingston describes the experiences of the women of her youth as they came to the United States from their native China.

China Men addressed similar issues among the Chinese-American men of Kingston's youth. The figure of Kingston's father dominates the book, as that of her mother in *Woman Warrior*. *China Men* also includes fictionalized histories of several members of Kingston's family and of the community she grew up in. The men in her book are shown slaving to earn meager wages building sugar plantations and railroads. They smuggle themselves into the United States in shipping crates and take on American names, such as Edison or Roosevelt.

Hong's *Hawai'i One Summer* (1987) is a collection of 11 essays originally issued as a limited hand-printed edition. Kingston describes Hawaii with high praise in topics ranging from surfing to house chores. The essays create a memoir of Kingston's years in Hawaii, where she underwent various incarnations, from war protester to virtual street person to respectable teacher.

Tripmaster Monkey: His Fake Book (1988) became Kingston's first pure novel. Through a young Chinese-American man, Wittman, in the 1960s in San Francisco, Kingston again takes on the issue of Asian-American life. Even though he is a fifth-generation American, the hero cannot earn full acceptance from white Americans. He identifies with the great poets of his generation, such as Allen Ginsberg. He is also an incarnation of the mythic Monkey King, the trickster character of Chinese legend who helped bring Buddha's teaching to China. Wittman is the one to bring China to America, which he plans to do with a theatrical production.

Through the Black Curtain, published in 1988, contained excerpts from *The Woman Warrior*, *China Men*, and *Tripmaster Monkey*.

Conversations with Maxine Hong Kingston, edited by Paul Skenazy and Tera Martin, was published in 1988. In this collection of interviews, Kingston talks about her life and her writing. In these conversations, Kingston discusses how her work wove in and out of fiction and nonfiction, memoir and imagination. She explains how she combined her parents' Chinese dialect with American slang, how she learned to explore her inheritance and find new relevance in her mother's "talk-stories," and how she developed the complex pairings of myth and memoir that fill her books.

Kingston earned numerous awards for her works, including the National Book Critics Circle general nonfiction award in 1976 for *The Woman Warrior*. *Time* magazine named *The Woman Warrior* one of the top ten nonfiction works of the decade in 1979. She earned the National Endowment for the Arts Writers Award in 1980 and 1982. She received the American Book Award for general nonfiction in 1981 for *China Men*. ◆

Kusama, Karyn

1968– ● FILM DIRECTOR

Karyn Kusama, a film director, became known for the great success of her debut film, the independently made *Girlfight*, a movie about female boxing that was released in 2000. Kusama was 32 years old.

Kusama struggled for several years to get her boxing picture made. She said that the source of her inspiration for the movie was observing young girls on the subways who looked terribly unhappy with the world. But the film project had difficulty getting off the ground due to a lack of financial backing and a lack

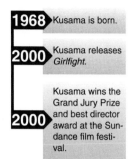

1968 ▶ Kusama is born.

2000 ▶ Kusama releases *Girlfight.*

2000 ▶ Kusama wins the Grand Jury Prize and best director award at the Sundance film festival.

of interest in the storyline. Kusama was inundated with suggestions to make the film about dancing or to cast a well-known beauty in the main role. Kusama refused to compromise and cast an untrained actress (Michelle Rodriquez) who had never boxed before and received some financing from filmmaker John Sayles. Sayles was executive producer of the movie and his wife, Maggie Renzi, co-produced it. The Independent Film Channel put in the rest of the film's $1 million budget. Kusama set out to make her film without starlets and frills.

Rodriguez indeed did train for her role as a boxer—and told reviewers that she really enjoyed it. In the story, Rodriguez played Diana Guzman, a troubled Hispanic teen from a bleak Brooklyn housing project who solves some of her problems by training to become a boxer.

Kusama acknowledged that *Girlfight* is a "sports movie," yet she saw it as much an exploration of gender, love, and power as a story of an athlete's evolution. *Girlfight* is a rite of passage story about a young woman finding discipline, self-respect, and love in an unexpected place—the boxing ring.

In Park City, Utah, on January 29, 2000, judges announced the winners of the Independent Feature Film Competition at the annual Sundance Film Festival. The Dramatic Grand Jury Prize was split between *Girlfight*, directed by Kusama and produced by Sarah Green, Martha Griffin and Maggie Renzi and *You Can Count on Me*, directed by Kenneth Lonergan and produced by John Hart, Jeff Sharp, Larry Meistrich and Barbara De Fina.

In addition to the Grand Jury Prize, Kusama also won the festival's Director's Award for *Girlfight*. After taking home the Grand Jury Prize at Sundance and being named best director, Kusama won the Young Cinema Award a few months later at the Cannes International Film Festival in France. ◆

Kwan, Michelle

JULY 7, 1980– ● FIGURE SKATER

Aworld-class figure skater since the age of 15, the Olympic silver-medal-winner Michelle Kwan has won legions of fans not only for her dazzling skills on the ice but also for her modest, spirited, and engaging personality. Never subject to the rumors of excessive or abusive training techniques that have dogged some of her peers, Kwan remains, in the words of former champion Peggy Fleming, "a wonderful example for our athletes today."

Michelle Wing Kwan was born on July 7, 1980, in Rancho Palos Verdes, California. As young children she and her sister were so thrilled by the speed and dynamism of their brothers on the ice hockey rink that they were inspired to learn how to skate. Donning her first pair of skates at the age of five, Michelle showed such promise that her father took on two jobs to help pay for her lessons, to which he drove her every weekend at the training center in Lake Arrowhead, California, a two-hour drive from their Torrance, California, home. Glued to the tele-

Michelle Kwan

vision as Brian Boitano went through his paces at the 1988 Calgary Olympics, Michelle vowed, at the age of seven, to occupy that spotlight herself one day.

Kwan's skating talent was so prodigious that she was skating in senior competitions by the age of twelve, when Frank Carroll coached her to a first place finish in the Gardena Spring Trophy in Italy and the U.S. Olympic Festival in San Antonio, Texas. In 1993 Kwan came in sixth at the U.S. Nationals, where she was the youngest senior entrant in two decades. Later in the year, she won the U.S. Olympic Festival in San Antonio. The following year she was runner-up at the U.S. Nationals, a result skewed by the assault on Nancy Kerrigan that benefited the winner, Tonya Harding, who was later implicated in the attack. Although her outstanding performance obscured by the media frenzy surrounding Kerrigan and Harding, she was named as an alternate to the 1994 U.S. Olympic team.

Kwan's next major goal was a slot on the 1998 Olympic team. After finishing second at at the 1995 U.S. Nationals and a fourth at the World Championships, followed by first place finishes at Skate America, Skate, Canada, the Nations Cup, and the U.S. Postal Service Challenge. In 1996 she won both

1980 Kwan is born in Rancho Palos Verdes, California.

1993 Kwan wins the figure skating competition at the U.S. Olympic Festival.

1994 Kwan comes in second at the U.S. National Championships.

1996 Kwan wins the World and U.S. figure skating championships.

1998 Kwan wins a silver medal at the Olympic Games in Nagano, Japan, and the World Championship.

2000 Kwan wins the World Figure Skating championship.

2001 Kwan repeats as world champion.

ethereal unworldy; spiritual.

the World Championships and U.S. Championships. Kwan's berth on the 1998 Olympic team now seemed secure.

However, in 1997, Kwan suffered unexpected reverses. At the U.S. Nationals Kwan fell several times during her long program and lost the gold medal to 14-year-old Tara Lipinski. Kwan then placed fourth in the short program at the 1997 World Championships. Marshalling her inner strength over the following two days, Kwan rebounded to win the gold medal for the long program and the silver medal for the overall competition.

With restored confidence Kwan enjoyed a superb year in 1998, easily besting Lipinski at Skate America and earning another gold medal at the U.S. Nationals in Philadelphia, where her magnificent performance elicited these words of praise from the skating coach Linda Leaver: "She has a unique style. It's **ethereal** and feminine. She seems to float over the ice. She hovers and skims, so you aren't aware of her over digging into the ice to get the height that she does on her jumps . . . She made the difficult look easy."

Kwan entered the 1998 Nagano Olympics as the heavy favorite for the gold medal, but Lipinski prevailed and Kwan went home with the silver. In 1999 she won gold medals in the Japan Open, the U.S. Nationals, Skate America, Skate Canada, and the 1998 World Championship. Although she finished second in the 1999 World Championships, many analysts consider her the top contender for the gold medal at the 2002 Winter Olympics in Salt Lake City, Utah. Kwan bolstered her hopes for gold by winning the World Championship in 2000 and 2001.

When not executing back-to-back triple jumps before worldwide television audiences, Kwan enjoyed relaxing at home with her collection of exotic dolls, which she said bring her good luck. She also enjoyed playing with her three pets: a cat and two cockatiels. Kwan also served as national spokesperson for the Children's Miracle Network. ◆

Lahiri, Jhumpa

1967– ● Author

Jhumpa Lahiri was born in 1967 in London, England, and grew up in Rhode Island. Both of her parents were born and raised in India, and Lahiri traveled there several times. Her father was a librarian and her mother was a teacher. As a child, Lahiri wrote extensive "novels" in notebooks, sometimes with her friends. She wrote for her school newspaper, but had stopped writing fiction by the time she went to college.

Lahiri graduated with a bachelor of arts degree in English literature from Barnard College in New York City. She applied to various graduate English programs but was rejected by all of them. In the meantime, Lahiri took a job as a research assistant at a non-profit institution in Cambridge, Massachusetts. She later said, "For the first time I had a computer of my own at my desk, and I started writing fiction again, more seriously. I used to stay late and come in to work on stories. Eventually I had enough material to apply to the creative writing program at Boston University."

Lahiri entered Boston University, where she received a master of arts in English. Unsure of what to do next, Lahiri went on to earn a master of arts in Creative Writing, a master of arts in Comparative Literature and the Arts, and a doctorate in Renaissance Studies.

The New Yorker published three of Lahiri's short stories in 1998, something of a record. These stories, as well as six others, came together in Lahiri's debut book, *The Interpreter of Maladies: Stories from Boston, Bengal and Beyond*, released in early

Pulitzer Prize for Fiction

When London-born Jhumpa Lahiri won the Pulitzer Prize for Fiction in 2000, she became the first person of Southeast Asian descent to receive this prestigious literary award. Equally extraordinary was that the 33-year-old author won for her very first published collection of short stories, *Interpreter of Maladies*. Although the author disavows any special authority on the subject of India, or of South Asia in general, many of her stories deal with the experience of Indian immigrants in the United States.

The Pulitzer Prizes are awarded annually to American writers, journalists, photographers, and composers who are judged to have published extraordinary work in the previous year. The tradition of the Pulitzer Prize began in 1904, when newspaper magnate John Pulitzer decided to set aside funds to be used to encourage excellence in all aspects of publishing, but particularly in journalism. He established a board that would select each year's prize recipients from a list of recommendations drawn from professionals in the various publishing disciplines: photography, journalism, fiction and non-fiction writing, and composition.

Nominees for the fiction prize are put forward by a jury of writers and editors, and the winner receives a modest monetary award. More important than the cash prize, however, is the professional recognition that the Pulitzer brings. Prize-winning authors like Lahiri find that their subsequent manuscripts are more likely to be accepted by prestigious publishing houses. More prosaically, they often find their books receiving far more critical attention, which translates into greater public awareness of their work, and thus greater sales not only of the prize-winning book but also of other works they may have published in the past.

1999. The stories in the collection were "A Temporary Matter," "When Mr. Pirzada Came to Dine," "Interpreter of Maladies," "A Real Durwan," "Sexy," "Mrs. Sen's," "This Blessed House," "The Treatment of Bibi Haldar," and "The Third and Final Continent."

The book brought Lahiri a number of accolades. Its title story was selected for both the O. Henry Award and *The Best American Short Stories*. In 1999, *The New Yorker* named Lahiri as one of the 20 best American fiction writers under the age of 40. On April 10, 2000, she was awarded the Pulitzer Prize for Fiction, the first person of South Asian origin to win an individual Pulitzer. In May 2000, "The Third and Final Continent," became one of three stories to win a National Magazine Award for Fiction for *The New Yorker*. Lahiri received a Transatlantic Review Award from Henfield Foundation and fiction prize from the Louisville Review. Lahiri's book went into a fourth printing, crossing the ocean to become a popular book in India.

Lahiri's stories drew richly from her visits to Calcutta, where her parents are from and where Lahiri visited frequently for extended periods of time. There she formed relationships with Indians, including her relatives. She developed strong ties over time, though it remained only a second home to her American home. Lahiri recalls that her parents never specifically sat her down and told her things about India, but it was always important to them to maintain strong social ties with Indians living abroad and visiting India. "The older I get," Lahiri said, "the more aware I am that I have somehow inherited a sense of exile from my parents, even though in many ways—superficial ones, largely—I am so much more American than they are."

But as Lahiri gained confidence, she began to set stories in the United States, and wrote about situations closer to her own experiences. In her stories set in America, Lahiri writes about Indian immigrants as well as their children. Her characters are culturally displaced immigrants who have grown up in two worlds simultaneously.

The first story in Lahiri's collection, "A Temporary Matter," narrates the story of a young Indian-American couple facing the heartbreak of the stillborn birth of their first baby. The story unravels complex emotions as the repairs on a faulty cable line in Boston lead to five days of hour-long powercuts. Shobha and Shukumar, immigrants from Bengal, cope with their disintegrating marriage, exchanging secrets that have driven them apart since the loss of their baby. "A Temporary Matter" was scheduled to be made into a film by one of India's top filmmakers, Mira Nair.

Marriage plays a role in many of Lahiri's stories. She touches on arranged and rushed marriages as well as marital betrayals and failing marriages. A woman in "Sexy," is involved in a hopeless affair with a married man. Mr. Kapasi has a regular job as an interpreter for a doctor who does not speak his patients' language, and Kapasi drives tourists to local sites of interest. His passengers in the story are Mr. and Mrs. Das—first-generation Americans of Indian descent—and their children. During the afternoon, Kapasi becomes enamored of Mrs. Das. She confides in Kapasi when she reads too much into his profession. "I told you because of your talents," she tells him after sharing a shocking secret.

1967 Jhumpa Lahiri is born in London, England.

1998 *The New Yorker* publishes three of Lahiri's short stories.

2000 Lahiri wins the Pulitzer Prize for Fiction, becoming the first person of South Asian origin to win an individual Pulitzer.

"I'm tired of feeling so terrible all the time," she says. "Eight years, Mr. Kapasi, I've been in pain eight years. I was hoping you could help me feel better; say the right thing. Suggest some kind of remedy." Kapasi has no cure for what ails Das—or himself.

Critics praised Lahiri's stories as moving and authoritative pictures of culture shock and displaced identity. As the narrator of the last story, "The Third and Final Continent," comments, "There are times I am bewildered by each mile I have traveled, each meal I have eaten, each person I have known, each room in which I have slept." Lahiri has captured a universal experience, applying to so many in today's mobile world. Many readers can relate to having grown up, left home, fallen in or out of love, and experienced being a foreigner.

Lahiri lived in New York City. ◆

Lau, Fred H.

JULY 26, 1949– ● POLICE CHIEF

> "I love gadgets. I love toys. Just about every single time a new kind of phone came out with a new technology, I'd ask to take a look at it."
>
> Fred H. Lau, speaking to *San Francisco Chronicle* staff writer Christian Berthelsen, November 26, 2000

On January 26, 1996, Fred H. Lau was sworn in as the 35th chief of police of San Francisco, California. Lau, a San Francisco native, was among the highest-ranking law enforcement officials of Asian-American descent at the time of his ascension to the head of the San Francisco Police Department. Born July 26, 1949, Lau spent his childhood in San Francisco and enrolled at San Francisco State University in 1969. During his first year there, Lau became involved with various student protest demonstrations and strikes that characterized the landscape of college campuses all over the nation, and especially in the San Francisco Bay area. During this time, students engaged in sit-ins, marches, and other forms of protest to signal their opposition to American involvement in the Vietnam War, and a general dissatisfaction with school administration and authority. Police were sometimes called in to disperse protests and marches, and Lau later joked that during his time on campus, he was most likely "chased around by some of the people who (now) work for me."

As Lau ironically pointed out, he withdrew from San Francisco State to join the San Francisco police force in 1971. He worked his way through the ranks and was named chief of po-

Fred Lau (center) is sworn in as San Francisco police chief in 1996.

lice in 1996 at the age of 46. Lau headed a force of over 2,000 officers, presided over ten district police stations and precincts, and security for the San Francisco International Airport; Lau oversees these duties and activities with a budget of over $230 million.

Lau's leadership and vision as the chief of police concentrated on developing a more cooperative relationship between the police department and the citizens they protected. Lau and other leaders within the department established a group called Citizens' Academy, which aimed to introduce members of the community to the different methods and reasons behind various police actions and policies. Another program, Citizens on Patrol, encourages neighborhoods and police officers to work in tandem to develop agendas and ideas for better policing and communication between the police department and citizens. As chief during the late 1990s and early part of the 2000s, Lau worked to incorporate new technology to help improve efficiency in the work his police force did, as well as the ability to respond quickly to various situations. Lau has also instituted

1949 Fred H. Lau is born on July 26.

1996 Lau is sworn in as San Francisco's 35th Chief of Police.

1997 Lau completes his college degree.

various mentoring programs in which police officers work individually with college students interested in pursuing law enforcement as a career, as Lau once was.

Lau also returned to San Francisco State to complete the degree program he had abandoned to join the police force. Lau completed work on a bachelor's degree in 1997, the same year in which he was formally inducted into the San Francisco State University Alumni Hall of Fame. Lau joined luminaries such as Mayor Willie Brown, actress Annette Benning, journalist Pierre Salinger, and many others also in San Francisco State's hall of fame. ◆

Lee, Ang

OCTOBER 23, 1954– ● FILM DIRECTOR

Ang Lee was born in October 23, 1954, in Pingtung, Taiwan. Lee's father was the principal of his high school and had high expectations for Lee, but Lee failed the entrance exams for college in Taiwan. Instead he enrolled at the Taiwan Academy of Art, where he became interested in acting. He then served two years in the Taiwanese military inspecting fishing boats.

In 1978, at the age of 23, Lee enrolled at the University of Illinois at Urbana-Champaign. His limited English kept him out of many speaking roles, but he still pursued acting. Lee also pursued film. Having access to American cinema, he discovered that the versions of American films he had seen in Taiwan were quite different from the originals, because they had been edited by Taiwanese censors. After receiving his bachelor of fine arts degree in theater, Lee went on to the graduate film program at New York University (NYU) and was a classmate of the famous director Spike Lee.

When Lee's parents decided to visit him in the United States in 1983, Lee phoned his girlfriend, Jane Lin, who was still at the University of Illinois working on her doctorate in microbiology. He proposed marriage to Jane, setting the date for the following week. Lee thought getting married would be a special event for his family. Unfortunately, the city hall wedding disappointed Lee's family, but Lee used his wedding as source material for his later movie *The Wedding Banquet*.

While at NYU, Lee created *Fine Line* as his thesis film. The story was about an Italian trying to escape the Mafia and a Chinese person trying to escape the Immigration and Naturalization Service. An actor in the movie recalled later that Lee did not speak much English and would say things like "Less," "More," or "Stand here." Nevertheless, the film was voted best student film in 1984, the year Lee graduated.

After graduating, Lee signed with an agent from the William Morris Agency. He had planned to go back to Taiwan, but his wife had a baby and the couple stayed in New York. Lee spent the next six years working on two screenplays, suffering what is referred to in Hollywood as "development hell," continually pitching ideas to studio executives. Lee did not fit the Hollywood system, behaving quietly instead of being aggressive. The six years of professional inactivity were depressing for Lee. His wife tried to help him stay focused, but Lee spent many hours watching television. Lee also became obsessed with cooking, a later theme of his movies.

In 1990, Lee submitted two scripts to an annual screenplay contest held by the Taiwanese government. His scripts placed first and second in the competition, and a Taiwanese production company gave him $480,000 to help make his first film. He signed up with a young production company that specialized in producing low budget films.

In 1992, Lee completed his first feature-length production. *Pushing Hands*, shot in Yonkers, New York, tells the story of an old **tai chi** master who must adjust to living in America with his son, who is married to a white woman. The father speaks no English and stays home all day with his daughter-in-law, who is a novelist. Within the house, the two wage a cold war that leaves the son/husband caught in the middle. *Pushing Hands* was not released in theaters in the United States until 1994, but it was very successful in Taiwan.

Lee's next project had a budget of $750,000. Lee based the script for *The Wedding Banquet* (1993) on the experiences of a young, gay, Taiwanese-American friend of his. In the film, the character marries a Chinese woman to satisfy his parents and to help the woman obtain American citizenship. The plot becomes comic when the groom's delighted parents decide

1954 Lee is born in Pingtung, Taiwan.

1992 Lee completes his first feature-length production, *Pushing Hands*.

1994 Lee's third film, *Eat Drink Man Woman*, is released.

2001 Lee accepts an Academy Award for best Foreign Language Film for *Crouching Tiger, Hidden Dragon*.

tai chi an ancient Chinese form of meditative movements practiced as exercises.

to come to New York from Taiwan for the wedding and the banquet.

The film won the Golden Bear Award, the top prize at the Berlin Film Festival, and it became the most successful film to date in Taiwan. In the United States, it earned nearly unanimous approval. The film was nominated for an Academy Award and a Golden Globe for best foreign-language film, because much of its dialogue is in Chinese. It earned worldwide appreciation, and the gross receipts for the film exceeded its $750,000 cost 30 times over, making it proportionally the most profitable film of 1993.

Lee's third film was *Eat Drink Man Woman* (1994). Set in Taipei, it focused on Taiwanese and Chinese cuisine and addressed intergenerational concerns within Asian culture. The film earned Lee a second consecutive Academy Award nomination for best foreign-language film. With its extensive dramatization of the delights of Chinese cooking, *Eat Drink Man Woman* was a culinary treat. Platter after platter of luscious food is uncovered in the film, with great puffs of steam. For authenticity, Lee employed three full-time chefs on his set to prepare the dishes, most of which are delicacies that cannot be found in even the best of restaurants. Over 100 different dishes appear in the film, and the preparation of many is shown in detail.

On a whim, producer Lindsay Doran sent Lee the screenplay for *Sense and Sensibility* (1995), which was based on the Jane Austen novel and had taken actress Emma Thompson five years to write. Lee accepted the project.

Lee's cast included Emma Thompson, Hugh Grant, Kate Winslet, and Alan Rickman. Lee led the cast in exercises based on tai chi, which he had been studying ever since he made *Pushing Hands*. Lee also assigned Winslet reading material and piano lessons. In addition, to avoid unrealistic melodrama in Thompson's crying scene at the end of the film, Lee instructed the actress not to face the camera.

In 1997, after playing at the Cannes Film Festival, Lee's fifth film, *The Ice Storm*, was released in the United States. Starring Kevin Kline, Sigourney Weaver, Joan Allen, Elijah Wood, and Christina Ricci, the film painted a bleak portrait of well-to-do families in suburban Connecticut in 1973. Lee researched American middle-class culture of the 1970s, which added to the film's authenticity. However, a complaint from many reviewers was that Lee left his characters' emotions unexplained. Lee said it was the first movie of which he was very proud.

In 2000, Lee became a household name with the release of the ravishingly beautiful martial arts epic, *Crouching Tiger, Hidden Dragon*. The movie earned ten Academy Award nominations, including nomination for Best Picture. It was also nominated for best Art Direction, Cinematography, Costume Design, Directing, Film Editing, Foreign Language Film, Musical Score, Song, Best Picture, and Writing.

On March 25, 2001, Lee attended the awards ceremony and proudly accepted awards with his collaborators in the categories of Art Direction, Cinematography, Foreign Language Film, and Musical Score. *Crouching Tiger, Hidden Dragon* also earned six trophies in 13-nominated categories at the annual Golden Horse Awards, Taiwan's top movie awards.

Lee, his wife, and their two sons live in Westchester County, New York, not far from New York Medical College, in Valhalla, where Jane worked as a researcher. Lee classified himself as a New York filmmaker, and in January 1996, he established the Ang Lee Fellowship for graduate film students at New York University. ◆

Lee, Bill Lann

1949– ● ATTORNEY

When President Bill Clinton nominated Bill Lann Lee to head the civil rights division of the Department of Justice in 1997, it sparked a firestorm of controversy in the Senate and began another round of the contentious debate over affirmative action.

William Lann Lee was born in 1949 in Harlem, a predominantly African American neighborhood in the borough of Manhattan in New York City where Lee's father ran a laundry. Lee later recalled, "My father was a big influence on me, and he suffered a lot." Notwithstanding his volunteer army service during World War II, the elder Lee was hard pressed to find an apartment after the war because of his Asian heritage. "This was before I was born," Lee said, and he was turned down and they told him it was because he was a 'Chinaman.' After I was born, I remember that it was customary for him to be called 'dumb Chinaman.' He was denigrated. There was that type of verbal abuse."

Inspired by his father's resiliency in the face of racial discrimination, the young Bill Lann Lee was determined to excel

Organization of Chinese Americans

The Organization of Chinese Americans (OCA) was founded in 1973 as a nonprofit, non-partisan group dedicated to protecting the civil rights of United States citizens of Chinese descent. In addition, the organization is an active force in the larger issue of civil rights for all Asian Americans. Its primary goals are to increase participation by Chinese Americans in the political process and to influence legislation and government policy in matters of particular interest to the Chinese American community.

The OCA is based in Washington, D.C., and has 40 additional chapters scattered throughout the country. Through its programs it promotes political action, provides advocacy for social justice and equal rights, and seeks to educate the broader public about the heritage and accomplishments of Chinese Americans. In this way the OCA hopes to help combat prejudice and ignorance, and to broaden the public's awareness of the contributions of Chinese culture and society to the nation.

The OCA sponsors a number of awards that recognize the contributions of individual Chinese Americans, as well as members of other Asian ethnic groups. In addition, the OCA administers scholarships to support the college careers for young Chinese American students who have demonstrated academic excellence, community involvement, and leadership abilities.

> *"In civil rights in particular, conciliation, mediation, when people can actually sit down at the table and agree on remedies, that sends a message. The message is we can work together. That is an important message to send."*
>
> Lee, interview in *New York Times*, November 6, 1997

in life. His first-rate academic record in school earned him admission to the prestigious Bronx High School of Science, where he graduated near the top of his class and won a scholarship to Yale University, which recruited him as part of an affirmative action program to seek out minority students. Lee vindicated Yale's confidence in him by graduating magna cum laude and Phi Beta Kappa in 1971.

In the fall of 1971, Lee enrolled in Columbia Law School, where he hoped to train as an advocate for the oppressed and disadvantaged. He soon found himself discouraged by the dry and tedious details of case law, which seemed utterly alien to the pressing issues of social justice to which he was devoted. Lee later recalled, "The only thing I understood was the legal methods course. We had that for the first two weeks, and then we didn't have it anymore." Intending to drop out, the dispirited Lee met with the dean of students, who coaxed him into staying with the offer to work as an assistant to Jack Greenberg, Thurgood Marshall's successor as the director of the NAACP's legal defense fund. "I didn't know who Jack Greenberg was, or what the NAACP was," Lee said, but when he found out, he decided to stick it out at Columbia.

Lee's first assignment for the NAACP was helping Greenberg to write a textbook, which he found just as tedious as his coursework. Lee asked to be put to work on real cases, and Greenberg agreed, but only so long as it was on Lee's own time. So, in the intervals of editing the book, Lee helped to churn out **briefs** for the defense fund's lawsuits. Lee now remembers the punishing schedule fondly, as a labor of love. "Back then, I thought it was a great deal," he later said. "In retrospect, it was probably exploitation."

Much of Lee's work was in the South, where he grew to appreciate the courtliness and congeniality of the local legal community despite the lingering racial parochialism. When he first arrived to work on a case in Macon, Georgia, in the late 1970s, he recalled that people "just thought I was a man from the moon." He said that when he returned in the mid-1990s, however, "I'd jump in a cab, and the taxicab drivers would say, 'YKK?'" And Lee was stumped by the initials until he learned about the local zipper factory by that name. "They assumed I was a Japanese executive with the YKK zipper factory. I tell the story to show how the country and the South have changed so fast. They once thought I was a man from the moon. Now they think I'm a Japanese business executive."

When President Clinton nominated Lee for a position in the Deparment of Justice, Republican opponents cited his longstanding support of affirmative action. Senate majority leader Trent Lott said, "I want to make it clear I do not believe Bill Leann Lee should be assistant attorney general—even in an acting capacity—because of his positions advocating racial preferences and timetables." But Lee's supporters were equally vociferous; Senate minority leader Tom Daschle hailed the appointment, commenting that "it's regrettable that Bill Lann Lee isn't already serving as permanent head of the civil rights division."

The deciding voice in this discordant chorus was that of President Clinton, who avoided a pitched battle in the Senate by naming Lee acting assistant attorney general for civil rights on December 15, 1997, a tactic that enabled Clinton to renew Lee's appointment every 120 days until the end of his administration. Brushing aside criticism of Lee's views on **affirmative action,** the president said, "His views on affirmative action are my views on affirmative action: no quotas, no discrimination, no position or benefit for any unqualified person. But mend, don't end, affirmative action, so that all Americans can have a fair chance at living the American Dream." At the announcement ceremony a grateful Lee stressed the nation's proud heritage of civil

1949 Lee is born in New York City.

1971 Lee graduates from Yale University and enters Columbia University Law School.

1972 Lee goes to work as a volunteer for the NACCP Legal Defense Fund.

1974 Lee graduates from Columbia University Law School.

1983 Lee starts work as Western regional counsel for NAACP Legal Defense Fund.

1997 Lee is named acting head of the civil rights division of the U.S. Department of Justice.

briefs documents submitted by attorneys to a court of law explaining and arguing their side of a particular case before that court.

affirmative action government policy of reserving a set number of positions in the workplace, schools, or other areas for minorities.

rights achievement, extending from Eisenhower's civil rights office to Kennedy and Johnson's fight for civil rights legislation during the 1960s.

It was a justifiably proud moment for Lee, who had witnessed his own father's struggle to maintain dignity in the face of racial **epithets** and who later reaped the fruits of affirmative action in gaining admission to Yale University.

Lee remained at the Justice Department until the end of the Clinton administration in January 2001. ◆

epithets disparaging or insulting words or phrases.

Lee, Brandon

1965–MARCH 31, 1993 ● ACTOR AND MARTIAL ARTS EXPERT

Brandon Lee was born in 1965 in California to Bruce and Linda Lee. His father, Bruce, was a legend in the field of martial arts who had used his skills and charismatic presence to become one of the world's leading action film stars. When Brandon was just an infant, his father moved the family back to Hong Kong so that Bruce could expand his film career. Lee was raised speaking Chinese and English, and when he was only two years old, he was already training with his father in the martial art known as Jeet Kune Do.

Brandon Lee

Lee lived a happy childhood until the fateful year of 1973, when his father mysteriously collapsed and died. Doctors eventually ruled that he had died after swelling in the brain that was supposedly caused by taking painkillers, but many people have never been satisfied with that ruling. A large cult developed around Bruce Lee that worshiped his martial arts skills and that firmly believed he was murdered for teaching the public the secrets of certain martial arts that had previously been closely guarded within the Asian community. Bruce was also supposedly the first victim of what came to be known as the Lee family curse. According to cult lore,

Lee incurred the wrath of local demons when he moved into a house in outside Hong Kong, who then cursed him.

After his father's death, Brandon Lee moved back to the United States with his mother. There, he was no longer the happy, confident child he had been in Hong Kong. He missed his father terribly, and it led to problems in school and in other areas. "When I was growing up, we moved around a lot," recalled Lee, "and whenever I'd get to a new school, there'd be somebody there trying to (beat me up)." Lee tried to continue his martial arts studies so he could defend himself, but when he attended a class at age nine, he ran crying from the room after spotting his father's poster hanging from a wall of the **dojo** where the class was held. Not only did he miss his father, but the pressure of living in his shadow was immense also.

Things did not get much better for Lee in high school. He was kicked out of the first two that he attended, and he was expelled from a third, the wealthy Chadwick School in Palos Verde, California, for bad behavior just before he was to have finally graduated. Finally, at his fourth high school, Lee received his diploma.

Lee then decided he wanted to follow in his father's footsteps. While he had dreamed of being an actor since he was a child, he did not begin to take steps to make that a reality until after he graduated. He signed up for acting lessons, and continued to improve his martial arts skills. He enrolled at Emerson College in Boston, which specialized in the performing arts. At the same time, he took acting lessons in New York. At age 20, Lee thought he was ready to try to make it as an actor, so he moved to Hollywood.

Immediately, Lee learned that he would have trouble landing any substantial acting jobs. With his father's legacy looming large, Lee was discouraged to discover that filmmakers only wanted him for low-budget martial arts pictures that required little or no acting. Initially, that upset Lee greatly, but eventually he realized there were worse things that could happen than for him to follow in his father's footsteps. He changed his minds about martial arts roles and accepted a role on the made-for-television film, *Kung Fu: The Movie*, which starred David Carradine in a return to the role of martial arts expert that he had played earlier in the "Kung Fu" television series.

Lee determined that, if he was going to give in and follow his father's career, he might as well do it right. Still facing problems landing jobs in Hollywood, Lee moved to Hong Kong,

1965 Lee is born in California.

1973 Lee moves back to the United States with his mother after his father dies under very mysterious circumstances.

1985 Lee is determined to follow in his father's footsteps, so he moves to Hollywood to begin an acting career.

1987 Lee stars in Hong Kong's *Legacy of Rage*, his first starring role.

1989 Lee stars in his American breakthrough film, *Showdown in Little Tokyo*.

1993 Lee dies after accidently being shot to death while working on the film *The Crow*.

dojo a training school for various martial arts.

You know, for years I was in my father's shadow, and I resented it. I wanted to be an actor, not do martial arts films. But it finally dawned on me–I am who I am, and I might as well accept it. Once I realized that, doors started to open for me.

Brandon Lee, posthumously, in *Premiere* magazine, July 1993

where martial arts movies were plentiful and always available. There, he made his first full-length martial arts picture, *Legacy of Rage* (1987), which was filmed entirely in Cantonese. In 1989, Lee returned to Hollywood to film *Showdown in Little Tokyo*, which co-starred well-known action star Dolph Lundgren. That latter film proved to be a turning point for Lee as it proved to studio executives that the young actor had the ability needed to play the leading man in standard action films.

Lee's career was definitely on the upswing after *Little Tokyo*, which he followed up in 1992 with the action movie *Rapid Fire*. After that film, Lee signed a three-picture contract with Twentieth Century Fox studios and worked tirelessly to promote *Rapid Fire*. For Lee, it was a dream come true. The budding star thought, for the first time, that he was out of his father's considerable shadow.

Lee's next movie role was supposed to take him from being a star of lesser known action films to being a genuine movie star. He was cast as Eric Draven in the film adaptation of the popular comic book, *The Crow*, which told the tale of a murdered rock musician who returned from the grave with supernatural powers in order to avenge his own murder and to assist others who had been unjustly murdered or victimized. The film had plenty of action and fighting scenes, but it was a big budget studio production that was a far cry from the cheap martial arts films of Hong Kong.

Things seemed to be going perfectly in Lee's career, when out of nowhere, tragedy struck. Most of *The Crow* as already finished, but every step of the way had brought a new accident or unfortunate incident. The film's producers were trying to stretch their budget as far as they could, and this meant working the cast and crew for long hours for days at a time. Tired people make mistakes, and that was certainly the case on the set of *The Crow*. On the very first day of filming, a carpenter was almost electrocuted to death. Another crew member accidently stuck a screw driver through his hand, while a stunt man fell off a roof and suffered from broken ribs. Filming in Wilmington, North Carolina, during the heart of the rainy winter season, many scenes were shot outdoors in the cold rain, late at night, which wore everybody down and led to an increased number of mistakes.

After almost two months of nonstop filming, the worst possible accident happened on March 30, 1993. The cast was working on a scene in which Lee, as Draven, walks into his apartment and finds a group of attackers about to rape his girlfriend. Before he can do anything, he is shot and killed by the intruders, falling at the door of the apartment and scattering the groceries he was carrying. On cue, he was shot, but instead of play-acting, Lee fell to the ground in real pain, the victim of a terrible mistake. Blanks were supposed to be used in the pistol, but somehow a small bullet known as a "dummy tip" was left in the gun, and that bullet was fired at Lee. It pierced his stomach, exploded through a number of key organs, and came to a stop next to his spine. Lee was rushed to New Hanover Regional Medical Center, but it was too late—he died of the gunshot wound at the hospital after five hours of surgery, with his fiancée Eliza Hutton at his side early the next morning.

To followers of the Lee family, Brandon's death was just the latest manifestation of the Lee family curse. Conspiracy theorists floated the idea that both Bruce and Brandon had been killed for dark reasons that involved their martial arts prowess. Lee was buried on April 3, just two weeks to the day before he and Hutton were set to be married. Fans remembered that in Bruce's movie *Game of Death*, there were scenes that seemed to predict that he would lose a son at some point in his life. Fans were also quick to note the eerie similarities between Lee's death and the plot of *The Crow*. After Lee's death, the film was on hold for some time, but the studio eventually finished the movie in June 1993, and released it in May 1994. Critical reviews of the movie were mixed, but it found a strong cult following that will last for years, if not decades. ◆

Lee, Bruce

NOVEMBER 27, 1940–JULY 20, 1973 ● MARTIAL ARTIST, ACTOR

The legend of Bruce Lee not only survived his sudden and untimely death but was enlarged by it. On the brink of international superstardom when he was suddenly felled by a **cerebral edema** at the age of age 32, this avatar of kung-fu cool inspired an entire generation of cinematic martial arts vigilante avengers; David Carradine, Chuck Norris, Steven Seagall, and Jackie Chan all rode to fame on a wave set into motion by Bruce Lee.

Lee's father, Lee Hoi Chuen, was a popular opera star in Hong Kong. On November 27, 1940, while he was on tour in

cerebral edema
an abnormal accumulation of serous fluid in the brain.

Bruce Lee in action.

Gaelic of or relating to the language of and speech of the Celts in Ireland, the Isle of Man, and the Scottish Highlands.

New York, his wife, waiting for him in San Francisco with their three sons, gave birth to another boy. Unable to consult with the father about the name, the mother accepted the doctor's suggestion of Bruce, which means "strong one" in **Gaelic**. The family wasted no time in launching Bruce's acting career, finding work for him as a three-month-old extra in the 1941 film *Golden Gate Girl*.

Notwithstanding the success of the father's tour, the family missed their native land and returned there later that year despite the city's occupation by the Japanese. Young Bruce's precocious film career continued apace in Hong Kong, where he appeared in another film when he was four years old. Two years later, he was on the big screen again.

With a steady stream of movie roles to feed his growing ego, the precocious and adventurous young Lee vented his creative energies in two oddly conflicting areas: street gangs and dance. While risking death or imprisonment through the former, he refined his increasingly self-conscious sense of style and grace through the latter. These two activities dovetailed nicely in Lee's growing fascination with the Chinese martial art of kung fu, especially the variant called wing chun, based on the techniques of a Shaolin Buddhist nun. But Lee's creative desire to fashion his own version of the exacting discipline led to his expulsion from the school.

If nothing else, Lee's walk on the wild side of Hong Kong's streets served as a useful method-acting exercise for this still-thriving film career, in which he was frequently typecast as a troubled adolescent or young street tough. An increasingly hot property thanks to his uniquely enigmatic, stoic good looks, Lee was offered a lucrative movie contract by Run Run Shaw, a powerful Hong Kong film producer. At the same time that Lee announced to his mother that he planned to accept the offer, he was picked up by the police for street fighting. Determined that her son obtain his diploma, Mrs. Lee packed him off to the United States to finish high school.

Lee landed in Seattle and proceeded to graduate from the high school in Edison, Washington. He then enrolled in the University of Washington, where he majored in philosophy, supporting himself by waiting tables and giving dance lessons. He soon began offering kung fu lessons to his classmates, one of whom, Linda Emery, became his wife in 1964.

Shortly after their marriage, Lee and Linda moved to California, where Lee founded a school offering instruction in his original variant of kung fu, which he called jeet kune do. The venture proved so successful that Lee eventually opened schools in Oakland and Seattle. He also persisted with his acting career, landing a recurring role in *The Green Hornet* television series as Kato, the Hornet's Asian kung-fu-fighting sidekick. Although the series was cancelled after only one season, Lee's role registered strongly enough with Hollywood's casting agents to keep him afloat with a smattering of guest roles on series such a *Longstreet* and *Ironside*. He also landed a feature-film role in *Marlowe* (1969).

Despite his sporadic success in Hollywood, Lee felt stalled by the limitations of typecasting as an Asian second banana, so in 1971 the Lee family—by then augmented by the birth of two daughters—moved to Hong Kong. There Lee signed a contract to appear in two feature films, one of which was later released in the United States as *Fists of Fury*. Propelled by Lee's powerful screen presence as a devoted student bent on avenging the murder of his kung fu instructor, the film became the most profitable in Hong Kong's history. His next outing, The *Chinese Connection* (1972), made even more money and enabled Lee to found his own film company, Concord Pictures.

1940 Lee is born in San Francisco.

1964 Lee marries and moves to California to open martial arts schools and pursue acting.

1971 Lee and his family move to Hong Kong, where Lee signs on to star in two feature films.

1972 Lee's movies become successful enough that he founds his own production company, Concord Pictures.

1973 Lee is found dead of an apparent cerebral edema.

Martial Arts

The wide range of martial arts, from *tai kwon do* to *aikido*, all have their earliest origins in a discipline that, according to tradition, began as the invention of Shaolin Buddhist priests in China, in the late 5th century A.D. At about that time, a holy man traveling from India is said to have traveled to the temple, spreading Buddhism to the people he encountered along the way. This visitor introduced techniques for meditation and physical training and, most importantly, the concept of *chi*.

Chi, an intrinsic energy source that can be cultivated by breathing and meditation, is a central part of all the martial arts. Through training and strengthening the chi, an individual can harness its energy and use it to increase his or her power and bodily control. The Shaolin monks who learned this discipline developed a style of fighting called *kung fu*, which means "hard work and perfection." Over the next few hundred years they became a formidable fighting force in service to the Chinese emperors. It is from this tradition that Bruce Lee drew upon to develop his own style, called *jeet kune do*, which also incorporates elements from many other martial arts styles.

A part of the earliest kung fu tradition came to be that, once a student had mastered a certain degree of competency, he would go out into the world to learn and to improve his skills. In this way, knowledge of the Shaolin techniques were brought to Japan, Okinawa, and Korea, where local variations were eventually developed. In Japan, these variations include judo, a fighting style that focuses on throws, holds, and other wrestling maneuvers. Karate, on the other hand, is an Okinawan martial arts style, more focused on kicking and striking blows. In Korea, tae kwon do was developed, with its primary emphasis on foot and leg movements.

Today, the martial arts have spread throughout the world, with major competitive venues in the United States, Europe, Asia, and Africa. While many practice the martial arts (or *wu shu* in Chinese: "fighting arts") as a sport, others seek the disciplines for their meditative and spiritual aspects.

The first of Lee's self-produced and directed projects was *Way of the Dragon* (titled *Return of the Dragon* in the United States), starring a young Chuck Norris. Lee was a wave of creative energy about to break upon the vast mass American audience, and he knew it. As he told a reporter in 1973, "I hope to make . . . the kind of movie where you can just watch the surface story, if you like, or can look deeper into it."

On July 23, 1973, those vibrant hopes were snuffed when Lee was found dead at the age of 32, only three weeks before his fourth film, *Enter the Dragon*, made its sensational debut in the United States. The coroner's report gave the cause as a cerebral edema that resulted from a reaction to an analgesic he was taking for back pain.

But so *pedestrian* a death somehow seemed an affront to the iconic power of Lee's life, and the rumor mill went into overdrive: he was taken out by hit men, he had been poisoned, he had crossed powerful figures in the underworld or the Hong Kong film industry, and so on, as Lee's mystique blossomed in the rarefied air of adulation reserved for the young, the beautiful, and the talented who die at the peak of their powers. ◆

pedestrian commonplace.

Lee, Chang-rae

JULY 29, 1965– ● AUTHOR

Chang-rae Lee was born in Seoul, Korea, on July 29, 1965. His father was Young Yong Lee, a doctor, and his mother was Inja (Hong) Lee. Lee moved to the United States in 1968 at the age of three. As in many immigrant families, Lee's father came over first then sent for Lee, his mother, and his sister a year later. Lee's father established a successful psychiatric practice in Westchester County, New York. Lee grew up in a **bilingual** household and attended the exclusive Phillips Exeter Academy for high school. He earned his bachelor's degree at Yale University in 1987.

bilingual the ability to speak two languages fluently.

Lee's first job after college was on Wall Street, analyzing stocks. After one year, he left to pursue a writing career. He went on to earn a master of fine arts degree from the University of Oregon in 1993 and immediately became an assistant professor of creative writing there. He later taught writing at Hunter College of City University of New York.

Lee's first novel, *Native Speaker* (1995), published when he was only 29, earned positive reviews and more than six major literary awards. The hero of the story is Henry Park, a Korean-American from an affluent New York suburb, whose father has worked hard in his grocery stores to give his family a good life. Park earns money spying on prominent Korean Americans for high-level politicians and businessmen. The novel explores the discomfort Park experiences when he is asked to snoop into the life of a popular city councilman.

Native Speaker showed how it feels to be a perpetual outsider in one's adopted country. Themes in the book are love, loss, family, identity, and language. Critics praised Lee's uniquely original treatment of the American myth of immigrant potential. They

also lauded his skill as a writer, praising his lyrical language and vivid descriptions.

Lee's second novel, *A Gesture Life* (1999), resulted from his research into one of the most notorious war atrocities of modern times. During World War II, the Japanese created a system of forcing Korean women to have sex with Japanese soldiers. These women were called "comfort women." When Lee first learned about these women, he became shocked at the terrible details of the lives of the comfort woman. He traveled to Korea to interview women who had survived their sexual slavery.

Inspired by a newspaper article, Lee had planned to write a story of one woman forced into sexual slavery during the war. But then he found a reference to a book by a Japanese man who had been a "recruiter" of comfort women. This led Lee to write *A Gesture Life* from the point of view of a man. Lee created the lead character, Franklin "Doc" Hata, a Japanese man of Korean descent leading a seemingly tranquil life in a small American town. He is a retired shop owner, but is filled with painful memories. Hata slowly begins to recall the horrors of World War II, during which he worked as a medic to care for the comfort women.

Lee exposes the issue of comfort women in an intimate and compassionate way, concerning himself with the psychological effects of the atrocity on both the women and the soldiers. *A Gesture Life* features the endlessly fruitful American theme of mixing cultures and the resulting conflicts of identity. Hata tries desperately to assimilate in the small American town of Bedley Run. "I had assumed," he says, "that once I settled someplace, I would be treated as those people were treated, and in fact I was fully prepared for it. But wherever I went—and, in particular, here in Bedley Run—it seemed people took an odd interest in telling me that I wasn't unwelcome."

A Gesture Life earned even higher praise than *Native Speaker* did. According to Andrew O'Hagan in *The New York Times Book Review*, "The accretion of wisdom in Lee's novel is stunning. . . . *A Gesture of Life* is . . . an achievement. It's a beautiful, solitary, remarkably tender book that reveals the shadows that fall constantly from the past, the ones that move darkly on the lawns of the here and now."

Donna Seaman, in *Booklist*, said, "This portrait of a man whose soul has cauterized would resonate in the plainest of tellings, but the glory of Lee's prose—its perfect pitch and pacing and the blazing intensity of each startling scene—makes this a work of inestimable moral and artistic power."

In South Korea, Lee feels like "a long-lost citizen." He has mixed feelings about visiting his homeland. "There's something about walking around people who look like you. It shouldn't be that, but it feels like that. I'm different from them, but I look like them so it raises interesting questions."

Lee married Michelle Branca, an architect, in 1993. He spent three or four hours each day writing in his New Jersey home that he shared with his wife and daughter. In 2000, he was writing his third novel. Set partly in Asia, the story centered on an American trying to put his life together after the Korean War. Lee also served as Director of the Master of Fine Arts Program at Hunter College, where he taught writing workshops and seminars in literature and researched a third novel.

By 2001, Lee had finished a screenplay based on his second novel for Hong Kong filmmaker Wayne Wang. He also wrote regularly for such publications as *The New York Times Magazine*, often about one of his favorite subjects, food.

Lee earned many honors, including more than eight honors and prizes for *Native Speaker*. They included the PEN/Hemingway Award, the American Book Award, and the Barnes & Noble Discover Award. *Time* magazine named *Native Speaker* one of the best books of 1995, and it was translated into Korean and Italian. In 1999, *The New Yorker* magazine named Lee one of America's best fiction writers under 40. ◆

Lee, Jason Scott

1966– ● ACTOR

Jason Scott Lee was born in Los Angeles in 1966 to a third-generation Chinese-Hawaiian family. His mother was Chinese and his father was Chinese-Hawaiian. The family moved when Lee was two to the Hawaiian island of Oahu when his father, a former military man, found a job with a telephone company.

Lee became interested in acting when he returned to Los Angeles at the age of 19. There he enrolled in an academic program at Fullerton Community College, but he soon turned to acting after taking an extracurricular class.

In an unusual turn of events, Lee secured an acting job from his first audition. Comedian Cheech Marin cast Lee as an illegal

1966 — Jason Scott Lee is born in Los Angeles.

1992 — Lee becomes well-known from his lead role in the film *Map of the Human Heart*.

1993 — Lee becomes a star from his lead role in *Dragon: The Bruce Lee Story*.

1994 — Lee plays Mowgli in the film version of Rudyard Kipling's *The Jungle Book*.

Asian immigrant trying to pass as a Chicano in the film *Born in East L.A.* Lee followed this with bit parts in TV and film, including a brief appearance in *Back to the Future Part II*.

Lee's great step forward occurred when he acted the lead role in the film *Map of the Human Heart* (1992). Lee starred as a half-white Eskimo named Avik opposite Anne Parillaud, star of *La Femme Nikita*, who played a half-white Indian named Albertine. The movie unfolds as a great love story, a terrifying war story, and a tender tale of human feelings and relationships, as the action moves from the cold Arctic north, to calm Montreal, and finally to Europe in the inferno of war. *Map of the Human Heart* became an international art house hit and brought Lee his first major name recognition.

When Lee went on to audition for *The Last of the Mohicans*, the casting director thought he looked too Asian to play a Mohican. However, the casting director recommended Lee for the lead in *Dragon: The Bruce Lee Story* (1993), the movie that made Lee a star. Lee found the role very challenging, and was not even sure he was right for it. Nevertheless, Lee trained in the martial art Jeet Kune Do for seven weeks just for the screen test. When he got the part, he trained four more months with former Bruce Lee student, Jerry Poteet. "I remember being on my knees weeping for days and wondering how I was going to pull this off," Lee said. He managed to perform most of his own stunts in the film.

Dragon: The Bruce Lee Story changed Lee's life dramatically, focusing his attention on spiritual enlightenment, he said. "Dragon brought me an understanding of what the body is capable of. The kind of energy you can generate mentally and command your body to respond with is incredible. Personally, it helped me to challenge myself; I saw my limitations and was able to move past them. What hit me the hardest was the seeking, that Bruce Lee was a man who kept on searching. It was almost like there was a demon inside him that drove him to such levels of excellence."

Lee's next major film was a disaster in many ways. In *Rapa Nui* (1994), Lee starred as Noro, a Polynesian tribal prince. Directed by Kevin Costner, the move was beset by problems during filming and then flopped at the box office.

guerrilla one who engages in irregular warfare tactics, especially as a member of an independent unit.

"I worked for five months on *Rapa Nui*. It seemed it would be a great **guerrilla** adventure, but it was a nightmare, much more physically demanding than my starring stint in *Dragon*. It was the most difficult thing I've ever worked on." The filming suffered from the rugged terrain and thunderstorms. For one scene, Lee stood on a plateau and was swept into the ocean by a huge wave. He suffered deep wounds and shock.

Lee went on to play the young Indian Mowgli in the film version of Rudyard Kipling's *The Jungle Book* (1994). Lee and most of the cast and crew became sick while on location in India. Lee also had little time to prepare for his role, which included handling animals. A wolf even bit Lee on the chest during the project.

Lee trained seriously for his roles by running, swimming, and practicing martial arts. He was a serious surfer and gymnast. Lee believed in the theraputic qualities of herbs and healers and was interested in becoming a herbalist. "It's a blessing to live in Hawaii," he said, "which is a very healing place." ◆

Lee, Mary Paik

AUGUST 17, 1900– ● AUTHOR

Mary Paik Lee's life became known through her autobiography, *Quiet Odyssey: A Pioneer Korean Woman in America*. Lee's book tells the story of her family being forced by Japanese soldiers to leave their home in Korea and to immigrate to the United States. Sucheng Chan, a professor of history and Asian American studies at the University of California, Santa Barbara, discovered Lee's story in 1986, when Lee was 86 years old. Her son, Allan Lee, had mentioned to Chan that his mother had written an autobiography.

When Chen read the manuscript, she became excited to find such a rare first-person written record of Asian immigration. Chen interviewed Lee in her San Francisco apartment and became amazed at her vivid memory for details. As a historian, Chen also knew she had found a rare sample of a still-living Korean who had been one of the 7,000 or more pioneers who had come from Hawaii between 1902 and 1905. Chen edited Lee's manuscript and also wrote a 40-page introduction. The University of Washington Press published the book in 1990.

When Paik Kuang Sun (later Mary Paik Lee) was born on August 17, 1900, in Korea, an American Presbyterian minister baptized her, as her family had converted to Christianity shortly

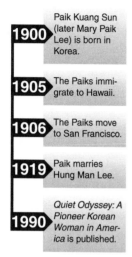

1900 Paik Kuang Sun (later Mary Paik Lee) is born in Korea.

1905 The Paiks immigrate to Hawaii.

1906 The Paiks move to San Francisco.

1919 Paik marries Hung Man Lee.

1990 *Quiet Odyssey: A Pioneer Korean Woman in America* is published.

before her birth. Her paternal grandfather was a teacher who also raised mulberry bushes and owned a vegetable stall in the village market. Her grandmother learned to read and loved to share the Bible with others. Kuang Sun never knew her mother's parents, as they were a poor family in a distant village and had given their daughter up to an arranged marriage.

After Japan's victory over Russia in the Russo-Japanese War, Japan began taking control of Korea. During this tyrannical reign, the Japanese took over Korean farms and businesses and used the nation for their own ends. The Japanese forced the Koreans to take Japanese names, and they prohibited the use of the Korean language. Koreans were forced to aid the Japanese war effort during World War II, and some were sent to work in mines and factories. Others were drafted into the Japanese armed forces.

When Kuang Sun was five years old, the Paiks were forced by Japanese soldiers to leave their comfortable home and their extended family. With only their clothes, a bit of food, and some bedding, they trekked to Inchon, the nearest large city. From Inchon, the Paiks boarded a boat with the promise of work in Hawaii. They immigrated to Hawaii, arriving May 8, 1905, and were never able to return to their homeland. Nearly all of the Koreans who came to Hawaii worked in the sugarcane fields, which was very difficult. Kuang Sun felt somewhat at home in Hawaii, though, since everyone she met was Asian. Her second brother was born later in 1905. After one year in Hawaii, the Paiks moved on to California where more agricultural work was available.

When little Kuang Sun stepped off the boat in San Francisco on December 3, 1906, she and her family were met by a group of young white men who taunted them, laughing at them and spitting in their faces. Kuang Sun was upset and asked her father why they had came to a place where they were not welcome. He father told her that when the first American missionaries arrived in Korea, they had also been taunted. Children had thrown rocks at the missionaries and called them "white devils" because of their blue eyes and light hair. Her father said that the missionaries just paid no attention to the tormentors, showing that they were better than those who laughed at them were. He said that in America they must study hard and show the Americans that they were just as good as they. Kuang Sun never forgot her father's lesson.

Kuang Sun's mother, Song Kuang Do Lee, helped support the family by cooking for 30 single men who worked in the citrus groves. Asians were not allowed to live near whites, so the Lees lived in shacks in Asian settlements. Kuang Sun took her first paying job at the age of six and worked until she was 85 years old. Although Kuang Sun went to school, she also helped her parents wash laundry, and she worked as a house servant. The Paik family changed locations every year or so to find work so they could feed and clothe their family that grew to 10 children.

The Paiks suffered from laws that prohibited Asians from renting or buying property. They often saw "whites only" signs meant to keep Asians out of certain areas. One year the family ate only biscuits and water. Through it all, her father worked at backbreaking and sometimes life-endangering jobs. However, he always gave to others in need.

Mary, as she became known, grew into a hard-working, honest, and caring young woman. She soon met Hung Man Lee (born 1892) who was also an immigrant from Korea. Hung Man worked as a foreman on a large rice farm, and a mutual friend introduced the young couple. On their first date, with permission from Mary's father, the couple went to a movie. She had never been in a theater. After they sat in a good seat, an usher came to tell them to move to the Asian section. The couple left in embarrassment. Their bond as American outsiders helped them to forge a union, though, and on January 1, 1919, they were married in a Presbyterian church.

Hung Man worked long hours waste-deep in water in the rice fields, and his skin developed a lifelong rash. The young family moved to Anaheim hoping to find other work. They remained in agriculture for most of their lives. The Lees had two sons, Tony and Allan. After age-related illness overcame him, Hung Man died at age 83 in 1975. Mary wrote, "He left me a priceless legacy, more valuable than material things. He gave me a feeling of great solace that makes life worth living and that enables me to carry on alone."

Mary Paik Lee often spoke up about what she believed to be right, particularly when it came to racism. Her autobiography was written with the intimacy of an oral history and her memories bring to life the rare experience of a Korean-born child growing up on the West Coast before 1910. Chan's extensive introduction and appendix help readers gain a detailed historical and cultural context. ◆

"Mother was a gentle person. She never indulged in gossip, never had harsh words for anyone. She knew a lot but never bragged about it. Father was full of vitality then. He had all kinds of ambitious plans for our future and was always telling us funny stories and jokes. He was also a very practical person, always looking for ways to improve our situation no matter how hopeless the conditions."

Mary Paik Lee, in *Quiet Odyssey: A Pioneer Korean Woman in America*

Lee, Samuel

AUGUST 1, 1920– ● OLYMPIC DIVER

Sammy Lee was the first male athlete to win two Olympic gold medals in the platform diving event, winning in the 1948 and 1952 Games. Lee was also the first non-white American to win an Olympic gold medal in high diving. He also won a bronze medal in springboard diving.

Samuel Lee was born August 1, 1920, in Fresno, California, where his parents had emigrated from Korea. Lee and his two sisters grew up hearing their father say that a "life without dreams is like a bird without wings." At age 12, Lee began dreaming of Olympic glory when he saw the flags of the world lining the streets of Los Angeles, where the 1932 Olympic Games were held. That summer, Lee discovered diving and declared that someday he would be crowned an Olympic champion.

Lee experienced prejudice in his Los Angeles suburb and was the only Asian-American at his school. He trained during a time when non-whites were only allowed into public swimming pools once a week. After the non-whites swam, the pool was drained and disinfected. However, Lee had heroes and mentors to show him the way. One of them was Hart Crum, a local black athlete, and another was Irishman Jim Ryan, an ex-Olympic coach who became Lee's hard-driving coach. They encouraged Lee to persevere despite the odds.

Lee also became inspired at age 16 by two winners at the 1936 Olympics, held in Berlin, Germany. He heard on the radio that a Korean, Song Kee Chung, had won the men's marathon. Also, track and

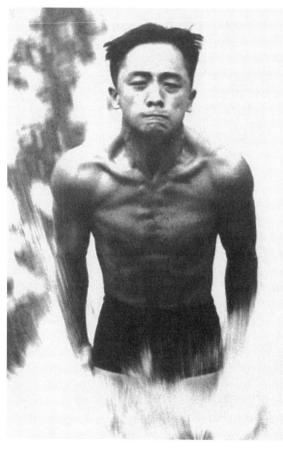

Sammy Lee executing a dive during the 1948 Olympic Games

field star Jesse Owens shamed racist Nazi Germany by winning four gold medals. Lee perfected his diving skills. The rigorous discipline it required helped him later to get through what he called one of "the most traumatic" experiences of his life, medical school.

Lee attended Occidental College in Los Angeles, and became an expert platform diver, a skill only the very best divers attempt to master. At age 22, Lee earned the national diving championship in both the 10-meter platform and the 3-meter springboard. Standing only 5 feet, 1 inch, Lee used his compact stature in his dives, tucking tighter and turning faster than his opponents did. Able to twist and spin faster than his taller competitors, Lee began to do dives nobody had attempted before. These included the forward three-and-a-half somersault and the reverse two-and-a-half somersault.

Lee went on to the University of Southern California School of Medicine, fulfilling his father's dream that he become a doctor. Lee briefly retired from diving, but returned to competition in 1946 and again won the national championship in the platform event. Lee successfully completed his medical studies, and eventually became an ear, nose, and throat specialist.

After his 1947 graduation, Lee joined the United States Army. He continued diving, and qualified for the 1948 Olympic Games in London. There he won a gold medal in the platform competition and a bronze in the springboard. He made history by doing the forward three-and-a-half somersault, his final dive, using a tuck position. Olympic crowds in London were thrilled by Lee's skillful sportsmanship. He was the first Asian-American ever to win gold at the Games.

After the Olympics, Lee returned to medicine, serving as a doctor in the Korean War. He was promoted to the rank of Major. Lee rarely competed over the next four years, but the coach of the U.S. diving team asked Lee to compete in the upcoming Olympics. Receiving permission from his superiors, Lee decided to go.

At the Olympic trials, the 31-year-old doctor had 54 points more than his nearest rival in the platform event, easily qualifying for the 1952 Olympics in Helsinki, Finland. Even as the oldest competing diver, Lee won the gold medal in the platform, becoming the first male to ever win two gold medals in that event. His triumph occurred on August 1, 1952, his 32nd birthday. He became the first male diver in history to win multiple

1920 Lee is born in Fresno, California.

1948 Lee becomes the first nonwhite American to win an Olympic gold medal in high diving.

1952 Lee becomes the first male athlete to win two consecutive Olympic gold medals in the platform diving event.

1990 Lee is elected to the U.S. Olympic Hall of Fame.

gold medals at the Olympics. He also was the oldest diver to ever win in platform diving.

In 1953, Lee retired from competitive diving, but he remained involved in the sport. When the war ended, he toured the Far East putting on diving exhibitions. He coached the 1960 U.S. Olympic team and the 1964 Japanese and Korean squads. In 1979, Lee became the first foreign coach to be invited to China to evaluate their diving program. Lee coached U.S. Olympic champion Bob Webster and the legendary Greg Louganis, 5-time Olympic medalist. Louganis, an American diver, dominated the sport of men's diving in the 1980s. Louganis won gold medals in both springboard and platform diving at the Olympic Games in 1984 and 1988.

In 1953, Lee received the James E. Sullivan Memorial Award, becoming the first non-white to be presented with the outstanding "amateur athlete of the year award." The award comes from the Amateur Athletic Union (AAU), a leading nonprofit organization that promotes and develops amateur sports and physical fitness programs in the United States. The AAU annually presents the James E. Sullivan Award to the nation's outstanding amateur athlete. The award is named for an early AAU executive.

In 1968, Lee was elected to the International Swimming Hall of Fame and to the U.S. Olympic Hall of Fame in 1990.

Lee's book *Diving* was published in 1979. ◆

Lee, Tsung Dao

NOVEMBER 24, 1926– ● PHYSICIST

Tsung Dao Lee shared the 1957 Nobel Prize in physics with Chen Ning Yang. They proposed that the "conservation of parity," a basic principle of nuclear physics, did not hold true in some cases.

Tsung Dao Lee was born on November 24, 1926, in Shanghai, China, and became the third of six children of Tsing-Kong Lee, a businessman, and Ming-Chang Chang Lee.

Lee studied at the Kiangsi Middle School in Kanchow, Kiangsi province, from which he graduated in 1943. He then attended the National Chekiang University in Kweichow province. In 1945, the Japanese invasion forced the university to move to K'un-ming to join other relocated institutions, which together became the National Southwest Associated University. Lee followed, and at the Associated University he met Chen Ning Yang, who would become his collaborator and fellow Nobel Prize winner.

Lee earned a bachelor of science degree in physics in 1946. His brilliance in physics won him a Chinese Government Scholarship that enabled him to study at the University of Chicago, where he studied under famous physicist Enrico Fermi. Lee's friend Yang also became a graduate student in physics at Chicago.

Tsung Dao Lee

Lee's success at Chicago won him a stipend from the university to complete his doctorate, which he did in 1950. His thesis was entitled "Hydrogen Content of White Dwarf Stars." For several months in 1950, Lee served as research associate in astrophysics at Yerkes Astronomical Observatory, at Williams Bay, Wisconsin.

From 1950 to 1951, Lee served as research associate and lecturer in physics at the University of California in Berkeley. Lee was reunited with Yang in 1951, when he accepted a fellowship at the Institute for Advanced Study in Princeton, New Jersey. He remained on the institute's staff until 1953.

Lee quickly became a widely known scientist, especially for his work in statistical mechanics and in nuclear and subnuclear physics, having solved some long-standing problems of great complexity. Lee investigated the subject of parity nonconservation, which earned him the Nobel Prize. He also studied statistical mechanics, nuclear physics, field theory, hydrodynamics, astrophysics, and turbulence.

Lee resigned from the institute to accept an appointment as assistant professor of physics at Columbia University in 1953. Dr. J. Robert Oppenheimer, director of the institute stated: "We saw him . . . leave with great regret. He [is] one of the most brilliant theoretical physicists we have known. His work in statistical mechanics and in nuclear and subnuclear physics has brought him worldwide renown, and justly. He has solved some problems of long standing and of great difficulty. His work has

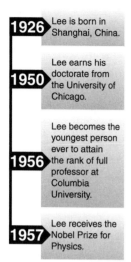

1926 Lee is born in Shanghai, China.

1950 Lee earns his doctorate from the University of Chicago.

1956 Lee becomes the youngest person ever to attain the rank of full professor at Columbia University.

1957 Lee receives the Nobel Prize for Physics.

shown a remarkable freshness, versatility, and style." By 1956, at age 29, Lee became a full professor at Columbia, the youngest person ever to attain that rank at the university.

In 1957, at barely 31 years of age, Lee became the second youngest scientist ever to receive the Nobel Prize for Physics. (The youngest was 25-year-old Sir Lawrence Bragg, who shared the physics prize with his father in 1915.)

Lee and Yang became the first Chinese scientists to receive the Nobel Prize for Physics. Together they had disproved the parity principle, which held that a mirror image of a nuclear reaction was identical with the reaction. As a result of Lee's and Yang's theories, the principle of the symmetry of space was destroyed.

When Lee and Yang first questioned the validity of the parity principle, which held that each object in nature was balanced with a corresponding mirror image that obeyed the same physical rules, they presented a challenge to an accepted basic law of nuclear physics. The parity rule, which was formulated in 1925, was so firmly supported by experimental data that few scientists would question its factuality. Physicists tried to make all their observations fit the parity principle.

The limitations of the parity principle became apparent in explaining the characteristics of k-mesons, subatomic particles produced by the giant atom smashers. These atom smashers were the cosmotron at Brookhaven National Laboratory in Upton, New York, and the bevatron at the University of California in Berkeley. Scientists saw that the pattern into which the k-mesons disintegrated was irregular. Because this behavior did not conform to the principle of parity, Lee and Yang insisted that it was not the fault of the k-mesons, but the fault of the rule of parity.

The two collaborators suggested experiments to test their calculations. At the laboratories of Columbia University, radioactive cobalt was cooled so that its thermal motions were reduced to a minimum. A magnetic field was applied so that the spinning cobalt nuclei fell parallel to the applied magnetic field. According to parity, as they spun, half of their electrons should have gone toward magnetic north and half toward magnetic south. What actually happened was that far more electrons came out the south end of the nuclei. The scientists verified that cobalt nuclei emit electrons from one end. This showed that one end of the nucleus is different from the other, something never known before. This defied the principle of parity. Particles would now be referred to as "right-handed" or "left-handed."

The success of the Lee-Yang experiments began a new era in physics. With the elimination of parity, scientists could now gain new insight into a great deal of confusing scientific information gathered since the end of World War II. Abolition of the parity law also opened new fields of research and encouraged hope of progress toward Albert Einstein's goal of a single unified theory.

In addition to the Nobel, Lee and Yang also jointly received the 1957 Albert Einstein Commemorative Award in science of Yeshiva University and the science award of the Newspaper Guild of New York. Lee was elected a fellow of the American Physical Society and the Academia Sinica, a research institute of Nationalist China. He was also elected a member of the National Academy of Sciences. Princeton University awarded an honorary doctor of science degree to Lee in 1958. Together with Yang, Lee wrote several prominent articles in *The Physical Review*.

Since 1979, Lee has worked to promote academic exchange between physicists of China and the United States.

Lee married Hui-Chung Chin (known as Jeannette), a university student, in 1950, and the couple had two sons, James and Stephen. Colleagues described Lee as shy and reserved, and his appearance as boyish. Lee had brown eyes and black hair, stands five feet seven inches tall, and weighed 135 pounds. Just plain thinking was Lee's main entertainment, but he also liked to relax by reading mystery novels and listening to music. He became a United States citizen in 1963. ◆

"Through your consistent and unprejudiced thinking, you have been able to break a most puzzling deadlock in the field of elementary particle physics where now experimental and theoretical work is pouring forth as a result of your brilliant achievement."

O. B. Klein of the Royal Swedish Academy of Sciences presenting the 1957 Nobel Prize in physics to Lee and Yang

Lee, Wen Ho

1939– ● NUCLEAR SCIENTIST

Although the Chinese-American nuclear scientist was never formally charged with spying, and although the government ended up dropping nearly all of its lesser charges against him—all of which pertained to the mishandling of classified information about America's nuclear warhead technology—nagging questions persist about his activities: Even if it was never proved that Lee passed on nuclear secrets to the

Wen Ho Lee in front of his home after being released from solitary confinement.

probable cause legal phrase signifying a reasonable ground for supposing a criminal charge is well founded.

Chinese, why was he downloading so much information about nuclear technology from the computers of Los Alamos? Was Lee a dedicated scientist who was targeted by overzealous prosecutors because of his ethnic heritage, or was he a wiley spy who managed to beat the rap?

A minor nuclear scientist at the Los Alamos National Laboratory in New Mexico for two decades, Lee saw his life of quiet scholarly research blown sky-high in March 1999, when *The New York Times* published a story that revealed the Justice Department's probe of alleged leaks of critical nuclear weapons technology to China. Lee had been the target of covert surveillance since 1996, when U.S. officials became convinced that China had come into possession of the design of the W-88, the powerful miniaturized nuclear warhead that is considered among the "crown jewels" of U.S. nuclear technology. The source of the revelation was a "walk-in" Chinese official who passed documents to the CIA indicating detailed Chinese knowledge of the design specifications of the W-88. Not everyone in the U.S. intelligence community was convinced of the authenticity and reliablity of the documents, but the FBI and the Department of Energy (DOE), proceeding on the assumption that the secrets had indeed been betrayed, believed that the likeliest source of the security breach was the weapons lab at Los Alamos, where most of the data were stored.

Assigning the case to second-level agents, the FBI launched the inquiry in 1996, focusing mainly on Lee among the 12 Los Alamos scientists with access to the data. But Attorney General Janet Reno, knowing the difficulty of obtaining dispositive evidence in spy cases, viewed the whole undertaking sketpically, and when FBI agents requested permission to search Lee's computer in 1997, her staff turned them town because of the lack of clear-cut "**probable cause**" evidence against Lee. The

FBI went over the staff's head to take its case directly to Reno, who seconded her staff's refusal.

The FBI vented its frustration among members of Congress, where Republican opponents of Reno began to monitor the investigation closely. The investigation languished throughout 1998, but the FBI did finally arrange to have Lee take a lie-detector test administered by a private security company, which judged his denials of any improprieties to be truthful. However, FBI agents looking at the same data concluded that Lee was lying, so the DOE reassigned Lee to a less sensitive area of Los Alamos, where he would be working with unclassified materials.

On March 6, 1999, *The New York Times* published a front-page story about the probe without, however, naming Lee as its target. Fearing that Lee was on to their investigation and would begin to cover his tracks, FBI agents descended on Lee's residence on March 7 in the hope of extracting a confession on the spot. Even though Lee steadfastly maintained his innocence, the next day Secretary of Energy Bill Richardson fired Lee for minor security violations unconnected with the W-88 case. It was then that Lee's name leaked to the press, typically juxtaposed with the appositive phrase "the suspected Chinese spy" even though no charges had been brought against him.

A subsequent FBI search of Lee's office turned up three computer tapes on which top-secret weapons codes had been downloaded. Computer analysts believed that Lee had transferred huge amounts of nuclear weapons design data from this classfied computer in the X Division to unsecured sections of the department's computer system. He then made 10 backup tapes of the information, only three of which have been found.

By now intense pressure was mounting from Congress to file formal charges against Lee. In White House discussions of the case, the main concern was not so much in nailing Lee as in explaining the loss of such critical nuclear secrets to the Chinese. One administration official recalled, "We didn't know any other way to [find out what happened to the tapes]. The whole goal was to try to figure out what happened to them." On December 10, 2000, Lee was finally charged with 59 counts of mishandling national security data. Glaringly absent from the list of charges was **espionage**, which the Justice Department deemed unprovable with the available evidence.

The government then asked that Lee be denied bail and held in solitary confinement, where he remained for the next

1939 Wen Ho Lee is born in Taiwan.

1970 Wen Ho Lee receives his doctorate in mechanical engineering from Texas A&M University.

1971 Wen Ho Lee joins the staff of the Los Alamos National Laboratory in Los Alamos, New Mexico.

1972 Wen Ho Lee is charged with 59 counts of mishandling classified government information.

1973 Wen Ho Lee spends 278 days in solitary confinement awaiting trial; in September, 58 of the 59 counts against him are dropped for lack of evidence.

espionage the practice of spying to obtain information about plans and activities, especially of foreign and/or enemy governments and nations.

It was an un-likely outcome for the career of a dedicated scientist and family man.

five months, passing the time reading Russian novels, writing a math textbook, and taking brisk walks during the one hour per day that he was allowed out of his cell. It was an unlikely outcome for the career of a dedicated scientist and family man who had been so highly regarded by his colleagues and neighbors.

Born in Taiwan in 1939, Lee earned his degree in engineering from Taiwan Provincial Cheng Kung University in 1963. In the spring of 1965, he enrolled at Texas A&M University, where he obtained his M.A. degree in mechanical engineering in 1966 and his doctorate in 1970. C. F. Kettleborough, one of Lee's professors there, remembered him as "a pretty good hard worker." In 1978 Lee and his wife joined the staff at the Los Alamos National Laboratory. The Lees prospered in New Mexico, sending their two children to college and acquiring two houses on the outskirts of Albuquerque just as investments.

Lee gradually worked his way into increasingly sensitive areas of nuclear-weapons research. In the late 1980s he was assigned to a team studying nuclear triggering mechanisms. A colleague from that period told a reporter, "He was a classic staff scientist, not in management, quietly working away." Another nuclear weapons scientist described him this way: "Lee was a behind-the-barn scientist [who was] never interfacing with the public or the government."

Had he read it in a newspaper, Lee might have pondered the bitter irony of that assessment as he now faced a life in prison as the most famous suspect in a nuclear weapons case since Ethel and Julius Rosenberg were tried, convicted, and executed for passing atomic bomb secrets to the Soviets in the early 1950s.

In contrast to the juggernaut of evidence and political pressure that sealed the fate of the Rosenbergs, however, the wheels were already coming off the case against Lee during the summer of 2000. In July the judge ruled that the defense could use sensitive information in making its case in court, a decision that gave prosecutors pause about the costs and benefits of parading such data in a public forum. And the judge permitted Lee's attorneys to gain access to FBI documents that might reveal whether he had been the target of racial profiling.

The final blow to the government's case came the following month, when FBI agent Messmer acknowledged making misleading statements at Lee's bail hearing that helped to secure the scientist's prolonged pretrial confinement. Judge Parker, already disinclined to believe that Lee had downloaded any truly secret information, was now at his wit's end and would likely have proved a most unfriendly jurist to the prosecution. The Justice Department then worked out an agreement with Lee's attorney's in which 58 of the 59 felony counts of the indictment would be dropped and announced the deal on September 10. As part of the bargain, Lee pled guilty to a single count of mishandling federal defense information and was sentenced to time already served.

As of late December 2000, the Justice Department was still looking into Wen Ho Lee's past. During his FBI interrogations, Lee disclosed that in the late 1980s and early 1990s he had served as a paid consultant to a Taiwanese businessman who later underwrote Lee's month-long visit to Taiwan's leading military research center, the Chung Shan Institute of Science and Technology, which has been a center of Taiwan's efforts to develop nuclear weaponry. While there in April and May of 1998, Lee claimed, he gave lectures on unclassified computer codes and accepted a $5,000 fee, which he neglected to report in accordance with lab rules. Investigators pursued the hypothesis that Lee's purpose in downloading the voluminous information from Los Alamos was to help his homeland to develop the armed might necessary to resist incursions by China.

The case against Wen Ho Lee was thus closed—for the time being. ◆

Lee, Yuan Tseh

NOVEMBER 19, 1936– ● CHEMIST

Yuan Tseh Lee was a Chinese-born American scientist who shared the Nobel Prize for chemistry in 1986 with American Dudley Herschbach and Canadian John Polanyi. Lee earned the prize for his development of the crossed molecular beam technique for studying chemical reactions. This technique involves creating high-speed jets of molecules or atoms that collide so that some individual molecules or atoms react with each other. This method yields information about the behavior of molecules or atoms that ordinary chemical reactions cannot provide.

Yuan Tseh Lee was born in Hsinchu, Taiwan, on November 19, 1936. His father Tse Fan Lee was an accomplished artist and

1936 Lee is born in Hsinchu, Taiwan.

1959 Lee graduates from the National Taiwan University.

1965 Lee earns a doctorate in chemistry from the University of California Berkeley.

1968 Lee accepts a position as a professor at the University of Chicago.

1974 Lee returns to Berkeley as a professor.

1986 Lee wins the Nobel Prize for chemistry.

his mother Pei Tsai Lee was a schoolteacher. Lee started his early education while Taiwan was under Japanese occupation—a result of a war between China and Japan in 1894. His elementary education was disrupted during World War II while the city populace was relocated to the mountains to avoid the daily bombing by the Allies. It was not until after the war, when Taiwan was returned to China, that Lee could attend school normally as a third year student in grade school.

His elementary and secondary education then became more fun. In elementary school, he became the second baseman on the school's baseball team as well as a member of the ping-pong team, which won a national championship. In high school, Lee played on the tennis team and played trombone in the marching band.

Lee also read a wide variety of books covering science, literature, and social science. The biography of Madame Curie made a strong impact on him at a young age. It was Madame Curie's admirable life as a great human being, her dedication toward science, and her selflessness that made him decide to be a scientist.

In 1955, with his excellent academic performance in high school, Lee was admitted to the National Taiwan University without having to take the entrance examination. By the end of his freshman year, he had decided chemistry was to be his chosen field. Although the facilities in the Taiwan University were less than ideal, the free and exciting atmosphere, the dedication of some professors, and the camaraderie among fellow students made up for it. He worked under Professor Hua-sheng Cheng on his bachelor of science thesis on the separation of the chemical element strontium and the element barium using the paper electrophoresis method.

After graduation in 1959, Lee went on to the National Tsing Hua University to do his graduate work. He received his master's degree on the studies of the natural radioisotopes contained in Hukutolite, a mineral of hot spring sediment under Professor H. Hamaguchi's guidance. Lee stayed on at Tsing Hua University as a research assistant of Professor C. H. Wong and carried out the x-ray structure determination of tricyclopentadienyl samarium.

Lee moved to the United States, and he entered the University of California at Berkeley as a graduate student in 1962. He worked under Professor Bruce Mahan for his thesis research on chemiionization processes of electronically excited alkali atoms. During his graduate student years, Lee developed an interest in ion-molecule reactions and the dynamics of molecular scattering, especially the crossed molecular beam studies of reaction dynamics.

Lee also studied chemistry under Dudley Herschbach at Berkeley. Upon receiving his Ph.D. degree in 1965, he stayed on in Mahan's group and started to work on ion beams. An **ion** is an atom that is charged because it has gained or lost electrons. Ions can be accelerated by electric fields to form high-speed beams of particles.

ion a charged atom that has either gained or lost electrons.

Lee worked on ion molecule reactive scattering experiments with Ron Gentry using ion beam techniques measuring energy and angular distributions. In a period of about a year he learned the art of designing and constructing a very powerful scattering apparatus and carried out successful experiments on a selection of chemicals. He obtained a complete product distribution contour map, a remarkable accomplishment at that time.

In February 1967, Lee joined Herschbach at Harvard University as a post-doctoral fellow. He spent half his time working with Robert Gordon on the reactions of hydrogen atoms and diatomic alkali molecules and the other half of his time on the construction of a universal crossed molecular beams apparatus with Doug McDonald and Pierre LeBreton. Time was certainly ripe to move the crossed molecular beams method beyond the alkali age. With tremendous effort and valuable assistance from the machine shop foreman, George Pisiello, the machine was completed in ten months and the first successful non alkali neutral beam experiment on selected chemicals was carried out in late 1967.

Lee accepted the position as an assistant professor in the Department of Chemistry and the James Franck Institute of the University of Chicago in October 1968. There he started an illustrious academic career. His further development as a creative scientist and his construction of a new generation state-of-the-art crossed molecular beams apparatus enabled him to carry out numerous exciting and pioneering experiments with his students. He was promoted to associate professor in October 1971 and professor in January 1973.

In 1974, Lee returned to Berkeley as professor of chemistry and principal investigator at the Lawrence Berkeley Laboratory of the University of California. He became an American citizen the same year.

In the ensuing years, his scientific efforts blossomed and the scope expanded. His world-leading laboratory contained seven very sophisticated molecular beams apparati that were specially designed to pursue problems associated with reaction dynamics, photochemical processes, and molecular **spectroscopy**. His laboratory consistently attracted bright scientists from all over the world. Lee took great pride in the fact that more than 15 of his former associates went on to serve as professors in major universities, and many others to make great contributions at the national laboratories and in the private sector.

spectroscopy the production and investigation of a spectra.

In 1986, Lee shared the Nobel Prize for chemistry with Herschbach and John Polanyi. Also that year, Lee received the Debye award of the American Chemical Society.

Lee and his wife, Bernice Wu Lee, whom he first met in elementary school, had two sons, Ted (born in 1963), Sidney (born in 1966), and a daughter, Charlotte (born in 1969). ◆

Lim, Shirley Geok-lin

DECEMBER 27, 1944– ● AUTHOR

Shirley Geok-lin Lim was born December 27, 1944, in Malacca, Malaysia. Her father, Chin Som, a petition writer, married Chye Neo Ang, who became Lim's mother and the family homemaker. In the tropical British colony of Malaysia, Lim grew up speaking three languages: English, Malay, and Hokkien. She developed a love of English and used that as her primary writing language.

Lim studied at the University of Malaya, where she earned a bachelor's degree with honors, in 1967 and studied at the graduate level until 1969. Lim immigrated to the United States in 1969. She earned a master of fine arts degree from Brandeis University in Massachusetts in 1971 and a doctorate in 1973. She married Charles Bazerman, a professor, in 1972. The couple had a son, Gershom Kean.

Lim taught classes at the college level beginning at the University of Malaya and then Queens College of the City University of New York, in Flushing. From 1976 to 1990, she was an associate professor at Westchester Community College of the State University of New York, Valhalla. Finally, she settled at the University of California, Santa Barbara, becoming professor of Asian American studies and English in 1990.

Lim published a great variety or works, including poetry, short fiction, criticism, autobiographical essays, and a novel. She wrote from the unique perspective of being an Asian woman as well as a Westerner.

Lim's career as a writer was helped greatly by a number of prestigious prizes. She won a Fulbright scholarship from 1969 to 1972 and grants from the National Endowment for the Humanities in 1978 and 1987. After a number of other poetry and other writing prizes, Lim won the American Book Award in 1989 for *The Forbidden Stitch*. The first Asian American women's anthology published in the United States, *The Forbidden Stitch* included the work of writers Chitra Divakaruni, Diana Chang, Jessica Hagedorn, Marilyn Chin, Nelllie Wong, Mitsuye Yamada, among its 80 contributors. It also included an extensive bibliography of Asian American women's work.

Lim's other works include her own poetry, essays, and short fiction—some of which is included in other collections and some in her own books. She also edited several collections of works by others. Her work includes: *Crossing the Peninsula and Other Poems* (1980); *Another Country and Other Stories* (1982); *No Man's Grove and Other Poems* (1985); *Modern Secrets: New and Selected Poems* (1989); *Reading the Literatures of Asian America (Asian American History and Culture)* (1992); *Approaches to Teaching Kingston's the Woman Warrior (Approaches to Teaching World Literature, No. 39)* (1992); *One World of Literature* (1992); *Nationalism and Literature: English-Language Writing From the Philippines and Singapore* (1994); *Monsoon History: Selected Poems* (1995); *Among the White Moon Faces: An Asian-American Memoir of Homelands (Cross-Cultural Memoir Series)* (1996); *Two Dreams: New and Selected Stories* (1997); *What the Fortune Teller Didn't Say* (1998); *Power, Race, and Gender in Academe: Strangers in the Tower?* (Editor, 1999); *Asian-American Literature: An Anthology* (1999); *Tilting the Continent: Southeast Asian American Writing* (Editor, 2000); *Transnational Asia Pacific: Gender, Culture, and the Public Sphere* (Editor, 2000).

In 1996, Lim published *Life's Mysteries: The Best of Shirley Lim*, a collection of short stories. After writing short stories about the paradoxes inherent in Southeast Asian and Asian-American life for almost 30 years, this collection presented a selection dating from 1967 to 1990.

"Rarely does Lim draw conclusions or point to any moral. There's little elaborate characterization and no melodrama in these tales, and the effect is consequently reserved and cool. This may sound harsh, but many of these stories are likely to appeal more to those who, like the author, have the double experience of Southeast Asian and Western life, than to the ordinary international reader." Bradley Winterton, review of *Life's Mysteries: The Best of Shirley Lim*, in the *Far Eastern Economic Review*, 1996

1944 ▸ Lim is born in Malacca, Malaysia.

1973 ▸ Lim earns her Ph.D. from Brandeis University.

1989 ▸ Lim wins the National Book Award for *The Forbidden Stitch*.

1996 ▸ Lim publishes *Life's Mysteries: The Best of Shirley Lim*, a collection of short stories.

The perceptive and carefully crafted stories were mainly about and narrated by women. Even in the abundance of female Asian-American writing, Lim stood out, both for her seriousness and for her commitment to her past. In "The Bridge," rational Western values are set into conflict with the ancestor-pleasing, spirit-placating world of old Malacca, Lim's birthplace. The opposition is presented through the vehicle of a teenager caught between these two worlds, her traditional family on the one hand, her Western-style school with its English headmaster on the other.

Lim creates a similar balancing act in "The Touring Company." A young woman studying Shakespeare's *A Midsummer Night's Dream* remembers acting the part of a fairy in a production by a touring company at school when she was 10 years old. The two experiences, the analytic and the magical, fuse in her thoughts about love and her relationship with a boyfriend.

In "Another Country," a striking story about the experiences of a hospital patient, illusion is balanced with reality—the illusion of how people appear and the reality of how they are. In "All My Uncles," memories from childhood are transformed into a plain, semitransparent art. A piece of childhood recollection, the final effect is of the Peranakan traditions of Peninsular Malaysia in conflict with the skeptical regard of a Westernized mind scrutinizing life so far away from an American academy.

The blend of Asian and Western is reflected in so many of Lim's tales, and it is not accidental. "Much of my writing life is composed of negotiating multiple entities, multiple societies, multiple desires, and multiple genres," said Lim in an interview with *Contemporary Authors*. ◆

Lin, Maya

OCTOBER 5, 1959– ● ARTIST

aesthetic having a particular sensitivity and affection for a particular art.

Having achieved world fame at 21 with her controversial design for the Vietnam Veterans Memorial in Washington, D.C., Maya Lin has been trying ever since to recede into the modest repute of a serious architect and sculptor who is celebrated for the **aesthetic** worth of her work rather than the volume of the controversy it engenders. She once told a reporter that she was "terrified that at twenty-one I might already have outdone myself. You really can't function as a celebrity. Entertainers are celebrities. I'm an architect, I'm an artist, I make things. I just love the fact that I can make a work and put it out there and walk away from it and then look at it like everybody else."

Lin was born on October 5, 1959, in the college town of Athens, Ohio, where the talents of her parents—both Chinese immigrants—coalesced into a very creative family. Her father was a ceramic artist and the dean of fine arts at Ohio University, where her mother taught literature. Maya was a precocious, solitary youth, given to working on pottery projects in her father's studio and taking long walks in the woods to brood on the **existentialist** literature she discovered in high school. Although Lin was interested in art from early childhood, she never felt any prodding to follow in her father's footsteps. She told an interviewer, "I was lucky. There was never any pressure from my parents to become anything I didn't want."

Lin retained her literary and philosophical interests as an architecture major at Yale University. Influenced by the existentialist preoccupation with death, she often wandered New Haven's Grove Street Cemetery, photographing headstones. Her fascination with mortality led her to countless European cemeteries during her junior year in Europe and into a course in **funerary** architecture in her senior year back at Yale. The professor asked each of his students to submit designs to the competition for designs for a proposed memorial to Vietnam veterans in Washington, D.C. After traveling to Washington to photograph the site, Lin settled on a conception that would blend in with the surrounding natural environment. She later commented, "You had to do something respecting the idea of opening the earth, letting the earth embrace you. The idea came simply—not as a brainstorm."

The distinguished panel of judges reviewing the roughly 1,500 submissions from around the country finally settled on Lin's design: a simple wall of polished black stone inscribed with the names of some 58,000 men and women who were killed in the war or declared missing in action. One of the judges said of Lin's conception, "It reflected the genius loci, the spirit of the place, and went beyond it to echo the national trauma arising form the Vietnam War and its aftermath. It thus became a memorable work of art in itself. And that seems to be essential in all great works of landscape architecture."

1959 Lin is born in Athens, Ohio

1980 Lin's design chosen for the Vietnam Veterans Memorial in Washington, D.C.

1995 A film on Lin's life and work wins the Academy Award as best documentary of the year.

existentialist an adherent of exitentialism, a philosophical movement that embraces various doctrines but centers on the individual existence in the unfathomable universe and the plight of individuals who must act without truly knowing what is right and wrong.

funerary associated with burial.

Not everyone agreed, however. The design triggered a howl of protest from many veterans' groups, some of which publicly vilified Lin's design as "a degrading ditch," a "wall of shame," and a "black gash." Some of the criticism was accompanied by racial and sexist slurs. The bitterness of the controversy led the panel to reevaluate all the entries, and it reaffirmed Lin's as the best.

By the time the project was finished in 1980, Lin had moved on to Harvard's graduate program in architecture. But the hailstorm of criticism left her roiled and unfocused. "I believed that this was going to help people," she told a reporter. "The only thing that really hurt me was when people said it was my ego getting in the way of letting anything change the design." Distracted from her coursework, Lin left Harvard to take a job at a Boston architectural firm in 1983. In the fall of that year, she returned to Yale as a graduate student.

Yale awarded Lin her master's degree in 1985 and her doctorate in 1987, by which time she had moved to the Lower East Side of Manhattan. That winter the Southern Poverty Law Center asked her to design a memorial to those who had died in the struggle for civil rights. Lin immersed herself in the history and iconography of the American civil rights movement. Inspired in part by the biblical imagery of the speeches of Dr. Martin Luther King, Lin designed a large, solid granite disk engraved with the names and events of the fight for racial equality. Behind the disk is a nine-foot granite wall inscribed with the following quotation from Dr. King: "We are not satisfied and we will not be satisfied until justice rolls down like water and righteousness like a mighty stream." Both pieces are covered with a thin veil of constantly running water. Visitors are attracted to the water, through which they can trace the inscriptions with their fingers.

Despite her involvement with these high-profile projects of political pedigree, Lin abjures any political intent in her work. She told an interviewer, "I would hesitate to call myself a political artist. If anything, I prefer 'apolitical.' I don't choose to overlay personal commentary upon historical facts. I'm less interested in presenting my opinion than in presenting factual information allowing the viewer the chance to come to his or her own conclusions." And that is not the only label Lin rejects— she also resists being pigeonholed as an architect: "When I was 21 years old, I was labeled 'architect' because I was an architecture student when I did the Vietnam Memorial. I want to be more of an artist who happens to build architecture. I'm not even licensed to be an architect," she laughingly told a reporter.

In the past decade Lin has demonstrated her versatility on a variety of widely praised projects: the renovation of two floors of a building to accommodate a new Museum of African Art; several private residences; a sculpture at Yale to honor the university's women, called The Women's Table; a 14-foot-long clock for New York's Pennsylvania Station; a pure earth sculpture, The Wave Field, for the University of Michigan; an installation piece for the Cleveland Public Library; and a sculpture for New York's Rockefeller Foundation. She has also designed a line of furniture for Knoll.

The subject of a 1995 Oscar-winning documentary, Lin divided her time between her house in Vermont and loft in New York City, where she operated her own design firm out of a modest office in an old building. ◆

Ling, Lisa

AUGUST 30, 1973– ● ACTRESS

Lisa Ling has already combined more success, fame, and world travel than most people could hope to wedge into several lifetimes. Before signing on as of the four cohosts of ABC television's popular daytime chat show *The View*, Ling has accumulated an impressive media resume as a cohost of the nationally syndicated teen magazine show *Scratch*, as a continent-hopping reporter for Channel One News, and as a documentary producer.

Ling was born on August 30, 1973, in Sacramento, California, and grew up in nearby Carmichael. Hers was an unremarkable middle-class upbringing—her father, now retired, was an aviation supervisor and her mother still runs a Taiwan-based immigration business from her home in Los Angeles. Ling's traditionalist parents disapproved of her youthful interest in broadcast journalism. But she persisted in looking for opportunities, even in high school. As Ling told a reporter, "I'm probably one of the most obnoxious and boisterous people that they have ever met so they just said, 'You know what? You can probably pull it off.'"

Ling's first foray into television journalism came at age sixteen, when she auditioned successfully for one of four hosting

1973 Ling is born in Sacramento, California.

1989 Ling, only sixteen years old, is chosen to be one of four hosts of *Scratch*, a nationally syndicated teen magazine show.

1999 Ling becomes one of the cohosts of *The View*, a daytime talk show on ABC television.

spots for *Scratch*, a youth magazine show based in Sacramento that went into national syndication after its first year on the air. She found out about the audition from her high school speech teacher. Ling's reports for Scratch enabled her to travel extensively on weekends throughout the country during her junior and senior years. In retrospect she values the experience although she regrets the amount of time it subtracted from her studies. "*Scratch* was a great experience for me," Ling has commented, "but I don't think I'll ever want to do anything like that again because it was totally entertainment based. It really difficult to learn anything of substance form a show like that. I learned to perform in front of the camera, and I was able to gain a lot of confidence from that."

Well into her third year on *Scratch*, Ling's syndicated broadcasts caught the eye of the director of Channel One, a national news show for teens that is shown in thousands of high schools and middle schools across the country. The director flew her out to New York for an audition, offered her the job, and was ready to help her move to New York when the entire operation shifted to Los Angeles, where Ling enrolled at the University of Southern California (USC) to begin her college education while working at Channel One. At the time she found it difficult to balance her professional and educational priorities. The juggling act proved impossible to sustain, and Ling dropped out of USC during her junior year.

No mere newsreader in her seven years at Channel One, Ling filed eyewitness reports from some two dozen countries— including Afghanistan, Iraq, Vietnam, Cambodia, Algeria, China, India, Iraq, and Japan—filing first-hand reports on diverse cultures and historic events such as the cocaine trade in Colombia, the threat to the Brazilian national rain forest, and the plight of the exiled Dalai Lama. In 1996 Ling joined a *Time* magazine team investigating a Russian company suspected of illegal trade in nuclear weapons, snaring the first-ever televised interview with the head of the shadowy Russian operation.

Ling's journalistic ambitions led her to undertake several documentary projects for public television, most notably an exposé of conditions in the Los Angeles County Jail, a poignant recounting of her 13-year-old cousin's struggle with liver cancer, and a four-part series on globalization—all while maintaining dean's list grades at USC.

When ABC's popular daytime show *The View*—a breezy lifestyle and celebrity-interview chatfest—began seeking a replacement host in 1999, Ling sprang at the opportunity, ready for a change from the globe-hopping demands of her job at Channel One. After a nationwide auditioning process that encompassed more than three thousand hopefuls, Ling was among the handful of finalists who qualified for an on-air audition, which in Ling's case subjected the aspiring cohost to endure a televised navel-piercing, about which Barbara Walters commented, "She thought it was wonderful. I thought it was disgusting." Walters' distaste notwithstanding, Ling got the job.

Although delighted with her network TV duties, Ling also longs for an eventual return to serious journalism. "I think that there are a lot of nice and interesting celebrities. But if I could choose, I'd want to interview Fidel Castro or Saddam Hussein or Tony Blair."

Ling lived in New York City. ◆

Liu, Lucy

DECEMBER 2, 1968– ● ACTRESS

Since making her first big splash in 1998 as scowling attorney-femme fatale Ling Woo on the Fox Television series *Ally McBeal*, Lucy Liu has gone on to scale the heights of Hollywood with her co-starring role in the 2000 feature-film version of the 1970s TV classic *Charlie's Angels* (2000).

The daughter of Chinese immigrants, Liu never dreamed of becoming a Hollywood sex goddess while growing up in Queens, New York, where she was born on December 2, 1968. "The popular girls were all blondes," she later told a reporter. "I wanted to be Barbie, and I was as opposite to Barbie as you could get." Before coming to the U.S., her parents held important jobs in China—her father was an engineer and her mother a biochemist—but their unfamiliarity with English obliged them to scuffle for sales positions in the United States. Liu did not speak a word of English until she entered kindergarten but soon found herself immersed in the language and culture of her parents' adopted homeland. Although Liu never wanted for the basics as a child, her parents worked long hours to maintain their home. As she later told a reporter, "My mom had so many jobs. I was pretty much a latchkey kid. Just come home from school and watch television." At the age of 14, Liu even found

1968 ▶ Liu is born in Queens, New York.

1998 ▶ Liu is cast as a cut-throat attorney on the Fox television series *Ally McBeal.*

1999 ▶ Liu costars with Mel Gibson in the feature film *Payback.*

2000 ▶ Liu stars in the feature-film reprise of the 1970s television series *Charlie's Angels.*

herself working part-time in a factory to help the family make ends meet.

After graduating from Stuyvesant High School in 1986, Liu moved on to New York University but found the atmosphere too "dark and sarcastic" for her taste, so she transferred to the University of Michigan, where she majored in Chinese Language and Culture while also taking some art performing arts classes. In her senior year at Michigan, Liu auditioned for a small role in a production of Alice in Wonderland but was chosen for the lead. That surprising success convinced her to have a go at making it as an actress and moved back to New York to begin the round of acting classes and auditions while working at a series of odd jobs that included secretary, aerobics instructor, and restaurant hostess.

With only one significant professional engagement to show for her time in New York—a supporting role in the Broadway drama M. *Butterfly*—Liu headed for Los Angeles in hopes of breaking into television and film. Amid another grueling treadmill of day jobs and auditions, Liu's talent began to attract some small TV roles, initially walk-ons on series such as *Beverly Hills, 90210* (1990), *NYPD Blue* (1993), *ER* (1994), and *The X-Files* (1993). In 1995 she was cast in a recurring role on *ER*: Mei-Sun Leow, an AIDS victim with a young child. Those parts led to a meatier role as an earnest college student on the short-lived sitcom Pearl in 1996. That appearance proved a springboard for Liu's first feature-film appearance, in *Jerry MacGuire* (1996).

After plodding through a series of small roles on the big screen, Liu made her breakthrough on the small screen. In 1997 Liu auditioned for the role of Nelle Porter on the hit Fox series *Ally McBeal*. Although the role went to Portia de Rossi, the writer-producer David E. Kelley was so taken with Liu's reading that he wrote a part especially for her in a subsequent episode. Audience reaction was so positive to Liu's portrayal of the menacing, scheming lawyer Ling Woo that the character became a regular on the series. As Liu commented, "I guess [Kelley] saw, you know, some kind of energy that I could bring to the Ally McBeal cast to cause a little conflict, a little trouble."

With her success on "Ally McBeal," Liu's career hit the fast track, although she risked typecasting with her role as a professional sadist in the Mel Gibson vehicle *Payback* (1999). Liu managed to step out of the sultry siren pigeonhole as a hitchhiker in *Play It to the Bone* and as the kidnapped Princess Pei Pei in Jackie Chan's western. *Shanghai Noon* (2000). Liu was intrigued by the parallels between the princess and the cold-blooded lawyer she plays on television. "What I really like is there's a strength in her character, she's not just a damsel in distress." As a student of the martial-arts discipline Kali-Eskrima-Silaxtpert, Liu was delighted to have the chance to work with the legendary Chan.

Liu's first star vehicle came in *Charlie's Angels* (2000), in which she received coequal top billing with Cameron Diaz and Drew Barrymore in the cinematic re-creation of the campy 1970s TV series about an improbably gorgeous trio of **doughty** crime fighters.

Liu relaxed off the set with a variety of creative endeavors: she dabbled on the accordion but devoted serious attention to art and photography; her mulitmedia works were shown at the Cast Iron Gallery in New York City. ◆

> *"Things are getting better in Hollywood for ethnic actors. There are more credible roles, not race-specific. It's improving."*
>
> Liu, interviewed by Jeff Hayward, Ling Woos Hollywood, *New Letter*, Aug. 25, 2000.

doughty marked by fearless resolution.

Locke, Gary

JANUARY 21, 1950– ● POLITICIAN

When Gary Locke was elected as Washington State's chief executive on November 5, 1996, he became the first Chinese-American governor in U.S. history and the first Asian American governor of a mainland state.

The second of five children, Gary Locke was born in Seattle, Washington, on January 21, 1950. His grandfather had emigrated to Washington from China but then returned to his homeland. Locke's father, James, resettled in Seattle in the late 1930s. After serving in General George Patton's 5th U.S. Armored Division in Europe during World War II, James traveled to Hong Kong, where he married and then returned with his bride to Seattle, where they opened a restaurant.

The Lockes worked punishing seven-day weeks to provide for Gary and his siblings, who grew up in a low-income housing project for World War II veterans. Despite the many hours he spent helping out in the family restaurant, Locke maintained excellent grades in school and became an Eagle Scout. In his senior year he was elected student body chairman and graduated as class valedictorian. He obtained a scholarship to Yale University, from which he graduated with a degree in political science in

Gary Locke

juris doctorate title
conferred upon
graduates of law school.

1972. Locke went on to study law at Boston University, taking his **juris doctorate** degree in 1975.

Locke spent the next several years as a deputy prosecutor in King County. In 1982 he ran successfully for the Washington State House of Representatives, where he proved an effective member of the House Judiciary and Appropriations Committees, chairing the latter in his last five years as a representative. In 1993 Locke was elected chief executive of King County, the state's largest county, and successfully tackled a complex array of problems that included expanding mass transit and limiting urban sprawl while trimming the county budget.

In 1996 he entered the Democratic gubernatorial primary and won by a handy margin against Seattle's mayor, Norm Rice. In the words of one political commentator, "Gary Locke can use the story about being a son of immigrants to connect with everybody. It tells us how wonderful we are, what a wonderful country this is. It's not a positive to talk about the history of black-white relationships. It doesn't make white voters feel good."

In the general election Locke's opponent was the staunchly conservative fundamentalist Christian Ellen Craswell, who railed against the sinfulness of homosexuality and advocated castration of sex offenders. By contrast, Locke supported full civil rights for homosexuals, legal availability of abortion, and affirmative action. Faced with this stark contrast, the voters handed the more progressive and tolerant Locke a landslide despite a barrage of negative Republican attack ads that marred the last few weeks of the contest. As the nation's first Chinese-American governor and the first Asian to head a mainland state government, Locke attracted considerable national media attention, especially after he was introduced by President Bill Clinton during the State of the Union address in 1997.

Locke was re-elected by a wide margin in 2000 despite charges by his Republican opponent, talk-show host John Carlson, that the governor lacked leadership skills. Locke won 58 percent of the vote against Carlson's 40 percent. Many political commentators pointed to Locke's record of accomplishment in education, economic development, and welfare reform as the keys to his victory.

Locke's biggest challenge as governor came not from political opponents but from the wrath of nature. On February 28, 2001, a broad swath of Washington State was rocked by an earthquake which registered 6.8 on the Richter Scale, the most severe tremblor to hit the region in 50 years. Because the quake originated along a fault that was 30 miles underground, it did not wreak the kind of death and destruction occasioned by the earthquake that hit Los Angeles in 1994. The Seattle quake did, however, inflict upwards of $2 billion in property damage in a heavily populated region that includes Seattle, the state's largest city. The quake's epicenter was Olympia, the state capital, which suffered such severe damage that the governor and hundreds of state workers were displaced from their offices in the 74-year-old state capitol building, which bore an ominous crack in its dome. Three days after the quake, the governor and his staff were still operating out of the Emergency Operation Center.

Governor Locke married Mona Lee Locke, a former television news reporter in Seattle. They had two children: Nicole, born on March 9, 1997, and Dylan James, born on March 13, 1999. ◆

1950 Locke is born in Seattle, Washington.

1972 Locke graduates from Yale University with a BA in political science.

1975 Locke takes his law degree from Boston University.

1982 Locke is elected to Washington State House.

1993 Locke is elected chief executive of King County, Washington.

1996 Locke is elected governor of Washington state.

2000 Locke is re-elected governor of Washington state.

Ma, Yo-Yo

OCTOBER 7, 1955– ● MUSICIAN

With a radiant smile and effortless charm to complement his stunning virtuosity, the cellist Yo-Yo Ma is among that rare breed of classical musicians who have burst the narrow confines of serious-music connoisseurship to command an admiring audience among the general public. As one critic put it, "The entire music world seems to adore Yo-Yo Ma, his cello playing, his boyishly buoyant presence, and his ability to suggest that a well-integrated personality need not preclude a questing artistic spirit."

Ma's distinguished musicianship is a family heritage—his father was a distinguished violinist, composer, and scholar, and his mother an opera singer. The younger of two children, Ma was born on October 7, 1955, in Paris, his father's home since the 1930s, when he emigrated from Shanghai. Both Yo-Yo and his older sister were first-handed violins, but the younger sibling sought to assert his individuality with a larger instrument and thus hearkened to the cello, which he began playing at the age of four thanks to his father's ingenuity. He fashioned a mini-cello by attaching an end pin to a viola. Under his father's patient guidance, Yo-Yo began by memorizing two measures of a Bach cello suite each

Yo Yo Ma performing.

197

1955 ▶ Ma is born in Paris, France.

1978 ▶ Ma wins Avery Fisher Prize.

1984 ▶ Ma wins the first of many Grammy awards.

1999 ▶ Ma collaborates on composition and performance of score of Oscar-winning film *Crouching Tiger, Hidden Dragon*.

etudes pieces of music used for the practice of technique.

day, an assignment he mastered with such ease that by the age of five he had memorized three Bach cello suites. A year later, he played one of those suites at his first public performance, at the University of Paris.

In 1962 the Ma family moved to New York City, where Yo-Yo's father had accepted a job teaching musically gifted children. It was at Mr. Ma's school that the renowned violinist Isaac Stern—whose child was one of Mr. Ma's students—first heard Yo-Yo's precocious mastery of the cello. Stern immediately referred him to Leonard Rose, an esteemed cellist who taught at the prestigious Juilliard School. Ma's prodigal gifts also dazzled the legendary Pablo Casals, whose raves led to Ma's first appearance on national television as a featured artist on Leonard Bernstein's American Pageant of the Performing Arts in 1963.

At the age of nine—when he debuted at Carnegie Hall—Ma began his studies with Leonard Rose and Janos Scholz, who remained Yo-Yo's teachers for the next seven years. Rose later said of his pupil, "By the time Yo-Yo was 11 or 12, I had already taken him through the most difficult **etudes**. He may have one of the greatest techniques of all time. I'm always floored by it."

Yo-Yo attended high school at the Professional Children's School in New York City, from which he graduated at the age of fifteen. He then entered the college program of the Juilliard School but transferred to Columbia University the following year. Ma's dissatisfaction with Columbia's program led him to transfer yet again, this time to Harvard University, where he explored music history and theory. Ma credits his theory teacher, Luise Vosgerchian, with helping him to mesh his formidable intellect with his musical instincts, which he honed with frequent performances at Harvard and environs.

Ma began performing in earnest after graduating from Harvard, giving more than a hundred performances in his first year. Ma's blossoming reputation crested in 1978, when he was awarded the coveted Avery Fisher Prize, which brought him the opportunity to appear with the New York Philharmonic, the Chamber Music Society of Lincoln Center, and other major U.S. orchestras. He has since appeared with some of the world's leading ensembles, including the Chicago Symphony, the Pittsburgh Symphony, the Los Angeles Philharmonic, the Boston Orchestra, the Philadelphia Orchestra, the Royal Philharmonic, the English Chamber Orchestra, the Berlin Philharmonic, the Orchestre National de France, the Vienna Philharmonic, and the Israel Philharmonic. On the concert stage Ma has been a featured collaborator with many of the stars of the classical music world, including Itzhak Perlman and James Levine, whom he joined for a special PBS performance of Mendelssohn's Sonata in D Minor; the violinist Young-Uck Kim, with whom he played in the "Isaac Stern and Friends" series at Carnegie Hall and the Kennedy Center; and his own series of concerts, "Yo-Yo Ma and Friends," a popular attraction at New York's Alice Tully Hall.

Ma's recorded output has been no less impressive. Since his first Grammy Award, which he received in 1984 for Bach: Suites for Unaccompanied Cello, Ma has won Grammys for his 1985 renditions of concertos by Elgar and Brahms and his sonatas with Emmanuel Ax; his 1989 collaboration with the Baltimore Symphony; a 1993 pairing with Ax; and for his 1998 CD "Premiers: Cello Concertos." In 1997 Ma was named Artist of the Year in the annual awards conferred by *Gramophone* magazine, which declared, "In a year of quite extraordinary diversity, the cellist Yo-Yo Ma has shown that the boundaries of 'classical' music need not be as restraining as he has vaulted spectacularly from classical cello concertos to bluegrass music via a disc of tangos to a host of specially composed works featuring his remarkable talent. . . . With Ma, there is only one category of music—the kind he wants to make." Ma's defiance of conventional musical boundaries is evident in such diverse projects as his 1999 CD "Soul of Tango," a 1999 recording of traditional American fiddle music ("Appalachia Waltz"), and his collaboration with composer Tan Dun on the original score for the Oscar-nominated film *Crouching Tiger, Hidden Dragon*.

Ma's devotion to the classical **repertoire** has proved compatible with a lively interest in new directions for serious music. He has been an enthusiastic supporter of a computer-cello hybrid called the hypercello.

Ma and his wife, Jill, lived with their two children, Nicholas and Emily, in Winchester, Massachusetts. ◆

> *"By the time you go on the stage, you already know everything that you know. You have to be free enough to say, 'O.K., my mind's a blank, I'm not going to make any decisions' and then go on. That, for a classical musician, is the scariest thing."*
> Ma quoted in The Economist, February 15, 1992.

repertoire a supply of skills of an individual performer.

Matsui, Robert T.

SEPTEMBER 17, 1941– ● POLITICIAN

His two-decade tenure on the pivotal Ways and Means committee of House of Representatives explains a good deal of Robert Matsui's exceptional influence in the Congress. He has also helped to shape policy in important

Robert Matsui

pittance a small amount
or portion.

legislation in areas as diverse as public health, social security, tax policy,
and international trade.

The Sacramento native was born
Robert Tadeo Matsui on September
17, 1941. His father, Yasjui, ran a
small produce business, but after the
outbreak of World War II had to sell
the family house and his business for
a **pittance** when Mr. and Mrs. Matsui, who were born in America, were
rounded up along with thousands of
others Californians of Japanese descent and herded into detention
camps for the duration of the war.
Matsui was so young that he retained
few memories of the three-and-a-
half-year incarceration, but the experience was a crushing blow to his
parents. As Robert later told an interviewer, "I remember how shame-
ful I felt sitting in a classroom and
having the teacher point to me and ask if I was one of those
who had been in the camps. The implication was that I had
done something wrong."

As the Matsuis tried to piece together their shattered lives
after the war, young Robert harbored dreams of following in
the footsteps of the celebrated lawyer Clarence Darrow, who
made his reputation fighting for prominent progressive causes.
Matsui entered the University of California at Berkeley in
1959 and during his college years found himself inspired by the
spirit of youthful idealism that pervaded the country during the
John F. Kennedy administration. After graduating with a degree in political science in 1964, Matsui enrolled in the Hastings College of Law, from which he earned a juris doctorate in
1967.

Later that year Matsui went into private law practice in
Sacramento, just getting by on the referrals he garnered from
local friends and family. When a redistricting plan created a
vulnerable seat on the Sacramento City Council in 1971, Matsui entered the race and was elected by an impressive margin,
garnering 54 percent of the vote in a field of nine candidates.
The following year Matsui shored up his political credentials by

chairing the reelection campaign of Congressman John E. Moss, a job he handled so effectively that Moss brought him back to chair his next two campaigns as well. Meanwhile Matsui had been re-elected to the City Council in 1975 and became vice mayor in 1977. The following year Moss announced his retirement from Congress, and Matsui leaped into the fray, easily overtaking two better-known opponents in the primary and gliding to an easy victory in the general election.

Assigned to the Judiciary Committee in his first term, Matsui campaigned actively for his first choice, the Commerce Committee, and was invited onto that panel six months into his first term. Matsui's interest in commerce reflects his overall political profile, which is liberal on social issues but centrist-to-conservative on economic policy, an outlook that serves him well among his **constituents,** who, since 1992, have awarded majorities to Republican presidential candidates despite the slight majority of registered Democrats in the district.

Matsui joined the powerful Ways and Means Committee in his second term and there he remains to this day, having since become the committee's ranking Democrat on international trade police, in which capacity he has been a persistent defender of free trade, defending **NAFTA** and the **WTO** against labor-backed opposition within the ranks of the Democrats. He is also the ranking member of the Subcommittee on Human Resources, which plays an important role in shaping the nation's social policy.

As the representative of a state whose economy is heavily bound up with defense contractors, Matsui has unsurprisingly been a champion of robust military expenditures, although he did vote against funding for the MX missile system in the mid-1980s, was a vocal opponent of the Reagan administration's interventionist policies in Central America, and voted against U.S. participation in the 1991 Gulf War.

Matsui's **fealty** to the Democrats' liberal social agenda was reflected in several key votes throughout the past 20 years: his 1982 vote to siphon some $5 billion from the military budget to shore up the Medicare program; his support for the ill-fated Equal Rights Amendment to the Constitution; his support for two-thirds overrides of several of President Reagan's vetoes of civil rights legislation; his support for sanctions to speed the end of **apartheid** in South Africa; and his vigorous support for the Family and Medical Leave act, signed into law by President Clinton.

1941 Matsui is born in Sacramento, California.

1964 Matsui graduates with BA from the University of California, Berkeley.

1967 Matsui takes his law degree from Hastings College of Law.

1971 Matsui wins a seat on the Sacramento City Council.

1978 Matsui is elected to the United States House of Representatives.

NAFTA North American Free Trade Agreement; a treaty involving the United States, Mexico, and Canada.
WTO World Trade Organization.

fealty fidelity; obligation.

apartheid an official policy of segregation and inequality against non-European groups in South Africa.

For the past eight years, with the unaccustomed luxury of a fellow Democrat in the White House, Matsui worked effectively on helping to pass key elements of the Clinton legislative agenda: the economic-stimulus/deficit-reduction package to which Democrats attribute the booming economy of the 1990s; the North American Free Trade Agreement; fast-track negotiating authority for the president on trade agreements; and Permanent Normal Trade Relations for China.

In recognition of his decades of legislative skill, Matsui was showered with numerous accolades: the 1989 Chubb Fellowship from Yale University; Claremont College's outstanding legislator award in 1990, 1992, and 1994; the Excellence in Public Service Award from the American Academy of Pediatrics in 1992; and the Small Business Council Congressional Award in 1988.

Congressman Matsui lived in Sacramento with his wife, Doris, and their son, Brian. Doris Matsui was the Director of Government Relations at the law firm of Collier, Shannon, & Scott. ◆

Matsunaga, Spark

OCTOBER 8, 1916–1990 ● POLITICIAN

Spark Matsunaga was born Masayuki Matsunaga on October 8, 1916, on Kauai Island, in Hawaii, to parents of Japanese descent. As a schoolboy attending the public schools on Kauai he acquired the nickname of "Spark"; he liked it so well that he made it his legal name when he became an adult. Matsunaga was a good student, impressing his teachers in elementary and high school with his hard work. He was initially drawn to the teaching profession, and upon graduating from Kauai High School in 1937 he went on to attend the University of Hawaii, where he received his degree in education in 1941.

Matsunaga combined his educational pursuits with a commitment to fulfilling his obligations as a citizen, and so along with his regular course work he also served in the University of Hawaii's Reserve Officer Training Corps (ROTC). A part of his ROTC obligation was to assume a commission in the military after receiving his diploma. In June of 1941, therefore, Sparks fulfilled this obligation by accepting an army posting that sent him to the Hawaiian island of Molokai. Like all members of the armed forces at that time, he was extremely aware of the conflict in Europe, where Hitler was achieving early successes against his neighboring countries. The United States, however, had not yet resolved to enter the European conflict, and Matsunaga's outfit was on peacetime status for the next several months. All this would change, and change dramatically, on the morning of December 7, 1941, with Japan's surprise attack on Pearl Harbor.

Japan's attack raised great suspicions among white Americans about the loyalty of American citizens of Asian descent. This distrust was particularly strong on the West Coast and in Hawaii, and Japanese-Americans in particular were looked upon as potential traitors. Hundreds of thousands of Japanese Americans were rounded up and placed in interment camps where they could be efficiently monitored. Many lost their homes, farms, and businesses in the process. This decision was grossly unfair, for there was no evidence of treasonable behavior to justify it, and throughout the years of World War II, no other ethnic group was treated this way; neither German Americans nor Italian Americans were similarly rounded up, although their nations of origin were equally at war with the United States and its allies.

Like their civilian counterparts, Japanese-Americans in the military found that their loyalty was suspected; they were removed from their units while the War Department decided what to do with them. Matsunaga was taken from Molokai and stationed instead at Fort McCoy, Wisconsin. Matsunaga, and many other Japanese-American servicemen, petitioned then-president Franklin D. Roosevelt for the opportunity to prove their loyalty and to serve their country as they had been trained to do. In 1942, their efforts were finally successful, and Roosevelt permitted 1,500 Japanese-American soldiers to form the 100th Infantry Battalion; Matsunaga was selected for this unit and began training for combat duty.

The 100th Infantry Battalion saw action in France and in Italy. Matsunaga served with bravery, as did many of his fellow soldiers in the battalion. Wounded twice in combat, Matsunaga was honored with two Purple Hearts, along with a Bronze Star for courage in battle. When his injuries made it impossible to return to the battlefield, Matsunaga returned home to the United States and began a career on the lecture circuit, speaking tirelessly of the loyalty of Japanese-Americans and protesting the

1916 Matsunaga is born on Kaui Island, Hawaii.

1941 Matsunaga and other Japanese American military personnel are removed from active duty after Pearl Harbor is attacked.

1942 Matsunaga joins the 100th Infantry Battalion, the first all Japanese-American unit in the U.S. Army.

1954 Matsunaga runs for his first public office, a seat on the Territorial Legislature for Hawaii.

1962 Matsunaga wins his first federal office, U.S. Representative for the state of Hawaii.

1976 Matsunaga wins his first election to U.S. Senate.

1990 Matsunaga dies in Honolulu, while still serving as U.S. Senator for Hawaii.

Spark M. Matsunaga Institute for Peace

In 1986, in recognition of his lifelong commitment to the cause of peace, the University of Hawaii's board of regents dedicated its newly formed Institute for Peace to Senator Spark M. Matsunaga, the state's first federal-level elected official of Japanese descent. Today, the Spark M. Matsunaga Institute for Peace carries on its mandate to promote nonviolent conflict resolution and compassionate engagement between nations. The Institute seeks to achieve its goals through classes, seminars, research, publications, and lectures. Its founders recognize that a peaceful world cannot come about without active efforts to understand and reduce the roots of conflict.

The Institute had its origins in a 1984 international conference of university presidents. There, University of Hawaii's president, Albert Simone, was inspired by a talk urging conference attendees to take the lead in helping to rid the world of war through teaching peace-making and peace-keeping skills. Fired with enthusiasm for the task, Simone returned to his university to enlist the support of faculty and alumni, and two years later the new Institute was opened. In naming the new research center after Senator Matsunaga, the university had chosen a fitting representative of its principles, for the senator had spent many years actively working toward the establishment of a national Institute of Peace in Washington, D.C., and had devoted his life to promoting compassion, tolerance, and cooperation across the wide range of diversity that makes up American society.

internment camps in which many Japanese-Americans were still being held.

Matsunaga's commitment to fair treatment for Japanese Americans became a lifetime crusade, but it was not his only contribution to American life. He returned to Hawaii in 1946, where he became briefly active in veterans' affairs. In that same year he met and married his wife, Helene, and when his military service was fulfilled he decided to return to college, entering Harvard Law School in 1948.

Matsunaga opened a law practice in Hawaii upon graduation, but at the same time he took the first steps toward entering politics. Running as a Democrat, in 1954 he was elected as a representative in the Territorial Legislature, and became a leader of the movement that would ultimately win statehood for Hawaii in 1959.

In 1962, Matsunaga set his sights on higher public office, and ran for a seat in the United States House of Representatives. He became an outspoken champion of veterans' issues, and was particularly vocal on the subject of minority rights, advocating not only for Japanese-Americans but for all minority groups in American society. He moved on from the House to a seat in the U.S. Senate in 1976, where he was instrumental in establishing the United States Peace Institute, which would eventually be renamed in his honor.

While Matsunaga is closely associated with his work on behalf of minority groups and in particular as an advocate of the Japanese-American community, his interests were broader than that. He strongly supported legislation to protect the environment, particularly laws supporting the use of renewable energy sources, and in 1990 he succeeded in getting Congress to pass the Matsunaga Hydrogen Research and Development Act. He was also a strong supporter of the space program, particularly advocating cooperative research and exploration involving the U.S. and the Soviet Union.

Matsunaga's experiences during the early years of World War II made him particularly sensitive to injustices against Japanese-Americans, especially those who had been interned in the detainment camps of the war years. As a senator, he was finally in a position to pursue this issue at the legislative level. In the 1980s he successfully argued for compensation for survivors of the camps and, perhaps more significantly, elicited a public acknowledgement and apology from then-president, Ronald Reagan.

Senator Matsunaga died in office in 1990. His last official act as a senator revisited his environmentalist concerns, when he cast his vote in favor of renewing the Clean Air Act in 1990. In recognition of his years of public service and his commitment to peace, the University of Hawaii established the Spark M. Matsunaga Institute for Peace, dedicated to scholarship that explores nonviolent conflict resolution. In the years since his death, his wife and children have continued his legacy of public service, and his son Matthew (the youngest of five children) followed in his father's footsteps by pursuing a political career of his own; in 1992 he was elected to his first term as a state senator for Hawaii. ◆

> *"Throughout his career Sparky worked to ensure that all Americans enjoyed the fruits of liberty and understood our shared responsibilities for keeping our country free and strong."*
> U.S. Senator Daniel Akaka, 1998, in *Honolulu Star Bulletin*.

Mehta, Zubin

APRIL 29, 1936– ● CONDUCTOR

Zubin Mehta was born in Bombay, India, on April 29, 1936, on the first anniversary of the founding of the Bombay Symphony by his father, the celebrated violinist,

Zubin Mehta,
conducting.

Mehli Mehta. His family is Parsee, descendants of the Zoroastrians who fled from Persia to India in about 600 A.D. to escape
their homeland's conquest by Muslims.

Mehta received his first musical training at an early age, beginning his studies of violin and piano at the age of seven. He
also began training as a conductor, and by the age of 16 he led
his first symphony orchestra for a benefit concert performance
by the Bombay Symphony. The concert, held in 1952, was dedicated to the memory of those who died in the Hungarian Revolution. This alliance of art to politics and to humanitarian
issues has become a characteristic theme of Mehta's entire professional career.

In college, Mehta pursued a medical degree. Music always
came first for him, however, and at the age of 18 he enrolled in
The Vienna Music Academy. The Academy's orchestra had no
need for his violin or piano skills, so in order to join the symphony he mastered playing the double bass. At the Academy,
Mehta trained under one of the most highly regarded conductors of the time, Hans Sworowsky of the Vienna State Opera,
and further enhanced his understanding of his art through frequent visits to the Viennese opera and concert halls.

Upon graduation from the Vienna Academy in 1958, Mehta had his professional debut with the Vienna Philharmonic. In that same year he entered an international conducting competition held in Liverpool, England. Upon winning first prize, he became guest conductor of the Royal Liverpool Philharmonic for a year. He followed this success by returning to the Vienna Philharmonic as guest conductor.

The year 1961 brought several important events for Mehta. The now 25-year-old conductor returned to England once again, to make his London debut. This occasion was an important first for the Indian-born conductor, for it was the first time an artist from any of the former English colonies ever appeared with a major British orchestra. In the same year, Mehta also moved permanently to the United States, establishing a home in Los Angeles, California. In addition, Mehta traveled to Israel to serve as guest conductor for the Israel Philharmonic Orchestra. This began what would become a lifelong association between the conductor and the Israeli Philharmonic, although he would not be formally appointed as its musical director until 1977. This year also marked the beginning of a six year appointment as conductor of the Montreal Symphony (1961-1967).

With Los Angeles as his home base, Mehta continued to build his international reputation. He accepted the post of conductor for the Los Angeles Philharmonic, where he served from 1962 through 1978, the first five years dividing his time between the California coast and Montreal. This double appointment marked two new firsts: Mehta was the first conductor ever to lead two major North American Symphonies simultaneously, and the youngest conductor ever appointed to lead the Los Angeles Philharmonic.

While leading the Montreal Symphony, Mehta met and ultimately married Carmen Lasky, a Canadian opera singer. The 1960s were a busy decade, as Mehta toured with his two orchestras and guest conducted with many of the world's leading symphonies. In 1964 he debuted as conductor of an opera, presenting a performance of *Tosca* at Montreal. In the following year he conducted *Aida* at the Metropolitan Opera in New York City. Throughout the decade he maintained his close connection with the Israel Philharmonic as well, and in 1967 even broke off a Metropolitan Opera tour in order to race back to Israel to lead his beloved IPO during the Six-Day War.

This commitment came as no surprise to those in the music world who knew Mehta well. From his very first days with the

1936 Mehta is born in Bombay, India.

1952 Mehta performs in public for the first time, conducting the Bombay Symphony Orchestra.

1961 Mehta becomes a permanent resident of the United States and begins his lifelong association with the Israeli Philharmonic Orchestra (IPO).

1981 Mehta becomes the IPO's musical director for life.

1990 Mehta conducts the first of the wildly popular "Three Tenors" concerts for American public television.

2000 Mehta receives the Padma Vibhushan, India's second highest civilian award.

Throughout the 1980s and 1990s Mehta continued his heavy schedule of touring and performing.

IPO he had strongly identified with both the orchestra and with Israel. From the start he was committed to take the small, undeveloped orchestra and build it into a world class body of performers, recruiting outstanding talents from Israel and, as time went on, from Jewish performers throughout the Soviet Union as well. The IPO has always had a reputation for performing in times of national crisis, performing nightly during the 1973 Yom Kippur War and during the Gulf War when Iraqi missiles fell on Israel in 1991, driving the populace into bomb shelters.

As the 1960s ended, Mehta's political commitments led him to once again imbue his professional life with his principles. Strongly against the war in Vietnam, Mehta called on his musician colleagues to form volunteer orchestras, which he took on tour throughout the United States to perform at anti-war concerts on college campuses. His interest in music outside of the classical tradition led him into a film collaboration with the legendary Frank Zappa, with whom he worked on Zappa's independent film *200 Motels*, a documentary-style film about life on tour in England which featured appearances by such pop luminaries of the day as Ringo Starr and Keith Moon.

The late 1960s saw another important change in Mehta's personal life. He had met actress Nancy Kovack, who is perhaps best known for her television appearances on such 1960s hits as "Star Trek," "Batman," "Voyage to the Bottom of the Sea," and "The Man From U.N.C.L.E." In late 1969 Mehta divorced his first wife to marry Kovack. Through his second wife he found himself marginally involved in the Whitewater investigations against President Clinton during the late 1990s, when it was alleged that Linda MacDougal, in a former job as Kovack's secretary, had misappropriated money through the use of one of Mehta's credit cards.

In 1977 Mehta's long association with the IPO became formalized when he was appointed the orchestra's musical director, and in 1981 he was named its "director for life." In 1978 he was named conductor of the New York Philharmonic as well, a position he retained until 1991.

Throughout the 1980s and 1990s Mehta continued his heavy schedule of touring and performing throughout the world. In high demand as a guest conductor, he has led London's Philharmonic and New Philharmonia, the Berlin Philharmonic, and the Maggio Musicale Fiorentino, among others. He has worked with the leading lights among performers, including

Yo Yo Ma, Midori, Itzhak Perlmann, and Jessye Norman. Among the many important concerts he conducted were the 1988 joint performances by the New York Philharmonic and the Moscow State Symphony Orchestra, held in Moscow's Gorky Park, and the Sarajevo Symphony Orchestra and Chorus, which he led in a performance of Mozart's *Requiem* at the bombed-out site of the former Yugoslavia's National Library. The latter concert, telecast to 26 nations, was a benefit performance, and the proceeds were donated to the United Nations Fund for Refugees. In 1994, Mehta achieved another first, bringing the Israel Philharmonic Orchestra to perform in India.

Mehta was always highly popular with audiences for both his exuberant style and his repertoire of light romantic and early modern classics, from Mozart, Bach, and Bruckner to Bartock and Schoenberg. His expressiveness at the podium helped make the music broadly accessible, as audiences could take their cues from his gestures. In 1990 he broadened his base of fans by conducting the orchestra behind the first of the Three Tenors performances, where he showed himself to be the equal in stagecraft to Placido Domingo, Luciano Pavarotti, and Jose Carreras.

Mehta showed no sign of slowing down or slipping from the public eye. In recognition of his contributions to Israel's musical heritage, he was granted honorary doctorates from Hebrew University in Jerusalem, Tel Aviv University, and the Weizmann Institute. He was also the only non-Israeli to be awarded the Israel Prize. In 2000, he was honored by the government of his homeland, India, which conferred upon him the Padma Vibhushan, "Special Decoration of the Lotus," which is the second highest civilian honor offered by that nation. ◆

Merchant, Ishamel

DECEMBER 25, 1936– ● PRODUCER, DIRECTOR

Ishmael Merchant was born Ishmael Noormohamed Abdul Rehman on December 25, 1936, in Bombay, India. The son of well-to-do parents, he attended good local elementary and high schools, and earned his bachelors degree from St. Xavier's University in Bombay. After graduation he moved to the United States to attend business school, and earned a degree in business administration from New York University. He

1936 Merchant is born in Bombay, India.

1960 Merchant makes his first film, a short feature entitled *The Creation of Woman.*

1961 Merchant, as producer, forms a partnership with James Ivory, as director, creating Merchant Ivory Productions (MIP).

1963 Merchant and Ivory release their first feature film, *The Householder.*

1985 Merchant and Ivory win numerous Academy Awards for their first E.M. Forster film, *A Room with a View.*

1993 Merchant opens a restaurant in New York City and makes his feature-length film debut with *In Custody.*

fledgling one that is new or inexperienced to a particular subject or craft.

was drawn to the film industry from the start, and with his earliest work he demonstrated an extraordinary talent. His first effort, a short film that he directed and co-produced in 1960, entitled *The Creation of Woman*, won an Academy Award nomination and was submitted for the Cannes Film Festival in 1961.

This early work was of signal importance not only because it was Merchant's first film, but also because it provided the opportunity for the formation of one of the cinema's most prolific and enduring teams. While traveling to Cannes, the young Indian filmmaker met a **fledgling** California director named James Ivory, and the two struck up a friendship. A few months later they met again, when James Ivory was traveling in India on a commission for the New York Asia Society to film a documentary on the city of Delhi.

The two renewed their friendship and began talking about the possibilities of working as a partnership. Ivory's skills lay in directing, while Merchant was a gifted administrator and financial manager. Merchant came up with a novel idea. Many major film studios in the United States and Europe had large accounts of rupees that could not be converted to local currencies due to India's laws governing the conversion of its money. The only way that the studios could realize the value of the money in these accounts was to spend it in India. Merchant proposed to Ivory that the two collaborate on making English language films in India for worldwide distribution by the major studios in England and the United States. The studios would get value from their otherwise useless rupees, along with a marketable product, and Merchant and Ivory would have access to funding to make films that they believed in.

Ivory agreed to Merchant's plan, and in late 1961 the two formed Merchant Ivory Productions (MIP). They immediately set to work on their first project, a feature film entitled *The Householder*, based on a novel by a German-born author named Ruth Prawar Jhabyala. The film, released in 1963, launched the new company to critical acclaim, but while it was positively received it did not receive a broad enough distribution to make the Merchant-Ivory name familiar to most theater-goers. It did, however, help to consolidate the MIP team, as Jhabyala signed on to serve as screenwriter on future MIP productions.

The Householder explored the subject of cultures in conflict, particularly the confrontation between English and Indian ways of life as it is played out in post-colonial India. This theme was explored further in the next several films produced by Merchant and Ivory, including *Shakespeare Wallah* (1965) which follows the fortunes of a touring English repertory troupe traveling through India. The films made by Merchant and Ivory during the 1960s were admired by critics if relatively unknown by most movie-goers, and the team soon decided to explore other themes in order to try to broaden their audience appeal. In the early to mid-1970s they had a few failed efforts, including *Savages* (1972) and *The Wild Party* (1975). For the remainder of the 1970s they turned away from theatrical films and instead concentrated on projects for television.

In the 1980s, however, they returned to feature films, this time with a new thematic and stylistic focus. They decided to concentrate on bringing literary classics to the screen, convinced that there was a largely untapped audience tired of a steady diet of action-adventures and witless comedies and hungry for intelligent, thought-provoking films. They turned to 19th century British novelist E. M. Forster for inspiration, and in 1986 they released *A Room With a View*, based on Forster's novel of the same title. The film was a major success, winning the Academy Awards for Best Screenplay, Best Art Direction, and Best Costumes.

The awards brought MIP far greater media attention than they had ever before enjoyed, and suddenly the audience for their films expanded from a few art-house afficionados to a much more mainstream public. They continued to mine literature for film subjects, returning to Forster's novels to make *Howard's End* (1992) and other films, but also drawing from such writers as Tama Janowitz, whose *Slaves of New York* became an MIP film in 1989.

Merchant's role in Merchant Ivory Productions was, throughout the first decades of the company's existence, largely restricted to the production side of the enterprise, while Ivory handled the directorial duties. However, in the 1990s Merchant decided to try his hand at directing on the 1993 feature film *In Custody*. While not as successful as the earlier MIP films directed by Ivory, it showed that Merchant had not lost the skills he had last displayed back in the early 1960s. Ivory remains the primary directorial talent for MIP, but Merchant has not overruled the possibility of taking on future directorial projects.

Merchant shares a household with his business partner in the Hudson River Valley region of New York State. Although the two remain committed to their work in films, in the 1990s

Merchant began branching out into other areas of business. A gourmet cook, Merchant made it a hobby to collect and experiment with recipes, particularly of Indian foods, and in 1993 he opened up a restaurant. Although his film schedule kept him very busy, he nonetheless found time to write and publish a series of gourmet cookbooks as well. ◆

Midori (Goto)

OCTOBER 25, 1971– ● VIOLINIST

Midori Goto was born in Osaka, Japan, on October 25, 1971. A true child prodigy, her career as a violinist was more or less preordained given her family background: her mother is Setsu Goto, herself a respected professional musician. Midori would be exposed to music from the cradle, and she herself has acknowledged that she cannot remember a time when music did not form an important part of her life. When she was three years old she made it clear that she wanted to play the violin, and her mother presented her with her very first instrument. From the first, Midori seemed to have an unusual ability, and one year later her mother began giving her formal lessons. Thus far, Midori's story reads like that of many another musician, for early training on an instrument is a common trait among those who grow up to become esteemed performers.

Midori's case is unusual, however, for within a very short time it became clear that she was more than merely talented. Rather, her ability was equally matched by a sophistication of skill and a degree of discipline that was far greater than anyone could expect from one so young. Her family was the first to be aware of her extraordinary gift, but by the time she was ten years old the whole world was let in on the secret. Her talent was already impressive enough to have earned her the opportunity to study at the Julliard School of Music in New York City, which is where she was practicing when, in 1982, Zubin Mehta heard her play and signed her to perform with the New York Philharmonic Orchestra on New Year's Eve.

There was no advance announcement of her appearance, so when this very young but precociously poised young girl stepped out on the stage at Lincoln Center and began to play a

Paganini concerto, the audience was stunned into surprised silence. The concert seemed doomed to disaster; as she played, suddenly a string snapped on her violin. Cooly she began again with a replacement instrument, only to have the same thing happen again. Summoning a third, she launched once more into the Concerto, playing it flawlessly to its end. The audience, taken as much by her enormous composure as by her talent, erupted into a standing ovation.

Midori's debut propelled her to international celebrity overnight, but stardom did not come without extreme effort. Her practice schedule was grueling, even at so young an age; she was routinely practicing for six or seven hours daily. Her regimen could be extremely frustrating, playing a piece or just a fragment of a piece for hours on end, struggling to master it. Through the daily grind, it was her profound love of music that kept her going.

After her astounding debut, Midori was highly sought after as a guest performer for prestigious orchestras throughout the world. She traveled throughout the world, playing in concert halls from Europe and North America to Japan, and in 1990 she made a triumphal debut appearance at Carnegie Hall. She also signed an early recording contract, and released numerous performances on record, cassette, and CD. Her recordings, featuring works by composers as diverse as Tchaikovsky, Bartok, and Elgar, brought her into creative collaboration with many other highly talented musicians, including the pianist, Robert MacDonald, with whom she has toured many times.

Midori's youth and great stage presence made her a natural for television, and her appearances in that medium also helped to increase her popularity. She appeared on the *Tonight Show* with Johnny Carson in the early days of her career, and performed in a number of concerts televised by PBS and carried to worldwide audiences. She was a featured performer in the opening ceremonies of the 1992 Winter Olympic Games.

Midori began garnering honors and awards early in her career. In 1984 she was honored with the Suntory Hall Award, a prestigious honor sponsored by Japan's Suntory Corporation. In 1988 the Japanese government honored her as "best artist of the year," and later awarded her its Crystal Award in recognition of her many contributions to the field of performing arts. In the United States she has received the Dorothy B. Chandler Performing Arts Award, presented to her by the Los Angeles Music Center in 1990, and in the following year New York's governor,

1971 Midori Goto is born in Osaka, Japan.

1982 Midori performs in public on New Year's Eve with the New York Philharmonic.

1991 Midori receives the Asian-American Heritage Month Award from New York Governor Mario Cuomo.

1992 Midori founds Midori & Friends, a nonprofit organization to benefit education in the arts for children.

Child Prodigies

To be a child prodigy is to be more than merely "gifted." Prodigies are not only exceptionally talented or smart; they are also highly precocious, displaying an ability to use their skills in ways that are decidedly *not* childlike. Perhaps the best-known child prodigy of all time is Wolfgang Amadeus Mozart, who by the age of three had already composed extraordinarily sophisticated musical pieces and performed for the royalty of Europe.

Like Mozart, Midori is typical of child prodigies in that her area of precocious performance was music (music and mathematics are the two fields most frequently associated with prodigies). Like all child prodigies, she combined a great talent with an adult's degree of mastery and discipline, as was evident in her first concert performance in Osaka at the age of six.

When prodigies are identified, they are soon closely identified with their particular talents—it comes to define their very lives. The people around them frequently encourage them strongly to concentrate on maintaining and developing their gift, and often they come to believe that it is their precocity in performance that makes them special. Sadly, this can lead to a profound sense of alienation, as they acutely sense their difference from their peers. A further problem is frustration: they often find themselves bored by any pursuits unrelated to their particular gift, and this can lead to behavioral problems.

Child prodigies face great expectations, but often receive little understanding from the public which so claims to appreciate them. Often treated as little adults and frequently fawned over, it would seem that they lead charmed lives. But the very nature of their gift brings with it a very real fear: many prodigies eventually come to realize that, as they leave childhood behind, their precocity will seem less remarkable. The fortunate ones, like Midori, develop a mature talent that itself earns recognition and respect. Others, like the unfortunate Mozart, burn out early.

Mario Cuomo, presented her with that state's Asian-American Heritage Month Award.

Although Midori's touring and performance schedules are extremely heavily booked, she has always made time to lend her name and her presence to social causes that she considers important, particularly the encouragement of musical education for children. This dedication brought her much public recognition, including awards such as the Spirit of the City Award (1995), jointly sponsored by the city of New York and the Cathedral of St. John the Devine; The National Arts Awards, presented to her by Americans for the Arts in 1998; and the Encore Award, sponsored by the Arts and Business Council and conferred upon Midori in 1998.

Of all her community involvements, however, Midori is most closely involved with her foundation, Midori & Friends, which is dedicated to fostering growth, self-esteem, and creativity in children through exposure to the arts, and especially through music. The foundation sponsors regular televised performances, carried by the cable arts channel, Ovation, and works directly and indirectly with school and community groups to further the cause of musical education in both public and private schools. The foundation, established in 1992, goes well beyond simply sponsoring concerts, providing instructional materials and an interactive website for teachers and classes to use in their own music education programs. The focus is not entirely placed on education, however. Midori seeks to overcome the other factors that get in the way of inculcating a love of music in young people. Availability and accessibility are two important issues that the foundation attempts to address by providing support for free public performances by noted musicians throughout the country.

When Midori entered her 20s, she could no longer properly be called a child prodigy, but if anyone feared that she would lose her popularity or that her extraordinary gifts would begin to seem less impressive, they soon learned there was little to worry about. Midori remained one of the finest violinists currently performing, and she worked hard to expand her talents and her range. She is particularly excited about working with new composers, and actively seeks out innovative works. Her own musical tastes were **eclectic**, embracing not only classical pieces but also jazz, folk, and pop. While her concerts tended to feature a limited range of composers, Brahms, Beethoven, Dvorak, and Bartok among others, she was also excited by the works of such less canonical composers as Ellen Zwilich, Ned Rorem, and Philip Glass.

Midori remained highly active in her career and in her foundation work, but was not exclusively driven by a need to make music. Somehow she managed to find time away from her roughly 80 scheduled performances per year and her foundation work to attend college and graduate school at New York University, where she studied psychology, not music. She made her home in New York City. ◆

> *"Midori has charm, vitality and enormous technical skill. . . . There is subtlety of gesture in Midori's playing, a depth of emotional expression and a surprising level of pure physical power."*
> The Washington Post, February 6, 1993

eclectic encompassing a variety of categories into one entity.

Min, Anchee

1957– ● WRITER

Anchee Min was born in Jiangxu Province, in China, in 1957, and grew up during the years of China's Cultural Revolution. Both her father and her mother were teachers. Their profession made them suspect in the eyes of the

1957 Min is born in Jiangxu Province, China, during the early days of the Cultural Revolution.

1974 Min is sent to Red Fire Farm, a youth collective assigned to grow cotton on the shores of the China Sea.

1975 Min is selected to perform in Madame Mao's Opera, *Red Azalea*.

1976 Weeks after filming begins on *Red Azalea*, Mao dies and Min is arrested as a follower of Madame Mao.

1984 Min escapes to the United States with the help of actress Joan Chen.

1990 Min receives her M.F.A. degree from the Chicago Art Institute and begins her career as a writer.

1995 Min's memoirs of growing up in communist China, *Red Azalea*, is published to great critical and public acclaim.

2000 Min sells her third book, a fictionalized biography of Madame Mao, is bought for publication with an advance of $150,000.

state, which had declared all professionals and intellectuals to be enemies of the state. Rather than a normal education, Chinese schools during the Cultural Revolution were supposed to focus their efforts on indoctrinating the children in the teachings of China's dictator, Chairman Mao Tse Tung. Min was taught to be an enthusiastic member of the Little Red Guard, a junior version of the adult militaristic and highly political organization. She was a leader of her own Red Guard group by the time she was 14 years old.

In China during the 1950s and 1960s, one part of the standard indoctrination program was that all good citizens were responsible for acting as watchdogs over the speech and behaviors of others. When a neighbor, acquaintance, or even a family member committed an act that violated the teachings of Mao, a loyal citizen was expected to denounce the errant individual to the government as a reactionary. The types of actions that could bring down such a judgement were often seemingly minor: even something as simple as having a relationship without the approval of the state was considered an act of treachery, and practicing any form of religion was forbidden. The danger of being informed upon was very real, so much so that Min's own mother kept the fact that she was a Christian from her daughter for 27 years.

Min's mother's fears were not unfounded. The children of Min's generation had been subjected to this type of indoctrination since infancy, and were fully capable of denouncing anyone who violated Mao's teachings. Indeed, when still quite a young child, Min discovered that a teacher whom she dearly loved was carrying on an unsanctioned affair. To Min, her duty was clear, and she informed on her teacher: the teacher and her lover were arrested and later killed.

In 1974, when Min was 17 years old, she was assigned to work on a collective farm, the Red Fire Farm, on the coast of the China Sea, where she and thousands of other young people, aged 17 to 25, were set to the task of growing cotton. The work was hard: the salty soil supported only the poorest of harvests, leeches were a constant pest, and food supplies were so scanty that starvation was always nearby. Nonetheless, Min worked hard and soon became a leader on the farm. Soon, however, she would find a way to leave the farm for the life of an actress.

The 1960s and early 1970s were a period in which Chairman Mao's concubine, Jiang Ching, held a great deal of power within China. An actress herself before she gained Mao's favor, it was she who was the orchestrator of the policies of the Cultural Revolution. Jiang, who was referred to as Madame Mao, wrote and directed a number of operas that were thinly veiled celebrations of her own importance. These operas were filmed by Shanghai Television for broadcast throughout China. In 1975, one of these operas, titled *Red Azalea*, was being cast, and Madame Mao's agents were scouring the countryside for talent. Min was recommended by a supervisor, who was a cultural advisor to Madame Mao, and was awarded the role not for any particular talent but because she suited Madame Mao's esthetic image of a proper peasant woman.

Min was brought to Shanghai, where she received some training in acting technique and began to learn her role. Her acting career was over as quickly as it started, however, for within weeks of the start of filming, in 1976, Mao died. The political cadre that took Mao's place at the head of the nation, known as the Gang of Four, immediately took steps to consolidate their power, and among their first acts was to declare Madame Mao a traitor and to throw her into prison. Min, because of her involvement with Madame Mao's opera, was declared a follower of Madame Mao and sentenced to menial work at the television studio for eight years.

Though not imprisoned, Min's sentence was nonetheless arduous, and after years of overwork she fell ill with tuberculosis. During her time at the studio, she had been befriended by one of the actresses, who fled China for the United States when Mao died. As Min's situation worsened, this actress, known to American theater-goers as Joan Chen, encouraged her young friend to try to come to the United States as well. In 1984, permission was finally granted, and Min left China believing that she would never return.

Min settled in Chicago, speaking no English and uncertain as to what would happen next. She had had little formal education, but during her time at the television studio in Shanghai she was exposed to Chinese literary works and was determined to learn to become a writer. She had a friend fill out an application for her to enter the Chicago Institute of Art, claiming excellent English language skills, but in truth she could speak only a few words, so when she arrived on campus she was told to leave and to try again only after she had sufficiently mastered English to handle the coursework. Six months later she once again presented herself on campus, having worked spent the time determinedly learning the language. This time she was able to meet the required level of skill, and she began her studies in English literature. By 1990 she had not only earned her bachelor of fine arts degree, but had picked up her master's degree as well.

All told, Min spent ten years in Chicago, first as a student, and then as a fledgling author. She entered a writing contest sponsored by the Mississippi Valley Review and won. This opened doors for her in the world of publishing. In 1995, she sold her first book, *Red Azalea*, a memoir of her life growing up during the Cultural Revolution. The book was an immediate success, making *The New York Times* best-seller list and garnering glowing reviews. In 1997, Min published her first novel, *Katherine*, which told the story of an American ESL teacher in Mao's China, and she followed this success by selling the manuscript for her next book, *Becoming Madame Mao*, for a $150,000 advance. This latter book is a fictionalized biography dealing with the life of the concubine who came to the power of life and death over the people of China. Min's books have sometimes been faulted for their periodic lapses in language, but they have enjoyed a wide readership and have earned the author many important fans. One such fan, Oprah Winfrey, bought the movie rights to *Katherine*.

Min eventually moved from Chicago to settle in Los Angeles, where she felt somehow closer to her homeland. As her success and fame grew, she began looking for ways to use them for the betterment of others. Recalling the poor education she received as a child, she took advantage of her early fame to return to China by promoting better schooling for women and children. She remained an active advocate of the importance of education, motivated not only by her own experiences during her childhood but also by respect for her parents, who remained dedicated to the teaching profession even during the grim years of the Cultural Revolution. ◆

Mineta, Norman

NOVEMBER 12, 1931– ● POLITICIAN

When Norman Mineta's brief tenure as Bill Clinton's Secretary of Commerce ended on January 20, 2001—the first cabinet position ever occupied by an Asian American—the Washington veteran barely broke stride as he took the reins of George W. Bush's Department of Transportation, capping a long and distinguished career of public service in that saw him rise from the San Jose City Council to become the mayor of San Jose, an eleven-term U.S. Congressman, and then back-to-back terms in the Cabinet.

A native of San Diego, California, Norman Y. Mineta was born on November 12, 1931, to Japanese immigrant parents. His father owned an insurance agency and afforded a secure middle-class upbringing to his son that was disrupted by the trauma of the mass relocation of Japanese-Americans to detention camps for the duration of World War II. It was as a 10-year-old detainee that he was befriended by a man who later became an important political associate—Alan Simpson, the future senator from Wyoming.

At the war's end the family picked up the pieces of its previous life and Norman went on to excel academically at San Jose High School. After graduation he enrolled at the University of California at Berkley, from which he graduated in 1953 with a Bachelor of Science degree in business administration. His love of country unshaken by his family's wartime detention, Mineta enlisted in the army upon his graduation from Berkley and served for until 1956, when he returned to civilian life to run his father's insurance business.

In 1962 the civic-minded Mineta first answered the call of public life as a member of San Jose's Human Relations Commission. From there Mineta ascended the rungs of city government: he was elected to the San Jose City Council in 1967 and became mayor in 1971. After a three-year term in City Hall, Mineta waged a successful campaign for the U.S. Congress, where he served with distinction for the next two decades.

While in the House of Representatives Mineta became an important force in shaping the nation's transportation legislation, especially airline deregulation and the 1991 law which opened up the federal highway trust fund for application to mass transit projects. He also made his mark in civil rights, most notably in his coauthorship of the Americans with Disabilities Act; his cosponsorship of a bill that mandated voting assistance to citizens with poor English skills; and his 1988 bill calling for an official U.S. government apology and financial restitution for survivors of the Japanese-American internment camps of World War II.

Upon retiring from the House in 1995, Mineta became a vice president of the Lockheed Martin Corporation, one of the

1931 Mineta is born in Sacramento, California.

1953 Mineta graduates with a BA from University of California, Berkeley.

1967 Mineta is elected to the San Jose City Council.

1971 Mineta is elected mayor of San Jose.

1974 Mineta is elected to the United States House of Representatives.

2000 Mineta serves in President Clinton's cabinet as Secretary of Commerce, becoming the first Asian-American cabinet member.

2001 Mineta is chosen by President Bush to serve as Secretary of Transportation.

Asian Pacific-American Heritage Month

In 1977 a bipartisan bill was introduced into the U.S. House of Representatives, setting aside the first 10 days of May as Pacific/Asian Heritage Week, in recognition of the contributions made by one of the nation's fastest-growing population sectors. This initiative was initiated in the House by representatives Norman Mineta of California and Frank Horton of New York, and was taken up in the Senate by Daniel Inouye and Spark Matsunaga, both of Hawaii. Renamed Asian/Pacific American Heritage Week the following year, the proclamation of an annual celebration of the diverse peoples and cultures of Asian descent was officially passed and signed by President Jimmy Carter on October 5, 1978.

Each year, schools, community groups, and federal agencies took the first week of May to celebrate and explore the art, languages, customs, contributions, and histories of peoples who trace descent from any and all of the cultures of the Pacific Rim. The diversity of peoples is immense, and the historical sweep of participation in American life by immigrants from Asia, and their descendants, provides rich material for a range of activities that includes dance performances, art exhibitions, lectures, seminars, and other such public offerings. Parades are held in many communities, and a proliferation of websites offer educational materials on the vitality of the Asian Pacific American community, both in the past and in today's world.

At the end of the 1980s, leaders of the Asian Pacific-American community sought further recognition, and on May 7, 1990, President George Bush responded by signing a proclamation declaring the whole month of May to be Asian Pacific-American Heritage Month.

largest defense and transportation contractors. During his tenure at Lockheed, Mineta retained a toehold in public life as head of the 21-member National Civil Aviation Review Commission, created by Congress to address the nation's mounting problem in civilian air transport. The commission's report, issued in December 1997, made headlines with its characterization of the nation's airport congestion as verging on "gridlock." In 1998 Mineta also headed a committee established to evaluate the performance of the Federal Aviation Administration, concluding that the agency's chronic inefficiency and disorganization required fundamental changes in its administrative structure.

In July 2000, when Transportation Secretary William Daley resigned to run Al Gore's presidential campaign, Clinton named Mineta to replace him for the six-month remainder of his term. As the first Asian-American to serve in the Cabinet, Mineta said of his appointment, "This says to everyone, it is possible to attain these heights. I am hoping that this will pave the way for others who aspire to high positions, whether it's in the public sector or the private sector." Mineta was asked to prolong his financial sacrifice when the newly elected George W. Bush asked Mineta, a Democrat, to join his cabinet as Secretary of Transportation, a job he had turned down Bill Clinton offered it to him in 1992, at which time Mineta preferred to remain in Congress to head the Public Works and Transportation Committee. But in 2001, Mineta accepted Bush's nomination, which was greeted enthusiastically by government officials of both major parties. Vice President Dick Cheney, who administered Mineta's oath of office, said, "Very few Americans have served in the Cabinets of two presidents. Far fewer have done so under presidents of different parties." ◆

Ming, Jenny

1955– ● BUSINESSWOMAN

J enny Ming was born in 1955 on the Island of Macao, a former Portuguese colony near Hong Kong. When she was nine years old she moved with her parents and four siblings to San Francisco, where her father found work as a printer. Ming attended the local schools, where she was a good, hardworking student. Her family was not wealthy, and to earn extra money in high school, Ming held part-time, weekend jobs as a bank teller and, later, as a sales clerk at the local Macy's department store.

Even while still in high school, Ming had already begun to show evidence of the skills and interests that would contribute so greatly to her success as an adult. In high school home economics classes she learned to sew, and discovered that she loved working with fabrics and fashion. She also displayed an early entrepreneurial streak, setting herself up as a seamstress and advertising for clients through the local newspapers.

When the time came to consider college, Ming's parents hoped that she would pursue a degree in **pharmacology,** believing that a career as a pharmacist would provide her with a secure future. Ming, however, had little interest in pharmacy, for by now she was certain that she wanted to find a career that would use her abilities and interest in clothing and fashion. She attended San Jose State University, in San Jose, California, and

pharmacology the science of drugs.

immediately began a course of study that would lead to a degree in home economics. Her coursework focused on textiles, and she received her B.A. degree in the spring of 1978.

After graduation, Ming recognized that she needed more background and training in management if she were to eventually achieve her dream of a successful career in the fashion industry. She took a management trainee position for Dayton Hudson Corporation, working in one of the Mervyn's chain stores, where she learned about the managerial side of the industry. She quickly distinguished herself and was soon promoted to the position of buyer in the linens and junior wear department.

Ming remained with Dayton Hudson Corporation for eight years, building a solid reputation for herself within the industry. One of the suppliers with whom she dealt was clearly impressed by her drive and vision, and recommended that Millard S. Drexler, chief executive of The Gap, Inc., consider hiring her on as a buyer for his highly successful chain of youth-oriented, casual clothing stores.

From the start of her association with The Gap, Ming stood out for her innovative marketing style. Her training in textiles and her early experience as a seamstress seem to have conferred upon her a strong intuitive sense of what customers want. Her early decisions showed that she was able to see the big difference that small changes can make. For example, prior to her coming on-board at The Gap, the chain only marketed its popular T-shirts in a limited range of colors, and treated them as purely a summer item. Ming, however, knew that teenagers—the age group targeted by The Gap stores—wore T-shirts all year round, and that more color choices would mean more individual purchases. Her intuition was correct, and T-shirt sales jumped dramatically once her new policy was adopted.

As a buyer, Ming was firmly committed to staying aware of trends in youth fashion. Whenever she traveled, she always made it a point to visit cafes and other student hangouts, and she kept herself current with youth-oriented magazines, trying to spot potential fads. She was so successful that she was rewarded with a promotion to vice-president in 1989, just three years after joining the firm.

In the late 1980s and early 1990s, Gap, Inc. expanded its operations. It acquired the Banana Republic chain, and positioned these new outlets as an upscale alternative to The Gap, aimed at a slightly older clientele. In 1994, Gap, Inc. launched a new chain, Old Navy Stores, this time targeting more budget-conscious consumers, but still retaining a very strong commitment to the youth market. Ming was an eminently logical choice to head up this new chain in The Gap empire, and she was named president of Old Navy in April 1999.

Ming has always enjoyed the respect and admiration of her colleagues within The Gap, Inc. empire, particularly for her ability to look beyond the obvious when making marketing decisions and selecting fashions for the stores to carry. Her understanding of the kinds of clothes that her target customers like have served her in good stead in her work at Old Navy: the chain, already 450 stores strong, is expanding rapidly throughout the country. She was behind the decisions to carry the highly popular fleece pullovers, baggy pants, and multi-pocketed cargo pants that enjoyed success during the late 1990s. Her accomplishments are clear in the sales figures: the Old Navy stores make up only 16 percent of the total stores operated by Gap, Inc., but brought in about 35 percent of the larger company's total sales in 1999. ◆

Mink, Patsy

DECEMBER 6, 1927– ● POLITICIAN

Patsy Mink managed to combine hard-headed persistence and dedicated idealism into a notable career of public service, courageously vaulting over racial and gender barriers to become the first Asian-American woman to serve in the United States Congress and then using her legislative eminence to fight for her deeply held convictions about racial tolerance and social justice.

She was born Patsy Takemoto in Paia, a tiny village on the island of Maui in Hawaii, one of two children of, Suematsu Takemoto, a civil engineer, and, Miitama, a housewife. From the earliest years Patsy excelled in school, first at the Hamakuopo Grammar School and, after the fourth grade, at the Kaunoa English Standard School. Even as a child she began to sense the importance of public service, inspired in part by the fireside chats of President Franklin Delano Roosevelt. She later recalled, "It occurred to me that one had to find a reason for one's existence. It seemed to me that possibly the highest

Patsy Mink

achievement is to find a place in life that permits one to be of service to his fellow men."

Patsy's youthful ideal of service centered on medicine, a goal that propelled her to the top of her class at Maui High School, from which she graduated in 1944 as student body president and class valedictorian. She then enrolled in the premed program at the University of Hawaii, where she was active in the Pre-Medical Students Club and the on the varsity debating squad. She spent the first half of her junior year studying at Wilson College in Chambersburg, Pennsylvania, and the second half a the University of Nebraska, where she had friends who, she hoped, could help her get into medical school. While there she was appalled to find herself in an "international house" populated entirely by students of color; her ensuing letter of protest to the student newspaper about this overt segregation helped to overturn the university's segregated housing policy. The fruits of victory were short-lived, however, for illness forced her to return to Hawaii the following year.

By the time she returned to the University of Hawaii for her senior year, Patsy was developing a passion for philosophical studies but nevertheless took her degree in zoology and chemistry in 1948. She then set about applying to medical school but received nothing but rejection letters. She later commented, "I wish someone has told me then that medical schools in the U.S. didn't admit women students—except for one all-female school." The dejected Mink took a job at the Honolulu Academy of Arts, then headed by a woman who suggested to Patsy that she might have better luck applying to law school. Patsy took her advice and was accepted at the University of Chicago School of Law, from which she graduated with a juris doctorate in 1951.

In her last year of law school Patsy married John Francis Mink, a hydrologist and geologist. Pregnant with their first child, Patsy set out to find legal work, only to face a series of frustrating rebuffs. She later recalled, "My reaction was disbelief that just being a woman was a disqualification for a job." After a six-month stint in the library of the University of Chicago Law School, Patsy gave birth to her daughter, Gwendolyn, and the family moved to Hawaii. John went to work as a hydrologist for the Honolulu Board of Water Supply, and Patsy was admitted to the bar in 1953, but only after waging a successful battle to overturn a discriminatory statute that deemed her a resident of her husband's home state.

As the island's first woman lawyer of Japanese descent, Mink once again found job offers scarce, so she simply started her own law firm while teaching law courses at the University of Hawaii. Determined to find a path to combating the racial and gender prejudice she had encountered, Mink found herself drawn to politics and began attending local meetings of the Democratic Party. Warming to the political milieu, she founded the Oahu Young Democrats and later the Hawaii Young Democrats, zealously campaigning for the party's 1954 slate of candidates.

After working as the staff attorney of the Hawaiian territorial legislative session in 1955, Mink was inspired to run for office, and in 1956 campaigned for a seat in the Territory of Hawaii House of Representatives, to which she was elected by a comfortable margin, becoming the first Japanese American woman to serve in that body. On her first day there she established her reputation as a passionate advocate for peace and justice by proposing a resolution of protest against British nuclear tests in the South Pacific.

After Hawaii achieved statehood in 1959, Mink ran for the U.S. Congress. Despite her loss to Daniel Inouye, she remained active in party affairs, playing a prominent role in the state delegation to the 1960 convention and serving as vice president of the National Yong Democratic Clubs of America. She ran successfully for the state Senate in 1962, and two years later ran again for the U.S. Congress, this time winning an easy victory. "I had worked from 1959 to 1964 to win a seat in the U.S. Congress," Mink later told an interviewer. "It was a huge task. My first thoughts at my victory were relief and vindication that I did not let my family and friends down."

1927 Mink is born in Maui, Hawaii.

1956 Mink is elected to the Hawaiian state legislature.

1965 Mink begins service as member of the United States Representatives.

1977 Mink is appointed and confirmed Assistant Secretary of State, OES.

1978 Mink is elected president of Americans for Democratic Action.

1983 Mink is elected to the Honolulu City Council.

1990 Mink is again elected to the U.S. Congress.

Mink served 12 distinguished years in the House, contributing significantly to legislation that advanced the causes of women, minorities, working people, and the environment. She was also one of the Democratic Party's most ardent opponents of the Vietnam War, and was among the American contingent to the Paris Peace talks in April 1972 in order to try to hasten a settlement.

In 1976 Mink resigned from her House seat to run in the primary for Democratic nomination for the U.S. Senate. After losing to Congressman Msayuki Matsunaga, the candidate of the party **machine,** Mink soon found herself back in Washington as Assistant Secretary of State for Oceans and International, Environmental, and Scientific Affairs for President Jimmy Carter. After two years in that post, Mink returned to Honolulu, where she served two years on the Honolulu City Council. Two unsuccessful campaigns followed: for the governorship in 1986, and for the mayoralty of Honolulu in 1988. Mink's political fortunes rebounded in 1990, when she waged a successful campaign for the House seat opened up by Daniel Akaka's decision to run for the Senate. There she has remained ever since, serving on a variety of committees, including Education and Labor and Government Reform. She also serves on the Congressional Caucus for Women's Issues. ◆

machine in politics, the organization of a political party usually controlled by one person or group through which strategy is made and patronage given.

Morita, Pat

JUNE 28, 1932– ● ACTOR, COMEDIAN

Long before his breakthrough role as Mr. Miyagi, the oracular karate instructor of *The Karate Kid* (1984) (and its sequels), Pat Morita had become an enduring presence among Hollywood's stable of comedic performers, forging a solid reputation first as a stand-up comedian and later as a character actor in movies and television series such as *Sanford and Son* and *Happy Days*.

Morita managed to forge his comic persona out of a relentlessly bleak childhood. The younger of two children of migrant farm workers, he was born Noriyuki Morita on June 28, 1932, near Berkeley, California. On top of the poverty and rootlessness of his family's life, Morita was afflicted at the age of two with spinal tuberculosis and spent nine years confined in a shoulders-to-knees body cast while under treatment at the Weimer Joint Sanatorium and, later, at the Shriner's Hospital in San Francisco. The young "Nori" Morita made the best of his debility, cultivating a rich fantasy life. As he later recalled, "So I made puppets out of socks to entertain the nurses and other kids. In many ways, who knows? If it weren't for my disease, I might not be where I am today."

Determined to confound the doctors' expectations that he would never walk again, Morita applied himself with unrelenting tenacity to his physical therapy regimen, and by the age of 11 he was able to walk out of the hospital to rejoin his family. Unfortunately, Morita was destined to escape one form of confinement only to face another—the year was 1943, in the middle of World War II, when most of the 110,000 Japanese-Americans on the West Coast were being held in internment camps. It was in two such facilities in Arizona that Morita spent the rest of the war with his family, first in Arizona and later in California. Morita later recalled the bitter ironies of this bleak wartime setting: "I remember doing the Pledge of Allegiance at the beginning of the school day. It was in a barracks. . . . [I remember] by English class; and looking out the window and seeing the American flag waving, juxtaposed against a guard tower in the background, I had this sense of 'What's this all about?' Why am I saying, 'Liberty and justice for all.'"

After the war, the Morita family opened a restaurant in a mostly black section of Sacramento, California (Japanese food was understandably out of favor in those days). Nori devoted himself to the family business, first as a waiter and later as an **emcee** at Morita-catered parties, where he first discovered his ability to entertain large crowds with his witty patter.

But Morita placed his show-business dreams on the back burner and took a job with an aerospace company, where he rose to become head of computer programming. After several years on the job, however, Morita grew restless, dreading the

Pat Morita

"My fame is largely due to young people, they're the first ones to discover me. You know why? I'm the same height."
Morita, interview, Ottawa Sun, September 25, 1999

emcee master of ceremonies at a performance or event.

1932 Morita born near Berkeley, California.

1967 Morita appears in first major feature film, *Thoroughly Modern Millie*.

1984 Morita wins Oscar nomination for his role as a karate instructor in *The Karate Kid*.

paucity small quantity.

prospect of spending the rest of his life in one job with one company. Remembering his facility with the wedding audiences, at the age of 30, with a wife and two children to support, he walked out of his job and embarked on a career as a comic.

Taking the short, snappy name "Pat," the diminutive Morita (he stands only five feet, three inches tall) made the rounds of the comedy clubs, promoting himself as "the hip Nip." He soon established a solid reputation that led to guest appearances on a number of TV variety and talk shows. That exposure resulted in a minor role in the major Hollywood musical film *Thoroughly Modern Millie* (1967), but despite a smattering of subsequent supporting film appearances, Morita's main media exposure came from television appearances. In the 1974-75 season Morita landed a regular supporting role in the NBC comedy series *Sanford and Son*; the following year he landed what became his best known television role, Arnold, on ABC's *Happy Days*.

Throughout the late 1970s and early 1980s, Morita wended his way through the "B" entertainer circuit: guest appearances on TV dramas, comedies, and talk shows, along with continued stand-up work in comedy clubs. But Morita was basically treading water until 1983, when he auditioned for the role that transformed him from semiobscure comic to cult figure: Miyagi, the karate sage of *The Karate Kid*. But the role did not land in his lap. Studio executives were initially skeptical about casting a comedian in this pivotal dramatic role, but Morita's impassioned pleas and convincing readings—he was called back five times during auditions—finally secured him the role of a lifetime.

Upon its release in 1984, *The Karate Kid* garnered respectable reviews but proved a major box office bonanza, spawning three sequels, all of them featuring Morita: *The Karate Kid II* (1986), *The Karate Kid III* (1989), and *The Next Karate Kid* (1994). His box office appeal firmly established, Morita became a familiar supporting feature-film presence found other film work throughout the late 1980s and early 1990s despite an overall **paucity** of roles for Asian Americans. For one season he was the star of a television detective series *O'Hara* (1987-88); his recent film highlights include *Even Cowgirls Get the Blues* (1994).

By the late 1990s, Morita's career began to slow down, but he continued to enjoy the adulation of young people who still snapped up *The Karate Kid* features at video stores. As he told a reporter in 1999, "Part of what comes with the territory of fame is a lot of intrusiveness. But I've got a philosophy about that. You either learn to do it well and handle it, or you're a putz. My fame is largely due to young people, they're the first ones to discover me. You know why? I'm the same height." ◆

Mow, William

APRIL 18, 1936– ● ENGINEER, ENTREPRENEUR

William Mow was born Mow Chao Wei in Hangchow, China, on April 18, 1936. His father, Mow Pan Tsu, was a career military officer in the Nationalist government prior to the Communist revolution, and at 28 had achieved the rank of general in the Chinese Air Force. His duties made it necessary for the family to move frequently, to Shanghai, Taiwan, and then Chensu, but wherever they lived William and his five brothers were educated in the best available schools.

In 1949, when China was in the midst of its revolution and the mainland Nationalist forces were about to fall to Mao Tse Tung's advancing army, the Mow family fled to Taiwan, where the Nationalist government set up its independent, Kuomingtan government, under the leadership of Chaing Kai-Shek. Mow's father was given a diplomatic post and in 1949 was sent to Washington, D.C., as a representative of the Nationalist government.

In the United States, Mow and his brothers enjoyed the benefits of their status as the sons of a diplomat, including education in the best schools in the area. Although Mow began his sixth grade year with very little knowledge of English, he displayed an early talent for mathematics and succeeded in graduating with the rest of his peers. In 1951, however, the family suffered a severe reversal of fortunes. Mow's father became involved in a dispute with his government in Taiwan and was summarily dismissed from his post. Worse, he was accused of wrongdoing, and Kuomingtang agents were sent to arrest him and bring him back to Taiwan for trial. To avoid arrest, Mow's father fled to Mexico, and his mother was left to raise the six Mow sons on her own.

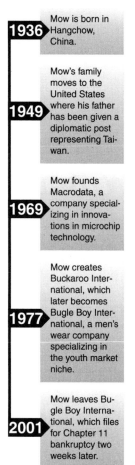

1936 Mow is born in Hangchow, China.

1949 Mow's family moves to the United States where his father has been given a diplomatic post representing Taiwan.

1969 Mow founds Macrodata, a company specializing in innovations in microchip technology.

1977 Mow creates Buckaroo International, which later becomes Bugle Boy International, a men's wear company specializing in the youth market niche.

2001 Mow leaves Bugle Boy International, which files for Chapter 11 bankruptcy two weeks later.

prospectus a printed proposal describing a potential business enterprise.

Mow's mother moved the family to Great Neck, New York, closer to where Mow was then a boarding student at the Riverdale Country School. There she established herself in business, opening up a restaurant called the Yangtze River Cafe. Mow has since claimed that these years, and his mother's restaurant, set the stage for his earliest entrepreneurial efforts. He came home for the weekends, and on Sundays, while he prepared to return to school, his parents would pack up 20 egg rolls from the restaurant to take along with him. Rather than keep them as a treat for himself, he started selling them in the school snack bar, where they proved popular enough to earn him a quarter apiece.

Mow did well in high school, and in 1956 he enrolled in Rensselaer Polytechnic Institute, a prestigious engineering college in Troy, New York. While there he met a young Taiwanese woman, Margarita Liu, and the two were married in 1961 in the same year that he graduated with a bachelor's degree in Electrical Engineering. Upon graduation, Mow attended Brooklyn Polytechnic to study for his master's degree while working as a research associate at the Institute. He received his master's in 1963, then took a job as logic engineer for Honeywell Corporation, where he worked for a few years before moving on to work toward his doctorate degree at Purdue University, in West Lafayette, Indiana.

In 1967, with his doctorate in Electrical Engineering in hand, Mow joined Litton Industries as a program manager. Unfortunately, within two years the company began suffering severe reversals, and in 1969 Mow realized that layoffs were imminent. Convinced that he had some real contributions to make to the fledgling computer industry, Mow put together a **prospectus** for a company that would develop innovative technology involving microchips, and began looking for investors. The result was Macrodata, which Mow founded and for which he served as both chairman and chief executive officer.

While at Macrodata, Mow was directly involved in research and design, and was personally responsible for many of the early advances achieved in the fledgling microchip technology in those pre-Apple, pre-PC years. He enjoyed early success as one of the first few pioneers in the field serving such giants in the computer field as IBM and NEC, and in 1975 he received recognition for his work when Purdue University recognized him as Outstanding Electrical Engineer. By the second half of the 1970s, however, the industry began to change as more and more people began to get involved in high-technology electronics. Macrodata, like many high-tech start-ups then and now, was undercapitalized, and although his inventions were of such **seminal** importance in the development of the microchip that they were (and still are) celebrated in museums, Mow eventually had to sell the firm. Realizing $1.1 million dollars on the sale, Mow began to look for new fields to conquer.

Mow next became interested in taking his talents in an entirely new direction: merchandise importing. He founded Dragon International in 1976, a company that specialized in brokering goods imported from Asia to companies in the United States. When Mow realized that this new enterprise was not enough to absorb all his creative energies, he began thinking about additional projects.

Mow became interested in creating his own line of apparel, and in 1977 he created Buckaroo International, which later became Bugle Boy International. As with his work in computer technology, Mow was somewhat ahead of his time in this new endeavor, because he was among the first to see the need for modern industry to understand and work with the emerging global economy. He built up a worldwide network of sources for materials and manufacturing, and this network was what enabled his new company to achieve explosive growth. Within a decade, from the early 1980s to the end of 1990, sales figures for his Bugle Boy operation grew from less than $10 million annually to well in excess of $500 million and showed no signs of slowing. Mow predicted that Bugle Boy would achieve $1 billion in sales by 2001.

The fashion industry is a volatile one, however, and Mow's success was preceded by several years of uncertainty in which he nearly lost his, and his investors, money. The stresses of this period damaged his marriage, and he and his wife began growing apart. In 1981 his wife filed for divorce, and Mow subsequently married a young woman, Rosa, whom he had met several years earlier while on a visit to the Taiwan offices of his import company.

In the 1990s, Mow began to achieve recognition not only for his entrepreneurial success but also for his philanthropy. In that decade he was awarded the Juvenile Diabetes Foundation's Father of the Year Award and was named Outstanding Electrical Engineer by Purdue University. In addition, he was inducted into the World Trade Hall of Fame in recognition of his work to further the development of the global economy. As late as 1999,

As with his work in computer technology, Mow was somewhat ahead of his time in this new endeavor.

seminal beginning.

articles were appearing throughout the business media proclaiming the likelihood that Mow's extraordinary success would continue for the foreseeable future.

Unfortunately, the start of the new century was unkind to many companies, both old and new. When the "market meltdown" of 2000 hit, it devastated old and new corporate entities, and Bugle Boy, Incorporated was no exception. From its high-flying days in the late 1980s, the company found itself in crisis, and in January 2001, Mow left the organization. Two weeks later, Bugle Boy, Inc., filed for Chapter 11 bankruptcy, citing debts totaling more than $75 million. Although his company failed, Mow's contributions to technology and to business remain important. As an early innovator in microchip technology, he has been responsible for some extremely important breakthroughs. Through his work in importing and his involvement with Bugle Boy International, he has been instrumental in furthering the development of the global economy. He has expressed a casual interest in eventually leaving the business world completely behind in favor of playing a role in U.S. diplomacy. ◆

Mukherjee, Bharati

JULY 27, 1940– ● AUTHOR

Brahmin a Hindu of the highest social state.

Bharati Mukharjee was born on July 27, 1940, to a Hindu **Brahmin** family in Calcutta, India. She was the second of three daughters born to Sudhir Lal Mukherjee and his wife, Bina Banerjee. The home in which she lived until she was eight years old was a large one, a shared household of more than 40 relatives. During her eighth year, however, her father took a job in England, taking his family with him to stay in London for the next several years.

As was to be expected in an upper-class family like hers, Bharati and her sisters received the benefits of an excellent education. She attended the University of Calcutta, graduating in 1959 with B.A. (with honors). She then went on to do graduate work at a university in Barada, India, where she earned her Master's degree in English and Ancient Indian Cultures in 1961.

With degree in hand and seeking to enhance her writing abilities, Bharati attended a writer's workshop sponsored by the

University of Iowa in 1961, then enrolled in the Fine Arts program at that university to earn a further graduate degree. She originally intended this visit to North America to be a short one, for her family expected her to return home and enter into a marriage that her father had arranged according to tradition. However, in early September 1963, Mukharjee met and fell in love with a fellow student in her degree program, a Canadian writer named Clark Blaise. The two were married after a courtship of only two weeks.

The newly-married pair remained in Iowa for another five years, during which time Mukherjee completed a master of fine arts program and began work on her doctorate degree in English and composition. In 1968, while Mukherjee was still working on her dissertation (she received her Ph.D in 1969), the couple moved to Montreal, Canada. Mukherjee took steps to become a naturalized citizen of that country, which she gained in 1972. She wrote of her time in Canada as the "hardest of her life" for, as a "visible minority," she faced much discrimination. Nonetheless, while teaching at McGill University, she worked at her writing steadily, publishing her first novel, *The Tiger's Daughter* in 1971 and beginning work on a second, *Wife*, which was published in 1975. In addition, she began work on a series of short stories which would eventually be published under the title *Darkness*, in 1985.

By 1980 Mukherjee had had enough of the constant acts, small and large, of discrimination she faced in Canada, and emigrated to the United States in hopes of finding greater acceptance there, ultimately being sworn in as a permanent resident. She took a series of short-term teaching appointments at universities and colleges around the country, all the while continuing with her writing. In 1986 she was able to concentrate more

Bharati Mukherjee

1940 Mukherjee is born in Calcutta, India.

1961 Mukherjee attends writer's workshop at University of Iowa, remaining to do graduate work.

1963 Mukherjee marries Clark Blaise of Montreal, Canada.

1968 Mukherjee moves to Canada to teach at McGill University.

1971 Mukherjee publishes her first novel, *The Tiger's Daughter.*

1980 Mukherjee leaves Canada to become a permanent resident of the United States.

1986 Mukherjee wins grant from National Endowment for the Arts.

1989 Mukherjee joins the writing faculty of the University of California, Berkeley.

fully on her creative projects for she received a grant from the National Endowment for the Arts, and relieved her of the need for expending so much of her energies on teaching duties. She remained strongly tied to academia, however, and in 1989 joined the faculty of the University of California at Berkeley, where she held the title of Distinguished Professor. Her husband was on the faculty at the University of Iowa. Bukherjee was the mother of two sons, Bart Anand and Bernard Sudhir Blaise.

Mukherjee's stated goal in her writing was to develop what she called a "new immigrant literature" which explores the conditions faced by Asians who come to live in North America. Her principle theme was the changing roles that such immigrants, particularly women, must learn to play in order to succeed in a new world and a new culture. Her work had a broad readership, and she received generally positive critical attention. Some critics, however, faulted Mukherjee for presenting an unrealistic vision of immigrant life.

Mukherjee had little patience for this type of criticism. She wrote strong characters whose personal virtues and strengths permit them to negotiate the difficulties of coping with the new social and cultural expectations they face in their adopted country, and pays less attention to the externally imposed barriers to success that are faced by many immigrants. This aroused critical ire, as was her insistence on presenting her characters, regardless of their social and economic standing, as thoughtful, literate beings. In doing so, her critics charged her work with being overly optimistic and unrepresentative of the immigrant experience. In addition, they took her to task for drawing upon Western literature, rather than the literature of her homeland, for inspiration.

Mukherjee responded to her critics by charging them with marginalizing immigrants by insisting that literature dealing with the subject must always present a particular vision of their lives. Rather than using her work to present a litany of hardships suffered and failures forced upon immigrants, she wrote about strong women who are, ultimately, survivors, who learn to negotiate the conflict between two worlds, two homelands, and two cultures. She charged that critics who insisted that only one view of immigrant life should prevail in literature were guilty of trying to appropriate the lives and culture of immigrants, and particularly those of South Asian women in North America.

Mukherjee objected to charges that there is something inappropriate in the influence of Western literature that appears in her work. She argued that it is far more inappropriate to restrict the creative and intellectual lives of people, real or fictional, to the literary traditions of the lands of their birth. After all, she argued, humans are thinking creatures, capable of absorbing lessons, values, and insights from all sources to which they are exposed, and capable of then synthesizing this information into something new and meaningful. To insist otherwise is to "ghettoize" cultures, locking them forever in separate worlds of experience and thought. It was Mukherjee's goal to use her work to break free from this monocultural view of individual life and to present, instead, a more integrated understanding of the multicultural elements that immigrants face.

This concern with the marginalization of immigrants and their experience was a powerful aspect of Mukherjee's writing and teaching. She was outspoken in her distaste for the trend toward "hyphenizing" minorities. To her, an appellation such as "Asian-American" constituted a kind of self-imposed marginalization, a voluntary setting apart of oneself, because the name itself marks a person as somehow different from or other than "real" Americans. At the same time, such a designation provides no real information about the richness of culture, tradition, and experience that is unique to any individual who is called by the name, for "Asian" refers to such a broad range of cultures, from Chinese and Japanese to her own background of Bengali. For Mukherjee, the great variety of individual experience was a kind of wealth, which her literature tried to celebrate, and she had no patience for those who would prefer to work in stereotypes, however well-intentioned those stereotypes may be. ◆

Natori, Josie

MAY 22, 1947– ● BUSINESSWOMAN

J osie Natori was born Josie Cruz on May 22, 1947, in Paloso Verdes, just outside of Manila, in the Philippines. She was the oldest of six children born to Felipe F. Cruz, a wealthy Manila contractor. She grew up in extremely comfortable circumstances, and attended the best local schools before heading off to college in 1964. While a child she developed an early interest in music, and began studying the piano at the age of four. She attended Manhattanville College, in Purchase, New York, a small (1,400 students), exclusive private school that in 1964 had an all-woman student body. Josie earned her undergraduate degree in 1968 and began looking for an appropriate career.

Josie's first employment was with Bache Securities, a job she took not for any particular love of the world of high finance, but simply because she was offered a position there. Although she had no overwhelming interest in the field, she was very good at her work, and was soon hired away by Merrill Lynch, a major investment firm. Within six months she had so distinguished herself that she was given the responsibility of opening the firm's Manila branch office, and in 1974, when she was 27 years old, was named vice president of investment banking.

While working at Merrill Lynch, Josie Cruz met a fellow investment banker, Ken Natori, a third-generation Japanese-American. The two discovered that they had much in common and soon married. One thing that they shared was a mutual boredom with their careers, and together they decided that they would go into business for themselves. It was one thing to know that they were ready to make a change, but at the start they

1947 Natori is born in Paloso Verdes, Philippines.

1968 Natori graduates from Manhattanville College and begins a career in investment banking.

1977 Josie and Ken Natori found Natori Company; Josie assumes the position of CEO and president.

1984 Natori has her first perfume named after her.

1997 Natori rents Carnegie Hall for a gala celebration marking her 50th birthday.

acumen skill.

were unsure just what sort of business they wanted to start up. The two started looking into a number of possibilities, even considering buying a car wash or opening a McDonald's franchise, when Josie was struck with an inspiration, drawn from her background in Manila: she would take traditional Philippine clothing, with its bright and intricate embroidery, and bring it to a broader market.

Thus, in 1977, the Natori Company was born. The enterprise started small, as Josie gathered samples and began attempting to interest buyers in major United States department stores. She had her first major stroke of luck in New York City, where Bloomingdales became interested in the samples she showed to its buyers, and placed an order. From that simple beginning, success came quickly; by the year 2000 the young company had grown to a $50 million business, specializing in lingerie and leisure wear. The company opened offices in Manila and New York, and a salon in Paris.

The Natori line of clothing, featuring original designs, nonetheless remained true to the traditional garments that inspired Josie to begin with, featuring delicate embroidery and intricate detailing. She also branched out somewhat, adding fragrance design to her many accomplishments; in 1994 Avon, the cosmetics company, launched her first namesake perfume, "Natori," and followed it in 1998 with a second perfume, "Josie." She and her husband explored the potential of e-commerce, intending to bring their business **acumen** to bear on developing an Internet presence for their company.

Josie's success soon won her and her company a great deal of public attention. As C.E.O. of Natori Company, she was one of a handful of Asian-American women occupying highly influential positions in industry. She was honored with the Ellis Island Medal of Honor for her success as an immigrant who rose to the top of her profession in American business. She was also been named a trustee of the Asia Society, an organization that is dedicated to furthering Asian-American interests in society and in politics, and she has served as a commissioner for the White House Conference on Small Businesses. Among the issues with which she became involved was the transformation of the workplace to accommodate the needs of working mothers. In interviews and on the lecture circuit, her overriding message to young people who dream of success in business was to stress the importance of hard work and a strong drive to be the best at whatever they do.

A multimillionaire, Josie Natori enjoyed the success that her company has brought her. It enabled her to provide her son, Kenneth, with a comfortable home and an excellent education, and to give back to her community and to the institutions that have been helpful to her throughout her life. Among the latter was her alma mater, Manhattanville College, to which she has returned on occasion to speak to students about career possibilities. More personally, she enjoyed the opportunities for self-expression that her success in business has brought. On her 50th birthday, for example, she stunned New Yorkers when she rented out Carnegie Hall for the evening and hosted a party for more than 2,500 "close friends and family," during which she dusted off her childhood skills as a pianist and offered a concert of Schumann and Rachmaninov, accompanied by a full orchestra. She, her husband, and her son, Kenneth, made their home in New York City. ◆

Ngor, Haing

MARCH 22, 1940?–FEBRUARY 25, 1996 ● PHYSICIAN, ACTOR

The actual date of birth for Haing S. Ngor is uncertain; sources differ substantially, listing dates as early as 1940 and as late as 1947, and even Ngor himself has given conflicting birth dates in interviews. On his tombstone, however, the date of March 22, 1940, is inscribed, and we know at least that, sometime in the 1940s, long before the Vietnam conflict brought Cambodia to the attention of most Americans, Haing Ngor was born in the village of Samrong Yong, just south of the Cambodian capital city of Phnom Penh.

Ngor was born into a comfortable home, the son of a prominent man who was able to provide his son with access to a fine education. He was raised a Buddhist, and attempted throughout his life to embody a vow of his faith: "to enlighten for the sake of all living things." Ngor became a physician, specializing in **obstetrics**, and over time he built up a respectable practice in Phnom Penh. To understand what happened to him later in life, however, more than a simple recitation of life events is required, for Ngor's life in the United States was very much the product of much larger forces, intimately bound up in events arising out of his homeland's involvement in the Vietnam War.

obstetrics a branch of medical science dealing with birth.

1940 ▶ Ngor is born in the village of Samrong Yong, Cambodia.

1975 ▶ Ngor, along with the other two million residents of Phnom Penh, is driven into forced labor in the countryside by the Khmer Rouge.

1978 ▶ Ngor and his niece, Ngim, flee Cambodia and arrive in Thailand.

1980 ▶ Ngor and Ngim gain approval of their petition to immigrate to the United States, settling in Los Angeles.

1984 ▶ Ngor wins Academy Award for role of Dith Pran in *The Killing Fields*, publishes memoir entitled *A Cambodian Odyssey*.

1996 ▶ Ngor is shot to death by burglars in front of his home in Los Angeles.

In the 1960s, Cambodia was being drawn ever closer to the fighting in Vietnam, where North and South were locked in a civil war. Cambodia's then-ruler, Prince Sihanouk, attempted to keep his country out of the fray, but the United States, which had allied itself with South Vietnam, was convinced that North Vietnamese forces were using trails through eastern Cambodia in order to supply their troops, and the U.S. wanted to cut off that source of supplies. The United States eventually tired of Sihanouk's refusal to cooperate with American objectives and, in 1970, supported military general Lon Nol in his successful bid to take over the government. Prince Sihanouk was exiled, and Lon Nol took an active part on behalf of the U.S. government objectives in the region. As part of his cooperation, he mobilized the army, and Ngor was called into service as a medical officer.

American bombing in Cambodia, however, had an unanticipated effect; in the countryside where the bombs were falling, the peasantry soon rose up in rebellion against Lon Nol, finding their leader in a charismatic revolutionary called Pol Pot. Soon, Pol Pot had an army of peasants with which to challenge Lon Nol's rule, and in 1973 this army, called the Khmer Rouge, began scoring victory after victory against the government's troops.

Pol Pot, and by extension his army, subscribed to a devastatingly brutal variant of Maoist philosophy, in which all intellectuals and professionals were considered enemies of the people. As the Khmer Rouge captured village after village, they conducted wholesale purges of the educated classes. By 1975 they had swept through the country, and marched victoriously into Phnom Penh itself, forcing Lon Nol to flee for his life.

For those who, like Haing Ngor, were unable to flee, what followed were three years of utter terror. Ngor, as an educated, professional man and a member of Lon Nol's army, was in grave danger. He was, in fact, imprisoned and tortured for his military service, and the only way for Ngor to avoid summary execution was to deny his training, claiming to have been a taxi-driver instead; he even went so far as to hide his eyeglasses, which were considered to be proof enough that he was a member of the enemy class.

Ngor was herded with the rest of Phnom Pehn's 2 million residents out into the countryside, where he was forced do hard labor in the rice fields by day and endure the Khmer Rouge indoctrination sessions in the evenings. All around him he saw people die of overwork, disease, and starvation. He was helpless to use his training to save them. The bitterest irony of all was to be forced to stand by idly as his pregnant wife, Chang My Huong, died of complications during labor; had he attempted to help, he would simply have added his own death to the deaths of his wife and newborn child. The Cambodian countryside came to be known as "the killing fields," and between 1–2 million people died in the 3-1/2 years of Pol Pot's rule.

Escape seemed hopeless for Ngor until 1978, when North Vietnam launched an all-out offensive against Cambodia and toppled Pol Pot's regime. The Khmer Rouge still ruled in the countryside, but without their leader their control was no longer quite so absolute. Ngor saw his chance; he had lost most of his family, but managed to find a niece, Ngim, who was 11 years old and had lost her entire family during the chaos of the Pol Pot years. With her he fled across the Cambodian border into Thailand and together, two years later, they made it to the United States.

In the United States, Ngor found that his medical degree was useless. He and his niece, who took the American name of Sophie, settled in Los Angeles and became actively involved in refugee work. He soon became a respected member of the Chinatown community in which he lived, and it was there that his life took an unforeseen turn. In 1982, plans were in the works for a major motion picture about *New York Times* journalist Sidney Schanberg and Cambodian journalist and translator Dith Pran and their experiences during and after the fall of Phnom Penh. During preproduction, the casting director saw Haing Ngor at a Cambodian wedding, and knew that he had found the perfect person to play the role of Dith Pran. The movie, released as *The Killing Fields*, was a powerful **evocation** of the horrors of life under the Khmer Rouge, and garnered seven Academy Awards after its release in 1984. Among the award winners was Haing Ngor, who took the honors for Best Supporting Actor, thus launching a wholly unexpected career. When the time came for him to give his award acceptance speech, he eloquently dedicated his Oscar to the memory of his lost family.

Ngor never played another role as important as that of Dith Pran. In the same year that *The Killing Fields* was released, he published his own memoirs, entitled *A Cambodian Odyssey*, and took minor roles in a variety of films, including Oliver Stone's *Between Heaven and Earth*. Nonetheless, he earned a substantial living, and was able to put some of his money to good use, funding two

The casting director saw Haing Ngor at a Cambodian wedding, and knew that he had found the perfect person to play the role of Dith Pran.

evocation imaginative re-creation.

medical clinics in Cambodia and supporting refugee causes in the United States.

What should have been a time of ease and pleasure after the horrors Ngor endured in the killing fields was cut short on the evening of February 25, 1996. Ngor was standing by his car, having just arrived home, when he was accosted by muggers who demanded his money and valuables. Although he willingly gave them his Rolex watch and his cash, he refused to part with a small locket, for it contained a photograph of his late wife. Angered by Ngor's refusal, his assailants shot him dead. ◆

Nguyen, Dustin

SEPTEMBER 17, 1962– ● ACTOR

Dustin Nguyen was born Nguyen Xuan Tri on September 17, 1962, in the city of Saigon, Vietnam. That he would grow up to become an actor was perhaps preordained, given that both of his parents were well-known actors themselves in Vietnam. His mother, My Le, was an accomplished dancer as well, and his father, Xuan Phat, combined writing and producing with his own acting skills. Xuan Phat was a very popular radio and television personality in Saigon, in the 1960s and early 1970s, and was sometimes called "the Vietnamese Johnny Carson."

Nguyen was the oldest of two sons, both of whom enjoyed the benefits of growing up in a wealthy family. Nguyen attended the best schools, where he routinely earned such high grades that he consistently ranked near the top of his classes. Like most well educated Vietnamese, he was fluent in Vietnamese and French.

The years of Nguyen's early childhood were a time when the United States was building up an increasingly large presence in South Vietnam, of which Saigon was the capital. Nguyen's father was closely associated with the American cause in Vietnam; he worked for the U.S.-controlled radio station, and was widely known for his vocal anti-communist, pro-American broadcasts. As long as the United States remained committed to maintaining its military presence in the country, the fortunes of Nguyen's family were largely secured. In April 1975, however, that security ended abruptly.

By the early-1970s, the United States' commitment to the Vietnam war was faltering, as it became clear that there was little to no possibility of ever securing a decisive military victory and, back home, anti-war protests grew ever more vocal. In 1975, President Gerald Ford declared that he was pulling the troops out of Vietnam, and in April Saigon collapsed, soon to be occupied by victorious North Vietnamese troops. Because Nguyen's father had been a highly visible proponent of the United States, he knew his family was unlikely to survive for long under the new political regime. He packed up his family and together they fled to Vung Tan, a seaside town where American ships were waiting offshore to evacuate the last American forces and those Vietnamese nationals who could manage to find a place on board.

Nguyen was only 13 years old when he found himself on the beach outside of Vung Tan, separated from his family. With a friend from Saigon, he was desperately trying to find his way aboard the ships when the North Vietnamese opened fire on the beach, killing hundreds of the would-be refugees as they frantically tried to escape. Nguyen himself nearly failed to make it to safety; he saw his friend shot to death beside him. Nguyen and the rest of his family were among the lucky ones that day, however, for they all made it onto the American ships and were evacuated, stopping first at Guam and then traveling on to a refugee camp that had been set up in Fort Chaffee, Arkansas.

The family remained in the refugee camp for a time, unable to leave until they could find American sponsors who would help them get settled in their new country. The Methodist Church, which was very active in helping find such sponsors for the Vietnamese refugees, eventually found a sponsoring family for Nguyen and his family in Kirkwood, Missouri, and in late 1975 they left the camps to get established in their new home. Nguyen's parents could no longer practice their former careers and took what work they could get; his mother initially taking a job as a cleaning woman, his father finding work as a janitor.

The family's new circumstances were dramatically different, and in addition to the financial hardships, they also faced the difficulties of trying to establish themselves in a country whose traditions and language were wholly new to them. Nguyen, although fluent in French as well as Vietnamese, spoke almost no English; what little he managed to pick up he learned from the children's television program *Sesame Street*. When he was enrolled in the local public school, he entered his eighth grade

1962 Nguyen Xuan Tri (Dustin Nguyen) is born in Saigon, Vietnam.

1975 Nguyen and family flee Vietnam after the fall of Saigon to the North Vietnamese Army.

1979 Nguyen wins the Midwest Tae Kwon Do Championship and earns a black belt.

1980 Nguyen moves to California and begins taking acting lessons.

1985 Nguyen gets first television acting jobs, including a guest appearance on "Magnum, P.I."

1987 Nguyen is signed as one of the young lead actors on the Fox Network's hit show, "21 Jump Street."

class able to speak only a handful of words. He felt very isolated, not only because of the language barrier but also because there were very few Asians in the state, and only two in his school. He understood little of what was going on in class, and his teachers were ill-prepared to help him.

The family worked hard to overcome all the obstacles that they faced as immigrants to a very foreign culture, and soon they met with a degree of success. Within a year of arriving in Missouri they had bought a house and Nguyen had picked up enough English to once again begin earning good grades in school. Still, Nguyen felt set apart and had few friends. To overcome his sense of isolation, he enrolled in classes in tae kwon do, taught through a local martial arts school. He became quite proficient in the sport, and began entering competitions, advancing to a black belt and winning the Midwest **Tae Kwon Do** Championship in 1979, when he was 17 years old.

Tae Kwan Doe Korean martial art resembling karate.

Nguyen's family continued to prosper. Although they never resumed their acting careers, both of his parents found better paying work, his mother as supervisor of the alterations department in a local clothing store, his father as a machinist in a heating and cooling factory. Nguyen continued to do well in his studies, graduating from high school in 1980, then heading to southern California to attend Orange Coast College, in Costa Mesa. He originally planned to fulfill his parents' wishes by earning a degree in engineering but, while still a student he began taking acting classes. No longer interested in his engineering studies, Nguyen threw himself into acting with enthusiasm, and soon began to look for work in his new-found profession. He dropped out of college before earning his diploma, seriously disappointing his parents, and began making the rounds of auditions for television and film projects. At about this time he began using the name Dustin Nguyen, recognizing that his Vietnamese name was not likely to find favor with casting directors or audiences.

Dustin was fortunate in finding a relatively important role early in his career. In 1985 he was signed for an episode of a hit television show, *Magnum, P.I.* Shortly afterward, he landed a recurring role on a highly popular soap opera, playing the character "Suki" on *General Hospital*. He remained with the show for seven months, until his character was written out of the storyline. Nguyen was then signed to do several guest appearances on a variety of series, including a spot on another hit show, *The A-Team*.

Nguyen's big break came in 1987, when he was cast in a new youth-oriented dramatic series, *21 Jump Street*. The break-out star of that show, Johnny Depp, got most of the attention from the press, but Nguyen's character, "Harry Ioki," soon developed a large fan following as well. For the next few years, Nguyen enjoyed the life of a true teen idol, in part because there were so few highly visible Asian actors on television at the time. He remained with the show throughout its run, but by the 1989-1990 season the show's ratings were beginning to drop and the lead actor, Depp, announced plans for leaving to make movies, so Nguyen realized that it was time to move on.

After leaving *Jump Street*, Nguyen continued taking roles in television and films, but discovered that there are few opportunities for Asian actors outside of certain stereotyped roles. He has appeared as a guest star on several major television series, from *Murder, She Wrote* and *Kung Fu: The Legend Continues* to *SeaQuest DSV*, and he has acted in several films, among them *Heaven and Earth* (1993) and *Virtuosity* (1995), starring Denzel Washington. In 1998, Nguyen's popularity soared when he landed the role of Johnny Oh in *V.I.P.*, a top-rated series starring Pamela Anderson as the head of a Los Angeles bodyguard agency. Nguyen lived in Los Angeles, where he was active in community issues, using his celebrity to support anti-drug and anti-gang programs in the city. ◆

Noguchi, Isamu

NOVEMBER 17, 1904–DECEMBER 20, 1988 ● ARTIST

American artist Isamu Noguchi was born Isamu Gilmore on November 17, 1904, in Los Angeles, California, to writer and editor Leonie Gilmore and Japanese poet Yonejiro (Yone) Naguchi. His parents never married, and Isamu's first years were spent in the United States with his mother; his father lived in Tokyo. In 1907, Leonie Gilmore and her son traveled to Japan and settled in Tokyo with Naguchi, but the arrangement did not work out for long. In 1910, mother and son moved to the Tokyo suburb of Onori, where they stayed briefly and Isamu attended local schools, then moved on to the seaside town of Chigasaki. Although Isamu's parents were still unmarried, they maintained a relationship, and soon had another child together, a daughter whom they named Arles, in 1912. This seems to mark the end of the relationship between Isamu's parents, however, for in the following year his father married a Japanese woman who worked in his household.

Intending to settle in Chigasaki for awhile, Leonie Gilmore decided to build a house there, and hired a contracting firm to do the work. Isamu, then nine years old, was fascinated by the craftsmen who took on the job and whenever he was home from school he enjoyed watching and learning from construction team, serving as an unofficial builder's apprentice. Once the house was completed, however, the family did not remain there long. In 1916 Leonie, deciding that her son would eventually be going to high school in the United States and recognizing that he would need more exposure to instruction in English, took Isamu out of the Japanese school he had been attending and sent him instead to a Jesuit-run middle school, St. Joseph's College, in Yokohama, moving the entire family there in the following year.

In 1918 it was time for the now 14-year-old Isamu to go to high school, and his mother decided to enroll him as a boarding student at the Interlaken School in Rolling Prairie, Indiana. Soon after his arrival there, however, the school was closed down and he was sent to stay with a family in LaPorte, Indiana, where he attended the public high school. Here he showed a marked artistic talent, particularly in sculpture. To develop that talent further, he spent the summer before he started college in an apprenticeship with an eminent artist of the time, Gutzon Borglum, who is best known for creating the carvings of the presidents on Mount Rushmore.

In the fall of 1922, Isamu entered Columbia University, planning to study for a degree in medicine, but remained strongly drawn to the world of art. He enrolled in evening sculpture classes offered through the Leonard da Vinci Art School in lower Manhattan, and soon was ready to exhibit his first works. At the urging of his teachers at the art school, Isamu left Columbia before completing his degree and committed himself to a full-time career as an artist.

Isamu established himself in a studio in the Greenwich Village area of Manhattan, and quickly set to work, exhibiting some of his important early pieces at the National Academy of Design, in Washington, D.C., and the Philadelphia Academy of Fine Art in 1925 and 1926. Meanwhile, he began exploring other avenues of artistic expression, and began what would become a lifelong involvement in theatrical design, costumes and sets. At the same time, Isamu actively sought to learn more about contemporary trends in sculpture, visiting the many galleries and museums in New York, and becoming particularly interested in the very modern work of Constantin Brancusi.

In 1927, Isamu won a Guggenheim Fellowship that enabled him to travel to Europe to further expose himself to the artistic movements of the day. He got no further than Paris, however. He remained in Paris for most of the next two years, living in Montparnasse and meeting many of the artists who lived and worked there, including Alexander Calder, Morris Kantor, and Brancusi. He remained in Paris for most of the next two years, establishing his own studio while working as assistant to Brancusi. When his fellowship funds ran out, however, he had to return home, arriving back in New York at the end of 1928 and setting himself up in a studio at the top of Carnegie Hall.

In 1929 Isamu had his first solo exhibition of his modernist sculpture in New York, and his work drew the attention of many of the city's leading artists and intellectuals. Two early admirers who would become extremely important to Isamu in the years to come were inventor and architect R. Buckminster Fuller and dancer Martha Graham. Isamu found Fuller's visionary philosophy particularly suited to his own emerging *esthetic*.

For all his critical success, Isamu received few commissions for his modern sculpture, and found it necessary to support himself with portrait work. Between commissions, he traveled with Fuller on a lecture tour through the northeast. The early 1930s were a time of much travel, and Isamu visited Paris, Moscow, and Beijing to expand his artistic horizons. During his travels, he began working in a variety of new media, moving beyond the stone and wood of his sculpture to explore ink and brush work and pottery. He ended this period of travel with his first return to Tokyo since his departure to attend high school. He met with his father, their first meeting in more than 12 years, and learned about the principles of creating Japanese gardens.

On his return to New York, Isamu began using his father's name, Noguchi, rather than Gilmore. The next decade was a time of great productivity in a wide variety of artistic formats, from costume and set design for Martha Graham to large scale public works commissioned by the Arts Project of the National Recovery Act and industrial projects for such clients as the Zenith Radio Corporation and the Ford Motor Company. He also began designing fountain installations and presented some

The early 1930s were a time of much travel, and Isamu visited Paris, Moscow, and Beijing to expand his artistic horizons.

After World War II ended, Noguchi threw himself back into his work.

of his first modern furniture designs at an exhibition for the Museum of Modern Art. During this period he also traveled to Mexico City, where he collaborated on the creation of a 72-foot political mural.

In 1941 Noguchi was living in Hollywood, California, when the Japanese attack on Pearl Harbor occurred. During this period, most Japanese-Americans on the West Coast were forced to leave their homes and enter relocation camps as a result of anti-Japanese feelings in the American population at large. Because of his prominence Noguchi was exempt from mandatory relocation, but he voluntarily spent two months at one of the camps as part of his effort to bring attention to the plight of Japanese-Americans during the war years. To further this cause, he formed the Nisei Writers and Artists Mobilization for Democracy.

After World War II ended, Noguchi threw himself back into his work, and the next several decades saw him completing many of his most important projects. He continued to collaborate with the theater, producing sets and costumes for productions by Graham and by George Balanchine, designing fountains, gardens, and furniture, and completing sculptures for public and corporate clients. In 1949 he received a Bollinger Foundation grant to write a book on "environments of leisure." The book was never written, but Noguchi used the funds to subsidize the costs of another bout of extended travel, visiting several European countries before moving on to Egypt, India, and Southeast Asia. He once again returned to Japan, where he found his work to be highly respected, and he received numerous commissions for work. During this period he met an actress named Yoshiko Yamaguchi, whom he married.

Noguchi continued his traveling, this time accompanied by his wife, but when the couple attempted to return to the United States in 1953, Yoshiko was prohibited from entering the country, due to charges that she was a communist sympathizer. Noguchi spent the next few years fighting the government on this issue, and the two were forced to live apart, he in New York, she in Europe. Noguchi's career throughout this period remained unaffected by his personal problems, however, and his furniture designs and gardens in particular were winning great acclaim.

In 1957 the years of separation proved to be too much for the relationship between Noguchi and his wife, and the two were divorced. Throughout the remainder of the decade and well into the 1960s, Noguchi was busy with a great variety of projects, from gardens and playgrounds to furniture, stage sets, costumes, and memorials. In 1961 he opened a studio in Long Island City, and in 1966 he established the Akari Foundation, dedicated to the support of artistic exchanges between the United States and Japan.

In 1968, the first Noguchi retrospective was held at the Whitney Museum in New York. This year also saw the publication of Noguchi's autobiography, *A Sculptor's World*. The artist, now in his 60s, showed no sign of slowing down, and over the next 12 years he took on a great many commissions, primarily fountains and gardens but also individual sculpture pieces. In 1981, however, Noguchi's thoughts began to turn to creating a lasting legacy of his work. Noguchi bought the land adjacent to his studio in Long Island City and began making plans for what would ultimately become the Isamu Noguchi Garden Museum, a 13-gallery facility housing some 240 works and built around a garden in which many of Noguchi's sculptures are placed. The Museum opened to the public in 1985.

Somewhat slowed down by age, Noguchi took little outside work while he devoted his energies to making the Garden Museum a reality. Nonetheless, the art world did not forget him. He received a number of awards during the next few years, including Japan's Kyoto Prize (1986), the National Medal of the Arts (1987), and the Award for Distinction in Sculpture, granted by the Sculpture Center in New York (1988). Noguchi died in his Long Island City home on December 20, 1988, at the age of 84. ◆

Onizuka, Ellison

JUNE 24, 1946–JANUARY 28, 1986 ● ASTRONAUT

Ellison Onizuka was born on June 24, 1946, in the town of Kealakekua, on the Hawaiian island of Kona, to Masanitsu and Mitsue Onizuka. As a child he attended the local public schools, graduating from Konawaena High School in 1964. He was 11 years old when the launch of Sputnik by the Soviet Union made headlines in the news media throughout the country. The United States responded to the challenge of *Sputnik* by launching a concerted drive to match and even beat the accomplishment of the Soviet Union, and like many young people at the time, Ellison was fascinated by the prospect of someday being a part of the American space program.

Unlike most of his peers, who dreamed of space but never really expected to go there, Ellison decided to take practical steps toward achieving his goal. He knew that he would have to acquire specialized knowledge and training before he could hope to qualify for the space program, and he chose his college and course of study with the specific aim of maximizing his chances to one day become an astronaut.

Onizuka attended the University of Colorado, where he majored in aerospace engineering, earning his bachelor's degree in 1968 and his master's degree the following year. In addition, he knew that astronauts were at the time drawn from the ranks of the military, specifically the Air Force, so he signed up for the four-year ROTC program on campus in preparation of taking up a commission in the Air Force upon graduation. His work at college and in graduate school was distinguished, and earned him membership in the Triangle Fraternity and the Tau Beta Pi

Sputnik Soviet satellite launched into orbit around the Earth in 1957, causing alarm among United States officials that the Soviet Union was winning the space race during the Cold War.

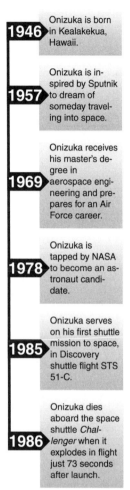

1946 Onizuka is born in Kealakekua, Hawaii.

1957 Onizuka is inspired by Sputnik to dream of someday traveling into space.

1969 Onizuka receives his master's degree in aerospace engineering and prepares for an Air Force career.

1978 Onizuka is tapped by NASA to become an astronaut candidate.

1985 Onizuka serves on his first shuttle mission to space, in Discovery shuttle flight STS 51-C.

1986 Onizuka dies aboard the space shuttle *Challenger* when it explodes in flight just 73 seconds after launch.

and Sigma Tau engineering honor societies (the two societies have since merged into a single organization).

While in college, Onizuka met a young woman named Lorna Leiko Yoshida, of Naalehu, Hawaii, and the two fell in love. They were married, and in 1969 had their first child, a daughter whom they named Janelle Mitsue. They had a second child, a son whom they named Darien Lei Shizue, on March 11, 1975.

Because of his outstanding performance in the ROTC program, Onizuka was offered a commission in the United States Air Force immediately upon graduation from his graduate program in December 1969, and he commenced active duty in January 1970. He was ordered to report to the McClellan Air Force Base in California, where he was assigned to the Sacramento Air Logistics Center. His duties required him to participate in flight tests and systems safety engineering, and he became familiar with most of the state-of-the-art aircraft of the day.

Onizuka knew that he was going to have to log a significant amount of flight time if he hoped to qualify as an astronaut, and so he attended the United States Air Force Flight School from August 1974 to July 1975. The course of study was rigorous, involving not only flying instruction but also training in conducting systems tests in-flight. Nonetheless, Onizuka enjoyed the challenge, and turned in a top-notch performance.

After completing flight school, Onizuka was immediately assigned to Edwards Air Force Base, again in California, where he was appointed to the Test Pilot School staff there; he soon earned the position of chief of the engineering support section and took up teaching duties as well. At the same time, he participated in test flights as well, logging more than 1,700 hours of flight time.

Throughout his career, Onizuka maintained a solid record of excellence, earning many honors along the way. He became a member of the Society of Flight Test Engineers, the Air Force Association, and the American Institute of Aeronautics and Astronautics. He was presented with numerous awards for his service in the Air Force, including the Commendation and Meritorious Service Medals, the Outstanding Unit and Organizational Excellence Awards, and the National Defense Service Medal.

Onizuka's hard work and planning paid off in January 1978, when he was selected as an astronaut candidate by the National Aeronautics and Space Administration (NASA). He was immediately signed up for a year of training and evaluation, which he completed in August 1979. He was selected to participate in the launch of the first Space Shuttle, STS-1, joining the support teams at the Kennedy Space Center in Florida in 1980 and working there until the shuttle's launch and return in 1981. He handled similar duties for the second shuttle launch in that same year.

It would be several years before Onizuka had the opportunity to move from support crew to the shuttle cockpit, during which time he worked in a number of technical capacities, from software testing to payload development. However, on January 24, 1985, he finally realized his dream, and was selected to serve as mission specialist on the *Discovery* space shuttle in the first mission flown for the Department of Defense. The flight gave Onizuka ample time to truly appreciate his first visit to space, for the shuttle made a full 48 orbits of the Earth before returning to the Kennedy Space Center three days later.

With one shuttle flight under his belt, Onizuka looked forward to further opportunities, but there would be only one more shuttle crew on which he would serve. He was selected to serve as one of the mission specialists on shuttle flight STS-51L, propelled by the *Challenger* shuttlecraft, set to launch in January 1986. This would be the first of a proposed series of shuttle flights that would include a civilian crew member, S. Christa McAuliff, who was participating in a newly developed NASA program called "Teacher in Space." The shuttle team had an exciting array of scheduled activities, including monitoring the transit path of Halley's Comet and the transmission of daily educational segments, taught by McAuliff, for use in the nation's schools. The flight was scrubbed several times due to a variety of technical and weather related problems, but on January 28, 1986, the *Challenger* was given the go-ahead for launch.

This *Challenger* launch generated perhaps the most excitement about the space program felt in the United States since the very first space flights of the 1960s. Millions watched on television as Commander M. J. Smith, pilot Francis R. Scobee, payload specialist Gregory Jarvis, Ms. Christa McAuliff, and mission specialists Judith A. Resnick, Ronald E. McNair, and Ellison Onizuka lifted off for their historic flight. In little more than a minute, however, excitement turned to horror: the *Challenger* exploded in mid-air just 73 seconds after leaving the launching pad, killing everyone on board.

The *Challenger* disaster had a devastating effect on NASA's space program, forcing all scheduled launches to be scrubbed for the next two years while inquiries were conducted into the cause of the accident. Weather conditions on the day of the

With one shuttle flight under his belt, Onizuka looked forward to further opportunities.

flight, and a faulty piece of equipment, called an O-ring, were ultimately blamed for the accident. Ellison Onizuka, who had spent his life pursuing his dream of exploring space, would doubtless have been greatly saddened that the accident had such a chilling effect on the space program in which he served, but he would no doubt be thrilled with the progress that has since been made with Spacelab and the *Soyuz* and *Mir* projects, and the continuation of space exploration as a whole. ◆

Ono, Yoko

FEBRUARY 18, 1933– ● ARTIST

Although best known to the general public as John Lennon's widow, the musician and artist Yoko Ono had forged a reputation as a serious visual artist long before her destiny merged with that of the legendary Beatle. As a pioneering member of the avant garde "Fluxus" circle in New York city in the 1960s, she helped to trigger the wave of creative energies that paved the way for the popular musical and cultural experimentation of the late 1960s.

Yoko Ono was born in Tokyo, Japan, on February 18, 1933. The daughter of a well-to-do banker and socially prominent mother, she was raised mostly by nannies and maids. She recalled her childhood as one of material wealth but emotional poverty: "When I wanted to see my father," she told a reporter, "I would have to call his office and make an appointment."

As a young child Ono was as passionate about poetry and writing as she was averse to music, which was force-fed her by her father, an amateur pianist. An indifferent student, she would often pretend to be sick to avoid classes. During World War II she looked after her younger siblings in the country quarters to which they were confined during

Yoko Ono

the Allied bombing of Tokyo. Yoko enrolled in Gakushuin University in Tokyo to study philosophy while being, in her own words "a closet song writer." She left the university in 1951 to join her family when they relocated to Scarsdale, New York. Yoko enrolled in nearby Sarah Lawrence College in Bronxville, New York. She seldom attended classes there, preferring to concentrate on the poems and short stories that she regularly sent out to major publications in return for a ballooning collection of rejection notices.

Unpublished but still harboring **inchoate** artistic ambitions, Ono left Sarah Lawrence after three years without a degree and landed in New York City, where, in 1957, she met and married Toshi Ichiyanagi, a Japanese musician. During her seven-year marriage to Ichiyanagi, Ono gradually fruitfully cultivated her associations among New York's avant-garde artists who helped to promote her art and "events" at various small but influential redoubts in the recesses of Greenwich Village; among her early fans were such underground eminences as John Cage, Max Ernst, Andy Warhol, Jasper Johns, and Peggy Guggenheim. The highlight of that period was the six-month Chambers Street Series that began in December 1960. A seminal forum for the mixed-media installations that pervaded the 1960s art scene, this "Fluxus" grouping of artist sought to demolish the formal boundaries that separated one art form from another. A typical effort of this period was Ono's "Bicycle Piece for Orchestra" (1962), which featured 100 cyclists circling the stage.

In 1964 Ono left Ichiyanagi and married the experimental film director Anthony Cox. In the words of one journalist, "During those years, Yoko bounced around from project to project, living closer to her art than to her husbands. . . . Yoko's works at that time included some of her more way-out conceptual items—art items that are created partly by the artist and that must be completed in the mind of the observer." The paucity of public and critical recognition often left her in despair, leaving her colleagues in doubt about the depth of her commitment. A friend recalled, "People just didn't believe she was serious about art, figuring she could always go home to Mom and Dad." Ono's most notable success in those years was a book, *Grapefruit* (1964), that featured prints of her conceptual artworks.

Ono met John Lennon at an art exhibition in London in 1968. There was an instant spark between them, and within a year they were married. Ono's omnipresence at the Beatles' recording sessions and business meetings was widely regarded as

1933 Ono is born in Tokyo, Japan.

1951 Ono's family emigrates to Scarsdale, New York, and Ono enrolls at nearby Sarah Lawrence College.

1962 Premiere of Ono's mulitmedia performance artwork *Bicycle Piece for Orchestra*.

1969 Ono marries John Lennon.

1989 The Whitney Museum of American Art holds a major retrospective of Ono's art.

2000 New York's Japan Society organizes a retrospective of Ono's artwork.

inchoate partly in existence.

"All my works are a form of wishing. Keep wishing while you participate."

Yoko Ono

a major factor in the breakup of the legendary foursome, an interpretation not entirely disputed by Lennon himself. As he told a reporter in 1972, "Meeting Yoko was . . . meeting somebody with the same interests, with a brilliant mind, who had the same kind of vision I had. . . . When Yoko came into my life, nothing else seemed important. . . . Her work and her way of life and her mind and *Grapefruit* just blew my mind open, and I saw that what I was doing with the Beatles was just trivia."

The marriage quickly evolved into a symbol of masscult countercultural iconography, with the full complicity of the media-savvy celebrity lovers, most notably at their spring 1969 "be-in" in their hotel room in Toronto, Canada, where they created the song that soon became the anthem of the antiwar movement, "Give Peace a Chance." Their ensemble, The Plastic Ono Band, performed a concert in Toronto the following fall, recording the proceedings for release as the best-selling album *Live Peace,* the third Lennon-Ono collaboration (the others were *Unfinished Music No. 2* and *Wedding Album*); all three albums contained original compositions by Ono, many of which addressed hot-button issues of social protest and unrest.

Ono's substantial contributions to *Double Fantasy,* recorded a few months before Lennon's death, elevated her standing with fans and critics alike. Her departure from relentless avant-garde experimentation led to a more engaging sound. As Ono said at the time, "I came to a point where I believed that the idea of avant-garde purity was just as stifling as just doing a rock beat over and over. People were silent. I felt the lack of a sense of humor. John was doing this healthy beat music, and I got stimulated with that."

After Lennon's murder in December 1980, the grief-stricken Ono went into a long period of seclusion, devoting herself entirely to the rearing of her son Sean. By the middle of the decade Ono began recording new music and released albums such as *Rising* (1995) and *A Story* (1997). She also began creating art again and has been featured in a steady stream of gallery and museum exhibitions over the past fifteen years. In 1989 her works were included in a major retrospective at the Whitney Museum of American Art in New York. In 2000, New York's Japan Society organized an exhibition called "Yes Yoko Ono," which featured more than 130 artworks Ono has created since 1960. After four months at the Japan Society, the exhibition traveled to museums throughout North America.

Yoko Ono lived in Manhattan in the Dakota, the building into which she moved with John Lennon in 1973. ◆

Ozawa, Seiji

1935– ● CONDUCTOR

Seiji Ozawa was born to Japanese parents in Shenyang, China, in 1935. Even as a child he showed great musical talent, and received instruction on the piano at an early age. When he was old enough, he attended Tokyo's Toho School of Music, where he studied with Hideo Saito, an acclaimed conductor who taught Western music and technique. Ozawa flourished under Saito's instruction, upon his graduation in 1959 he was awarded first prizes in both composition and conducting. In that same year he competed in the International Competition for Orchestra Conductors, held in Besancon, France, and won first prize there as well.

At the competition, Ozawa was spotted by Charles Munch, who was then musical director for the Boston Symphony Orchestra. Munch was greatly impressed by Ozawa's talent, and invited him to come to Tanglewood Music Center in Massachusetts, where the Boston Symphony ran a summer educational program for young musicians. There Ozawa once again distinguished himself, winning the Koussevitzky Prize for Outstanding Student Conductor in 1960.

Ozawa then went to work with the Berlin Philharmonic, where he came to the attention of Leonard Bernstein, who was visiting there during a tour of Europe with the New York Philharmonic at the time. Bernstein was so impressed with Ozawa that he appointed the young conductor to the post of assistant conductor for the 1961-1962 season in New York.

Ozawa's work with the New York Philharmonic brought him an offer to appear as guest conductor for the San Francisco Symphony, which was his first professional performance in the United States, also in 1962. His excellence as a conductor brought him numerous further opportunities to conduct some of the most accomplished orchestras in North America and in Europe over the next several years. In 1964 he conducted the Boston Symphony Orchestra for the first time, in performances at Tangelwood. He was appointed musical director for the Chicago Symphony Orchestra's summer program, the Ravinia Festival, from 1964 to 1969, and for most of those years he served as musical director of Toronto during the regular seasons, from 1965 to 1969. In 1968 he had his debut at Boston's Symphony Hall.

Seiji Ozawa

The 1970s saw the beginning of what would become Ozawa's long formal association with the Boston Symphony Orchestra. He was named artistic director there in 1970, moving up to musical advisor in 1972 and, finally, assuming the full duties of musical director in 1973. He assumed this post on the departure of the much beloved Leonard Bernstein, with whom the Boston Symphony had long been identified, and some wondered whether or not he would be able to earn the great public affection that had been accorded his predecessor. Bernstein, after all, had built up a great deal of goodwill for his orchestra, particularly with his programs for making classical music more accessible to the public through his "Evening at the Pops" concerts on American public television (PBS) and programs offered through the area's schools. It was difficult in the mid-1970s to even think about the Boston Symphony without immediately thinking of Bernstein.

In the end, there was little reason to worry, for Ozawa's exuberant style and his commitment to carry on Bernstein's tradition of outreach to the broader public quickly earned him the favor of Boston's audiences. He further built his reputation, and the reputation of the Boston Symphony, through frequent tours throughout the country and the world, and through his practice, which continues to this day, of commissioning new works specifically for the Symphony to perform. He also continued Bernstein's tradition of public television specials, and in 1976 he won his first of two Emmy awards for a PBS series entitled "Evening at the Symphony." His second Emmy, which he received in 1999, was for a televised performance of the works of Dvorak, also performed by the Boston Symphony. Ozawa's long tenure as musical director in Boston ended in 2002, when he accepted the position of musical director for the Vienna State Opera.

Throughout his career, Ozawa built an increasingly important worldwide reputation. In addition to his work with the Boston Symphony Orchestra, Ozawa regularly conducted performances of the Berlin and Vienna Philharmonics, and appeared with the New Japan Philharmonic, and the Toronto and London Symphony Orchestras. He increasingly explored opera as well, appearing as conductor for performances at New York's Metropolitan Opera and La Scala, among others. He received numerous awards, including the Chevalier de la Legion d'Honneur, presented by French President Jacques Chirac, for his longstanding support of French composers and for his work at the Paris Opera. In addition, he received Japan's Jhouye Shu Award for lifetime achievement in 1994, and Musical America's Musician of the Year award in 1997.

One of the constant themes running through Ozawa's career in music was his profound commitment to education, clearly motivated by a belief in the need to train future generations. For example, in 1992 he co-founded the Saito Kinen Orchestra, in Matsumoto Japan, in memory of his early teacher, Hideo Saito, when he was a student at the Toho School. He expanded his televised performances beyond the Boston Symphony Orchestra specials, working with pop musician Bobby McFadden in a series of musical education programs aimed at school children that is carried on cable television throughout the United States. He also served as teacher and administrator at Tanglewood Music Center, the Boston Symphony's summer teaching facility in western Massachusetts, throughout his tenure as director of the orchestra. Commemorating his commitment to education, in 1994 the Tanglewood Music Center opened the doors to its new Saiji Ozawa Hall.

1935 Ozawa is born in Shenyang, China.

1959 Ozawa wins first prize in the International Competition for Orchestra Conductors.

1960 Ozawa attends Tanglewood Music Center, in Massachusetts.

1973 Ozawa begins his 25 year tenure as musical director of the Boston Symphony Orchestra.

1984 Ozawa co-founds the Saito Kinen Orchestra in Japan.

1998 Ozawa conducts a real-time, world broadcast of Beethoven's "Ode for Joy," simultaneously leading symphonies in Germany, Australia, the United States, Japan, North Africa, and China.

2002 Ozawa begins tenure as musical director of Vienna State Opera.

In 1998, Ozawa enjoyed a world-wide audience for his irrepressible conducting style when he led a real-time performance of Beethoven's "Ode for Joy" by five orchestras on five continents: Japan, the United States, Australia, China, and Africa. This performance, part of the celebrations surrounding the Winter Olympic Games held in Nagano, Japan, was seen by the largest single audience ever to enjoy an orchestral production. In Massachusetts, where he worked for so long to expand and improve musical education, Ozawa received recognition from many important institutions. The University of Massachusetts, the New England Conservatory of Music, and Wheaton College, in Norton Massachusetts, have all conferred honorary doctorate degrees upon him. ◆

Paik, Nam June

1932– ● ARTIST

June Paik was born Nam June Paik in Seoul, Korea, in 1932. Information on his early years as a schoolchild in Korea is limited, but he showed an early talent in art and in music. Among the composers he most admired was Arnold Shoenberg, whose works he first heard while still in high school. Unfortunately, Paik's interests in music and art would be interrupted for a time by the violence of the Korean War. Life in Seoul was becoming ever more dangerous, so Paik and his family eventually decided to flee the increasing hostilities in 1950, when Paik was 18 years old.

The family first made their way to Hong Kong, where they stayed briefly until they could find passage to Japan. They settled in Tokyo, where Paik was able to resume his studies by attending the University of Tokyo. There he explored esthetics and art history, earning his bachelor's degree in 1956. He wrote his senior thesis on the works of Shoenberg.

After graduation, Paik decided that he needed to broaden his understanding of Western music, so he moved to Germany, and enrolled in the music school of the University of Munich to study music theory. While still working on his degree, he attended the 1957 International Summer Courses for New Music in Darmstadt, Germany. This would provide the single most important influence on his developing artistic sensibilities, for there he made the acquaintance of avant garde composer John Cage, whose innovative work was a striking departure from traditional composition in principle and in technique. Paik was strongly attracted to the new approach to art that Cage and his

Nam June Paik alongside his installation "The Rehearsal."

followers were developing, an approach based on "happenings," which confronted its audience with a demand for interaction, as opposed to the simple, static viewing of exhibition pieces that had, to this point in time, been customary.

Paik threw himself into this new style of art with enthusiasm, exploring ways in which he could combine his dual interests of visual art and music. When he completed his work at the University of Munich and was awarded his degree, in 1964, it was only natural that he would then moved to New York City and throw himself into the vibrant art scene that was developing in Greenwich Village in the 1960s.

Paik's mentor, John Cage, had founded a group called Fluxus, which had drawn into its circle artists and performers as disparate as Allen Ginsberg and Yoko Ono. Paik became a prominent figure in the New York Fluxus group, and quickly became caught up in what came to be known as "performance art." He had become fascinated with the possibilities of incorporating television into his works, and in discovering ways to manipulate the medium. In 1963 he began with simple experiments, using the television as an object to be manipulated, dismantled, or otherwise altered. Soon, however, he saw the possibilities of using the medium itself to express his artistic vision, and began accompanying his presentations with audio as well. From these early explorations, Paik developed a wholly new field of artistic expression, and became known as the "father of video art."

Paik's first installation to make use of television was a space that he filled with 13 sets laid out on their backs and turned on, with each of their horizontal and vertical hold buttons tuned to different settings, resulting in a visual montage of shifting screen images. This use of flickering, random images on video screens has since become the signature of his art. So also is his incorporation of his first artistic love, music. Throughout his career, until her death in 1999, he frequently collaborated with Fluxus cellist Charlotte Moorman, who played an instrument he invented, a "video cello" into which television screens had been fitted.

Paik's work has always been forward-looking, and futuristic. As his art has matured it has involved ever more elaborate displays. In the 1990s, for example, he presented an installation entitled "Electronic Superhighway: Nam June Paik in the 90s," which included more than 500 working television monitors, simultaneously broadcasting game shows, news, cartoon clips, and other random images. The display spreads out over several rooms, all flooded in harshly flashing neon lights. Also part of the display are robot-like structures created from television parts and a futuristic "Cybertown" where all the mailboxes are equipped with computer keyboards.

While Paik's work received critical respect throughout his career, both in the United States and abroad, it was in the 1990s that he first began achieving formal honors. In 1993 he was awarded the Gold Lion Award for the best exhibition in the Venice Biennale. In New York, where his work is best known and most frequently displayed, 1996 was a particularly gratifying time for Paik, for he was awarded the city's Artist Award and was given the Medal of Freedom by New York City Mayor Rudolph Giuliani.

From his earliest exhibitions, Paik was a visionary whose work anticipated technological innovations that could barely be imagined four decades ago. He understood early on that video, then a relatively new medium, would ultimately come to infiltrate and eventually dominate life. His art commented on this future vision on two levels. First, the use of the physical

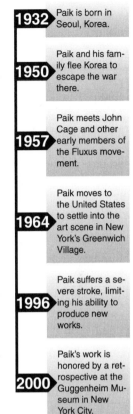

1932 Paik is born in Seoul, Korea.

1950 Paik and his family flee Korea to escape the war there.

1957 Paik meets John Cage and other early members of the Fluxus movement.

1964 Paik moves to the United States to settle into the art scene in New York's Greenwich Village.

1996 Paik suffers a severe stroke, limiting his ability to produce new works.

2000 Paik's work is honored by a retrospective at the Guggenheim Museum in New York City.

trappings of television and, later, other technologies such as faxes and computers as materials for the construction of his art made a general statement about the ways that our technology comes to define us. Second, and more **insidiously,** his selection and manipulation of images within his sculptures permitted him to comment directly and indirectly upon cultural issues. Thus, for example, his distortion of video images of Nixon as they flicker on the screens of one of his exhibits makes a political statement. Similarly, in an installation dedicated to the memory of his early mentor, John Cage, and his longtime collaborator, Charlotte Moorman, he uncharacteristicly refrains from incorporating sound, suggesting that they, now dead, have been silenced.

insidious subtle.

Paik's work, once at the cutting edge of the avant garde movement, found acceptance within mainstream art, and he inspired a generation of younger video artists to explore the territory that he pioneered nearly half a century ago. In 1996 Paik was forced to drastically cut back his work after suffering a stroke that severely limited his mobility. He remained involved in designing exhibitions of his work, however, and was an active consultant when the Guggenheim Museum in New York City staged a major retrospective of his art in 2000.

Pei, I.M.

APRIL 26, 1917– ● ARCHITECT

Ieoh Ming Pei was born on April 26, 1917, in Canton, China, into a wealthy family whose prosperity came from his father's success as a banker. As the first-born son of well-to-do parents, he received an excellent early education as a matter of course, and when he reached college age he was able to apply to the top universities of the world. He chose to attend Massachusetts Insititute of Technology (M.I.T.) in Boston, and arrived there in 1935 to begin his studies in architecture. He received his bachelor's degree in architecture in 1940, having so distinguished himself that he took high honors and several prestigious awards, including an M.I.T. Traveling Fellowship.

In 1942, after a couple of years of practical experience, Pei enrolled in the Harvard Graduate School of Design. There he studied under the legendary German architect Walter Gropius,

an important representative of the modern school of architecture. Six months later, Pei's education was interrupted by the United States' involvement in World War II, and Pei supported the war effort of his adopted nation by volunteering his services to the National Defense Research Committee, which was established in Princeton, New Jersey. In that same year he married an American woman, whom he had met in Boston.

I.M. Pei's glass pyramid in Paris, France.

Pei returned to Harvard in 1944 in order to complete his graduate degree, which he received in 1946. While working at his studies, and for a few years afterward, he supported himself by serving as an assistant professor for the graduate school from 1945 until 1948. In 1951 his work was recognized by Harvard when he was granted the Wheelwright Traveling Fellowship, administered by the university. These funds permitted him to take an extended tour through England, France, Italy, and Greece, where he studied the architectural work of the masters of the past.

Pei returned to the United States in 1954, this time with the intention of making it his permanent home. To this end he petitioned for citizenship, and became a naturalized citizen of

1917 Pei is born in Canton, China.

1935 Pei comes to the United States to study at Massachusetts Institute of Technology.

1942 Pei attends Harvard Graduate School of Design to study with architect Walter Gropius.

1955 Pei establishes his own architectural firm, I.M. Pei and Associates.

1984 Pei establishes a scholarship fund to support Chinese architectural students studying in the United States.

1986 Pei is awarded the Medal of Liberty by President Ronald Reagan.

1990 Pei retires from active involvement in the architectural profession, turning the business over to his partners in the firm.

the United States in that same year. In the following year he formed his own architectural firm, I.M. Pei and Associates, and spent the next several years establishing himself professionally, and in the 1960s he began work on a series of public and institutional projects that brought him widespread recognition and acclaim both within his industry and in the broader public as well.

The first of these important commissions was done for the federal government, which awarded him the assignment of designing the National Center of Atmospheric Research, to be built in Boulder Colorado. This project was completed in 1967, and was followed by a commission to design the East Building of the National Gallery of Art, in Washington, D.C., which took ten years to complete. Overlapping these two projects was a commission to design the John F. Kennedy Library in Boston, Massachusetts, on which Pei worked from 1965 to 1979.

In all, Pei completed over thirty large- and small-scale institutional projects, from churches, hospitals, and schools, to municipal buildings, libraries, and museums. While the bulk of his work was done in the United States, his services were sought out by governments and corporations throughout the world. His designs included the Museum of Modern Art in Athens, Greece; the Miho Museum in Shiga, Japan; the Grand Louvre, in Paris; Raffles City Hotel, in Singapore; and the Bank of China, in Hong Kong. In the United States, two of his better-known buildings were the Four Seasons Hotel in Manhattan and the Rock and Roll Hall of Fame in Cleveland, Ohio. In 1990 the then 73-year-old architect retired from active participation in his firm, which was renamed Pei, Cobb, Freed, and Partners.

In addition to his creative work, Pei was an active force within his profession, serving on a number of boards and committees that dealt with issues of concern to architects and designers. He served on visiting committees for Harvard, M.I.T., and New York's Metropolitan Museum of Art. In addition, he participated in many government panels dealing with public policy regarding architecture and public policy, including the Urban Design Council of New York City and the American Institute of Architecture's National Urban Policy Task Force. In 1966, President Lyndon Johnson appointed him to the National Council on the Humanities, and in 1980 he was appointed by President Jimmy Carter to the National Council on the Arts.

Beginning with the prizes and awards he won while a student at M.I.T. and Harvard, Pei earned recognition and many honors throughout his long career. He was granted honorary doctorate degrees within the United States from the University of Pennsylvania, Brown and Columbia Universities, New York University, and the University of Colorado, and U.C.L.A. awarded him its Gold Medal in 1990. Abroad, he was given honorary doctorates from the Chinese University of Hong Kong and the University of Paris.

Pei was highly honored within his professional field as well. He was made a Fellow of the American Institute of Architects, which awarded him its highest honor, the A.I.A. Gold Medal, in 1979, and elected to the American Academy of Arts and Sciences. In addition, he was a member of the National Academy of Design and the American Academy of Arts and Letters, and admitted as a Corporate Member of the Royal Institute of British Architects. In 1986, President Ronald Reagan presented him with the Medal of Liberty Award in recognition of Pei's many contributions to American society and culture.

In 1975 Pei was elected to the American Academy, a highly exclusive organization that restricts its membership to 50 at any one time. In 1978 he became Chancellor of the Academy, in which position he served until 1980. In 1982 he was awarded the Grande Medaille d'Or from the French Academie d'Architecture and in 1984 he was inducted into the Institut de France. In the following year he received that nation's Ordre des Arts et des Lettres. In 1993, with the completion of his work on the Grande Louvre, he was made an *Officier* in the Legion d'Honneur by the French president. In Japan, too, he was singled out for honors, in recognition of his work on projects that include the Miho Museum in Shiga. In 1989 Pei was awarded Japan's Praemium Imperiale by the Japan Art Association, in recognition of his lifetime of achievement in architectural design.

Pei's prolific career gave the United States and the world an extraordinary legacy of brilliantly designed buildings, but he has not been content to let that be his only gift to his profession. In 1983 he used the funds that accompanied his Pritzker Architecture Prize to set up a scholarship fund for Chinese architecture students to study in the United States, with the provision that they return to their homelands to practice their profession. ◆

Pran, Dith

SEPTEMBER 27, 1942– ● PHOTOGRAPHER

A survivor of Pol Pot's Cambodian holocaust of the 1970s, the photojournalist Dith Pran rose to prominence for the role he played as an assistant to *The New York Times* reporter Sydney Schanberg during those dark years, an experience that was memorably recorded in Schanberg's article "The Death and Life of Dith Pran" (1980), later retold in the award-winning movie *The Killing Fields* (1984).

Dith Pran was born on September 27, 1942, to a middle-class family in Siem Reap, a town in northwestern Cambodia that is near the famous religious monument Angkor Wat. His father was a supervisor of public works and road construction. Although Pran's native language was **Khmer,** by studying on his own he learned English well enough to get a job as an interpreter for the newly formed United States Military Assistance Command in 1962.

Khmer the official language of Cambodia.

___

Dith Pran

Three years later the Cambodian government broke formal diplomatic relations with the United States after several Cambodians were killed by bombs dropped by the U.S.-backed South Vietnamese Army. Obliged to seek other work, Pran became a guide director to the Angkor ruins for a local hotel. But the course of the war in Southeast Asia soon proved disastrous to the tourist industry. With North Vietnamese troops increasingly taking refuge in Cambodia, South Vietnamese troops began pursuing them there, accompanied by U.S. bombs. By 1970 the situation had so destabilized the country that Lon Nol seized power in a right-wing military coup and facilitated further attacks from U.S. bombing raids. The besieged populace became more supportive of the left-wing Khmer Rouge, and a bloody civil war ensued.

Driven out of the tourist business by the fighting, Pran moved his family to Phnom Penh, where he found work as an interpreter and guide for foreign correspondents, most notably Craig Whitney, *The New York Times* bureau chief in Saigon at the time. Through Whitney, Pran met Sydney Schanberg, a *Times* reporter who arrived in Cambodia in 1972 to cover the widening war. Pran soon became an indispensable right arm to Schanberg, and their professional association fostered a close personal bond. As Pran later commented to Schanberg, "It seems like we are born from the same mother. . . . We both have the same blood."

By 1973 Pran was working exclusively with Schanberg, at whose recommendation Pran was hired as a full-time stringer by the *Times*. Despite the intensity of Schanberg's demands on Pran's time and resources, the bond between the two was never frayed. As Pran later told Schanberg, "I never got angry, because I understand your heart. I also understand that you are a man who wants everything to succeed." Among Schanberg's journalistic successes made possible by Pran's resourcefulness, none was more important than Schanberg's account of the appalling desperation among the residents of Cambodia's mushrooming refugee camps, reportage that exposed the falsity of official U.S. government assurances that wartime dislocation of civilians in Cambodia was minimal. Pran's ingenuity and persistence also allowed Schanberg to land a scoop about U.S. bombing of civilians in Neak Luong in 1973, at a time when U.S. officials had sought to bar all reporters from the scene.

In April 1975, the U.S. embassy ordered all American citizens, including journalists, out of Phnom Penh as the Khmer Rouge drew closer to the embattled city. Schanberg and Pran decided to stay, judging that the United States had overestimated the danger and that the Khmer Rouge, once in power, would end its reign of terror. On April 17, after the surrender of the Cambodian government to the rebels, Schanberg and two other reporters were seized at gunpoint by Khmer Rouge soldiers and ushered into a car. Pran persuaded their captors to let him join them, fearing they would be shot if he were not present. He then managed to convince the soldiers, after two hours of desperate **entreaty,** that the three men were neutral French reporters and should be freed. The men then fled to what they

1942	Pran is born in Siem Reap, Cambodia.
1973	Pran becomes an assistant to Sidney Schanberg, *The New York Times* correspondent in Cambodia.
1979	Pran escapes from Cambodia and is reunited with Schanberg.
1980	Pran is hired as an apprentice photographer by *The New York Times*.

entreaty plea; urgent request.

Dith Pran Holocaust Awareness Project

Although it has been decades since Dith Pran made his escape from the killing fields of Pol Pot's Cambodia, the memory of the mass deaths, torture, and despair of those years remain a powerful force in his life. Driven to do what he can to keep such brutalities from ever being repeated, he established the Holocaust Awareness Project in 1996. Dith Pran serves as president of the project, and his wife Kim DePaul acts as executive director. The Project is based in Woodbridge, New Jersey.

The project is a non-profit, nonpolitical organization dedicated to educating American students of high school and college age about the Cambodian genocide that occurred from April 1975 until January 1979. Most of the work of the project is carried out by Dith Pran himself, who lectures tirelessly at high schools and colleges throughout the country, carrying the message that it is up to everyone to take a stand against the inhumanity of war and the horrors of genocide. An important part of his mission is carried out on his web site, at www.dithpran.org/, where he provides historical and current information about the situation in Cambodia, and recruits others to join him in his work.

In addition to speaking engagements and the web site, the project also disseminates books and articles on the subject of Cambodia and the mass killings that occurred there during the Pol Pot years. It is Dith Pran's hope that, by keeping the memory of the killing fields alive, future generations will be spared the devastation that the people of Cambodia suffered in the past.

thought were safe grounds—the French embassy—but the Khmer Rouge entered and ordered all Cambodians out of the building.

Pran was now herded together with millions of his countrymen who were being driven to the countryside under Khmer Rouge orders to empty all the cities, which they considered to be swamps of reactionary, decadent bourgeois culture. Pran survived by **feigning** a working-class background and meekly enduring his impressment into back-breaking 14-hour days of farm labor in a village 20 miles from Siem Reap. Limited to rations of a spoonful of rice per day, he and his fellow workers survived by eating insects, rodents, and tree bark.

feigning faking; impersonating.

In 1977 Pran won permission to transfer to the less **draconian** labor camp at Bat Dangkor, where the camp supervisor, disaffected from the brutal regime, permitted Pran to listen to Western radio broadcasts, from which he learned, in 1979, of the Vietnamese capture of Phnom Penh. Escaping and returning to Siem Reap, Pran found that his father and niece had starved to death and that his siblings and their families had been executed by the Khmer Rouge, among the 5000 corpses

draconian cruel measures.

crowded into what later became known as the surrounding "killing fields."

Under the Vietnamese administration Pran became the administrator of Siem Reap and, through a visiting European journalist, was able to get a message to Schanberg, who in 1976 had won the Pulitzer Prize for his reporting on the war in Cambodia. Later in 1979, when the Vietnamese found out about Pran's association with the *Times*, they relieved him of his duties. Fearing further retribution, Pran fled to a border village from which he and several other men trekked on foot for four days to cover the 60 miles to Thailand. Exhausted, ill, and bordering on starvation, Pran made his way to a refugee camp, where he got word to Schanberg of his escape.

At their tearful reunion on October 3, 1979, Pran said, "I am reborn. This is my second life." He was reunited with his family later that month in San Francisco, and, after a lengthy *convalescence*, moved to New York to begin an apprenticeship as a photographer for *The New York Times*, which supported the Pran family during Dith's training.

For the past twenty years Pran worked as a photographer for *The New York Times*, specializing in human-interest photos. His personal life was devoted entirely to exposing the brutal history of the Khmer Rouge guerillas, many of whom still occupy important government posts as part of the coalition government that took place free elections in 1993. Pran continued to dedicate himself to bringing the leading Khmer Rouge officials to justice as war criminals.

Pran lived in Woodbridge, New Jersey, with his second wife, Kim DePaul. ◆

"I'm not a politician. I'm just an innocent person who wants to tell his story to the world."
Pran, in interview with Josh Getlin of *The Los Angeles Times*, October 25, 1991.

Saiki, Patricia

MAY 28, 1930– ● POLITICIAN

Patricia Saiki was born Patricia Fukada on May 28, 1930, in Hilo, Hawaii. She attended the local public elementary and high schools there, and she excelled at her studies. In 1948, after graduating from high school, she entered the University of Hawaii, Manoa campus, graduating from there in 1952 with a degree in education.

Over the next 16 years Saiki worked in her chosen profession, teaching history at the junior and senior high school levels until 1968. She was always interested in politics, however, both because of her work as a teacher, and because of a strong personal commitment to public service. When, in 1968, Hawaii held its first constitutional convention, she was determined to play an active part. She therefore left her teaching position to take part in the convention, and at the same time she ran for a seat in the Hawaii House of Representatives, running on the Republican ticket as a moderate.

Saiki was successful in her first bid for public office, something of a feat in the largely Democratic state. The Democratic Party had monopolized political life in Hawaii since the 1950s, when Democratic voters became a large majority in reaction against what had been perceived as Republican insensitivity to minority issues in the past several decades. Saiki, while acknowledging some abuses in the past, took the position that the Republican Party had changed dramatically for the better in terms of inclusiveness, and felt that the overwhelmingly Democratic majority of political officeholders was unhealthy for the state in the long term.

1930 Saiki is born Patricia Fukada in Hilo, Hawaii.

1952 Saiki graduates from University of Hawaii, Manoa campus, with a degree in education.

1968 Saiki wins a seat in the Hawaii House of Representatives.

1974 Saiki wins seat in the Hawaii Senate.

1983 Saiki fails to win election for Lieutenant Governor, instead takes the post of GOP State Chairman.

1986 Saiki loses interim election to U.S. House of Representatives, but wins the general election in November of the same year.

1990 Saiki stands down from the House to make a failed bid for U.S. Senator, leaves elected office.

1991 Saiki is named an administrator for the Small Business Administration by then-President George Bush.

1993 Saiki leaves the Small Business Association for life in the private sector.

Saiki served as a state representative for six years and, having fully committed to a career in government, set her sights on her next goal: a seat in the Hawaii Senate. Once again, Saiki was successful, winning office in 1974 and serving as a state senator until 1983. She was a highly popular senator within her republican constituency, and soon began thinking of achieving higher political goals.

Saiki's visibility and name recognition served her in good stead in 1982, prompting the Republican Party to put forth her name as a candidate for the office of Lieutenant Governor. To run for office, she had to stand down for the state senatorial race for that year, ending her tenure in the state Senate. Unfortunately, for all her popularity within the party, this time she could not overcome the fact that Hawaiian voters overwhelmingly favor Democratic candidates. They did so in this election, handing Saiki an unaccustomed defeat. For the next two years, Saiki remained active within the Republican Party, serving as its state chairman until 1985. She did not run for office again during this time, preferring to bide her time until a good opportunity presented itself.

In 1986 that opportunity arose. Saiki was now a resident of Honolulu and Hawaii's First Congressional District. The incumbent U.S. Representative, Democrat Cecil Heftel, decided to run for governor of the state, vacating his office a few months prior to the end of his elected term in order to devote himself to his campaign. To fill his seat, a special election was called that summer, and Saiki was the Republican Party's logical choice to run for the office.

Once again, the predominance of registered Democrats in her district worked against her, and Saiki was defeated by Neil Abercrombie. Although Saiki did not win the special election, another was soon to be held in November, and the public exposure she earned in her special-election candidacy made her a logical choice for the Republican ticket in that race. She won the nomination easily, and then went on to beat her Democratic opponent, Mufi Hannemann, becoming the first Republican from Hawaii to serve in the U.S. House of Representatives since the state joined the union.

During her service in the House of Representatives, Saiki was a member of several important committees, including the Committee on Banking, Finance, and Urban Affairs; the Committee on Merchant Marine and Fisheries; and the Select Committee on Aging. She was active in championing causes important to her constituency back home. In particular, she was a co-sponsor of the legislation that led to President Reagan's 1988 apology to Japanese-Americans who had been interned in camps during World War II, and she helped in the successful fight to win compensation for the survivors of that ordeal. In addition, she was instrumental in passing a bill that authorized an expansion of the Hawaiian lands to be included in the Kiluea National Wildlife Refuge.

In 1990, Saiki was ready for yet another move forward in her political career. Democratic Senator Spark Matsunaga, highly popular with his constituency and long considered unbeatable by the Republican Party, had just died. Democrat Daniel K. Akaka had been appointed to fill out the late senator's term, but had to face a full-scale re-election campaign if he wanted to remain in the Senate. The Republican Party saw its best chance to win another seat in the Senate, counting on the fact that Akaka was far less well-known than his predecessor was. The party considered it highly possible that Saiki, with several years of service at the national level already to her credit, could beat Akaka. Saiki ran a tough race, but Akaka ultimately bested her in the general election. This ended Saiki's congressional career, but did not keep her from serving her party in other capacities. She was appointed by President George Bush to the position of Administrator for the Small Business Administration, where she served from 1991 to 1993.

In 1994, Saiki once again decided to run for elected office, this time with an eye to winning the governorship of Hawaii. Once again she beat all contenders within her party to win the nomination, and energetically launched herself into the general election campaign. Running in a three-way race against Democratic candidate Ben Cayetano and Frank Fasi, who ran on his own ticket (the "Best" Party), she faced an uphill battle, and ultimately lost. The traditional popularity of the Democratic Party once again worked against her, and the Fasi campaign **siphoned** off votes that she might otherwise have won. ◆

"My purpose in getting elected was not to be in power. . . . My purpose in running for office was to try to correct some of the inequities that I saw."

Patricia Saiki, 2001, Hawaii Republican Party web site.

siphoned drawing something off another source.

Saund, Dalip Singh

SEPTEMBER 20, 1899–APRIL 22, 1973 ● POLITICIAN

Dalip Singh Saund was born on September 20, 1899, in the town of Amritsar, in the India's Punjab district. He went to private boarding schools in India, then traveled

1899 ▸ Saund is born in Amritsar, Punjab, India.

1922 ▸ Saund receives his doctorate in mathematics from graduates from the University of California, Berkeley.

1949 ▸ Saund becomes a United States citizen.

1952 ▸ Saund wins a California judgeship.

1957 ▸ Saund wins a seat in the United States House of Representatives, and serves until 1962.

1973 ▸ Saund dies in Hollywood, California.

acquiesce submit or agree.

to Britain to study at Prince of Wales College. He returned to India to earn his bachelor's degree in 1919 at the University of Punjab, and came to the United States to pursue graduate studies in mathematics at the University of California at Berkeley. By 1922 he had earned both his master's and doctorate degrees.

At this time, immigration laws in the United States were actively discriminatory. Just the year before Saund finished his graduate studies, in fact, then-President Warren G. Harding had signed the Quota Immigration Act, which severely limited all immigration into the United States.

The anti-immigrant sentiment of the times had immediate consequences for Saund not only in his career possibilities but also in his personal life. While still in graduate school, Saund had married an American woman, an act that simply was not tolerated in most circles, and one that would soon have serious legal consequences. President Harding signed into law the 1922 Cable Act, which revoked the citizenship status of any American woman who married a foreigner. To compound the problem further, just one year later the Supreme Court ruled that Asian Indians were ineligible for citizenship because they were neither black nor white, the only two race categories recognized by the law at the time. It thus became impossible for either Saund or his wife to claim any rights as citizens of this country.

Given the attitudes of the time, it was not surprising that Saund would find work opportunities to be few, even for a man as educated as he. After several frustrating years of being turned away from professional positions, Saund gave up on working within his field and, in 1930, he became a lettuce farmer, the only way he could find to earn a living. From this he moved on to work with a chemical fertilizer company, distributing the product to the farms of California's Imperial Valley.

Saund did not simply **acquiesce** to the discriminatory treatment that he and his fellow immigrants faced. In the 1940s, inspired by his desire for greater equality for America's Asian Indian population, Saund founded the Indian Association of America. The focus of this organization was to influence American immigration legislation, with the hope of eventually getting citizenship rights extended to Asian Indians. His organization, along with the Indian League of America (founded by J. J. Singh) and the India Welfare League (founded by Mubarak Ali Khan), ultimately succeeded; in 1946 President Harry S. Truman signed the Luce-Cellar Act into law, granting citizenship to Asian Indians. In 1949, Saund himself became an American citizen.

At the same time in India, the leadership of Mahatma Gandhi had brought down the last of British colonialism there. This touched off a wave of Indian students coming to the United States, rather than attending British schools as had been the practice in the past. Most of these students were ineligible for citizenship (until after 1965), but the change marked a **burgeoning** community of Asian Indian intellectuals in the United States. Meanwhile, Saund, now a citizen, began a period of increasing political activism, working through established organizations such as the March of Dimes, and becoming an important actor within the Democratic Party.

burgeoning growing.

As soon as his citizenship status permitted him to do so, Saund also sought public office, winning a judgeship in Westmoreland County, California, in 1950. He was barred from taking his post, however, because he did not meet statutory requirements—he had not been a citizen long enough. He waited until 1952 and ran again, this time successfully being seated on the bench, where he served until 1957. Saund's political service earned him selection as a delegate to the Democratic National Conventions in 1952, 1956, and 1960, representing the state of California.

In 1957 he set his personal goals higher than local politics, and ran for Congress, seeking to represent the Imperial Valley congressional district in the United States House of Representatives. He won, becoming the first Asian-Indian to serve at the national level. He went on to serve three terms, leaving office after being defeated in 1962. Saund spent the next decade as a private citizen, withdrawing from the public eye and died on April 22, 1973, in Hollywood, California. He was buried in Forest Lawn Cemetery in Glendale, California. ◆

Sheng, Bright

DECEMBER 6, 1955– ● COMPOSER

Bright Sheng was born Sheng Zong-Lian in Shanghai, China, on December 6, 1955. His parents were not particularly musical, his father being a medical doctor and his mother an engineer. Sheng received early training in music, taking his first piano lessons from his mother when he was just four years old, but when the Cultural Revolution began in 1966, the family piano was seized by the Red Guards and he could no longer study at home. He attended local schools in Shanghai, where he received the general indoctrination that was a standard part of China's educational system during the era of the Cultural Revolution, but Mao Zedong's wife, Jiang Qing, fancied herself a patron of the arts, particularly music.

Because of Jiang Qing's sponsorship of musicians, Sheng avoided the normal fate of young people upon leaving high school, which was to be assigned to work as a peasant farmer on a rural collective. Instead, he was sent to Qinghai Province, in a part of Tibet that had been annexed to China, and there he was expected to work as a musician. He taught himself musical theory and experimented with composition, incorporating many elements of the local folk music in his own work. He stayed in Qinghai for seven years, and was then accepted by the newly formed Shanghai Conservatory of Music, where he studied Western-style musical composition.

With the death of Mao Zedong in 1976, it became easier for scholars and artists to travel outside of China. In 1982 Bright Sheng took advantage of this relaxation in policy to travel to New York, hoping to further his musical training. At this time he took the name by which he is known today, "Bright" being a rough translation of "Liang," which means "bright lights" in Chinese. He attended Queens College, City University of New York, and Columbia University, and he had the opportunity to work with such major talents as Leonard Bernstein, Chou Wen-chung, Hugo Weisgall, George Perle, and Mario Davidovsky.

Sheng's early experiences in China provided him with powerful inspiration for his creative work, which is strongly influenced by China's folk music traditions. Gerard Schwarz, director of the New York Chamber Symphony, commissioned Sheng's first orchestral composition, which resulted in a piece entitled "H'Un," ("Lacerations") a musical portrait of the Chinese Cultural Revolution, which Sheng had experienced firsthand. The piece premiered on April 16, 1988, and met with immense critical acclaim, even earning first runner-up for the Pulitzer Prize for Music in the following year. In no time at all, the piece was being performed by major orchestras from the

New York Philharmonic to the San Francisco Symphony and the Tokyo Philharmonic. Musical Director Kurt Masur included "H'un" among the pieces performed by the New York Philharmonic during its 1993 tour of Europe, and in 1994 it was a featured piece by the National Philharmonic of Poland during the 1995 Warsaw Autumn Festival.

The critics were overwhelmed by the power and emotionalism of this first symphony, and declared Sheng a major new talent. The great success of "H'un" brought Sheng a great many further commissions from prestigious American orchestral groups, including The Los Angeles Philharmonic, the Boston Symphony Orchestra, and the Seattle Symphony. Internationally, Sheng met with equal acclaim, as the Shanghai Symphony and Italy's Orchestra sinfonica dele' Accademia Nazionale de Cecilia, among others, sought to present the young composer's works. His compositions have been performed by such important musicians as cellist Yo-Yo Ma.

The 1990s saw an outpouring of work by Shen, with premiers of major pieces occurring throughout the United States. In 1992 he premiered his first opera, *The Song of Majmun*, performed by Chicago's Lyric Opera. In 1994, the Houston Symphony premiered his "Prelude for Orchestra," and in 1995 the Seattle Symphony performed *China Dreams* for the first time. In 1997, Carnegie Hall commissioned a work specifically for Yo-Yo Ma to perform with the National Traditional Orchestra. The result, *Spring Dreams*, premiered in New York and then toured the United States, further expanding Sheng's reputation as a world-class composer.

As Sheng's reputation grew, he received numerous offers to associate himself with some of the most important musical organizations in the United States. The San Francisco Symphony made him artistic director of its "Wet Ink 93" Festival in 1993, and that same year Sheng was invited to serve as composer-in-residence for the Santa Fe Chamber Music Festival. He accepted these posts while still serving a two-year stint, from 1992 to 1994, as composer-in-residence for the Seattle Symphony. For the 1994-1995 season he served as artist-in-residence at the University of Washington. Sheng has also served as guest conductor for a number of symphonies in the United States and abroad, including the San Francisco and Seattle Symphonies, the China National Symphony Orchestra of Beijing, and the Shanghai Symphony.

1955 Sheng is born in Shanghai, China.

1982 Sheng emigrates to the United States.

1988 Sheng's composition, "H'un" premiers, performed by the New York Chamber Symphony.

1992 Sheng's first opera is performed by the Chicago Lyric Opera.

1995 Sheng joins the faculty of the University of Michigan school of music.

Sheng has never forgotten his personal battle to secure a good musical education, and throughout his career has been generous in giving his time to performances at universities. This same commitment to education led him to accept a position on the faculty at the University of Michigan at Ann Arbor, where he has been a teacher since 1995. In addition, Sheng's work has been recorded widely, in performances by the Houston Grand Opera, the New York Chamber Symphony, the John Oliver Chorale, and by Yo-Yo Ma, who is the artist perhaps most closely associated with Sheng's work.

Sheng was been widely recognized for his work, most particularly by the United States and China. Among Sheng's many awards and prizes were a grant from the National Endowment for the Arts and awards from the American Academy and Institute of Arts and Letters, the Guggenheim Foundation, and the Illinois Council on the Arts. In China he was awarded first prize in the Art Song Competition (1979) and took both first and second prizes in the Chamber Music Competition (1980). ◆

Shinseki, Eric

NOVEMBER 28, 1942– ● U.S. ARMY CHIEF OF STAFF

Eric Shinseki was born on November 28, 1942, in the town of Lihue, on Kauai Island in Hawaii, just one year after the Japanese attack on Pearl Harbor. During this time, people of Japanese descent were classified as "enemy aliens," by the government and many were consigned to internment camps for the duration of World War II. Among Shinseki's family, however, the baselessness of these fears was clear: several of his uncles saw distinguished service in the fabled 442nd Regimental Combat Team, the all-Japanese unit formed to fight in the European theater, particularly in France and Italy. Shinseki grew up hearing his uncles talk of their service, and as he grew older he was inspired by both their pride and their patriotism to choose a military career for himself.

Shinseki gained his early education locally, and during high school he met the woman that he would one day marry: Patty Yoshinoba, a local beauty and homecoming queen. He graduated from Kauai High School in 1960, and then attended the United States Military Academy at West Point, graduating in 1965. Upon graduation he was assigned to Vietnam, where he served with the 25th Infantry for a one-year tour of duty, during which he was injured in battle and received the Purple Heart. He spent the following year in the hospital recovering from his injuries, and in 1969 he returned to Vietnam for another tour, this time with the 9th Infantry. Wounded once again, he returned to the United States in 1970 for another year-long stint in the hospital. Although he recovered from his injuries, a further posting to Vietnam was out of the question.

The next decade saw Shinseki busy on a number of fronts. He married his childhood sweetheart, and he entered into the graduate program at Duke University, where he earned his master's in English Literature. His career, too, continued to move forward, and he received a number of promotions within the Army's administrative hierarchy. In addition, Shinseki had the opportunity to display his leadership and excellence in the academic world, for he taught English at the U.S. Military Academy.

From 1982 to 1984, Shinseki was once again posted overseas, this time as commander of the 3rd Squadron, 7th Cavalry, and 3rd Infantry in Germany. He came back to the United States in 1985, but returned to Germany in 1987 for a two-year assignment as commander of the 2nd Brigade, 3rd Infantry. All told, he served more than ten years in Europe, in a variety of capacities. His leadership and commitment to excellence earned him the respect of both his superiors and his troops, and he was rewarded with regular military citations and honors throughout this period and, indeed, throughout his entire career.

Shinseki's honors and awards are extensive. He was awarded the **Distinguished Service Medal**, the **Legion of Merit**, the

Eric Shinseki

"His commitment to his duties and outstanding service to preserve and defend our nation's democratic principles have prepared him well."
Senator Daniel K. Inouye, on Shinseki's appointment as Army Chief of Staff, 1999

Distinguished Service Medal United States military medal awarded for exceptional service to the nation during war.

442nd Regimental Combat Team (RCT)

With the Japanese bombing of Pearl Harbor on December 7, 1941, public hysteria led to the suspicion that citizens of Japanese ancestry were potential traitors. Servicemen of Japanese ancestry were pulled from their assigned units and relocated far from the West Coast, and civilian Japanese Americans were classified 4C, meaning they were deemed unfit to be drafted into the army.

Many loyal Japanese American servicemen and women fought this prejudice, among them future senators Spark M. Matsunaga and Daniel Inouye. They petitioned the government for the right to serve their country, and on February 1, 1943, their petition was granted: the 442nd Infantry Regimental Combat Team, was formed. The 442nd Regiment consisted entirely of Japanese-American volunteers from Hawaii and the mainland.

After combat training at Fort Shelby, Mississippi, the regiment shipped out to Europe. The 442nd performed bravely in southern France and in Italy, and by the war's end it was the most decorated unit in the history of the United States. Its members, collectively, earned nearly 9,500 Purple Hearts, the medal awarded for having been wounded in combat.

Although the heroism of the 442nd was recognized within the military, white citizens back home were not so quick to drop their prejudices against Japanese Americans, even after the war. Japanese American war veterans returned to a society that still refused them service in hotels, restaurants, and stores. Many of the men of the 442nd went on to fight anti-Japanese prejudice through careers in public office, or by taking to the lecture circuit to educate the public about the contributions of Japanese Americans throughout the nation's history.

The legacy of the 442nd's heroic service to the country provided inspiration for succeeding generations of young people of all ethnic backgrounds, among them current Army Chief of Staff Eric Shinseki. General Shinseki has credited the brave example of the veterans of the 442nd with leading him to his career in the Armed Forces. Through their bravery, and their willingness to confront prejudice, they opened the way for later generations of Japanese Americans to serve their country at all levels of rank and responsibility in the Armed Forces.

Bronze Star a United States military medal awarded for heroic or meritorious service to the nation not involving aerial flights.

Legion of Merit United States military medal awarded for exceptionally meritorious conduct in the performance of outstanding services.

Bronze Star, and the Purple Heart, among others. In addition he earned the Parachutist Badge and Ranger Tab, along with numerous other commendations and insignia of rank.

In the 1990s, Shinseki's long and distinguished service won him ever-increasing recognition. In 1996 he was promoted to the rank of lieutenant general, and was named Deputy Chief of Staff for Operations and Planning. Just a year later, in 1997, he was awarded the rank of general, and set in command of the Army's European branch, overseeing the operations of the U.S. Army, Allied Land Forces, and NATO Stabilization Force, with specific command over troop activities in Bosnia-Herzogovina. In 1998 he followed up on these successes by becoming the Army's 28th Vice Chief of Staff. With such a distinguished service, it was not surprising that, in 1999, he received the highest career honor available when he was named Army Chief of Staff.

Shinseki's career can hardly be called unremarkable, however. Rather, it served as a testament not only to his own accomplishments but also to the distance the United States Army, and the broader American culture, have traveled since the year of his birth. As the first Japanese-American ever to rise to the rank of four-star general in the Army, he stands as a symbol for which his uncles fought in World War II: the right of Japanese-Americans to claim the status of first-class citizens.

When Shinseki's uncles and such decorated war heroes as Spark Matsunaga and Daniel Inouye were first denied the right to serve their country and later consigned to a segregated division within the army, the idea that a Japanese-American could ever rise to the highest positions of authority in the American military was nearly unthinkable. Nonetheless, these heroes provided Shinseki, and others of his generation, with the role models they needed to challenge lingering prejudices and insist on their fitness to serve. Shinseki's success in the army was of course due in large part to his own personal attributes of courage, capability, and commitment to excellence. But he himself acknowledged that his rise was made possible largely through the patriotism of his forebears, who refused to be sidelined during World War II and insisted upon taking their part in defending their country. ◆

1942 Shinseki is born in Lihue, Kauai, Hawaii.

1965 Shinseki graduates from United States Military Academy, begins his first tour of duty in Vietnam.

1970 Shinseki completes final tour of duty, Vietnam.

1982 Shinseki begins more than a decade of duty assignments in Europe.

1996 Shinseki becomes lieutenant general.

1997 Shinseki attains the rank of full general.

1998 Shinseki becomes Army Vice Chief of Staff.

1999 Shinseki is named 34th Chief of Staff, U.S. Army.

Shyamalan, M. Night

AUGUST 3, 1970– ● FILM DIRECTOR AND SCREENWRITER

M Night Shyamalan was born on August 3, 1970, in Pondicherry, India. When he was just eight weeks old, his parents N. C. and Jayalakshmi, moved to the United States, where they bought a home in a wealthy suburb of Philadelphia, Pennsylvania. His parents were both doctors—his father a cardiologist and his mother a gynecologist. Twelve other family members either worked as doctors or had

1970 Shyamalan is born in Pondicherry, India.

1978 Shyamalan makes his first films using his father's 8-millimeter camera.

1987 Shyamalan decides that he wants to become a filmmaker, not a doctor, and enrolls at New York University.

1992 Shyamalan graduates from NYU and marries his wife, Bhavna.

1993 Shyamalan's first film, *Praying with Anger*, is named the Debut Film of the Year by the American Film Institute.

1999 Shyamalan writes and directs *The Sixth Sense*, one of the most successful horror movies of all-time.

rudimentary primitive.

their doctor of philosophy degrees. Shyamalan was raised entirely in America, but every two years, he traveled back to India to visit his relatives there. The initial M in his name stands for Manoj, and his middle name, Night, is an Americanized version of his actual middle name, Nelliyattu.

As a result of having so many doctors in the family, there was pressure on Shyamalan when he was a child to follow in his parents' footsteps and become a physician. However, when he was just eight years old, Shyamalan picked up his father's Bell & Howell 8 millimeter film camera and began making **rudimentary** movies; from that point on, he knew what he wanted to do with his life. "He would call all the neighborhood kids into the backyard and create stories," recalls his mother. His father remembered his son's vivid imagination. "The plots [of his movies] would have one kid playing the richest man in India. Even then, he was telling ghost stories."

Once he decided he wanted to be a filmmaker, Shyamalan tried to model his career after that of award-winning director Steven Spielberg, who began making films at a very young age. Shyamalan attended private Catholic schools in Philadelphia and continued to develop his movie-making skills; by the time he was 16, he had completed 45 short films. When he turned 17, he gathered his family together and announced that, even though he had been accepted at several medical schools, he had decided to become a filmmaker.

Shyamalan decided to attend New York University, enrolling in the prestigious Tisch School of the Arts. While in school, he wrote seven full-length screenplays, and, upon graduating in 1992, he immediately began filming a semi-autobiographical film called *Praying with Anger*. That first film tells the story of an Indian student raised in the United States who is sent to a university in India for one year so that he can get in touch with his cultural roots. At the same time he was trying to make *Praying with Anger*, he had sold a script to Miramax Films for a movie called *Wide Awake*. Shyamalan actually used some of the money he was paid for *Wide Awake* to make *Praying with Anger*, finishing the latter film on a shoestring budget of $750,000, in large part because he was the film's writer, director, and lead actor. His commitment to the film paid off, as it was named Debut Film of the Year in 1993 by the American Film Institute.

After the critical success of *Praying with Anger*, Miramax had high hopes for *Wide Awake*, which focused on a 10-year-old

Indian boy who wants to find God so he can be sure that his deceased grandfather actually made it to heaven. Shyamalan and the studio disagreed about the tone the final cut of the movie would have, which delayed the film's release by two years. When it did come out, the movie was a commercial and critical failure, gaining little public attention.

Even after *Wide Awake*, Shyamalan was still highly thought of in Hollywood and had no problem finding work. He wrote one script for a movie called *Labor of Love*, that was about a widower who decided to walk across the United States to prove his love for his wife, and he also handled the script for the family movie, *Stuart Little*, which was a huge commercial success. All the time he was working on the *Stuart Little* script, however, Shyamalan was working on another script that was really his dream project. The script was for a horror film about a young boy who could see dead people all around him. After taking a year to write the script, Shyamalan sold it, with no changes, to Disney Studios for $3 million, which was thought to be a record for a film written without a contract at that time. In addition to being paid for writing the movie, Shyamalan's fee also included payment for serving as the film's director.

The film that Shyamalan sold to Disney was *The Sixth Sense*, which became one of the most popular movies of the year when it was released in 1999. Starring Bruce Willis and Haley Joel Osment (as the young boy), the film was heaped with praise and was nominated for Best Picture at the 2000 Academy Awards; Osment was also nominated for Best Actor and Shyamalan received a Best Director nod. As with many of his scripts, *The Sixth Sense* came out of Shyamalan's own life experiences, in this case his childhood fears. "I was a scared little child until I was 12 years old," he remembered.

Shyamalan knew, deep down, that *The Sixth Sense* was going to be a hit. Still stinging from the terrible reviews that *Wide Awake* had received, he set out specifically to create a stunning story that would translate into a stunning film. Of all the bad reviews *Wide Awake* received, the one that stuck with Shyamalan the most was that of Stephen Holden of *The New York Times*. Holden is a powerful critic whose opinion can make often make or break a new filmmaker's career, but Shyamalan refused to let Holden's bad review hold him back. "I decided I was going to write the greatest script, and everything was going to change. It's going to be mine, and they'll have to let me direct

A movie has to feel important to me on some level. I can't make a movie about a guy opening a pizza shop. But if you say that his dad came here from Italy with this dream of his own shop and the son is finally doing it, then you have something more than pizza. In a way, you have something about family and about spirituality.

M. Night Shyamalan, from *Written By* magazine, March 2000

because they won't get it any other way. I also had this fear that I was not supposed to this, not supposed to succeed. . . . So I just wrote and wrote. The first draft was bad, so I threw it out and started again on page one. Second draft, same thing. . . . It wasn't until about the fifth draft that I really began to figure it out. . . . It took me five more drafts to execute it right."

Shyamalan followed the overwhelming success of *The Sixth Sense* with another unconventional movie with supernatural overtones called *Unbreakable*, which starred Willis again, along with Samuel Jackson. Like *The Sixth Sense*, the film has a surprise ending that attempts to lead the audience to the point where they learn something about the meaning of life. The film, while not reaching the level of success that *The Sixth Sense* obtained, was a critical and box-office hit, cementing Shyamalan's place as one of Hollywood's most creative, and successful, young directors.

Shyamalan lived in Wayne, Pennsylvania (a suburb of Philadelphia), with his wife Bhavna and his two children. Shyamalan met his wife when he was just 17 years old, but he said that he knew from their first meeting that she was the person he would marry. "She was beautiful, innocent, and intelligent," he recalls. They were married shortly after Shyamalan graduated from NYU, when both were 22 years old. ◆

Sidhwa, Bapsi

AUGUST 1, 1938– ● AUTHOR

Parsi a descendent of Persian refugees principally settled in Bombay.

Bapsi Sidhwa was born August 1, 1938, in Karachi, India (which is now Pakistan). Her family was a **Parsi** family, which is a religious ethnic group that came from the Zoroastrians sect of 14th century Persia. The community is small, well-educated, and stays neutral on political issues. Bapsi's father, Peshotan, was in business and her mother, Tehmina, was an association president. Soon after Sidhwa was born, the family moved to Lahore, India.

When Sidhwa was only two years old, she contracted polio. Because she was sickly, she barely attended any school. She had an Anglo-Indian tutor at home who taught her to read and write English. When Sidhwa was 10, the tutor gave her a copy of Louisa May Alcott's *Little Women*. "The novel sent me into any orgy of reading from which I have still to recover," recalled Sidhwa later.

Sidhwa was a very shy child and hardly spoke. Instead, she lived in a world of books. She read everything—from comic books to magazines to classics like *Jane Eyre* and *The Pickwick Papers.* When she was 15, she went to Kinnaird College for Women and was delighted to find their library full of even more books she could read. Sidhwa graduated in 1956.

Besides books, one of the biggest influences on Sidhwa's early years was watching the partition of the Indian Subcontinent in 1947. She was just a young girl and was shocked to see the brutality and bloodiness. She was especially affected by the treatment of women during the fighting and would later become a strong advocate for downtrodden women.

Being a Parsi was difficult for Sidhwa because she was unsure how she fit in. "I felt marginalized as a Parsi in a predominately Muslim society. Some people . . . would say things like 'Can you be Pakistani if you're Parsi?' Whereas, to Indians, I am a Pakistani," said Sidhwa.

Because there are strict rules for how young women of the Parsi culture should live their lives, Sidhwa was expected to marry and have children. Following tradition, she married at age 19 to Gustad Kermani and moved to a Parsi community in Bombay. They quickly had two children, Mohur and Koko. Sidhwa lived these early years as she was expected to. Her husband was a successful businessman and Sidhwa was busy being the wife in this upper class family, performing volunteer work and playing bridge. The marriage, however, did not last. In 1963, Sidhwa married another Parsi businessman Noshir R. Sidhwa. The two lived in Lahore and Sidhwa lived much the same kind of life that she had with her first husband.

That all changed when Sidhwa was 26. She and her husband were invited to watch the army building a road from Pakistan to China. There, they heard a story about a girl who had been taken to marry a man she did not want to marry. The girl escaped, and the tribesmen took the escape as an insult and vowed to track her down. They found her and brutally murdered her. The story fascinated and galvanized Sidhwa, especially since she was so attracted to stories of women facing hardship. The event inspired her to write a novel called *The Bride.* It took her four years to get it all down on paper.

Sidhwa got an agent in the United States for her work, but success was still years away. She was told that people were

1938 Sidhwa is born in Karachi, India.

1947 Sidhwa witnesses the Partition of India.

1964 Sidhwa is inspired to begin work on her first book, *The Bride.*

1978 Sidhwa self-publishes *The Crow Eaters.*

1991 *Cracking India* is named a notable book of the year by *The New York Times.*

uninterested in the work of a Pakistani writer, and she received many rejection slips. Still, Sidhwa had discovered her calling. She wrote a second book called *The Crow Eaters*, the title of which comes from a nickname for the Parsees because of their supposed ability to talk noisily and vigorously like crows. The book was funny and entertaining, yet Sidhwa was still unable to find a publisher. Finally, she published the book herself, which finally led to a contract from an Indian publisher. The book made its way to England and the United States and brought acclaim for Sidhwa. However, the book was controversial within her Parsi community. They were offended by the title, and there was a bomb threat at a book launching in Lahore. But Sidhwa still continued writing. In 1983, she and her husband moved to the United States.

Her third novel, *Ice Candy Man*, (which was renamed *Cracking India* because her American publisher thought the former title sounded like it was a drug reference) made her an international literary figure. The book is about the Indian partition and is told through the eyes of a young girl named Lenny. In 1991, *The New York Times* named it a Notable Book of the Year.

Sidhwa became a naturalized citizen of the United States in 1992. Part of her decision to do so was because she discovered that she lost out on a writing award that was only open to U.S. citizens.

Sidhwa continued writing and teaching creative writing classes all over the world. She published *An American Brat* in 1994. In 1999, *Cracking India* was made into a movie, *Earth-1947*, directed by Deepa Mehta. She won numerous awards including the National Award for English Literature, a Bunting Fellow from Radcliffe/Harvard and a Lila Wallace-*Reader's Digest* grant of $100,000. Sidhwa was recognized as the leading Pakistani writer in the world. ◆

Sugiura, Kanematsu

JUNE 5, 1892–OCTOBER 21, 1979 ● BIOCHEMIST AND CANCER RESEARCHER

Kanematsu Sugiura was born on June 5, 1892 in the small village of Tsushima-shi, Japan, which is near the large city of Nagoya. He was one of seven children born to father Seisuke Sugiura and mother Miyono Aoki. His family was fairly well off, as his father worked a number of jobs, including dyemaker; he was also a **kendo** master and had at one time served as a samurai. When Sugiura was only eight years old, his father died of cancer, which had two lasting effects. First, it caused great financial hardship in the Sugiura household, forcing young Kanematsu to work as an apprentice in the hardware business. Second, it made an impression on the young boy that would later have a great influence on the medical work he undertook.

After several years of scraping by financially after his father's death, Sugiura's life took a turn for the better. In fact, as an adolescent, Sugiura got to experience things that most teenagers never did. When he was 13, his older brother, Kamasaburo, took a job in the United States serving as a Japanese translator for American railroad baron Edward Harriman, who had business dealings with the Japanese government. Harriman was one of the wealthiest men in the United States at that time, and had a number of interests. One of them was the martial arts, which he became entranced with after viewing a demonstration of **jujitsu** and kenjitsu. He was so enthralled by the ancient sports that he paid to have four Japanese boys—including Sugiura—travel to the United States to give live demonstrations to other members of his social circle, which just happened to include President Theodore Roosevelt and many prominent businessmen.

When Harriman offered financial assistance to any of the boys who wished to stay in America permanently, only Sugiura accepted the offer. He knew that he might never have another chance to attend American schools and to eventually attend university. Bravely, he set out on his own and moved to New York City, where he lived with the family of Harriman family physician William G. Lyle. In New York, he attended a public middle school and then moved on to Townsend Harris Hall High School, where he studied from 1908 to 1911. To earn money, he worked after school each day in the research laboratories of nearby Roosevelt Hospital.

Sugiura's life was again touched by cancer in 1909, when Harriman was struck down by the disease. Before his death, he contributed $1 million to fund the opening of the Harriman Research Laboratory (HRL), which was devoted to finding treatments—and hopefully a cure—for cancer. Sugiura decided that he would dedicate his life to trying to unlock the mysteries of the terrible disease that had killed both his father and his benefactor. He went to work at HRL full-time in 1911 as an assistant

1892 Sugiura is born in Tsushima-shi, Japan.

1905 Sugiura travels to the United States to help stage martial arts exhibitions, staying to attend high school and college in New York City.

1911 Sugiura takes his first job as an assistant chemist at Harriman Research Laboratories.

1917 Sugiura completes his master's degree at Columbia University.

1947 Sugiura is named an associate member of Sloan-Kettering; full membership follows in 1959.

1962 Sugiura retires from biochemistry as one of the most esteemed cancer researchers in history.

1977 Sugiura announces his support of the controversial drug laetrile in the newsletter *Second Opinion*.

kendo a Japanese sport of fencing with bamboo swords.

jujitsu an art of fighting without weapons using holds, throws, and paralyzing blows to disable or subdue an opponent.

chemotherapy the use of chemical agents in treating a serious physical or mental illness.

chemist, and in 1912, he became one of the first cancer researchers in the United States, concentrating on **chemotherapy**. He did this even before he had completed his college degree—after working all day, he attended night classes at the Polytechnic Institute of Brooklyn; he completed his bachelor of science degree in 1915. Two years later, he added a master's degree in chemistry from Columbia University.

After receiving his master's degree in 1917, Sugiura was promoted to associate chemist at HRL. However, shortly after the promotion, he found himself out of a job when the Harriman family withdrew its funding, forcing the lab to close. Sugiura was already so highly respected that he was immediately offered a job as an assistant chemist by Dr. James Ewing, who worked at what was then called Memorial Hospital for Cancer and Allied Diseases. Numerous name changes later, the hospital reached its current name, the Memorial Sloan-Kettering Institute for Cancer Research, which is one of the most respected cancer research facilities in the world. For Sugiura, it was the beginning of a lifelong relationship—he would remain at Memorial until his retirement in 1962, and even after he retired, he showed up at the hospital every day for years to assist others in their research.

Sugiura, who earned the title "Dr." only after being awarded an honorary degree from Kyoto Imperial University in Japan, was one of the first researchers to study the theory that powerful drugs and chemicals could be used to stop the spread of cancer. Sugiura also investigated different substances to see if they could be classified as carcinogens, and also was one of the pioneers in using X-rays and similar radiation treatments as a weapon against cancer. Additionally, he was among the first to experiment with tumor transplantation techniques, discovering procedures that were used for decades afterward. So prominent was Sugiura in the research community, and so important was his work, that he was not interned in prisoner of war camps during World War II, as were most Japanese-Americans. His travel was restricted, but he was allowed to go to his lab each day and continue the fight against cancer.

In 1947, Sugiura was named an associate member of Sloan-Kettering and was made the head of the Solid Tumor Section of the Division of Experimental Chemotherapy. He was named a full member of the institute in 1959 and, upon his retirement, an **emeritus** member. Even after his retirement in 1962, Sugiura remained very active in cancer research, lending his name and support to numerous causes.

emeritus holding an honorary title in retirement.

Sugiura was among the first cancer researchers to study the numerous compounds discovered after the end of World War II, such as **methotrexate**. In his later years, Sugiura found himself at the center of a controversy when he gave his stamp of approval to a drug known as laetrile. Thought by many, including most of the major scientists at Sloan-Kettering, to be a "quack" drug, Sugiura stuck by his belief that the drug provided limited, palliative care even when he came under intense criticism. He made public his acceptance of laetrile in an underground newspaper called *Second Opinion* in 1977, and his approval of the drug is considered by its supporters to be one of the most important endorsements in their fight to have the drug gain more widespread acceptance.

methotrexate a toxic anticancer drug.

Sugiura was married once, on October 20, 1923, to Zoë Marie Claeys. In his later years, he lived in Harrison, New York. He died on October 21, 1979 in White Plains, New York. ◆

Sui, Anna

1955– ● FASHION DESIGNER

Anna Sui was born in Dearborn Heights, Michigan, in 1955, although she guarded the exact date closely. Her parents, Grace and Paul Sui, were the first generation of her family to move from their native China to the United States. Paul worked as a structural engineer, while Grace stayed home to raise Anna and her two siblings.

Sui's mother had once studied art in Paris, and it became evident early on that Sui also had an eye for color and style. As a child, she would find issues of the fashion magazine *Women's Wear Daily*, which is generally only read by fashion industry workers and followers, and would also read more mainstream fashion magazines such as *Mademoiselle* and *Seventeen*. From the magazines, Sui would clip articles and advertisements that caught her eye. Nearly 40 years later, she still had many of those early clippings, which she kept in manila folders she called her "Genius Files." It was not uncommon for her to refer to those early clippings when seeking inspiration for one of her new designs.

One of the articles in her Genius Files influenced her in another way. It was a story in *Life* magazine about two young girls

1955 Sui is born in Dearborn Heights, Michigan.

1973 Sui attends the Parsons School of Design in New York.

1980 Macy's department store purchases six of Sui's clothing designs and features them in a *New York Times* ad.

1991 Sui holds her first runway show.

1993 Sui wins the Perry Ellis Award for New Fashion Talent.

1997 Sui launches a line of shoes called Anna Sui Shoes.

1999 Sui launches a fragrance and cosmetic line.

2000 Sui opens her third boutique in Asia, this one in Osaka, Japan.

kitschy appealing to somewhat lowbrow or popular taste in poor quality.

plaudits praise.

who attended school in New York and then moved to Paris, where they became successful fashion designers. Sui read the article, and then determined to follow in the girls' footsteps. In her hometown she was known as a flamboyant dresser, and she made many of her own clothes. When she graduated from high school in the early 1970s, she moved to New York and attended the Parsons School of Design. During her second year at Parsons, Sui quit school to go to work at a junior sportswear company, where she first worked as a designer. She supplemented her income by collaborating with photographer Steven Meisel, whom she met at Parsons. Meisel was already in demand as a fashion photographer (he would later become famous for his portraits of Madonna and other stars), so Sui worked for him as a stylist when he was hired to shoot fashion layouts for Italian magazine *Lei*.

Sui worked for a number of design companies in the 1970s before settling in at a women's sportswear company called Simultanee. During her spare time she continued to work on her own designs, and her big break came in 1980 when the department store Macy's purchased six of her designs and featured them in an ad in *The New York Times*. To Sui, the ad was a sign that it was time to take the plunge and break out on her own, which she did.

Throughout the 1980s, Sui slowly but surely grew her fashion design business, gaining clients while working out of her apartment. Her clothes were known for being fun and often **kitschy,** borrowing heavily from the pop culture influences that had such an effect on Sui as a child. "My clothes are about nostalgia and memories of my own childhood," she said once. Her next breakthrough came in 1991, when Meisel helped organize her first runway show, which is a trademark of all top designers. A fashion critic for *The New York Times* attended the show and gave it a rave review in the paper; finally, with the success of the show, Sui would be able to move out of her apartment and into a real fashion studio in New York's Garment District.

One year after the show, as **plaudits** for her clothes continued to pour in, Macy's—the store that first bought her designs in 1980—rewarded Sui by letting her open her own boutique in their Herald Square store. She also opened her own boutique in the SoHo district, which features furniture that was bought at flea markets and a wildly colorful paint scheme. In 1993, she won her first major fashion award when she was chosen to receive the CFDA Perry Ellis Award for New Fashion Talent.

In addition to being fun and colorful, Sui's clothes are notable because of their cost. At a time when most top designers charge thousands of dollars for every piece of clothing, original Sui dresses can still be bought for under $300. "She gives more fashion for the price than any other New York designer," said Bloomingdale's fashion director Kal Ruttenstein. Ordinary people love Sui for that reason, but top models love her for her sense of style. "I live in Anna's little dresses in the summer," said model Linda Evangelista. "They're feminine, flowing, and great fun."

Throughout the 1990s, Sui rapidly expanded her fashion empire. In 1997, she opened a boutique in Tokyo, the first of three Anna Sui boutiques that are now found in Asia; the other two are in Osaka, Japan. That same year, she also introduced a line of footwear for the first time under the name Anna Sui Shoes. In 1999, she opened a new boutique in Los Angeles, where she can be close to all of the film and television stars she has befriended after they wore her clothes to various award shows. That same year, she also launched a fragrance and cosmetic line. Her second fragrance, "Sui Dreams," was released in the fall of 2000. In addition to her boutiques, her clothes are now sold at more than 200 stores worldwide. ◆

Sui's style is rooted in the 1970s, with references to flower power hats, tiny Liberty floral prints, and to the ethnic trail. But she made it all seem fresh and modern. . . . The collection had a sunny spirit that made the downbeat, downtown collections on other runways seem like last year's trends.

The International Herald Tribune on Sui's Spring 1998 collection

Tabuchi, Shoji

1947– ● MUSICIAN

Shoji Tabuchi was born in 1947 in the town of Daishoji, Japan, which is in the Ishikawa prefecture near the bustling city of Osaka. The youngest of three children, Tabuchi was raised in an middle-to upper-class environment in which his father Shigeru was a successful businessman and his mother Yukie a stay-at-home mom. Tabuchi was the youngest child in the family; his sister Kazuko was three years older and his brother Masaya was two years older.

From an early age, Tabuchi's parents realized that he had an ear for music that should be encouraged and developed. At the age of seven, Tabuchi took his first violin lesson, which meant little to the indifferent child. Tabuchi had no real love for music at an early age, but his parents insisted he keep taking the lessons, which he did. Tabuchi's instructor was a disciple of the Suzuki method of instruction, which teaches that all children are innately able to play a musical instrument. That belief seemed to hold true for Tabuchi, who overcame his early indifference to become a very good violin player. Tabuchi jokes that his mother had to chase him almost every lesson day, and that "she became pretty good at climbing trees."

Tabuchi approached his studies with the same lack of enthusiasm that he approached his music lessons. Throughout elementary and high school, he went through the motions at school, earning fair grades. While he had plenty of friends in school, Tabuchi tended to go against the flow and do his own thing, demonstrating great individuality.

1947 Tabuchi is born in Daishoji, Japan.

1967 Tabuchi moves to San Francisco to attempt to make it as a country western musician.

1968 Tabuchi marries his first wife Mary Jo and moves to Kansas City, Missouri, to be near her family.

1970 Tabuchi begins a five-year engagement as the opening act for country star David Houston.

1980 Tabuchi signs a six-month contract to play at the Starlite Theater in Branson, Missouri.

1989 Tabuchi buys his own theater in Branson.

2001 Tabuchi continues to perform more than 450 shows a year at his theater in Branson.

When Tabuchi was 17, he attended a concert that forever changed his opinion of his music lessons and also forever altered the path his life would take. With a group of friends, Tabuchi attended a concert that featured American musician Roy Acuff and his Smoky Mountain Boys. Tabuchi had never really heard American country and western music, but he loved the songs that Acuff sang. He paid particular attention to violinist Howdy Forrester, a talented bluegrass musician who was a master violin player. When Tabuchi heard the offbeat sounds that Forrester produced, he was hooked. At his lessons, Tabuchi was often bored by playing the same songs over and over and instead spent time writing original songs or coming up with improvisations of existing songs, which greatly frustrated his teacher. Once he heard Forrester play, Tabuchi knew that he had done the right thing by following his own musical path and he also knew that he wanted to play the violin for a living. Gone was Tabuchi's plan to earn a business degree and work for a Japanese company; in its place was the dream of making a living playing country and western music in the United States.

The decision to concentrate on country and western was a wise one, as Tabuchi did not exhibit the exacting skill level needed to be a classical violinist. When he was 18, he joined a group of friends who also loved country music and formed a country western band called the Bluegrass Ramblers. Tabuchi and his bandmates became overnight sensations and minor celebrities in Japan when they won a nationwide band competition. As the leader of the group, Tabuchi became the biggest individual star in the band thanks to his talent and his striking appearance—he was almost a head taller than the rest of the band members. As a result, he was told he could perform on the Asahi television network whenever he liked.

Because country western music enjoyed only marginal popularity in Japan at that time, Tabuchi knew he would have to move to the United States if he ever hoped to be a star. In 1967, he decided it was time to make the move, although he feared telling his parents. His father, especially, expected that Tabuchi would follow his father's example and make a career in business. However, when Tabuchi told his mother he was leaving, he was surprised to learn that she actually supported him, and even gave him money.

Tabuchi traveled to America with friend and fellow musician Keiji Nozaki. The pair lived in San Francisco, which was at the height of the hippie and anti-Vietnam War movement. After gaining entry to the U.S. on a tourist visa, Tabuchi could not legally work as a musician, meaning he had to play at small clubs that would pay him under the table, or simply put a hat on the ground in which appreciative listeners could throw money. "I did not have a so-called good life there," Tabuchi recalls of his time in San Francisco. Money was always tight, and his poor English made it hard to land music gigs. The first band he and Nozaki formed, the Osaka Okies, folded when the homesick Nozaki returned to Japan. Tabuchi tried to form a second band, but that did not last long either. The early failures only strengthened Tabuchi's resolve.

One good thing did happen in San Francisco—Tabuchi met his first wife, Mary Jo. She was from the Kansas City, Missouri, area, where the couple moved after marrying in early 1968. Now that he was married, Tabuchi could legally work in the United States, and he quickly landed a full-time job playing the fiddle at a club in Riverside, Missouri, called the Starlite Club. On a trip to Nashville, Tabuchi looked up Roy Acuff, whom he had met after that fateful concert in Japan. Acuff remembered the personable Japanese musician, and quickly granted Tabuchi a coveted spot on the country western showcase, the Grand Ole Opry. The very same week he ran into Acuff, Tabuchi found himself performing on the stage of the Opry, a goal he had dreamed of for years.

From there, Tabuchi's music career gained steam. He and Mary Jo lived in Wichita, Kansas, for two years, where Tabuchi played numerous clubs. In 1970, he hooked up with successful recording artist David Houston, who signed Tabuchi to become his opening act. That partnership lasted five years. During those years, Tabuchi worked hard to become more than just a novelty act. He improved his showmanship and strengthened his blue-grass fiddling skills, but more importantly, he added vocals to his show. He knew that if he ever hoped to truly succeed, he would have to sing.

As his career took off, his marriage fell apart. Tabuchi simply says the two drifted apart, but it took some time. The couple had a child, Shoji John, in 1974, but just two years later, they officially separated. Their divorce was not final until 1986, but the two did not live together in the decade between the separation and the divorce. In 1975, Tabuchi ended his relationship with Houston and set out on his own, intent on becoming a headline act. He spent five years playing at clubs around the Midwest and southern United States, and he was making good money, but he still had not become the star he wanted to be.

During those years, Tabuchi worked hard to become more than just a novelty act.

In Branson, Tabuchi finally became a star.

In 1980, he moved to the rapidly developing town of Branson, Missouri, which was turning into a country music showcase. There, he was named the headliner act at the Starlite Theater. He also met up with an old friend named Mike Ito, who introduced him to his eventual second wife Dorothy. The two dated for several years, during which Tabuchi turned his six-month contract at the Starlite into a four-year stay. In 1989, Tabuchi decided it was time to be his own boss, and with the support of two financial backers, he bought his own theater in Branson.

In Branson, Tabuchi finally became a star. After a successful first year, Tabuchi invested his earnings into the theater, expanding it to its current 2,000-seat capacity and turning it into a lavish show palace. It is among the largest theaters in Branson—larger than those owned by Willie Nelson and other better-known country artists—and it is filled to capacity for almost every show. In some quarters, Tabuchi is known as the King of Branson. With Dorothy producing the shows and joining him on stage, Tabuchi gave patrons their money's worth every night, playing a three-hour set that included a break for autographs and a personal goodbye after the show. Shows include the 16-piece Shoji Tabuchi Orchestra, as well as dozens of back-up singers and dancers.

While much of Tabuchi's show now relies on Las Vegas glitz over country music, Tabuchi has still been recognized by the Nashville establishment for his musical talents. From 1984 to 1987, Tabuchi was named Instrumentalist of the Year each year at the Ozark Music Awards. In 1991 and 1992, he was nominated for a similar award by the much larger TNN/Music City News Country Music Awards. Tabuchi's fame spread as he was featured on a number of national television programs, including *60 Minutes*, *Lifestyles of the Rich and Famous*, *The Today Show*, and *Inside Edition*.

Tabuchi was one of the hardest working men in show business. He was the sole owner of the Shoji Tabuchi Theater, and he and Dorothy managed all aspects of their business. Together, the couple put on more than 450 shows a year that brought in nearly $20 million. For nine months out of each year, Tabuchi staged two shows a day, and almost every show was sold out. Inside the theater's gift shop, Tobuchi sold numerous videos of his performances at the theater and many compact discs of his music, which he recorded and sold himself. Almost all sales of his CDs happened right at the theater, but he still sold tens of thousands of records a year. There is no doubt that Tabuchi achieved all the goals he set for himself, and that he was one of the most successful country western stars in the world. ◆

Takaki, Ronald

April 12, 1939– ● Historian, Professor, and Author

Ronald Takaki was born April 12, 1939, in Honolulu, Hawaii. His grandparents were the first members of his family to emigrate from Japan to the United States, moving to Hawaii to work on the sugar cane plantations there. Takaki's parents remained in Hawaii, and he was raised there. He has fond memories of spending hour after hour surfing when he should have been studying, admitting that he was not "academically inclined." It was not until his senior year in high school that Takaki really became interested in a class and thought about pursuing his studies at college. The class covered religion and was taught by Dr. Shunji Nishi, who became Takaki's mentor. He actually arranged for Takaki to attend the College of Wooster in Massachusetts.

Takaki made the trip across the country to attend Wooster, where he received his bachelor's degree in 1961. Takaki's most vivid memories from his years at Wooster involved the reception he received from other students when they first encountered him. Many asked him when he first came to the United States, assuming because of the color of his skin that he must be a foreign student. Even though he was born and raised in the United States, he was not seen as an American by many of his fellow students, a situation that intrigued Takaki and spurred him to pursue studies regarding ethnic issues.

After graduating from Wooster, Takaki then moved to California to continue his studies, enrolling at the University of California's Berkeley campus, where he earned a master's degree and his doctorate in 1969. While completing his degrees, Takaki worked as an instructor of American history at the College of San Mateo from 1965 to 1967. From there, Takaki moved to the University of California at Los Angeles, where he served as an assistant professor of history for five years, leaving in 1972.

That same year, he took a job at his alma mater, Berkeley, where he would remain for nearly 30 years as a professor of

1939 ▶ Takaki is born in Honolulu, Hawaii.

1961 ▶ Takaki receives his bachelor's degree from the College of Wooster.

1969 ▶ Takaki completes his doctorate at the University of California at Berkeley.

1972 ▶ Takaki begins teaching at UC-Berkeley, where he founds the first graduate program in ethnic studies.

1979 ▶ Takaki writes *Iron Cages: Race and Culture in Nineteenth-Century America*.

2001 ▶ Takaki tours the country as a lecturer and making a presentation entitled *A Different Mirror: A History of Multicultural America*.

Ronald Takaki

ethnic studies. At Berkeley, he designed and directed the nation's first ethnic studies graduate program. He was the recipient of the Distinguished Teaching Award at Berkeley, and he
also received three honorary doctoral degrees from other universities.

During his distinguished career, Takaki wrote more than 20
books on ethnic topics. Many of his books focused on the immigration of Asian people to the United States and how well
they assimilate once they are in the country. He also wrote
books on slavery in pre-Civil War America, which proved to be
controversial. His first book was called A Pro-Slavery Crusade:
The Agitation to Reopen the African Slave Trade (1971), and studied the affects the abolition of slavery had on the American
South in the 1850s, as well as the movement that attempted to
reestablish slavery.

One of Takaki's most controversial books was 1979's Iron
Cages: Race and Culture in Nineteenth-Century America. In that
work, Takaki tried to build a case showing that the way white
Americans treated one racial group greatly affected the way
they treated other racial groups. While some reviews praised

Asian American Studies at American Universities

The field of Asian American Studies covers a broad, multidisciplinary field in an attempt to document and interpret the contributions of Asians and Pacific Islanders to American society. Students work in areas as diverse as the social sciences, education, business, literature, the performing and visual arts, and philosophy. In so doing, the students gain an appreciation for the diversity and complexity within Asian American culture.

The earliest Asian American studies programs came into being in the late 1960s and early 1970s at colleges and universities on the West Coast; the University of California at Davis, for example, first established its program in 1969. At the forefront of this movement were scholars such as Ronald Takaki, now a professor at the University of California at Berkeley, who noted that American cultural studies up to that time largely ignored the contributions of non-whites. These pioneers in the field of ethnic studies noted that this approach presented a false picture of the nation's rich, multicultural heritage, and they took action to institute greater diversity in university curriculums.

The first Asian American studies programs, like other specialized ethnic studies, only offered a concentration or, at best, a minor degree. Over time, however, a number of universities began to allow their students to major in Asian American Studies. Once again, the majority of such schools are found on the West Coast, with Stanford University, U.C. Berkeley, U.C.L.A., and U.C. Davis leading the way.

Since the late 1990s, university students across the country have intensified their insistence that the Asian American heritage be taught at their schools. In 1996, for example, students at Columbia University in New York City staged a hunger strike until their demands for such a curriculum be included in the course offerings. There has, however, been something of a backlash against all ethnic studies, and the Asian American programs have not been immune to these pressures.

the book, others thought it was flawed and inaccurate. C. Van Woodward wrote a scathing review of the book for the *New York Review of Books* in which he essentially accused Takaki of being guilty of racism himself. He argued that because Takaki essentially stated that whites constantly demonstrated the traits of "**rapacity**, greed, cruelty, inhumanity, brutality, malevolence, [and] demonic destructiveness," he was guilty of the same racial stereotyping that he spoke out against in the book.

rapacity ability to plunder or grasp excessively.

In his classes, Takaki taught tolerance and looked at ways that ethnic groups can work together. He believed that ethnic nationalism is self-defeating—that is, that dividing a larger ethnic group into smaller pieces is often a waste of time. "I think splintering as Asian Americans into just Koreans and Vietnamese and Filipinos . . . immobilizes us in terms of racial discrimination and in terms of the need to transform the world," he said. Continuing that thought, he believed that people should revel in their ethnic identities and not limit themselves to just one. They should "expand [their] identity and have multiple identities at the same time. [They] could be Vietnamese American, [they] could be working class American. All of those identities are not contradictory to each other. But I think the whole function of education is for us to be multiple identities, to be complex people."

Besides writing and teaching, Takaki was extremely active on the national lecture circuit. He appeared on national news shows on all of the major networks, and defended his views on multicultural education in several national debates against the likes of noted academics Nathan Glazer, Charles Murray, and Arthur Schlesinger Jr.

Takaki was married in 1961 and had three children. He was a member of the American Historical Association. ◆

Takei, George

APRIL 20, 1940– ● ACTOR

George Takei was born on April 20, 1937, in Los Angeles, California. Takei had a far from normal childhood. When he was just a year old, Japan bombed Pearl Harbor and went to war with the United States. Because Takei's parents were second-generation Japanese immigrants, they were caught up in American's anti-Japanese fervor after war was declared. Seeking to prevent Japanese espionage, the U.S. government rounded up Japanese-Americans living on the West Coast and made them move to detention camps.

Most Japanese went quietly to the camps, convinced they could do nothing to stop the process. Takei's mother, however, refused to go quietly. When the Takei family was sent to a camp in Arkansas, she renounced her U.S. citizenship. To punish her, the government moved the family once again, this time to a prison camp in California. Takei remembers little of his time in the camps, and although he has no negative memories of the experience, he admits that "for my parents, it was a terrible time."

After the war, the family was allowed to return to its home in Los Angeles. There, Takei did well at Mount Vernon Junior

George Takei as "Mr. Sulu" on *Star Trek*.

High School and Los Angeles High School. He was an excellent student who made friends easily, and it was at school that he first became interested in acting as a member of the Drama Club. Takei was so popular with his classmates that, despite continuing anti-Japanese sentiment, he was elected class president at both schools.

After graduation, Takei enrolled in the University of California at Berkeley. While Takei still had the acting bug, he agreed to go to Berkeley to study architecture to make his parents happy, as they were convinced that acting was not a very safe career. However, it was too late for Takei to undertake any other career—he was hooked on acting. As a summer job after his freshman year, he dubbed American voices into the soundtrack of Japanese science fiction movies such as *Rodan!* and *Rodan Meets Godzilla*.

Takei lasted at Berkeley for two years before admitting the obvious—he wanted to study acting as a career. To facilitate that, he transferred to the University of California at Los Angeles (UCLA), for its excellent acting program. Shortly after enrolling at UCLA, he was signed by an agent who knew of his

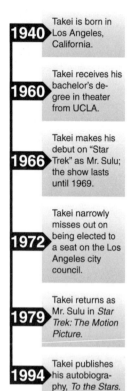

1940 Takei is born in Los Angeles, California.

1960 Takei receives his bachelor's degree in theater from UCLA.

1966 Takei makes his debut on "Star Trek" as Mr. Sulu; the show lasts until 1969.

1972 Takei narrowly misses out on being elected to a seat on the Los Angeles city council.

1979 Takei returns as Mr. Sulu in *Star Trek: The Motion Picture*.

1994 Takei publishes his autobiography, *To the Stars*.

voice-over work, and while he was still in school, Takei had his first television acting role on the show *Playhouse 90*. After switching agents, Takei continued to mix his studies with paying acting jobs, as he appeared in episodes of *Hawaiian Eye* and *77 Sunset Strip*. In his almost nonexistent spare time, Takei took additional acting classes at the Desilu Workshop, which specialized in television and film acting. One interesting sidelight about Takei's time at UCLA was that he starred in a film made by a young student filmmaker named Francis Ford Coppola, who went on to be one of the leading directors in Hollywood.

Takei graduated from UCLA in 1960 with a bachelor's degree in theater. After short stays in New York City and in England, where he studied Shakespeare, Takei returned to UCLA and began working on his master's degree in theater arts. While working toward his degree, he received the call that changed his life—Gene Rodenberry wanted to interview Takei for a part on the new science fiction show he was developing called "Star Trek."

Takei met with Rodenberry and interviewed for the part of astrophysicist Hikaru Sulu, better known as Mr. Sulu. Takei felt the interview did not go well, but to his surprise, he was offered the part. The show got off to a rocky start on NBC, with two different pilots being filmed, and underwent many changes in its first season. Among the changes was Takei's role on the show—Sulu was changed from astrophysicist to a helmsman, meaning he would have a very prominent role on the main deck, or bridge, of the spaceship Enterprise.

In its first two seasons on NBC, *Star Trek* did not do well in the ratings. Vocal fan protests kept the show on for one more season, but after that it was canceled. Little did NBC realize that it had just ended the run of the show that would launch a cult phenomena that includes four different television shows, nine motion pictures, dozens of novels, and hundreds of web sites, fan conventions, and merchandising spin-offs. Takei starred in all three seasons on television, plus the first six movies in the motion picture franchise. In addition, he regularly appeared at *Star Trek* conventions around the world, where fans of the show (known as "Trekkies") worship members of the original cast. Takei was not bothered by the sometimes fanatical devotion of the Trek fans. "The conventions grew to be big, big business, so the actors began to feel that we should participate . . . ," he told *Starlog* magazine. "Our speaking fees wound up supplementing our incomes in a very nice way."

Besides his role as Mr. Sulu, Takei had a very active acting career, appearing in more than 25 motion pictures and literally hundreds of television shows, usually as a guest star. Movies in which he appeared include *The Green Berets*, *P.T. 109*, and *Hell to Eternity*, while he has made appearances on television shows ranging from *3rd Rock from the Sun* to *MacGyver*, acting in both comedic and dramatic roles. In addition, Takei occasionally performed on stage, appearing in plays such as *Undertow* (in Scotland) and *Year of the Dragon* (in New York).

Besides acting, Takei was active in politics. After *Star Trek* was canceled, he hosted a Los Angeles talk show on PBS that discussed East/West relations. A lifelong Democrat, he served as a delegate to the Democratic National Convention in 1972, which was held in Miami, Florida. Takei twice ran for public office, barely losing out on his bid for a seat on the Los Angeles city council in 1973, then withdrawing from the race for a seat in the California assembly after one of his opponents claimed that the release of the first Star Trek motion picture gave Takei an unfair advantage. Even with those setbacks, he remained committed to public service, and held a position on the Southern California Rapid Transit District and as an active member of the Japanese American Citizens League and the Academy of Television Arts and Sciences. Takei also wrote a successful science fiction novel called *Mirror Friend, Mirror Foe*, and wrote his autobiography, which was called *To the Stars* and was published in 1994. ◆

My feeling was that [the interview] wasn't successful because of the way it was carried on. Gene didn't ask me a thing about my experience. We just discussed current events and the movies we had recently seen. I figured Gene was being polite, but that he wasn't interested in me.

George Takei, on his interview with *Star Trek* creator Gene Rodenberry for the role of Mr. Sulu, in *Starlog*, June 1981

Tan, Amy

FEBRUARY 19, 1952– ● AUTHOR

Amy Tan was born on February 19, 1952, in Oakland, California. Her parents, John and Daisy, also gave their daughter a Chinese name: En-mai, which means Blessing of America. John was an electrical engineer and a Baptist minister, while Daisy raised Amy and two boys. Tan spent all of her early years in the San Francisco Bay area, where she had an adolescence that was anything but typical. When she was 15, her brother Peter died unexpectedly of a brain tumor. To compound that tragedy, just six months later, her father also died from the same affliction.

1952 Tan is born in Oakland, California.

1973 Tan completes a double major in English literature and linguistics at San Jose State University.

1983 Tan quits a reporting job to begin working full-time as a freelance writer.

1987 Tan writes fiction for the first time, selling her first short story to G. K. Putnam publishing company.

1989 Tan's first novel, *The Joy Luck Club*, is released to strong critical and commercial response.

2001 Tan's fourth novel, *The Bonesetter's Daughter*, is released.

linguistics the study of language.

Getting through those two deaths was hard enough, but then Tan learned that her mother had kept a huge secret from her family, a secret that came to light only after the two deaths. When Daisy fled China to come to the United States, Chinese officials refused to grant her custody of the three children she had from a first marriage; they routinely refused to let divorced women have custody of their children. When Daisy met and married John in the United States, she could not bring herself to tell him about the three children she had back in China. After his death, however, she told Amy that she had two half-sisters back in China. Daisy's secret life had a great influence on her daughter, as Tan would later incorporate her mother's story into her works of fiction.

After the two deaths, a Chinese mystic told Daisy that she should get away from California to escape the evil influences that had invaded her life. She decided to spend time in Europe, so Tan and her brother lived there for three years, first in the Netherlands and then in Switzerland. Tan graduated from the exclusive College Monte Rosa International in Montreaux, Switzerland. At that point, Tan seemed to be overcome by anger over the death of her father and brother. She began associating with drug dealers who fit the hippie mold of that time period and was arrested at age 16. She nearly eloped to Australia with a mental patient who told her he was a German army deserter. Daisy decided that it was time to return to the United States.

Once in America, Tan attended Linfield College in Oregon, where she was taking pre-med classes so she could become a neurosurgeon, just as her mother desired. However, she soon realized she was not cut out for medicine and that she had a love for the English language and a strong desire to write. She changed her major to English literature and then bounced around at a couple different colleges, first transferring to San Jose City College and then switching to San Jose State University. At San Jose State, she completed two bachelor's degree in 1973, one in English literature and one in **linguistics.** She remained at the university to work on her master's degree in linguistics, which she completed in 1974. That same year, she married Lou DeMattei, whom she had met on a blind date.

After graduating, Tan had no intention of writing as a career. She took some additional coursework at two other California universities, but in 1976, she again experienced tragedy in her life when a good friend was murdered. Tan dropped out of school and began working with disabled children as a language development specialist at the Alameda County Association for the Mentally Retarded in her hometown of Oakland. It was the job her friend had wanted to hold when she was done with college. Tan held that job until 1980 and considers it to be an important time in her life. While working with the disabled children, Tan said that she rediscovered her humanity and learned to better understand people. "It was rewarding and sad and it helped me identify with many different kinds of people," she recalled later.

After that emotionally charged job, Tan took her first writing job in 1981, working as a reporter and editor for a publication called *Emergency Room Reports*. While on that job, she also began working as a freelance writer for corporate clients, writing press releases and other documents. Before long, she had enough clients to allow her to quit the reporting job and work full-time as a freelance writer, which she did in 1983.

In 1987, Tan experienced two important firsts. She met her two half-sisters from China for the first time, and, not long after that, began writing fiction for the first time. She started with short stories, treating her writing as a form of therapy. With her work weeks commonly running 80 or 90 hours, she found that the tension was building in her personal life and that she needed a release. She tried therapy, but her therapist did a poor job. She also tried her hand at jazz piano. Writing fiction was simply another way to escape from the pressure she felt to perform every day.

Tan had success with her very first short story, which landed her a spot in a writer's workshop and was noticed by G. K. Putnam publishing company, which purchased the story, called "Rules of the Game," and an outline that Tan had for her first novel. In 1989, Putnam's faith in hiring a new writer paid off in a huge way when Tan's first novel, called *The Joy Luck Club*, was an enormous hit with adult and young adult female readers. While not directly autobiographical, the novel does focus on Chinese American daughters and their Chinese mothers. The novel's **protagonist,** June, has recently experienced the death of her mother, so the book concentrates on how daughters and mothers have to work to bridge the gap between generations. It also tells of June's struggle as she tries to decide whether or not she should travel to China to meet her half-sisters for the first time to tell them first-hand of their mother's death. Clearly, that plot line is borrowed directly from Tan's own life.

I know I will always have some degree of depression. I still have to wrestle with it, but I see where it fits in with my mother's life, my grandmother's life, my own life. For a long time, I think I didn't know how to be happy, and I didn't trust happiness—I felt that if I had it, I would lose it. But today, I think I am basically a happy person.

Amy Tan, in *People Weekly,* May 7, 2001

protagonist the main character in a story.

The book was a critical and commercial success. It spent nine months on *The New York Times* bestseller list and received a number of awards, including the Gold Award for Fiction from the Commonwealth Club and the Bay Area Book Reviewers Award for best work of fiction. It was also a finalist for the National Book Award for fiction and was nominated for the National Book Critics Circle Award for Fiction. In 1993, the book was released as a major motion picture, for which Tan had helped write the screenplay.

Since the success of that first novel, Tan has been one of the most recognizable voices in women's fiction. Her second novel, *The Kitchen God's Wife*, also focused on mother-daughter relationships, this time in Shanghai, China. The book was directly based on conversations Tan had with her mother about her mother's difficult life in China. Tan's third novel, *The Hundred Secret Senses* avoided mothers and daughters and instead looked at the relationships between half-sisters. With *The Bonesetter's Daughter* (2001), Tan returned to the familiar territory of mothers and daughters. In addition to her novels, Tan has also written two children's stories—*The Moon Lady* (1992) and *The Chinese Siamese Cat* (1994).

In 2001, Tan revealed to the media that she had suffered from bouts of depression for much of her life that had led to suicidal behavior. Her writing and her marriage to DeMattei helped, but things did not get substantially better until 1993, when she began taking antidepressant medications. The drugs gave her "a footing," she says, and made her realize that her "problems [did not] have to keep [her] a prisoner." ◆

Tien, Chang-Lin

JULY 24, 1935– ● PROFESSOR, UNIVERSITY PRESIDENT

Chang-Lin Tien was born on July 24, 1935 in Wuhan, China. Born into a life of privilege, Tien was the son a wealthy Chinese banking official. Used to living in the lap of luxury and having everything a child could want, Tien's life changed drastically when World War II broke out. First, when he was just four years old, his family was forced to flee to Shanghai to escape from the invading Japanese army. Then, after the war was resolved and the Communist Party had risen to power, the Tien family was again forced to run to avoid being persecuted as an enemy to the state. This time, Tien and his parents moved to Taiwan, which was fighting to establish a free and democratic China in opposition to the communists.

With the move to Taiwan, Tien experienced an overnight change from a life of wealth and power to one spent in cramped quarters inside a small Taiwanese apartment. Tien's father had lost everything in his flight from the communists, and although he did resume his banking career, he died in 1952 and left his family in poverty, living as refugees. His future wife, Liu Di-Hwa, had also escaped to Taiwan, thanks to her father's position as a general in the Chinese army.

Tien realized at the age of 17 that he would have to work hard to escape a life of poverty, and he did. He took advantage of the educational opportunities that were available to him and was able to attend the National Taiwan University. There, he studied engineering, graduating with a degree in mechanical engineering in 1955. That degree was the first of several that Tien would earn in a lifetime dedicated to education. Anxious to advance his place in the world, Tien borrowed $4,000 shortly after graduation and moved to the United States.

Once he arrived in America, Tien enrolled first at the University of Louisville, where he earned his master's degree in mechanical engineering in 1957. That same year, he enrolled at Princeton University, where he added a master of arts degree before completing his doctorate in mechanical engineering in 1959. That same year, he began his teaching career at the University of California's Berkeley campus.

At Berkeley, Tien became the youngest professor ever to win the university's Distinguished Teaching Award, which he earned in 1962 at age 26 while working in his field of specialization, thermal radiation. Berkeley proved to be a perfect fit for Tien, and he remained there as the decades rolled by. As time passed, he found that, despite the numerous awards he won for his teaching excellence, he enjoyed the administrative side of academic life as much as he enjoyed teaching. From 1974 to 1981, he served as chairman of the mechanical engineering department, which led to a campus-wide post in 1983. That year, he became the school's vice-chancellor of research, a position he held for only two years before the desire to teach again led him back to the classroom.

Tien remained busy as a professor until 1988, when the University of California at Irvine approached him about becoming the school's vice-chancellor. Despite the fact that he had been

1935 Tien is born in Wuhan, China.

1955 Tien receives his first academic degree, a bachelor's degree in mechanical engineering from National University Taiwan.

1956 Tien moves to the United States, where he attends the University of Louisville and Princeton University.

1959 Tien accepts his first teaching position at the University of California at Berkeley.

1974 Tien is named chairman of the mechanical engineering department at Berkeley.

1988 Tien is named vice-chancellor at the University of California at Irvine.

1990 Tien is named chancellor of the University of California at Berkeley, a position he would hold for seven years.

1999 Tien is named to the National Science Board.

Asian Pacific American Institute for Congressional Studies

Headquartered in Washington, D.C., the Asian Pacific American Institute for Congressional Studies (APAICS) was founded by the Congressional Asian Pacific American Caucus in 1995. It is the only national nonpartisan organization dedicated to increasing Asian Pacific American participation in politics and in the formulation of public policy. Its board of directors are internationally respected members of the Asian Pacific American community, and in 2001 the chairman of the board was retired U.S. Navy rear admiral Ming E. Chang.

The Institute was created in recognition that the Asian and Asian-Pacific communities of the United States are growing rapidly and that, while comprising a great diversity of individual ethnic groups, they have shared concerns and interests. A key part of the Institute's mission is to make certain that national policy planning takes these concerns and issues into account. To accomplish this goal, the Institute sponsors demographic research, provides forums for the dissemination of information of ongoing policy issues, brings together representatives of the diverse Asian Pacific communities to discover common goals, and serves as an informational resource to these communities through its newsletter and web site. In addition, the Institute briefs legislators on issues of interest to the Asian Pacific communities, sponsors internships for college and graduate students interested in careers in public policy, and provides fellowships and scholarships.

The Institute is a not-for-profit organization, funded entirely by corporate, foundation, and individual donors. In order to protect its independent, non-partisan status, it accepts no funds from overseas sources, nor from political parties.

given an endowed position at Berkeley, he felt the Irvine job was too good to pass up and accepted the job. It proved to be a smart decision, as just two years later, his experience and success led to a dream job offer—the position as chancellor (equivalent to the presidency) of the University of California at Berkeley. With that appointment, Tien became the first Asian American to head a major U.S. research university.

Chang would serve as chancellor for seven years. His time as leader of the Berkeley campus was marked by a commitment to diversity. As a newly arrived student in the U.S. in the late 1950s, Chang had been puzzled by the incidences of black-white racism that he witnessed in the American South. As an Asian American, he did not know if he was expected to use the "Colored" accommodations or those for white people—after all, his skin was considered yellow. He was finally told to use the white facilities, but the memories of those times stayed with him. Tien instituted policies at Berkeley that ensured that nearly half of each incoming freshman class during his tenure was selected on the basis of diversity, not academic merit. And, his definition of diversity did not stop at race or skin color—Tien believed in including people who were different because of their sexual orientation, political beliefs, or other distinguishing characteristics. For his diversification efforts and for his sunny personality—he could often be seen mingling with students on campus and attending Cal athletic contests—Tien gained the respect and admiration of many students.

While Chang broadened Berkeley's student population, at the same time, he had to oversee difficult financial times in the California public university system. State funds totaling more than $30 million were cut from Berkeley's budget, which led to increases in tuition and other student fees, as well as teacher cut backs and the elimination of some education programs. Critics argued that Tien failed to respond to student and faculty concerns about the cuts. However, Tien tried to find alternate sources of funding whenever possible. His ties to the business and Asian communities led to multimillion dollar grants and endowments, such as the $4 million grant from San Francisco's Tang Foundation. During his administration, financial support from off-campus, nongovernment sources increased 35 percent over the previous chancellor, and private gifts to the university reached record levels. By the end of his seven-year stay as chancellor, Tien had raised more than $780 million in funds for the university he loved.

In 1997, Tien decided he had done all he could as Berkeley's chancellor and that it was time to return to teaching. Since stepping down as chancellor, however, he retained his ties to the Berkeley campus. In 2001, he was serving both as university professor and as the NEC Distinguished Professor of Engineering. In that role, Tien studied high-level scientific topics, such as microscale heat transfer, including the effects of short length scales, short time scales, and the material microstructure on thermophysical phenomena; and thermal radiation. Tien also served on the National Science Board, a position he was named to by then-President Bill Clinton in 1999.

Tien was successful in every endeavor he undertook, and won numerous awards, including the Max Jacob Memorial Award (the highest honor in his field) in 1981. In addition to the teaching awards, he received two rather unique honors. First, in December 1999, Chinese astronomers named an asteroid Tien Chang-Lin Star to recognize Tien's contributions to science. Two months later, the Chevron Corporation, for which Tien served as a board member, named its newest super oil

> *I don't call myself a role model. I am a very ordinary person. I do work hard and I do have principles and integrity. I try to do the best job as I can. I try to serve the people, including Asian Americans. But I am an American, and I think of America as a whole country—everyone is involved.*
>
> Chang-Lin Tien in *AsianWeek* magazine, two weeks before stepping down as Berkeley chancellor in 1997

tanker after Tien, christening the M/T Chang-Lin Tien in a special ceremony off the Korean coast that was attended by friends and family members.

Tien remained happily married and had three children, all of whom graduated from the University of California at Berkeley. When not working, Tien enjoyed playing golf and attending football games and other athletic contests. ◆

Ting, Samuel Chao Chung

JANUARY 27, 1936– ● PHYSICIST

Samuel C. C. Chung was born on January 27, 1936, in Ann Arbor, Michigan, where his parents K. H. and Jeanne Ting both attended the University of Michigan. When his parents finished their education, they returned to their home in China, where Ting was raised. Much like his parents, Ting proved to be a very smart child who blossomed into a well-educated and intelligent young adult. Even though he did not start his formal schooling until he was 12 years old due to World War II, he showed an aptitude in mathematics, science, and history, and followed in his parents footsteps by traveling to Ann Arbor in 1956 to attend the University of Michigan.

At Michigan, Ting earned a bachelor of science degree in both mathematics and physics in 1959. He remained in Ann Arbor for his graduate studies, completing his master's degree in physics in 1960 and his Ph.D. in physics in 1962. Also while in Ann Arbor, Ting met and married architect Kay Louise Kune in 1960.

After obtaining his doctorate degree, Ting was named a Ford Foundation fellow and went to work at the European Center for Nuclear Research (CERN) in Geneva, Switzerland. There he worked with Italian scientist Guiseppe Cocconi on a proton **synchrotron**, which accelerates protons so that they can be analyzed in many different ways. Two years at CERN led to a job as a teacher at Columbia University, where he worked with two other Chinese scientists. There, Ting continued his research in extremely high-level physics that very few people in the world even understand.

synchrotron an apparatus for imparting very high speeds to charged particles by means of combining high-frequency electric fields and low-frequency electric fields.

Ting became interested in the production of electron and positron pairs by photon radiation, which was part of a specialty field known as quantum electrodynamic theory, which concerns the interaction of matter and electromagnetic radiation. Ting was fascinated by a series of experiments conducted on the pairs at Harvard University, and in 1966 he took a leave of absence from Columbia to travel to Germany in order to replicate the experiments. Working with a team of scientists and a German synchrotron, Ting built a double-arm spectrometer and was able to confirm the results of the Harvard experiments, taking the work of the Ivy League scientists even further by verifying their results at distances as small as one hundred-trillionth of a centimeter.

Ting's work in Germany led him to the study of heavy protons, which he undertook after joining the staff at the Massachusetts Institute of Technology in 1969. Ting's work with heavy protons was an extension of his work with electron (a negatively charged particle) and positron (a positively charged particle) pairs; he simply was trying to locate new particles whose decay products resulted in electron-positron pairs. With a group of colleagues from MIT, Ting went to Long Island, New York, and built another version of the double-arm spectrometer that he had built in Germany, this time at the Brookhaven National Laboratory.

With the new spectrometer in place in the summer of 1974, Ting made a surprising discovery. When certain high-energy electron-positron pairs were shown to be present at 3.1 billion electron volts after one experiment, Ting realized that he had discovered a new particle, which he named J/psi. When Ting's experiment was easily duplicated in Italy, the results of his study were submitted for publication in the scientific journal *Physical Review*. When he discussed the upcoming article with a fellow scientist at Stanford University, Ting was startled to discover that the other scientist, Burton Richter, had made essentially the exact same discovery the same week, but in a different way.

Because the two men had independently reached the same end result, both were named the winners of the 1976 Nobel Prize in Physics. The award was remarkable because in scientific circles, it often takes years, sometimes decades, to receive the proper recognition for new discoveries. The two-year gap between finding the new particle and winning the Nobel Prize was perhaps a new record for that award.

The discovery of the J/psi particle started a renaissance in the study of fundamental particles. The fact that the lifespan of a J/psi particle was a thousand times longer than scientists had

1936 Ting is born in Ann Arbor, Michigan, although he is raised in his parents native China.

1956 Ting returns to the United States to attend the University of Michigan.

1962 Ting completes his studies at Michigan by obtaining his Ph.D. in physics; earlier he had completed bachelor degrees in physics and mathematics and a master's in physics.

1969 Ting joins the staff of the Massachusetts Institute of Technology.

1974 Ting and a team of MIT scientists discover a new particle that is named J/psi.

1976 Ting and Burton Richter receive the Nobel Prize in Physics for their simultaneous discovery of the J/psi particle.

1988 Ting receives the DeGasperi Award in Science from the Italian government.

quark a hypothetical particle that carries a fractional electric charge.

expected could mean only one thing—that there was a type of **quark** that existed that had never been discovered until that time. Quarks are one of the tiniest forms of matter, subatomic particles that comprise larger subatomic particles, and for many years, scientists thought that only three quarks existed. The new quark uncovered by the discovery of J/psi was called charm; one J/psi particle was thought to be made up of one quark (charm) and one antiquark.

Ting remained at MIT after his discovery of J/psi, but he was named the very first Thomas Dudley Cabot Institute Professor in 1977. As of 2001, Ting was still teaching at MIT. In addition to winning the Nobel Prize, Ting also received the Ernest Orlando Lawrence Memorial Award for Physics from the U.S. Energy Research and Development Agency in 1976 and the Eringen Medal from the Society of Engineering Science in 1977. In 1988, he was the recipient of another major scientific award when the government of Italy honored him with the De-Gasperi Award in Science.

Ting was a member of many scientific organizations, including the American Academy of Arts and Sciences, the U.S. National Academy of Sciences, and the American Physical Society. He belonged to several international bodies and received numerous honorary degrees during his career. He and his wife Kay lived in Massachusetts; the couple had two daughters. ◆

Trinh, Eugene Huu-Chau

SEPTEMBER 14, 1950– ● PHYSICIST AND ASTRONAUT

Eugene Huu-Chau Trinh was born on September 14, 1950, in Saigon, Vietnam. When he was only two years old, Trinh's father sent his family to live in Paris, France, when military tensions grew between South and North Vietnam. Trinh's father worked for the United Nations, which was active in the country in order to try to ease tensions between the two countries.

Trinh stayed in Paris until he was 18. He attended French schools, and in 1968, decided to move to the United States to attend college at Columbia University in New York City, which had offered him a full academic scholarship. Once there, he discovered that the tensions that caused him to leave Vietnam had followed him to the United States. The conflict that had been a minor skirmish in 1950 had turned into a full-blown war by 1968, with the North Vietnamese trying to unite the country under communism and the South, with its American allies, trying to keep democracy in place. The war was an unpopular one in the U.S., and student protests were common throughout the country—Columbia, in fact, was one of the main outposts of student unrest. Trinh tried to not become involved in the protests, but he did support the antiwar movement.

For the next nine years, Trinh concentrated on his academics. He graduated from Columbia in 1972 with a bachelor's degree in mechanical engineering, then enrolled in graduate school at Yale University in Connecticut. At Yale, Trinh earned three degrees—a master's degree in applied physics in 1974, a master's in philosophy in 1975, and a Ph.D. in applied physics in 1977. After completing his last degree, Trinh worked on the Yale campus for one year, then moved to California after he accepted a position with the prestigious Jet Propulsion Laboratory (JPL) at California Technical University.

Eugene Huu-Chau
Trinh

At JPL, Trinh specialized in experiments concerning **fluid mechanics,** which is the study of the motion of fluids (liquid or gas) and the principles of physics that affect that motion. To obtain accurate results, several of the experiments Trinh was conducting had to be done in a state of weightlessness, which occurs when there is a lack of gravity. The only way to achieve this while on Earth is to participate in flights sponsored by the National Aeronautic and Space Administration (NASA) in a KC-135 airplane. The plane flies in a pattern that is known as a parabola, and at the top of the parabola, weightlessness is temporarily achieved when the plane goes into free-fall. Using the NASA flights worked for some experiments, but Trinh knew that his best bet was to conduct his experiments in space, where weightlessness is constant. With the space shuttle program

fluid mechanics the study of the motion of liquid or gas fluids and the physics upon that motion.

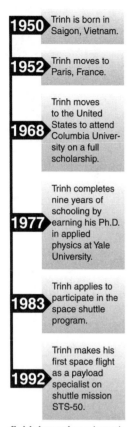

1950 Trinh is born in Saigon, Vietnam.

1952 Trinh moves to Paris, France.

1968 Trinh moves to the United States to attend Columbia University on a full scholarship.

1977 Trinh completes nine years of schooling by earning his Ph.D. in applied physics at Yale University.

1983 Trinh applies to participate in the space shuttle program.

1992 Trinh makes his first space flight as a payload specialist on shuttle mission STS-50.

fluid dynamics a branch of engineering concerned with the study of aerodynamics, the forces on an object moving through the air.

surfactants surface-active substances such as detergent.

making space travel easier and more common, Trinh applied to NASA to become an astronaut.

Trinh's application was received in 1983, and he was accepted two years later. In 1985, he was part of a group of scientists working on what was known as the drop dynamics module experiment. He almost reached his goal of flying on the shuttle that year, but he was chosen as an alternate to lead scientist Taylor Wang, and did not get a chance to fly. After a seven-year wait, Trinh earned another chance to serve on a shuttle mission, and this time he was selected to serve as a payload specialist. The shuttle mission for which he was selected would be NASA's first long-duration shuttle flight, as mission STS-50 intended to stay in space for 14 days. Tring would be part of the crew conducting a number of experiments as part of the U.S. Microgravity Laboratory (USML-1).

On July 9, 1992, aboard the space shuttle *Columbia*, Trinh began his mission. While flying in the KC-135 airplane, Trinh had logged more than 25 hours of what was called low gravity time, but on this one shuttle mission alone, Trinh would experience zero gravity of nearly 14 full days. Trinh's background in **fluid dynamics** paid off on the shuttle mission, as his job was to study the effects of fluid surface tension in low gravity. Specifically, he had to perform a series of experiments that tested the magnitude and strength of surface tension in conditions that were not available on Earth. Such experiments were made to improve the production of **surfactants**, which are used in hundreds of products as diverse as mayonnaise and detergents. The experiments also focused on environmental science, mimicking the transfer of gases into the atmosphere that occurs in each of the oceans on Earth.

Payload specialists on shuttle flights have an extremely busy schedule, and Trinh was no different. He worked a minimum of a 12-hour shift every day, with almost no break time. Still, Trinh took time to reflect on how lucky he was to make a trip that very few people get to make and to take in the breathtaking view of Earth from outer space.

In 1999, Trinh was named head of the Microgravity Research Division at NASA. Trinh was a member of several professional associations, including the American Institute of Aeronautics and Astronautics, the American Physical Society, and the American Society of Mechanical Engineering. He published more than 40 papers on fluid dynamics, microgravity, and other physics topics. When not working, Trinh spent time with his wife Yvette and their daughter, Claire, at their home in Culver City, California. ◆

Tsui, Daniel Chee

FEBRUARY 28, 1939– ● PHYSICIST

Daniel C. Tsui was born February 28, 1939 in Henan, China. As a child growing up in a remote village in central China, Tsui experienced drought, flood, and other hardships, including World War II. Even through the difficult times, however, he remembers his parents working to ensure that their house was a happy one. Like most people in the crowded village where he was born, Tsui's parents could not read or write, a situation they swore would not happen to their son. Thus, in 1951, when the opportunity arose to send Tsui to Hong Kong to attend school, the Tsui's jumped at it and sent Daniel away.

In Hong Kong, Tsui began his schooling at the sixth grade level. School was difficult for him at first because he did not recognize the **Cantonese** dialect that was spoken in Hong Kong at the time. Overcoming that obstacle represented a fond memory for Tsui, as many of his classmates generously pitched in to help him learn how to speak the local language. Those same students also included Tsui in many after-school activities.

Cantonese the dialect of Chinese spoken in and around Canton.

His second year in Hong Kong, Tsui attended the Pui Ching Middle School, which was well-known for its strong natural sciences curriculum. With war still out of control in China, many of the nation's best scholars had fled to Hong Kong, which meant that the schools in that city were stocked with the finest scholars and teachers in China. Some of the teachers struggled in the classroom because they were used to doing only research, but all had a great intellect and all urged the students to do the best they could in every subject.

Tsui graduated from Pui Ching in 1957 and, since he still could not return to China to see his parents due to the continuing turmoil, he signed a two-year agreement to teach in a government program designed to prepare high school graduates for the rigors of the University of Hong Kong. In 1958, Tsui learned

1939 ▶ Tsui is born in Henan, China.

1951 ▶ Tsui moves to Hong Kong, where he attends Pui Ching Middle School.

1958 ▶ Tsui moves to Rockford, Illinois, to attend Augustana College.

1967 ▶ Tsui completes his master's and doctorate degrees at the University of Chicago.

1968 ▶ Tsui moves to New Jersey to work at Bell Laboratories.

1981 ▶ Tsui and several colleagues discover the fractional quantum Hall effect.

1998 ▶ Tsui and his colleagues receive the Nobel Prize in Physics for discovering the fractional quantum Hall effect.

semiconductor any of a class of solids whose electrical conductivity is between that of a conductor and an insulator in being almost as great as that of a metal at high temperatures.

that he had been admitted to Augustana College in Rockford, Illinois. He knew of the small school because it was the one that his church's pastor had attended, and the pastor had helped arrange a full scholarship for Tsui if he could get to the United States. Tsui made all the necessary arrangements, and by the first week of September, 1958, he was in Rockford and enrolled in classes.

Tsui studied at Augustana for three years, a period he called "the best three years of [his] life.' Tsui chose physics as his major, in large part because Chinese scientists C. N. Yang and T. D. Lee had won the Nobel Prize for Physics at the University of Chicago in 1957. Proud Chinese students wanted to emulate Yang and Lee, and Tsui was no exception. While his studies at Augustana were difficult, he had more free time than he had ever had in his life thanks to the fact that he no longer faced a long daily commute and extensive church activities each day. He used that time to reflect on his spirituality and his Lutheran faith, "to make sense out of [his] life experience."

Tsui chose the University of Chicago for his graduate studies in physics. It was the complete opposite of small-town Rockford—a huge, exciting urban area that presented numerous academic and cultural opportunities. At Chicago, Tsui earned both his master's degree and his doctorate degree in physics, graduating in 1967. While at the university, he met physicist Royal Stark, whom he viewed as a mentor. Under Stark's tutelage, Tsui realized that his primary interest in physics was in the area of solid state research. Working as Stark's research assistant, Tsui concentrated on small-scale experiments, "tabletop experiments," as he called them. He learned how to make his own machines, from the engineering to the machining and soldering. When he felt that he had learned all he could at the university, he decided that he wanted to continue working in a research capacity, rather than take a job that would use his technical skills. As a result, he accepted a position with Bell Laboratories in Murray Hill, New Jersey in 1968.

At Bell Labs, Tsui discovered his true calling in physics was **semiconductor** research. Rather than work in existing areas, such as optics and high energy band-structures, he launched a whole new field of study that was called the physics of two-dimensional electrons, which examines the two-dimensional electron gas that is present in semiconductor interfaces. In 1981, Tsui, together with colleagues Horst L. Stormer and Robert B. Laughlin, made a groundbreaking discovery called the fractional quantum Hall effect, which deals with the movement of electrons in a conductor at the quantum level. Their discovery built on decades of work by other scientists, beginning with Edwin H. Hall, who first discovered the quantum effect that bears his name in 1879.

While other scientists had taken Hall's initial discovery and made many important discoveries of their own, none were more important than the leap forward that Tsui, Stormer, and Laughlin made. Sixteen years after uncovering the fractional effect, Tsui and his colleagues were recognized for their work when they were was awarded the 1998 Nobel Prize in Physics, the most prestigious award in science. Earlier, Tsui, Stormer, and A. C. Gossard were recognized with the American Physical Society's Oliver E. Buckly Condensed Matter Physics Prize in 1984. Tsui also won the Benjamin Franklin Medal in Physics in 1998. Tsui's work launched a new era in the study of many-body phenomena and has had far-reaching implications in many other areas of physics.

A year after discovering the fractional quantum Hall effect, Tsui decided that he wanted to rejoin the academic world and accepted a position as the Arthur Legrand Doty Professor of Electrical Engineering at Princeton University, where he still taught as of 2001. At Princeton, he turned his research efforts to the study of the electronic properties of metals, the surface properties of superconductors, and low-temperature superconductors. Tsui was elected to the National Academy of Sciences in 1987, and he remains active in many other scientific organizations.

Tsui lived in Princeton, New Jersey, with his wife Linda, whom he married in 1964. The couple had two children. ◆

Perhaps it was the Confucius in me, the faint voice I often heard when I was alone, that the only meaningful life is a life of learning. What better way is there to learn than through teaching!

Daniel Tsui, and why he left Bell Labs for Princeton University in 1982, quoted in *Les Prix Nobel,* 1998

Wang, An

FEBRUARY 7, 1920–MARCH 24, 1990 ● COMPUTER SCIENTIST

An Wang, whose name means "Peaceful King," was born in Shanghai, China, on February 7, 1920. The era in which he was born was known in China as "the Age of Confusion," and with good reason. Internal conflicts that pitted Chinese warlords against Nationalist leader Chaing Kai-Shek wracked the countryside, and that, combined with an aggressive Japanese military occupation following World War I, meant that the China of Wang's youth was a tumultuous place. His father, Yin Lu, taught English at a private elementary school on the outskirts of Shanghai, and he also practiced traditional Chinese herbal medicine. Both of Wang's parents (his mother's name was Zen Wan), as well as one of his sisters, were killed as a result of conflicts with the Japanese.

Wang was a bright child who was put to the test at an early age when he was forced to attend classes with third graders, even though he was only of kindergarten age. Even though he was two years younger than his classmates, Wang was one of the best students in his class, especially excelling in mathematics. When he was 16, he was still well ahead of other students his age, as he entered Chiao Tung University at that age. There, he studied engineering and graduated near the top of his class in 1940.

Upon graduating, Wang took a job as an engineering teaching assistant. However, he was angered by the Japanese occupation of his homeland, so he bravely volunteered to be part of a group of engineers who would sneak into enemy occupied land to build radio transmitters that could be used by Chinese Nationalists in their fight against the invaders. During the height

An Wang next to one of his company's computers.

of World War II, Wang worked at the Chinese Central Radio Works in Kweilin. Even as he fought against the Japanese, however, Wang realized that many of the Chinese Nationalist leaders were brutal men in their own right who would rule with an iron fist, so he jumped at a chance to work in the United States as part of a Nationalist program to send engineers abroad to learn the skills needed to rebuild the war-torn country.

Wang arrived in Newport News, Virginia, in June 1945. It was expected that he would work as an apprentice at one of the large American communications company so that he could learn the latest technology, but instead Wang decided to further his education by attending Harvard University. There, he complete his master's degree in 1946 and his doctorate in applied physics in 1947.

Wang remained at Harvard after his graduation and worked at the Harvard Computation Laboratory, which was run by computer pioneer Howard Aiken. There, Wang would make a discovery that changed the face of computing and that made him a wealthy man. The lab where he worked was home to the first **binary** computer in the United States, and owners of

binary something made of two parts or things.

today's modern personal computers would not have recognized the machine as a computer; it was 51 feet long, eight feet high, and very loud, as it relied on mechanical movement to make computations. Aiken and others realized that computers would never reach their full potential until someone created a method through which data could be obtained magnetically, instead of mechanically. All previous efforts to devise such a system had failed, because the only method that existed at that time for reading magnetic information actually destroyed the information as it was read. Aiken assigned Wang to attempt to solve the magnetic problem.

In a flash of inspiration that came to him as he walked across Harvard Yard, Wang solved the problem. His invention, the magnetic memory core, did in fact destroy information as it read it, just as the current magnets did. However, Wang realized that this was not a problem; because the computer "learned" the information as it destroyed it, it could immediately rewrite the information as it performed a computation. That way, data was constantly lost and regained, with no mechanical parts needed. It was the breakthrough the computing world had been waiting for, and it represented the first of 35 patents that Wang would register with the U.S. Patent Office during his career. Other computer scientists, most notably Jay Forrester of the Massachusetts Institute of Technology, used Wang's magnetic memory core to create a new system of randomly accessible memory that gave computers a much greater available memory in a much, much smaller space. It was the beginning of modern computing.

Wang decided that he had learned all he could at Harvard and that it was time to strike out on his own so he could make money off of his discoveries. With only $2,600 to his name, Wang rented a 200-square foot office in Boston and began developing commercial uses for his magnetic memory core. In its first year, Wang Laboratories earned $3,254, the first of more than 120 consecutive fiscal quarters—spanning three decades—in which the company increased earnings and revenue. Wang's personal life was also changing during this exciting time in his life. In 1949, he married Lorraine Chu, a fellow Chinese student at Harvard; the couple would have three children together. In 1955, Wang officially became an American citizen.

One of Wang's first contracts was an extremely high profile job—he built the new scoreboard at Yankee Stadium, one of the

1920 Wang is born in Shanghai, China.

1941 Wang begins working for the Central Radio Works, fighting the Japanese during World War II.

1945 Wang arrives in America and enrolls at Harvard, completing master's and doctorate degrees by 1948.

1951 Wang founds Wang Laboratories in Boston.

1956 Wang reaches a settlement with IBM over the use of his magnetic memory core.

1975 Wang leads his company through a period of unprecedented economic growth.

1990 Wang dies of cancer.

most famous stadiums in American sports. At the time, Wang was locked in a court battle with the giant company, International Business Machines (IBM), also known as "Big Blue." IBM was using Wang's magnetic memory core in almost all of their new products, and thus they decided to challenge his patents in court, claiming that the magnetic memory core should reside in the public domain. Even though IBM was 10,000 times the size of Wang Laboratories, Wang stood his ground and refused to cave in to the industry leader. He knew that IBM had to have his technology to stay alive, so he fought their lawsuits at every turn. Just as it seemed as if Wang had finally beaten IBM, the company produced a scientist who was challenging Wang's right to the patent, claiming that he had devised a similar invention. Wang knew the claim was bogus, but he also knew that his patience for court battle was running out. Negotiating from a position of strength, Wang settled for $400,000 from IBM, an enormous sum in 1956.

Wang invested that money back into his company and set about battling IBM in another arena—home office equipment. First he concentrated on newly invented desktop calculators, but when he sensed the market for those was waning, he turned to typewriters and word processing. He created an electronic typewriter that featured a memory system that made it easy to store and edit text; not only was it better than IBM typewriters, it was cheaper. Soon after that first electronic typewriter, Wang created a word processor that featured a television-like monitor upon which text was displayed as it was typed. Now common on today's personal computers, the monitor was a first of its kind, and Wang's word processing machines were a huge hit.

During the height of his word processor success in the 1970s and early 1980s, Wang Laboratories went through a period of phenomenal growth that averaged an almost unheard of 42 percent a year. Wang intended that his company would be handed down from generation to generation of Wang children, and even after it went public with a common stock offering, voting control of the company remained in the Wang family. However, things began to change for the worse in the mid-1980s. At that time, two new companies—Microsoft and Apple—were introducing relatively cheap and very powerful computers that fit on a desktop. They looked very similar to Wang's word processors, but the machines were much more powerful than that basic machine and could perform far, far more applications. Showing a stubborn streak and a bit of ego that had served him well earlier in his career, Wang did not move quickly enough to meet the new challenge, and when he did make moves, they often proved to be the wrong ones. By 1989, most of the company's top executives had left, and Wang was fighting to keep his once powerful company out of bankruptcy.

In 1990, with the future of the company still very much in doubt, Wang became ill and succumbed to a fast-spreading cancer of the esophagus. Perhaps it was best that he was not alive to see the company that he had founded from scratch hit bottom two years after his death when it declared bankruptcy. Under the guidance of Wang's son, Frederick, the company did survive the bankruptcy and remained in business, but it was radically downsized. Instead of being one of the leading players in the computer industry, Wang Laboratories instead worked in a few niche markets that proved to be fairly lucrative.

In addition to his lasting contributions to world science, Wang was also known for his charitable contributions. He made sure that he shared his vast wealth, estimated at more than $2 billion at one point, by supporting such organizations as the Wang Institute, the Wang Center, and Massachusetts General Hospital. From his humble beginnings, An Wang changed the face of American business and left a lasting legacy in the computer industry. ◆

Wang, Charles

AUGUST 18, 1944– ● ENTREPRENEUR AND COMPUTER PROGRAMMER

Charles Wang was born on August 18, 1944, in Shanghai, China. His family was quite wealthy by Chinese standards, as his father was a Supreme Court justice in that country. However, several years after the end of World War II, a communist revolution was underway that was sweeping across China. Wang's father wisely decided that it was time to leave the country, so he moved his family to the United States in 1952.

Wang was a hard-working child who did well in school. His first job was at the U.S. Post Office, where he worked part-time sorting mail. After graduating from high school, he attended Queen's College in New York City, where he graduated with a bachelor's degree in mathematics in 1967. Wang had no clear

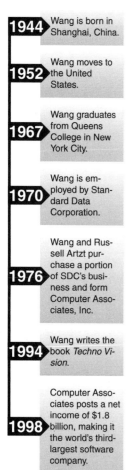

idea what he wanted to do for the rest of his life, and he settled on computers almost by accident. While reviewing the help wanted ads one day, he noticed that there were many ads seeking computer programmers. Realizing that so many vacant jobs meant that the field was growing rapidly, he told his mother right then he was going to be a programmer, even though he admitted he had no idea what a programmer did.

To learn just that, Wang signed on as a trainee at the Columbia University Electronics Lab—even though he did not have a computer background, the lab recognized that he was smart and he was a hard worker, and the rest he could learn through training. After four years at Columbia, Wang knew exactly what programmers did, and he took that knowledge to the large computer company, Standard Data Corporation. Wang worked at SDC for five years, learning how to service and provide software support for IBM mainframe computers (mainframe computers are very large and powerful computers that usually provide the power for a network of personal computers).

In 1976, Wang and coworker Russell Artzt decided to start their own business. To do that, they approached SDC about purchasing one portion of its software business that was underperforming. SDC was happy to sell off the less profitable sector, which Wang and Artzt renamed Computer Associates, Inc. (CA). In the new company, Wang was the salesman and Artzt was the technical expert. Wang had a brash New York City attitude that made him a perfect salesman in the highly competitive computer industry.

Wang and Artzt's first move as the heads of CA came to characterize the company's corporate philosophy. They identified a Swiss company that had a product that was perfect for the U.S. market. Since the Swiss had been unable to find an American distributor, they were more than happy to make a deal with CA. In exchange for stock in the fledgling company, Wang earned the right to produce the Swiss product in the United States. The act of trading stock for the rights to a product, or for ownership of an entire company, became Wang's trademark move. With Wang and Artzt working well as a team, CA thrived right from the start, and in 1981, it became a publicly-traded company.

Wang seemed to have a golden touch when it came to selecting companies to purchase and fold into the CA product line. He specialized in two things—first, identifying a niche area that was not being properly served, and then purchasing a company that could serve that niche while meshing with his other products; and second, ensuring that his clients could easily and efficiently operate their computer systems despite the vast number of different hardware and software solutions that existed.

He also had what some people called a ruthless streak, as he was not afraid to let excess employees go after he had made an acquisition. He realized that whenever he bought a company, certain jobs, such as those in accounting or marketing, were already being handled by his existing accounting and marketing staffs. What Wang was purchasing was the product—not the people. He would closely examine the new company to see just who was essential and who could be released, and often it was only the technology experts who survived a Wang takeover. While such moves may seem heartless, Wang was actually highly praised by the employees he kept because he provided excellent compensation and benefits to his employees, as well as a nurturing work environment that included such amenities as free breakfasts and free day care. Those who remained behind after a CA takeover became very loyal to their new employer.

By the late 1990s, Wang had turned CA into the third-largest independent computer company in the world, behind only Microsoft and Oracle. That fact may surprise many people, as Wang and Computer Associates were far less known than Microsoft. Whereas Microsoft founder Bill Gates took an active, and very public role as the leader of the computer industry, Wang was content to remain in the background and quietly do the things it took to make his company grow. It was estimated that CA acquired more than 60 rival companies, and it showed no signs of slowing down.

While Wang did not have as high a profile as Gates, he did match his rival in the important area of charitable contributions. Gates was well-known for the $3.5 billion he gave to charity in 1999, and while Wang was not be able to match that astronomical number, he routinely made very large donations to numerous causes. One of the largest was a donation of $25 million to the State University of New York at Stony Brook to build an Asian American cultural center. He chose Stony Brook because it was near CA's headquarters in New York. He hoped that the center would improve relations between eastern nations such as China and the United States.

Wang was married twice and had one daughter from his first marriage. In 1994 he wrote a book called *Techno Vision* that helped business leaders understand computers and networks. He lived on a huge estate on Long Island, New York. One of his favorite pastimes was playing basketball with old friend Russ Artzt, who remained part of the CA corporate team. Wang was also close to his brother Tony, who served as CA's chief operating officer. ◆

Wang, Garrett

DECEMBER 15, 1968– ● ACTOR

1968 Wang is born in Riverside, California.

1985 Wang graduates from Harding Academy in Memphis, Tennessee, and enrolls at UCLA.

1994 Wang receives his first big break in television when he is cast in the series *All-American Girl*.

1995 Wang becomes the second Asian character featured in the *Star Trek* group of television shows when he wins the role of Ensign Harry Kim on the new *Star Trek: Voyager*.

1997 Wang is named one of *People* magazine's 50 Most Beautiful People in the World.

Garrett Wang was born on December 15, 1968 in Riverside, California. His parents moved to the United States from China, and Wang had a Chinese name—Wang Yi Chung—in addition to his American name. As a child, his family moved around a lot, moving from Indiana, to Bermuda, to Memphis, Tennessee, where he spent the most time. After graduating from the Harding Academy in Memphis at age 16, Wang moved to Los Angeles to attend the University of California at Los Angeles (UCLA), where he majored in Asian studies.

It was at UCLA that Wang first became interested in acting, as he participated in university theater productions. He credited his acting teacher at UCLA, Jenny Roudtree, with making him believe that he could make it as an actor. At UCLA, Wang also played tennis well enough to consider playing the sport professionally, but after working with Roudtree, he decided to pursue a career in acting.

After graduating from UCLA, Wang became active in the Los Angeles-area theater scene. His first notable role came in the play "Porcelain," which was playing at the Burbage Theater. Wang played the lead role of John Lee in Chay Yew's play and received strong critical reviews for his performance.

In addition to his stage work, Wang was trying to break into either television or the movies, and he succeeded in television first. First came a series of commercials, including Burger King, which was his first, Big Red Gum, and Rice Krispies Treats. He got his first big break in 1994, when he was cast opposite star Margaret Cho in Cho's autobiographical comedy, *All-American Girl*. Wang played Cho's boyfriend in the series, but it was canceled midway through its first season.

After that failed effort, Wang was faced with his first big career decision. He auditioned for roles in a new *Star Trek* series that was preparing for launch on the UPN network, and at the same time he tried out for a role in the film *Cruz*, in which he would be playing a college dropout. When he received word that he had won both parts, Wang had to choose which he would accept. The "Star Trek" role would mean job security for years, while the film role could lead to a successful film career, which most actors would choose over a career in television. However, in the end, Wang decided that he did not like the character he would be playing in *Cruz*. Instead, he decided to take the role of Ensign Harry Kim in the new series, which was to be called *Star Trek: Voyager*. That was in 1995, and the show quickly became the top-rated show on the UPN network. After seven seasons, he was set to close out his run on the show when it filmed its farewell episode in May 2001.

As Ensign Kim, Wang became the first Asian-American actor to appear as a regular in one of the *Star Trek* series since George Takei played Sulu in the original *Star Trek* television series in the 1960s. It was a responsibility that Wang took very seriously. "I believe that I have a huge responsibility in being one of a very small number of Asian-Americans appearing in television regularly," he told one interviewer. "My goal now is to do the best job possible playing Ensign Harry Kim and to begin repaying my parents for the unaccountable financial support they have given me throughout the years."

Wang knew that playing Kim would be a unique opportunity, since *Star Trek* fans are known to be the most loyal in show business. As a result, Wang spent quite a bit of time fleshing out the character of Harry Kim, providing him with a depth that would make him more memorable.

Besides his work on *Voyager*, Kim remained as active as possible in other acting venues. He had roles in the independent films *Ivory Towers* and *Hundred Percent*, and he also remained active in live theater. He performed in plays such as "Model Minority" at the Los Angeles Theater Center, "Woman Warrior" at the Mark Taper Forum, and "A Language of Their Own" at the Intiman Theater.

Wang's acting career led to a number of high profile, if less serious, awards as well. In 1997, *People* magazine named him to its annual list of the 50 Most Beautiful People in the World, and E! Entertainment Television named Wang one of the 20 Coolest Bachelors in the United States.

> *I hope because I've made it, a kid who looks like me can walk down the street and instead of [somebody yelling] "Hey Chinaman," they'll say "Hey, you kind of look like Garrett Wang!"*
>
> Garrett Wang in *People Weekly* magazine, May 12, 1997

Off screen, Wang enjoyed snowboarding, drawing, and writing. He was also active on the Star Trek lecture circuit, regularly attending conventions and other shows. ◆

Wang, Vera

JUNE 27, 1949– ● FASHION DESIGNER

Vera Wang was born on June 27, 1949, to Cheng Ching and Florence Wang. Wang was born and raised in New York City, where her parents settled after fleeing China during World War II. Wang's father was a brilliant scientist who, upon arriving in the United States, studied chemical engineering at the Massachusetts Institute of Technology. However, to provide a better living for his family, Wang switched to a career in business, in which he also succeeded. He rose to the position of chairman of the U.S. Summit Company, and he would later be one of the primary investors when his daughter launched her own clothing company. Wang's mother worked as a translator at the United Nations. Wang had one brother, named Kenneth, who later took over his father's business.

Thanks to her family's wealth, Wang had the best education that money could buy and was also afforded opportunities to participate in many extracurricular activities. She attended prestigious private schools, such as the Chapin School in Manhattan, and when she decided that she wanted to become a professional ballerina, she enrolled at the School of American Ballet. At the age of seven, Wang's lifelong goal changed when she received a pair of ice skates for Christmas. Instead of being a ballerina, Wang wanted to be a professional figure skater, and she nearly attained her goal. She received instruction from some of the best trainers in the United States, and when she was a teenager, placed fifth in the U.S. Nationals junior

Vera Wang

pair championships with partner James Stuart in 1968 and 1969.

Wang thought she had a realistic chance to skate at the Olympics, but after Stuart decided to skate singles instead of pairs, she decided that it was time to hang up her skates and attend college. Again, she had the financial standing to attend the best schools, enrolling at Sarah Lawrence College. Wang elected to study art history, which led to spending her junior year abroad at the Sorbonne in France. Wang later graduated with a bachelor's degree in art history, a degree that her parents thought was very impractical.

After graduating, Wang remained in the city and landed a job at the fashion magazine, *Vogue*. There, her good taste and eye for fashion allowed her to rise quickly through the ranks, and at 23, she became the youngest editor in the magazine's history; by her mid-20s, she was a senior fashion editor. Wang was good at her job, and she loved it. She was able to travel to some of the world's most beautiful cities, and socialize with leading fashion models and other celebrities at the best clubs and restaurants. It was an exciting, glamorous job, and Wang remained at *Vogue* for 16 years.

In 1987, Wang decided it was time for a change, and she decided to put her experience a fashion editor to work designing her own line of clothes. She took a job as a designer with Ralph Lauren's company, where she served as a design director for women's accessories. In 1989, she married businessman Arthur Becker, a move that changed her professional life as much as it changed her personal life. When she was preparing for the wedding, she could no find a wedding gown that she liked—they were all too frilly and not elegant enough for her tastes. After the wedding, she went back to work at Ralph Lauren, but after just six months, she decided to open her own design company that would specialize in wedding gowns.

Bankrolled by her father's investment, Wang opened Vera Wang Bridal House, Ltd. in the Carlyle Hotel in Manhattan in 1990. In the beginning, she offered gowns made by other designers as well as her own, but she was working on new designs as fast as possible so that she would not have to rely on others. Within a year, Wang was in demand as one of the leading wedding dress designers in the country. Her gowns featured a simple elegance and lavish materials, as well as a bit of sexiness that was often lacking from wedding gowns. Wang created ready-to-wear dresses that were available in boutiques around the country that

1949 — Wang is born in New York City.

1972 — Wang, at age 23, becomes the youngest editor ever at *Vogue* magazine.

1987 — Wang leaves *Vogue* after 16 years and goes to work as a designer for Ralph Lauren.

1989 — Wang marries businessman Arthur Becker.

1990 — Wang opens Vera Wang Bridal House, Ltd., which specializes in designing fashionable wedding gowns.

1993 — Wang introduces a full line of evening wear to compliment her wedding gowns.

1994 — Wang receives international attention when she designs the costumes for Olympic figure skater Nancy Kerrigan.

They were over-the-top and ornate and looked like wedding cakes. I wanted something more elegant and subdued, but there wasn't anything. I realized the desire to fill that niche.

Vera Wang, on why she started designing wedding gowns, in *Biography* magazine, June 1998

ranged in price from roughly $2,000 to $5,000, but she really became famous for her custom designs. Wang's name spread quickly thanks to all of her fashion and celebrity friends from her days at *Vogue*, and before long, her dresses were seen on some of Hollywood's most famous brides, including Holly Hunter, Mariah Carey, and Elizabeth Shue.

Since becoming famous for her wedding designs, Wang has also branched out into other areas. In 1993, she introduced a line of evening wear. Once again, the stars flocked to her designs, and leading actresses such as Halle Berry and Sharon Stone wore Vera Wang gowns to the Academy Awards and other ceremonies. In 1994, Wang combined two of her lifelong loves—clothes and ice skating—when she designed American Olympic figure skater Nancy Kerrigan's skating outfits. Other endeavors included a series of designer Barbie outfits for toymaker Mattel, and a line of housewares and linens. Shoes and a fragrance line were expected to follow.

Wang lived in New York with her husband and their two adopted daughters, Celine and Josephine. She was still very close to her family, as her brother lived in the building next to hers and her parents were just blocks away. She and her husband also owned homes in Southhampton, New York; Pound Ridge, New York; and Palm Beach, Florida. In her spare time, she enjoyed golf and shopping. She was also active in the Asian Society of New York and devoted time and money to a number of charitable causes. ◆

Wang, Wayne

JANUARY 12, 1949– ● FILM DIRECTOR

Wayne Wang was born January 12, 1949, in Hong Kong, China. His family arrived in Hong Kong just six days before Wang's birth, as they had been forced to flee mainland China to escape the communist takeover that swept through their homeland. Wang's father was forced to flee because he was part of the educated elite who were in the most danger when the communists took over—he was an engineer and businessman who was far more comfortable with Western culture than he was with the communist regime. Wang's father loved American films, and even named his son after American actor John Wayne.

Wang was raised in Hong Kong, where he attended private religious schools as a child, which is where he learned to speak English. When he turned 18, his mother urged him to move to the United States, as the political situation in Hong Kong was worsening thanks to the instability in the region caused by the Korean and Vietnam wars, and by the ruthlessness of the communist regime, which was led by Mao Tse Tsung. Upon arriving in the U.S., Wang enrolled at Foothill College in California, where he studied painting. There, Wang succeeded in his studies, but he felt tremendous pressure as one of the few Asian students on campus. "I developed a lot of insecurity about being Chinese there," he remembers.

After two years at Foothill, Wang continued his art studies at the California College of Arts and Crafts in Oakland. He soon switched from painting to filmmaking, however, and he eventually graduated with his master's degree of fine arts in film and television. Wang's parents were initially disappointed with their son's career choice—they wanted him to be a doctor or engineer, not an artist. They were at least partially appeased when he switched from painting to film. "When I got into film, my dad was actually glad because he loves movies so much," says Wang, "and he said at least I wasn't going to be a painter starving in the streets."

After graduating, Wang returned to Hong Kong, which has a thriving film industry. Jobs were plentiful, and Wang had no trouble breaking in, initially working on small films and on television series. When he did not advance as quickly as he would have liked, he returned to the United States, settling in San Francisco, where he made films that focused on the plight of Chinese immigrants. Using his own experiences as his guide, Wang successfully directed his first film, called *Chan Is Missing* (1982), on a tiny budget of just $22,000. The movie told the story of two Chinese cab drivers in San Francisco who were trying to find a man named Chan, with whom they had invested $4000, only to have him disappear. The film was a surprise critical success, earning more than $1 million dollars.

The success of *Chan Is Missing* meant that Wang would no longer have to work with tiny budgets. His next film, *Dim Sum* (1984), told the story of four Chinese women who met each week to play the Chinese game, **mah-jongg.** The film especially concentrated on the relationship between one of the players and her daughter, and the poignant storytelling that Wang demonstrated earned strong critical praise for the film.

1949 Wang is born in Hong Kong, China.

1967 Wang moves to the United States and enrolls at Foothills College in California.

1982 Wang directs *Chan Is Missing*, his first film.

1987 Wang directs his first "non-Chinese" film, called *Slamdance*, with Tom Hulce.

1993 Wang directs his biggest commercial picture, the screen adaptation of Amy Tan's *The Joy Luck Club*.

1999 Wang directs *Anywhere But Here* with Susan Sarandon and Natalie Portman.

mah-jongg a game of Chinese origin played by four persons with 144 tiles that are drawn and discarded until one player has a winning hand.

With each film, Wang's reputation grew in Hollywood, and after *Dim Sum*, he made his first film that did not feature Chinese American themes. Called *Slamdance* (1987), the movie starred Tom Hulce and Mary Elizabeth Mastrantonio in a psychological thriller. The film failed to generate much interest at the box office, but it was a critical success, as it was received a strong reception at the prestigious Cannes Film Festival in France.

Stung by the failure at the box office, Wang returned to Chinese American stories for his next two films. *Eat a Bowl of Tea* (1989) was set in 1940 Chinatown in New York City and dealt with the difficulties faced by a woman who is brought to live in New York after World War II by her Chinese American husband; the bride was portrayed by Wang's wife Cora Miao, a Hong Kong actress he had met in 1983. In an odd quirk, budget restraints forced Wang to use modern-day Hong Kong as a fill in for New York City in the 1940s. His next film, called *Life Is Cheap . . . But Toilet Paper Is Expensive* (1990), was called a "guerrilla gangster flick" by one critic. The movie tells the tale of Chinese American criminal sent to Hong Kong to deliver a briefcase to "The Big Boss." While essentially a crime story, the movie focuses on the cultural differences between Hong Kong and America and the problems those differences cause for the Chinese American protagonist. Wang used his own experiences in America as a basis for the cultural tension felt by the lead character.

Wang's next picture was his biggest commercial success. Teaming with Asian American author Amy Tan, Wang directed the screen version of Tan's successful novel, *The Joy Luck Club* (1993). Like *Dim Sum*, the book and the movie studies the relationship between Chinese-born mothers and their American-born daughters. The movie received strong reviews and also was a success at the box office, becoming one of the most popular mainstream Asian American films of all time. The only criticism leveled at the movie was its negative portrayal of Asian-American men, who are portrayed in a very unflattering light in Tan's story. Other Chinese American critics felt the film distorted Chinese myths and made light of Chinese culture. Still, Wang was optimistic that the film would pave the way for more big budget Chinese American projects. He hoped the film would "reach the heart of America" and added that "I don't think most of America knows that Chinese-Americans are just as American as they are."

Wang's projects since *The Joy Luck Club* veered away from large studio productions and featured small, independent films. Also, Wang felt that he wanted "to step away from the Chinese thing for a while." The low-budget film *Smoke* featured only one Chinese American character, and noted actor Harvey Keitel was the centerpiece of the movie. A sequel—or perhaps companion film is a more accurate description—to *Smoke* called *Blue in the Face* was also released in 1995. In 1997, Wang returned to Chinese themes in the film *Chinese Box*, which featured Jeremy Irons as a photojournalist who learns he has only months to live. Irons approaching demise is seen as an allegory for the demise of Hong Kong, which is about to shift from British rule to Chinese rule as the movie progresses.

In 1999, Wang returned to one of his most familiar themes mother/daughter relationships but in a much different way. This time, instead of addressing Chinese-American maternal relationships, Wang featured two of the top female stars in Hollywood—Susan Sarandon and Natalie Portman—in *Anywhere But Here*, which tells the tale of a mother and daughter struggling to survive in Beverly Hills. ◆

Wong, Anna May

JANUARY 3, 1905–1961 ● ACTRESS

Anna May Wong was one of silent films' most prominent Asian American stars. As such, she struggled against Hollywood's stereotypes of Asian women, and for most of her career the only roles available to her fit the formula of the evil temptress, or "dragon lady," who seduced white men but was ultimately rejected in favor of the virtuous white leading lady. Nonetheless, Wong's determination to succeed against considerable adversity helped to pave the way for her successors.

Born above her father's laundry business on Flower Street in Los Angeles on January 3, 1905, Anna May Wong started life as Wong Liu Tsong. She grew up one of seven siblings in the cramped quarters above her father's store. Her father, a strictly traditional man, was born in the United States, and spent his childhood in Michigan. (Her paternal grandfather immigrated to Sacramento from China during the Gold Rush.)

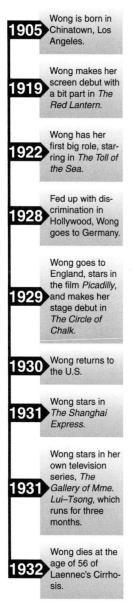

1905 Wong is born in Chinatown, Los Angeles.

1919 Wong makes her screen debut with a bit part in *The Red Lantern*.

1922 Wong has her first big role, starring in *The Toll of the Sea*.

1928 Fed up with discrimination in Hollywood, Wong goes to Germany.

1929 Wong goes to England, stars in the film *Picadilly*, and makes her stage debut in *The Circle of Chalk*.

1930 Wong returns to the U.S.

1931 Wong stars in *The Shanghai Express*.

1931 Wong stars in her own television series, *The Gallery of Mme. Lui–Tsong*, which runs for three months.

1932 Wong dies at the age of 56 of Laennec's Cirrhosis.

nickelodeon movie theater to which admission for a show was five cents.

Wong fell in love with the movies at an early age, and spent many afternoons at the neighborhood **nickelodeon.** Her interest in film and her dreams of stardom worried her father, who would have preferred that she concentrate more on her schoolwork. Despite his concern, however, she won her first role in 1919, a bit part in the film *The Red Lantern*. For her screen debut, she chose the name Anna May, keeping her family name Wong (although it would be several years before she would receive billing for a role). She continued to work as an extra without her father's knowledge; he found out when she was offered a small part in the film *Bit of Life*. While he disapproved, and insisted that she be accompanied on the set at all times by a chaperone, he did not forbid her from taking the role.

Wong's first big film was *Toll of the Sea* in 1922, an adaptation of *Madame Butterfly*. She continued to work in Hollywood for the next few years, appearing in various unmemorable films. She played Tiger Lily in J.M. Barrie's *Peter Pan*, but the role gave her little screen time. In 1926, she played in a movie called *The Silk Bouquet* (whose title was later changed to *The Dragon Horse*), a film of which little is known. Judging from the titles, and its disappearance from the record, it is likely that it was an all-Chinese production aimed at an exclusively Chinese audience.

Wong's career continued without any major breakthroughs, and, frustrated with the lack of opportunity for Asian-Americans in Hollywood, she decided in 1928 to move to Europe. In Germany, she starred in two films, then went on to England in 1929, where she acted in E.A. Dupont's *Picadilly* (the last silent film to her credit). She also made her stage debut in England in a play called *Circle of Chalk*. The work, based on a Chinese folktale, was created by playwright Basil Dean expressly for Wong; she starred opposite the as-yet unknown Laurence Olivier.

While in Europe, Wong taught herself to speak fluent German, French, and Italian. She found Europeans more progressive than Americans in their treatment of Asians. She was accepted into exclusive social circles, and career opportunities abounded. Nonetheless, she did not feel entirely at home there, and in 1931 Wong returned to California. She filmed *Daughter of the Dragon* in 1931 (a flop), then went on to star in perhaps her best-known feature, *Shanghai Express*, in which she took a supporting role to Marlene Dietrich.

Increasingly discouraged by Hollyood's attitude toward Asian-Americans after several rejections for roles, Wong returned to Europe, making three films in England, then touring

England and Ireland with **vaudeville** acts. She returned to the U.S. in the mid-1930s, where she had several more parts in films. She auditioned for the role of O-Lan in *The Good Earth* (one of the day's very few positive portrayals of an Asian woman) but lost the part to an Austrian born actress. She was offered a supporting part, but declined.

After this disappointment, Wong decided to make a long-planned trip to China. Her celebrity's welcome was allayed by criticism of what many Chinese considered her degrading portrayal of Chinese women. Many of her films had in fact been banned in the country. She stayed in China for ten months. Despite her study of the culture and language, however, she found that the cultural obstacles were too great to surmount; while in the United States, her features marked her as Chinese, and kept her from the unqualified success possible for white actresses, she was also too westernized to succeed in Chinese theater.

Wong remained single throughout her life. Her American upbringing left her unable to accept the Chinese model of marriage in which the wife is subordinate to the husband. Both her position at the interstices of two cultures and her independent spirit led her to the ultimate decision not to marry. She maintained a large house in Hollywood Hills, where she gave dinner parties, but for the most part lived a private life. In 1946, she was diagnosed with Laennec's Cirrhosis, and to protect her health, moved to Santa Monica to live with her brother, Richard Kim Wong. She continued to make movies in the 1940s, and in the 1950s turned her efforts to television. She had her own show, "The Gallery of Mme. Lui-Tsong", a crime drama which lasted for only three months. Her final film credit was *Portrait in Black* (also starring Lana Turner) in which she played a housekeeper.

Wong died of Laennec's Cirrhosis in 1961 at the age of 56. ◆

> **vaudeville** a stage performance consisting of acting, singing, and dancing.

Wong, B.D.

OCTOBER 24, 1962 – ● ACTOR

Throughout his career, B.D. Wong was dedicated to expanding the range of possibilities for Asian-American actors on stage and screen. Playing both traditional Asian roles and others, ranging from the lead in Peter Pan to a

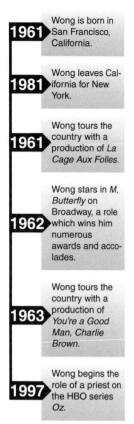

1961 Wong is born in San Francisco, California.

1981 Wong leaves California for New York.

1961 Wong tours the country with a production of *La Cage Aux Folles*.

1962 Wong stars in *M. Butterfly* on Broadway, a role which wins him numerous awards and accolades.

1963 Wong tours the country with a production of *You're a Good Man, Charlie Brown*.

1997 Wong begins the role of a priest on the HBO series *Oz*.

coolie an unskilled laborer or porter, usually in or from the Far East and hired for low wages.

priest in the HBO series *Oz*, he aims to create three-dimensional characters that transcend stereotypes.

Bradley Darryl Wong was born on October 24, 1962, in San Francisco, California, to second-generation Chinese American parents. The second of three sons, he grew up in the Sunset district, where at the time his was one of few Chinese families in the neighborhood. Growing up, B.D. and his brothers attended a Chinese American youth group and summer camp, an effort on their mother's part to instill them with Chinese cultural values.

Wong was bitten by the acting bug early, and during high school performed in a number of school and community productions. His parents were supportive, if somewhat concerned about the economic viability of a career in theater.

Throughout high school, Wong struggled with shame about his ethnicity. "I didn't have a strong sense of self as an Asian American," he admits in retrospect. When he auditioned for a lead role in a community theater production of *Anything Goes*, and was instead given the part of a **coolie**, Wong was forced to confront the obstacles and prejudices facing him, and to begin to develop the pride and self-respect he would need to succeed as an Asian American in Hollywood. He ultimately turned down the role of the coolie.

After high school, Wong spent one year at San Francisco State University, where he excelled at drama, but evinced little interest in his other subjects. He saved money, and in 1981 left for New York City. He supported himself by working odd jobs, performing in summer stock and dinner theaters, and dreaming of a big break. In 1985, he toured the country as part of the chorus in the show *La Cage Aux Folles*. The tour brought Wong back to the West Coast, and he decided to stay in Los Angeles, where he became a student of Donald Hutton.

It was in Los Angeles that Wong auditioned for his first major role, the lead in *M. Butterfly*. The 1988 Broadway production earned him a Tony Award, a Drama Desk Award, the Outer Critics Circle Award, the Clarence Derwent Award, and Theater World Award; he was the first Asian-American to receive several of these honors, and the first actor ever to have won all of them for the same performance.

After *M. Butterfly*, he turned his attention primarily to the movies, accepting roles ranging from a Chinese gang lord in *Mystery Date* to an assistant wedding coordinator in *Father of the Bride*. He was a gay artist in *And the Band Played On* and a geneticist in *Jurassic Park*. He played the brother of comedian

Margaret Cho in her television series "All American Girl," the first television situation comedy to center around an Asian-American family, and made occasional appearances on "Sesame Street," "The X Files," and "Chicago Hope."

Wong lived in New York, but his work frequently brought him to California. He divided his energy between stage and screen. In 1999, he played Linus in a Broadway production of *You're a Good Man, Charlie Brown*. Film roles included *Mulan*, an animated Disney feature in which he provided the voice of Captain Li Shang; *Seven Years in Tibet*, and *Executive Decision*. Wong also provided narration for several books on tape, including *Cloud Mountain* by Aimee E. Liu and David Guterson's *Snow Falling on Ceders*. His most prominent role is as a priest on the controversial HBO prison drama *Oz*.

As one of few openly gay Asian actors in Hollywood, Wong made a point of promoting fair treatment of both homosexuals and Asian-Americans; for example, when a white actor was cast to play an Asian character in "yellow face" in the Broadway play *Miss Saigon*, Wong risked his own reputation to speak out against this. Ironically, his vocal opposition to the casting, which earned him a good deal of negative publicity, was interpreted by many critics, who assumed he coveted the role, as self-interest. Several Asian American groups, however, commended him for taking a stand. Wong's social conscience was evident not just in his presence in the theater community, but also in his participation in various fundraising activities for AIDS organizations. ◆

Wong, Russell

MARCH 1, 1963– ● ACTOR

Russell Wong was known equally for his acting ability and for his heartthrob qualities. In 1995, he was named one of *People* magazine's "50 Most Beautiful People." Wong was proud of his Chinese heritage, and a number of his roles, including his parts in Wayne Wang's *Eat a Bowl of Tea* and in *The Joy Luck Club* explored some of the issues of being bicultural.

Wong was born in Troy, New York, on March 1, 1963, the fifth of seven children. His father, William Wong, immigrated

1963 Wong is born in Troy, New York.

1977 Wong moves with his mother and stepfather to Santa Monica, California.

1980s Wong appears on the television show *21 Jump Street*.

1989 Wong stars in Wayne Wang's movie *Eat a Bowl of Tea*.

1993 Wong plays an abusive spouse in *The Joy Luck Club*.

2000 Wong stars in *Romeo Must Die*.

to the United States from Shandung Province in China, and opened his own restaurant; he still owns two takeout restaurants in upstate New York. Wong's parents met in New York in 1950, when his father was a student at Columbia and his mother was a part-time music student. Wong's mother, Connie Van Yserloo, is an artist of mixed Dutch, French, Canadian, and Indian background. According to Yserloo, the two faced some prejudice as a mixed-race couple, but they were "young and in love."

Wong spent the first fourteen years of his life in Albany, New York. A born performer, Wong loved singing from a young age, and would entertain his family with renditions of everything from commercial jingles to "The Star Spangled Banner."

His parents divorced when he was seven, an event Wong termed "the most painful experience" of his life. His mother remarried when Wong was fourteen. Wong moved with his mother and stepfather to Santa Monica, California. Wong played football at Mariposa High School, then went on to Santa Monica City College, where he admits that he had little interest in academics. However, it was in college that he began to study dance and acting. While he enjoyed dancing, he found it difficult at first to overcome his inhibitions. When it came to acting, however, Wong was a natural.

Wong identified strongly with his Chinese background. When he was young, his father took the entire family on a trip to Asia, a formative experience for Wong, which he remembers fondly. Russell Wong's values were, in his own words, "very Oriental;" this was most evident, he says in the strong importance he placed on family. He had a very close relationship with his mother, whom he and his siblings helped support financially. (Most of his siblings pursued creative careers as well, and one brother, Michael, was a well-known actor in Hong Kong.)

Wong got his first break in the mid-1980s in the hit television series *21 Jump Street*. His first main role on the big screen was in Wayne Wang's 1989 film *Eat a Bowl of Tea*, in which he played a young Chinese American who returns to China in search of a bride. Other movies to his credit include *Taipan* (1986) and *China Girl* (1987). One of his best-known roles to date was in the 1993 film version of Amy Tan's best-selling novel *The Joy Luck Club*, in which Wong played an abusive womanizer. He starred in *Takedown*, released in 1999, a film based on the story of a computer hacker, and *Romeo Must Die* in 2000, a contemporary take on *Romeo and Juliet*. He has starred in such television shows as *The Equalizer, As the World Turns,* and *Touched by an Angel.* His latest television role was in the miniseries *Vanishing Son,* in which he played Jian-Wa, a Chinese immigrant who, along with his brother, uses martial arts to help people out of tight situations. While he was troubled by the danger of playing into stereotypes of Asian Americans, he tended to see the increasing presence of Asians in the media as a positive development overall. He says of his role in *Vanishing Son,* "I want to participate in bringing Asian men up to be leading actors, and to be a part of that. I think we're headed in that direction."

Despite his roles in acclaimed movies and television shows, Wong earned extra money dancing in music videos for artists such as David Bowie, Donna Summer, and Denise Williams, as well as performing with the Westside Ballet Company. His hobbies included martial arts and singing. Wong was also a practiced amateur photographer. While his first priority was to continue to grow as an actor, and to explore genres in which he has less experience, such as comedy, Wong envisioned trying his hand at producing and directing some time in the future. ◆

Wong-Staal, Flossie

1947– ● SCIENTIST

AIDS researcher Flossie Wong-Staal is one of the leading scientists in her field. In 1990, the Institute for Scientific Information named her the top woman scientist of the previous decade, and ranked her as the fourth most influential scientist under the age of 45, and a 1990 issue of *Scientist* declared her "one of the ten superstars of science." Wong's most prominent achievement was her discovery of the anatomy of the AIDS virus. She was also the first person, in 1984, to clone the virus.

Flossie Wong-Staal was born Yee Ching Wong in China in 1947. Wong's father immigrated with his children to Hong Kong in 1952, fleeing the communist regime. She was enrolled in Catholic school there, where the nuns decreed that the students should have English names. Wong's father, who was fluent in English, chose the name Flossie after a typhoon which had recently hit Hong Kong.

Flossie Wong-Staal

bacteriology the study of bacteria.

Flossie was an outstanding student in high school. The teachers at her school encouraged all their best students to go into science, and this is the direction in which she was steered. In 1965, she left Hong Kong for the United States, enrolling at the University of California, Los Angeles, where she majored in molecular biology. The field fascinated her, particularly for its newness and the exciting discoveries being made, and she continued with postgraduate work in the same area, focussing on **bacteriology**. In 1972, she moved to the University of California, San Diego (UCSD) for a two-year post-doctoral position, after which she found work at the National Cancer Institute in Bethesda, Maryland as part of Robert Gallo's team researching retroviruses. From 1973 until 1989, she was a Fogerty Fellow at the institute, and held the position of Section Chief of Molecular Genetics of Hematopoietic Cells in the Laboratory of Tumor Cell Biology.

During graduate school, Wong married a physician. Although they later divorced, she kept his name. They had two daughters, Stephanie, born in 1972, and Caroline in 1983. Wong-Staal raised the girls on her own, and was extremely proud of them. Because of the obstacles she faced as a Chinese American woman, (and being aware of the even greater limitations her own mother lived with in China), Wong-Staal was conscious to encourage her daughters to pursue their dreams, and to live by her own motto, "One should enjoy and find pride in what one does."

In 1990, Wong returned to California, where she was appointed chair of AIDS research at UCSD. She held the Florence Riford Professorship there, and in addition to her research taught medicine and biology. In 1994, Wong-Staal received a grant from the National Institutes of Health to establish the AIDS Research Institute at UCSD, which she co-directed with Douglas Richman, M.D. The institute, in addition to being a center of research, also provides clinical resources and education to the public.

Wong was interested in human retroviruses (such as HIV and leukemia) as tools to help understand to mechanisms of gene regulation and virus-host interaction. In terms of practical applications, she was concentrating on using this research in the development of an AIDS vaccine and therapy.

Wong was a pioneer in the field of gene therapy. This is a relatively new science, which involves inserting a new gene into a human cell in order to replace a defective or missing gene or to alter the DNA of a group of cells. HIV (the virus that causes AIDS) attacks T-cells, a vital part of the immune system. The technique with which Wong was experimenting involved introducing a new gene into the T-cells that represses the HIV. She experimented with mouse and bird viruses, genetically engineering them to produce proteins called ribozymes which destroy AIDS viruses. Wong encountered opposition from the Food and Drug Administration and the National Institute of Health. Gene therapy is still in experimental stages, and these organizations worry that the process could result in human mutations, cancer, or other adverse reactions. The first human trials began in the mid-1990s. The results were mixed, but as the technique is perfected, the future of gene therapy as a weapon in the fight against AIDS is promising. ◆

Woods, Eldrick "Tiger"

DECEMBER 30, 1975– ● PROFESSIONAL GOLFER

Tiger Woods first picked up a golf club at the age of nine months. Since then, it was a rare moment that he did not have one in his hands. His love of and dedication to the game, not to mention his remarkable talent, made him a worldwide icon.

Tiger's mother, Kultida, a Thai woman, met Earl Woods when he was serving in the United States Army during the Vietnam War. Earl brought her back to the United States with him in 1969. Tiger was born December 30, 1975. Kultida chose the name Eldrick, which she had created from the letters of both her and her husband's names. Earl Woods, however, had decided that he would call his son Tiger, after a friend he had made while serving in Vietnam, and the nickname stuck.

Tiger Woods

Tiger grew up in Cypress, California, in Orange County, 35 miles southeast of Los Angeles. He was raised as an only child (although he had three half-brothers from his father's previous marriage). Earl Woods was an avid golfer, and when he saw Tiger's aptitude and love for the game, he encouraged his son to play. Earl began taking the boy to the driving range when Tiger was only eighteen months old. At the age of two, Tiger won a competition for boys ten years old and under at the Navy Courses. That same year, he also appeared on "The Mike Douglas Show" with Bob Hope; the boy's precocious ability made him a curiosity.

Tiger began working with his first coach, Rudy Duran, at the age of four, playing at Heartwell Golf Park in Long Beach, California. When he was ten, he moved on from Duran to a new coach, John Anselmo. Tiger continued to work on his game, and to improve at an impressive rate. His obsession with the game was perhaps as impressive as his accomplishments. His mother says that she disciplined Tiger by taking away his golf clubs; she thus ensured that her son rarely misbehaved.

Woods attended Western High School in Anaheim, California. During this time, under the tutelage of the school's coach, Don Crosby, Woods cemented his reputation as the best junior golfer in the world. At 15, he was the youngest person to ever win the U.S. Junior Amateur tournament. In 1993, Earl Woods recruited Butch Harmon, director of the famous Lochinvar Golf Club in Houston, as his son's coach.

After high school, Woods enrolled at Stanford University. In the two years he spent there, he won a total of ten collegiate events. On August 27, 1996, Woods officially turned professional, and left college. As of 2001, he had won an astounding six USGA national championships, as well as the NCAA title.

Tiger Woods Foundation

Eager to use his success in golf as a means of improving the lives of disadvantaged children, especially those who live in America's inner cities, Tiger Woods established the foundation that bears his name in December, 1996. With funds from Tiger Woods himself, along with substantial corporate donations, the foundation has been able to provide a wide array of services and opportunities to the young people of the nation. Additional funds are raised through foundation-sponsored events, including the annual "Tiger Jam" benefit rock concert.

The foundation is headquartered in Los Alamitos, California. Under the leadership of Tiger's father, Earl Woods, who serves as foundation president, the organization has focused on improving the opportunities available to urban youth, and on strengthening the institutions of family and community. A key part of the foundation philosophy is its focus on teaching young people to assume responsibility for their lives, and helping parents to provide guidance and encouragement to their children.

The foundation carries out its mission in several ways. Central to its activities are the annual golf clinics that are held in urban centers across the country. In the clinics, small groups of local children are given the opportunity to meet with Tiger Woods and to learn the basics of the game from him. In conjunction with the clinics, participating communities hold a variety of fundraising events ranging from celebrity auctions to local concerts, and foundation personnel lead parenting workshops for local families. Of the money raised during the clinics, 90 percent is earmarked for the "Leave Behind" program: the money is left within the sponsoring community to address local needs pertaining to children, family, education, and health.

The foundation also administers three college scholarship funds: the William and Marcella Powell Scholarship Award, named for the first African-American couple to design, own, and operate a golf course in the United States; the Alfred "Tup" Holmes Memorial Scholarship, named for a man who was key in helping to desegregate the public golf courses of Georgia, and the National Minority Junior Golf Scholarship.

The awards, honors, and tournaments that Woods won are too lengthy to even begin to list. He was the youngest Masters champion ever, at the age of 21 (and the first of either African or Asian descent). He was named the Associated Press Male Athlete of the Year in both 1997 and 1999, and was the *Sports Illustrated* Sportsman of the Year for 1996 and 2000. He graced the cover of every golf magazine in the country, in addition to *Sports Illustrated*, *Time*, *Newsweek*, and others. He competed with and earned the highest accolades from the very golfers he himself emulates; Jack Nicklaus said of Woods, "There isn't a flaw in his golf or his makeup. He will win more majors than Arnold Palmer and me combined."

1975 Eldrick "Tiger" Woods is born in California.

1981 Woods gets his first coach, Rudy Duran, at the Heartwell Country Club.

1993 Woods begins working with coach Butch Harmon.

1996 Woods turns professional; named *Sports Illustrated* Sportsman of the Year.

1997 Woods is named Male Athlete of the year by both the Associated Press and ESPN.

2000 Woods spends all 52 weeks of the year as the top-ranked golfer in the world.

2001 Woods wins the Masters championship, and becomes the first golfer to hold each major professional championship simultaneously.

In April 2001, Woods won his second Masters championship in five years and became the first golfer in history to hold all of professional golf's major championships simultaneously, leaving many sports pundits and commentators to wonder if the feat was the greatest in the history of sports.

As a professional golfer, Woods won millions of dollars from tournament victories. He endorsed a number of companies, including Nike, Titleist, American Express, Rolex, Buick, and Wheaties.

While Woods was widely accepted in the upper echelons of the golf community, which was known for its racist and exclusionary attitudes, this was not the case from the beginning. Woods faced his share of racism, both on the golf course and off. When he used to play with his father, he noticed that rules about children not being allowed to play were selectively enforced; while Tiger was often kicked off the course, the regulations for white children were usually overlooked. Tiger attended a mostly white elementary school, and on his first day was tied to a tree by a group of older white boys, who taunted him with racial epithets. Thankfully, however, this traumatic experience was an isolated incident. Tiger was proud of his mixed racial and ethnic heritage; he coined the term "Cablinasian" to describe his background that includes white, black, Indian, and American ancestry. The media tried to pin him down and make him choose a single racial identity, but by refusing to do so, Woods became something of a trend-setter, and a poster child for the multiracial and multiethnic identity that was emerging in the United States. "My parents have taught me to be proud of my ethnic background," he said. "The media has portrayed me as African-American; sometimes, Asian. In fact, I am both." ◆

Wu, Chien-Shiung

MAY 31, 1912–FEBRUARY 16, 1994 ● PHYSICIST

Chien-Shiung Wu overcame considerable barriers as a Chinese American woman to become a world-renowned physicist, but she was also lucky enough to receive uncommon encouragement and support from an early age. Being in the **vanguard** ran in Wu's family; her father took

vanguard the forefront of a movement or action.

part in the 1911 revolution in China that unseated the Manchu dynasty, and was later the founder and principal of a private girls school—an anomaly in China at the time.

Chien-Shiung Wu was born on May 31, 1912 in a small town near Shanghai by the name of Luihe. She attended her father's school until the age of nine, when she left home to study at the Soochow Girls School, where she received a top-caliber education. The school emphasized Western subjects, and often hosted guest lecturers from American universities. In 1930, after graduating at the top of her class, Wu enrolled at Nanjing University, where she excelled in her studies, majoring in physics. She graduated in 1934, then taught for one year in a provincial university. She went on to do research in x-ray crystallography at the National Academy of Sciences in Shanghai, where she found a mentor, a female scientist who urged her to go to the United States to continue her studies at the postdoctoral level. Her family was supportive, and Wu left for the U.S. in 1936.

Wu settled in Berkeley, where she worked with E.O. Lawrence, a Nobel Prize-winning physicist in the area of nuclear physics. Racial discrimination made it difficult for Wu to obtain funding, but she nonetheless earned her doctorate in 1940. In addition to the discrimination she faced, Wu had the added hardship of being cut off from her family in 1937 when the Japanese invaded China. After graduating, she continued at Berkeley as a research assistant, but despite her outstanding work, could not find a better position.

In 1942, Wu married Luke Yuan, a fellow scientist whom she had met soon after arriving in the U.S. Together they moved to the East Coast, where Yuan took a job at RCA Laboratories in Princeton, New Jersey and Wu taught at Smith College in Northhampton, Massachusetts. She soon found a teaching position at Princeton University, which allowed her to be near her husband.

Wu's true calling was laboratory work, however, and in 1944, she found a job at Columbia University's Division of War Research. She worked on the famous Manhattan Project, using diffusion to separate **isotopes** of uranium, research that was used in the development of the atomic bomb.

When World War II ended in 1945, Wu received the first word from her family in many years. She and her husband considered returning to China, but when civil war erupted there soon after between the communists and the Nationalists, they decided to stay in the United States.

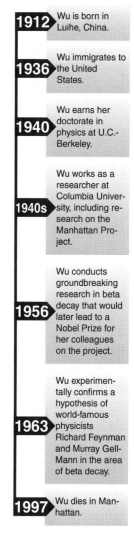

1912 Wu is born in Luihe, China.

1936 Wu immigrates to the United States.

1940 Wu earns her doctorate in physics at U.C.-Berkeley.

1940s Wu works as a researcher at Columbia University, including research on the Manhattan Project.

1956 Wu conducts groundbreaking research in beta decay that would later lead to a Nobel Prize for her colleagues on the project.

1963 Wu experimentally confirms a hypothesis of world-famous physicists Richard Feynman and Murray Gell-Mann in the area of beta decay.

1997 Wu dies in Manhattan.

isotopes any of two or more species atoms of a chemical element with the same position on the periodic table and atomic number, and virtually the same chemical behavior, though with differing atomic mass and physical properties.

In the late 1940 and early 1950s, Wu studied beta decay, doing experiments based on the theories of Enrico Fermi. She perfected previously performed experiments, proving Fermi's prediction of the speed at which electrons would exit an atom during decay.

Wu's best-known work, however, was her 1956 experiment that disproved previously held assumptions about the conservation of parity. Until then, physicists had believed that the laws of parity and symmetry that apply to large particles also held true for subatomic ones. Working with two other researchers, Tsung Dao Lee of Columbia University and Chen Ning Yang of the Institute for Advanced Study at Princeton, Wu discovered irregularities in the decay of a particle called K-meson. Wu worked separately from Lee and Yang at the National Bureau of Standards, using their observations, but she was forced to operate on limited funding and substandard equipment. Nonetheless, her groundbreaking work led to research that won the Nobel Prize for Lee and Yang in 1957.

In 1958, Wu became a full professor at Columbia University, where she continued her research in beta decay. In 1963 she experimentally proved a theory posited by world famous physicists Richard Feynman and Murray Gell-Mann. In 1973, Wu was named the first Pupin Professor of Physics at Columbia, a position she held until she retired in 1980.

Throughout her career, Wu won numerous honors, awards, and honorary degrees. She was the first woman to receive an honorary doctorate of science degree, as well as the first woman to receive the Comstock Award from the National Academy of Sciences and the Research Corporation Award, and the first woman chosen as president of the American Physical Society. She was also the first scientist to have an asteroid named after her within her lifetime. After retiring, Wu, traveled throughout the world and the U.S., lecturing at various universities, including in China and Taiwan. Wu died in February 16, 1994, in Manhattan at the age of 84, leaving her husband and a son, Vincent Yuan, who was a research physicist at Los Alamos National Laboratory in New Mexico.

Wu's legacy was a powerful one. Lee, her colleague and collaborator, said of her, "C.S. Wu was one of the giants of physics. In the field of beta decay, she had no equal." Throughout her career, and even after retirement, Wu was an advocate of women in the sciences, and pushed for a more female-friendly environment in the upper levels of the scientific community as well. ◆

Wu, David

APRIL 8, 1955– ● POLITICIAN

Representative David Wu's hard work and optimism allowed him to fulfill the traditional dream of the American immigrant, rising through his own initiative to a position of influence in his adopted country. Wu's firm belief in America as a land of opportunity led him to pursue a career in politics, and as a member of Congress, he pushed for legislation that treats newcomers to this country with justice and dignity.

David Wu was born in Taiwan on April 8, 1955. His family moved to the United States in 1961, when an executive order signed by President John F. Kennedy revised previous immigration quotas that had discriminated against Asians. Wu attended public school, then went on to Stanford University, where he graduated with a Bachelor of Science in 1977. He attended Harvard Medical School for a short time, then decided to go into law, receiving his degree from Yale in 1982.

Wu held a clerkship with a federal judge in Portland, Oregon, then went on to found his own firm, Cohen and Wu, in 1988. Based in Portland, the firm concentrated on high technology industries and small businesses. Wu built a reputation of empowering local businesses, helping them grow, and in the process, creating jobs for people in the region. His dedication to the Oregon business and technology communities served him well when he decided to run for office in 1998.

Wu won his district's congressional seat that year, becoming the first Chinese-American ever elected to the U.S. House of Representatives. He was re-elected to a second term which began January 3, 2001. His constituency stretches from Portland to the Pacific coast, including the counties of Washington, Clatsop, Columbia, and Yamhill, and parts of Multnomah and Clackamas. Wu was part of the New Democrat Coalition (NDC), a group of moderate House Democrats. Wu concentrated particularly on improving the state of the education system. His primary goals in this area included reducing class size and modernizing schools. He spearheaded an effort in his home state to hire 100,000 new elementary school teachers, to ease the burden of overcrowded classes in the early grades. Wu also served on the Subcommittee on Early Childhood, Youth, and Families. This group has jurisdiction over the Elementary and

1955 Wu is born in Taiwan.

1961 Wu immigrates with his family to the United States.

1977 Wu graduates from Stanford University with a Bachelors of Science.

1982 Wu earns a law degree at Yale University.

1988 Wu co-founds the Portland law firm Cohen and Wu.

1998 Wu runs for the U.S. House of Representatives, winning the First Congressional District of Oregon.

2000 Wu is reelected.

moratorium a legally authorized period of delay in the performance of a legal obligation or payment of debt.

Secondary Education Act (ESEA), which will soon be reauthorized. Wu hoped to achieve significant reforms in the process.

Wu also focused on the condition of American workers, and believed that one of the most effective ways of continuing to stimulate the economy was by funding job training and research. Wu was a member of the Subcommitte on Employer-Employee Relations, a body active in health care reform, among other issues. Wu was dedicated to preserving and strengthening Medicare and Medicaid programs.

Preserving the environment was also one of his priorities, and Wu sponsored a number of bills in this area. These included a **moratorium** on new mining activities on federal land; a law eliminating the use of the Savannah River nuclear waste separation facilities in South Carolina; and one terminating funding for the Fast Flux Test Facility at the Hanford Nuclear Reservation in Washington.

Wu also served on the Committee on Science; the Subcommittee on Technology; and the Subcommittee on Space and Aeronautics.

One of the issues in which Wu had the most vested, both personally and politically, was immigration policy. Wu supported legislation to adjust the Immigration and Nationality Act so that certain unaccompanied alien children in the U.S. would have temporary protected status, and to change the status of illegal immigrants who are under the age of 18. In light of recent allegations in the United States toward Asian Americans of espionage and illegal campaign financing, Wu also spoke out against a general sense of distrust toward Americans of Asian ancestry. Wu chaired the Congressional Asian Pacific Americans Caucus, which was founded in 1994 by then-Rep. Norman Mineta. The caucus attempted to ensure the rights of Asian-Americans, to educate people about the contributions of Asian-Americans in this country, and to provide scholarships and educational opportunities.

Wu and his wife Michelle had two children: a son, Matthew, and a daughter, Sarah. ◆

Yamaguchi, Kristi

JULY 12, 1971– ● FIGURE SKATER

Kristi Yamaguchi skated her way into the history books at the 1992 Albertville Winter Olympics; her skating was praised as equally distinguished for its artistic merit and its athleticism.

Kristi Yamaguchi was born July 12, 1971, in Hayward, California. Her parents, Jim, a dentist, and Carole, a medical secretary, were third-generation Japanese-Americans. Kristi's grandparents lost nearly everything they had during the internment of Japanese-Americans during World War II. Both her mother's and her father's families were sent to internment camps; her mother was born in a camp in Colorado. Nevertheless, Jim and Carole made a conscious effort to leave these hardships behind them and to raise Kristi, her sister Lori, and her brother Brett as proud Americans.

Kristi was born with a clubfoot, but corrective shoes left no trace of the early deformity. Inspired by the example of Dorothy Hamill, she began ice skating at the age of five. By

Kristi Yamaguchi

351

1971 Yamaguchi is born in Hayward, California.

1986 Yamaguchi and skating partner Rudi Galindo win the national title in pairs competition.

1992 Yamaguchi wins a gold medal at the World Championships in individual competition.

1992 Yamaguchi wins a gold medal at the Winter Olympic Games in Albertville, France.

1998 Yamaguchi is inducted into the Figure Skating Hall of Fame.

eight, she was training with Canadian coach Christy Kjarsgaard-Ness, who had her on the ice at 4:00 A.M. most days of the week. In addition to figure skating, Yamaguchi studied dance. Several years later, she took up pair skating with partner Rudi Galindo. Together, they won the U.S. Pairs Championship in 1986, the same year in which Yamaguchi came in fourth in the singles event. Two years later, she won both the singles and the pairs competitions at the World Junior Championships, and was named Up-and-Coming Artistic Athlete of the Year by the Women's Sports Foundation.

In 1989, Yamaguchi competed in the U.S. Championships, becoming the first woman in 35 years to win two medals (gold in pairs, silver in individual). Her singles routine was lauded for its technical difficulty and elegance. The following year, Yamaguchi entered the World Championships for the first time, where she came in sixth in singles and fifth in pairs. In 1989, Yamaguchi's coach moved to Edmonton, Canada; immediately after her high school graduation, Yamaguchi followed her there. Her partner Galindo moved as well, although their pairs coach, Jim Hulick, remained in San Francisco. The two skaters commuted back and forth often. Unfortunately, Hulick had been suffering from colon cancer, a disease that took his life in December, 1989. Yamaguchi lost her grandfather only five days later. She later said of the two men, "They were two big influences in my life as a skater. They used to be the happiest seeing me go on. They made me work harder." The double loss led her to quit pairs skating in May 1990 and concentrate solely on singles competitions.

This renewed focus paid off. In 1991, Yamaguchi placed second to Tonya Harding in the national championships, and the following year won the gold at the World Championships. In February 1992, she turned in her legendary performance at the Olympic Games in Albertville, France. The favored skater was Midori Ito of Japan; Yamaguchi, unfazed by the media and the pressure that many athletes felt at the event, was relaxed and focussed. Ito, clearly affected by the enormous expectations placed on her, fell during a triple Lutz, and Yamaguchi came away with the gold. She floated effortlessly through her performance to Strauss' "Blue Danube Waltz;" two days later, her routine to "Malaguena" did not go as smoothly—she fell on one jump—but nonetheless was solid enough compared to the other skaters to win her the gold.

Yamaguchi went on in March of that year to defend her title at the World Championships, becoming the first woman to do so since Peggy Fleming in 1968.

In September 1992, Yamaguchi decided to turn professional but continued working with Kjarsgaard-Ness, the same coach she worked with since the age of eight. Yamaguchi joined Discover Card's "Stars on Ice" revue in 1993, and regularly appeared in over 50 shows a year, performing with other figure skating luminaries, including Scott Hamilton and Katarina Witt. In 1998, she was inducted into the Figure Skating Hall of Fame.

Yamaguchi signed with numerous sponsors, from Dura-Soft contact lenses to Wendy's restaurants; appeared in fashion spreads in *Elle*, *Vogue*, and *Seventeen* magazines; and even made a brief appearance in the Disney movie *D2: The Mighty Ducks*. She also founded her own charity, the Always Dream Foundation, which contributes to various children's organizations in California, Nevada, and Hawaii.

On July 8, 2000, Yamaguchi married Bret Hedican, a defenseman for the Florida Panthers of the National Hockey League.

Yamaguchi continued to push herself to develop as a skater. As she told ABC Sports, "I feel fortunate to be in this era of growth in professional figure skating, because I love what professional skating has to offer. You can still experiment with different types of music, different choreography and costumes and that is what has been the challenge for me." ◆

> *"There may be two or three performances in your life that are absolutely on, where all the planets are lined up for you, and you feel that you're invincible. And I feel lucky that I had that happen."*
> from an interview with Donna De-Varona, ABC *Sports*, 9 March 1996, speaking of her performance in the 1992 Winter Olympics

Yamasaki, Minrou

DECEMBER 1, 1912–FEBRUARY 6, 1987 ● ARCHITECT

Diligence and passion led Minoru Yamasaki to a distinguished career in the field of architecture.

Yamasaki was not the first in his family to find success despite considerable odds. His father, who had been a landowner in Japan, immigrated to the United States in order to pursue other opportunities. Minoru was born in Seattle, Washington, on December 1, 1912. His family started out in a tenement with no hot water or indoor plumbing, but his father's

1912 Minoru Yamasaki is born in Seattle, Washington.

1934 Yamasaki graduates from the University of Washington with a degree in architecture and moves to New York City.

1935 Yamasaki gets his first job in the field, working for Githens and Keally.

1937 Yamsaki moves to Detroit to work for Smith, Hynchman and Grylls.

1938 Yamasaki starts his own firm, Yamasaki, Hellmuth and Leinweber (later Yamasaki Associates).

1939 Yamasaki's firm earns its first important job, designing the St. Louis Airport.

1940 Yamasaki Associates is hired (in conjunction with Emory Roth and Sons) to design the World Trade Center.

1987 Yamasaki dies at the age of seventy-three.

hard work (he often held two or three jobs at once) paid off, and soon they were living in relative comfort. In high school, Yamasaki excelled in math and science. He found his calling when his Uncle Koken, a recent graduate of the school of architecture at the University of California, showed the young Yamasaki his drawings. "Right then and there," Yamasaki recalled, "I decided to be an architect."

Yamasaki pursued this dream after high school, enrolling in the University of Washington's architecture program. While he breezed through the math and science courses, Yamasaki had to work particularly hard at his art and drawing classes. Later, building design gave him such difficulties that he nearly gave up architecture for engineering, but the encouragement of a professor persuaded him to keep going.

Yamasaki put himself through college by working summers in canneries in Alaska. The work was demanding and the pay meager, but the Great Depression, which made jobs scarce throughout the country, left him little choice.

After graduating from Washington in 1934, Yamasaki left the West Coast for New York. He could not find a job as an architect, and instead worked for a Japanese company, wrapping Noritake china dishes for distribution. He went to school at night, working towards a master's in architecture at New York University.

In 1935, Githens and Keally, a New York architectural firm, offered him a job. After one year, he was hired by Shreve, Lamb, and Harmon, who had designed the Empire State Building. There he worked on shop drawings, the sketches closest to the final stages of production.

In 1941, Yamasaki married Teruko Hereshiki, with whom he would have three children.

In 1943, Yamasaki found work with Harrison, Fouilhoux and Abramowitz (most famous for the design of Rockefeller Center). He went on to work at Raymond Loewy Associates, and then in 1945 moved to Detroit to head the design division of Smith, Hynchman, and Grylls. He founded his own firm, Yamasaki, Hellmuth and Leinweber, in 1949. Their first big contract was the St. Louis Airport in 1953. He went on to design three important buildings in Detroit: the American Concrete Institute, the Reynolds Metals Company offices, and McGregor Memorial Building at Wayne State University, as well as structures in places ranging from Japan to Saudi Arabia to New Delhi to Honolulu.

Yamasaki's firm continued to grow in size and reputation throughout the 1950s and 1960s. In 1962, he bested more than forty other companies to obtain a $280 million contract from the Port Authority of New York and New Jersey. In collaboration with another firm, Emory Roth and Sons, Yamasaki Associates (as the firm was then known) spent 14 years working on the design the World Trade Center, which would be, at the time of their completion, the tallest buildings in the world.

Yamasaki continued to distinguish himself in the field in subsequent years, designing the Century Plaza Towers in Century City, California, the Rainier Bank Tower in Seattle, and Saudi Arabia's Eastern Province Airport.

Yamasaki died of cancer on February 6, 1987, at the age of 73, leaving his wife; two sons, Taro (a Pulitzer Prize-winning photographer) and Kim; and a daughter, Carol Yamasaki Chakrin. ◆

"The purpose of Architecture is to create an atmosphere in which men can live, work, and enjoy."
Yamasaki Associate's website, www .m~yamasaki.com

Yan, Martin

CHEF

When chef Martin Yan came to the United States in the early 1970s, he brought the continent of Asia with him.

Yan was born in Guangzhou, China, shortly after the communist takeover of the area formerly known as Canton. He was interested in cooking from the time he was very young, and often helped his mother in the kitchen. At the age of 13, he left home and began working as an apprentice in his uncle's restaurant in Hong Kong. Thus began Yan's life as a self-proclaimed "**gypsy**," travelling and working in restaurants, learning about different regional and national cultures through their cuisines. He later attended the Overseas Institute of Cookery in Hong Kong.

At the age of 18, he left Hong Kong for Canada, then moved on to the United States, where he graduated from the University of California at Davis with an master's in food science. He moved to Canada to continue his training, eventually becoming certified by the Ontario Restaurant Association as a Master Chinese Chef. Yan held an honorary doctorate from

gypsy an individual who lives somewhat of a nomadic life.

1970s Yan immigrates to the U.S., earning a B.A. and an M.A. in food science from the University of California at Davis.

1978 Yan makes his first television appearance as a guest on a Canadian talk show; he is offered his own series.

1982 KQED in San Francisco buys the popular *Yan Can Cook* show.

1994 Yan wins a James Beard Award for Best Television Cooking Show.

1996 Yan wins a James Beard Award for Best Television Food Journalism.

aegis sponsorship.

Johnson and Wales University in culinary arts (an honor also bestowed upon fellow cooking all-star Julia Child).

In 1978, Yan was working as manager and head cook at a Chinese restaurant in Alberta, Canada. A Canadian television producer who tried his cooking booked Yan for a guest appearance on a talk show. The audience loved him, and he was soon after offered a deal to star in his own series, *The Yan Can Cook Show. Yan Can Cook* came under the **aegis** of the San Francisco public television station KQED in 1982. Since then it has become one of the nation's leading cooking shows. It is also broadcast internationally in 75 countries. In 1994, the show won the James Beard Award for Best Television Cooking Show, and in 1996, the James Beard Award for Best Television Food Journalism. The only cooking show that was on the air longer is *In the Kitchen with Julia Child.*

Yan also made appearances on various talk shows such as *The Phil Donahue Show, The Home Show,* and *Live with Regis and Kathy Lee.*

Yan wrote 12 best-selling cookbooks, including *A Wok for All Seasons* (1988), *Simply Delicious* (1993), *Martin Yan's Asia* (1997), and *Martin Yan's Feast* (1998).

In 1998, Yan signed a contract with Wente Vinyards in Livermore. As part of the marketing arrangement, he took part in events sponsored by the winery in the U.S., Europe, and Asia, and incorporated the company's wine into his cooking demonstrations. An important aspect of the agreement was the introduction of wine into the Asian market, where it still plays a less significant role than it does in Western cuisine. Yan was excited about the possibilities of various pairings that could enliven both the food and the wines. His own Asian cooking managed to borrow from Western cuisine without compromising the integrity of the original.

Yan lived in San Mateo, California, with his wife, Susan, whom he met as a student in college, and their twin sons. He taught Chinese and Asian cuisine at a number of schools, including the Culinary Institute of America, Johnson & Wales, the California Culinary Institute, and the New England Culinary Academy. Yan also contributed to the establishment of "Yan Can Cook" scholarship programs at these schools.

Yan's creative interpretations of various Asian cuisines made him famous not just in the U.S. and Canada, but around the world. He travelled extensively, exploring culinary secrets from Malaysia to Japan, from Canton to Singapore, and introduced them to home cooks through his widely distributed television show and his numerous cookbooks. His likeable personality and sense of humor, combined with his passion and wide-ranging knowledge, made Yan's show one of the most popular of its genre.

Yan generally filmed each year's 52 shows in a mere 13 days. He continued to travel extensively, spending at least one to two months of each year in China and other parts of Asia, and much of the rest of his time on the road in the U.S., teaching and promoting his products. He encouraged other cooks to approach the art with the same attitude he bring to it. ◆

Yang, Chen Ning

SEPTEMBER 22, 1922– ● PHYSICIST

In 1956, physicist Chen Ning Yang disproved what had previously been one of the fundamental assumptions in that field. Along with his partner Tsung Dao Lee, Yang discovered that the conservation of parity law, which states that elementary particles are always symmetrical, does not hold true in all cases. For this work, the two shared the 1957 Nobel Prize in physics.

Chen Ning Yang

Yang was born in the town of Ho-Fei, in Anhwei province in northern China on September 22, 1922. Yang was one of five children. His father, a professor of mathematics, got a job at Tsinghua University in 1929, and relocated the family to Beijing.

Tsinghua University was moved to the town of Kunming in 1937, when the Japanese invaded China. It was united with the National Southwest Associated University there, where Yang earned a bachelor's degree in physics in 1942. His thesis dealt with group theory and molecular spectra. Yang earned his master's there in 1944 with a thesis

on order-disorder transformations. It was at the university where Yang first met his future partner, Tsung Dao Lee, a fellow research student in the physics department there.

In 1945, the National Southwest Associated University awarded him a fellowship to study at the University of Chicago with world-renowned physicist Enrico Fermi. Upon arrival in the U.S., Yang decided to take an American name; he chose Franklin after Benjamin Franklin, and became known as Frank to his American friends. In 1948, Yang earned his doctorate with a thesis on angular distribution in nuclear reactions. He stayed on at Chicago for a one-year teaching position, then moved to Princeton University's Institute for Advanced Study. In 1950, he married Chih Li Tu, with whom he would have three children, two sons and a daughter.

Tsung Dao Lee had come to the University of Chicago a year after Yang, and earned his Ph.D. there in 1950. He and Yang began their intense collaboration a few years later, in 1953, when Lee found a position at Columbia University in New York, and Yang had a two-year stint as senior physicist at Brookhaven National Laboratory in Long Island. In 1955, Yang returned to his post at the Institute for Advanced Study, but two continued their work on the conservation of parity law. Theoretical physicists, Yang and Lee found fault with this law on paper; they then needed experimental support of their theory. They enlisted the help of Dr. Chien Shiung Wu, a physics researcher at Columbia. In 1956, she designed and performed the experiments that would prove Lee and Yang's theory and win them the Nobel Prize the following year.

Yang left the Institute for Advanced Study in 1965 to become the director of the Institute for Theoretical Physics at the State University of New York at Stony Brook. In the 1970s, he served as a board member for Rockefeller University, for the American Association for the Advancement of Science, and for the Salk Institute for Biological Studies in San Diego.

Yang expressed his pride in his Chinese heritage, and made yearly trips to his home country to encourage goodwill and understanding between China and the United States. He became a U.S. citizen in 1964.

Yang won numerous awards, including the Albert Einstein Commemorative Award from Yeshiva University in 1957 and the Rumford Medal for the American Academy of Arts and Sciences in 1980, and honorary degrees from schools such as

Princeton, the University of Minnesota, and the University of Durham. He was a member of the National Academy of Sciences, the American Philosophical Society, and the American Physical Society. Yang was most currently Albert Einstein Professor of Physics emeritus at the State University of New York at Stony Brook and distinguished professor at large for China University of Hong Kong. ◆

Yang, Jerry

1968– ● ENGINEER AND ENTREPRENEUR

Jerry Yang, electrical engineer and entrepreneur, founded one of the most successful Internet companies in the world. Yang was born Chih-Yuan in Taipei, Taiwan in 1968. His father died when he was two; his mother and grandmother immigrated to the United States in search of opportunity, bringing Yang (ten years old at the time) and his younger brother, Ken. Yang chose the name Jerry for himself upon moving to the U.S. The family settled in San Jose, California, where his mother, Lily, was a professor of English and drama.

Jerry was a good student, and earned straight A's through most of his schooling. He attended Stanford University, obtaining both a bachelor's and a master's degree in electrical engineering in four years, then enrolled in Stanford's doctoral program. He spent a good deal of time with long-time friend and fellow engineering student David Filo, looking for, as Yang says, "every single possible way of distracting ourselves from writing the thesis." This included everything from playing golf to researching hobbies on the Internet. Both Yang and Filo were fascinated with the potential of the Internet, and were particularly excited when the first unified browser, Mosaic, came out in late 1993.

In 1994, Yang and Filo began to collect their own database of their favorite sites for fun. Their headquarters was a trailer on the grounds of Stanford University. The enterprise grew quickly and, "before we knew it," Yang recalls, "we had people from 90 countries using this little thing that we had created." It began under the moniker "Jerry's Guide to the World Wide Web." Not wanting all the credit for himself, Yang changed the name to

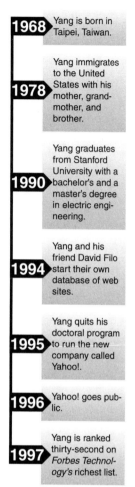

1968 Yang is born in Taipei, Taiwan.

1978 Yang immigrates to the United States with his mother, grandmother, and brother.

1990 Yang graduates from Stanford University with a bachelor's and a master's degree in electric engineering.

1994 Yang and his friend David Filo start their own database of web sites.

1995 Yang quits his doctoral program to run the new company called Yahoo!.

1996 Yahoo! goes public.

1997 Yang is ranked thirty-second on *Forbes Technology's* richest list.

nascent new; just beginning.

"David and Jerry's Guide to the World Wide Web," but Filo did not want his name in the title. The two played around with other names, settling on an acronym beginning with "Yet another," because (even as early as 1994) there were already a number of other directories and searches. "Yahoo" appealed to them for its self-deprecating tone, and its reference to the rude and uncivilized tribe from Jonathan Swift's *Gulliver's Travels*. (The entire acronym is Yet Another Hierarchical Officious Oracle.) They added the exclamation mark for good measure.

In 1995, several months before earning his degree, Yang dropped out of his engineering program to dedicate himself entirely to his business. That same year, Masayoshi Son, the head of Japan's Softbank, bought 20 percent of the **nascent** company; when its stock went public on April 12, 1996, Son bought another 17.02 percent. (Yahoo!'s value rose in its first day on the market from a starting price of $13 per share to close at $33 a share, the second-biggest first day gain in Nasdaq market history.) By this time, Yang and Filo each owned only 12 percent. Son put in place his own management team, appointing people to run the company. He kept Yang and Filo on, however, with the official titles of Chief Yahoos, as the source of inspiration and creativity.

Yang continued to do quite well for himself financially; in 1997, he was ranked 32nd on *Forbes Technology's* richest list; by May 1998, he was worth more than $800 million. He lived in a $1.9 million house in Los Altos, west of his childhood home of San Jose. He married his wife Akiko in 1997; a marketing consultant, she was a Costa Rican of Japanese descent. Yang and Filo used some of their earnings to make donations, including endowing their alma mater with a $2 million chair in the School of Engineering.

Yahoo! was threatened by recent downturns in the economy, particularly in the technology sector. Nevertheless, it remained one of the most popular web portals, and Yang remained idealistic about the possibilities of the Internet.

Despite yearly earnings in the hundreds of millions of dollars, and a lifestyle that had him frequently commuting between New York, Seattle, Los Angeles, and Tokyo, Yang was surprisingly down-to-earth. He remained partial to linen shirts and khaki pants; his offices in Mountain View, California, were cluttered with bicycles, Foosball, and other toys; and he still made it home for Sunday dinner at his mother's house. ◆

Yep, Lawrence

JUNE 14, 1948– ● AUTHOR

Born in San Francisco, California, on June 14, 1948, Lawrence Yep grew up in an African-American neighborhood in the city's West End. His parents, second-generation Chinese Americans, owned a grocery store. He commuted to school in Chinatown, where he still felt like something of an outsider, in part because he did not speak Chinese. He excelled in writing, and with the encouragement of an English teacher, began sending his stories to publishers before he was thirteen.

Yep spent one year at Marquette University in Milwaukee, Wisconsin. Homesick for California, he did not last long in the Midwest, but that year Yep had his first story accepted by a science fiction magazine, *Worlds of If*. (The publication later folded.)

Yep graduated from the University of California at Santa Cruz in 1970 with a degree in literature. Throughout his undergraduate years, he had several science fiction short stories and novellas published. A friend who worked at Harper and Row publishers (today HarperCollins) encouraged him to try his hand at science fiction for the children's market. Yep's first young adult novel, *Sweetwater*, was published in 1973.

After college, Yep went on to attend graduate school in English at the State University of New York at Buffalo. His doctoral thesis was titled "Psycholinguistic Strategies of William Faulkner's Early Heroes." In 1975, the same year that he earned his Ph.D., Yep published the novel *Dragonwings*, the story of a Chinese-American who built and flew a machine that was a precursor to the airplane. The book, which combines science fiction, fantasy, and historical fiction, received the prestigious Newbery Award, as well as the IRA Children's Book Award and the Carter G. Woodson Award. It was cited as one of the Notable Children's Books of 1971-1975, and as one of the Best of Children's Books for 1966-1978.

After earning his doctorate, Yep returned to California to look for a teaching position. Academic jobs were hard to come by, however, so he instead focussed his efforts on writing. His years in graduate school had trained him to approach literature from a detached, analytical stance, which he found somewhat

1948 Yep is born in San Francisco, California.

1966 Yep publishes his first story in the science fiction magazine *Worlds of If.*

1970 Yep graduates from UC Santa Cruz with a degree in literature.

1971 Yep publishes his first book, the young adult science fiction novel *Sweetwater.*

1972 Yep earns his Ph.D. in English from the State University of New York at Buffalo.

1973 *Dragonwings,* published the previous year, wins the Newbery Honor Award.

1991 Yep publishes *The Star Fisher,* a novel about his mother's childhood in West Virginia, and *Tongues of Jade,* his second book of retellings of Chinese folk tales.

stifling to the creative process. "It took me awhile to get back to just basic storytelling," he later remarked.

Yep used science fiction as a vehicle for exploring his own world through a new perspective. In much of his work, the alien from another planet becomes a metaphor for the Chinese as an alien in the United States, and the conflict that arises when two cultures collide. He also drew on both his own experiences and family stories. His mother grew up in West Virginia, a place to which Yep felt a strong ancestral connection that he explored in his novel *The Star Fisher,* published in 1991.

While still interested in the possibilities science fiction has to offer, Yep expanded his range beyond the genre. *The Rainbow People* and *Tongues of Jade,* published in 1989 and 1991 respectively, are collections of Yep's retellings of Chinese folk tales.

American Dragons: Twenty-Five Asian American Voices, which he edited in 1993, compiles stories, poems and essays by Asian-American writers such as Maxine Hong Kingston and Jeanne Wakatsuki Houston. Yep also experimented with theater, a medium in which he has found new territory to explore. He adapted his book *Dragonwings* into a play. Under the direction of Phyllis S.K. Look, the production was performed at Lincoln Center in New York and the Kennedy Center in Washington, D.C. in 1993. Yep continued to publish prolifically, often putting out several works in one year. Some of his most recent include *The Case of the Lion Dance* and *The Cook's Family,* both published in 1998.

For a period of several years in the 1980s, Yep taught creative writing and Asian American studies at San Francisco Bay Area junior college and at the University of California at Berkeley and at Santa Barbara. While he enjoyed the experience, he again returned to writing full time when he became involved in theater.

Yep lived with his wife, Joanne Ryder, also a children's book author, in San Francisco. ◆

Zakaria, Fareed

1961– ● SCHOLAR, EDITOR

Fareed Zakaria was, according to a 1999 issue of *Esquire* magazine, "one of the 21 most important people of the 21st century." If the accolade was somewhat premature, it was certainly not without precedent. Zakaria, the editor of *Newsweek International*, was a respected scholar in international politics, and wrote several books on the subject. And while Zakaria was not alone among immigrants to rise to prominence in American politics (some whom he admired include Henry Kissinger and Zbigniew Brzezinski), he was one of the few who have not come from a European background.

Fareed Zakaria was born in Bombay, India, in 1961. Fareed grew up in Bombay, in the wealthy district of Malabar Hill and his family lived in a mansion called Rylestone, which was built for the British high court judge during the time of the Raj. His father, Rafiq Zakaria, was a state minister from Maharashtra and deputy leader of the Congress Party (the party of then-Prime Minister Indira Gandhi, of whom he was a close associate). Fareed's mother, Fatima Zakaria, was Sunday editor of *The Times of India*. His parents often invited their friends—who included artists, intellectuals, and politicians—to the house for Urdu poetry readings. Zakaria attended the Cathedral School, where the 800 Indian students received a thoroughly English education.

Zakaria left India after secondary school to attend Yale University. He promptly fell in love with the United States, preferring its culture to the British.

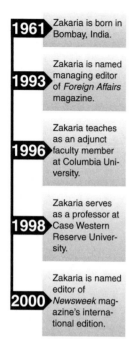

1961 Zakaria is born in Bombay, India.

1993 Zakaria is named managing editor of *Foreign Affairs* magazine.

1996 Zakaria teaches as an adjunct faculty member at Columbia University.

1998 Zakaria serves as a professor at Case Western Reserve University.

2000 Zakaria is named editor of *Newsweek* magazine's international edition.

adjunct professor a member of a university faculty who is not a full-time or tenured professor.

After receiving his degree in history, Zakaria went on to earn a doctorate in international relations from Harvard University. While there, he taught in the Department of Government and in the Core Curriculum, and ran the Project on the Changing Security Environment and American National Interests from 1991 to 1993.

In 1993, at the age of 28, Zakaria was named managing editor of *Foreign Affairs*, the journal of the organization Council on Foreign Relations. The magazine is released every two months in English and a number of other languages, and has the largest worldwide circulation of all journals on international politics and economics. Zakaria, the youngest person ever to fill the position, led the publication to increased circulation and influence. In addition to being a talented editor, Zakaria also wrote with distinction. He won an Overseas Press Club Award as part of a *Newsweek* reporting team. *Foreign Affairs* was also nominated for a National Magazine Award in 1997 for an article written by Zakaria entitled "The Rise of Illiberal Democracy." Other awards he has won include the prestigious Harvard MacArthur Fellowship and the John M. Olin Fellowship.

Zakaria also taught at the collegiate level. From 1996 to 1997, Zakaria was an **adjunct professor** at Columbia University; from 1998 to 1999, he taught at Case Western University in Ohio.

In October 2000, Zakaria, previously a contributing editor to *Newsweek*, was named editor of the magazine's international edition. His responsibilities included overseeing the magazine's content and direction. Upon hiring him for the position, *Newsweek* Editor-in-Chief Richard M. Smith remarked of Zakaria, "Fareed is a brilliant young writer and editor . . . [H]e will bring an inspiring vision and heightened impact to *Newsweek International* and our global coverage."

Zakaria continued to write his regular column for *Newsweek*, as well as occasional articles for *The Washington Post*, *The New York Times*, the *Wall Street Journal*, and *The New Republic*, among other publications. He was also the wine columnist for the Internet journal Slate.com.

In 1997, Zakaria co-edited the book *American Encounter: The United States and the Making of the Modern World Essays from 75 Years of "Foreign Affairs"* with James F. Hoge (his colleague at the journal). Zakaria's 1998 book, *From Wealth to Power: The Unusual Origins of America's World Role* explored the origins of the United States as a global power.

Zakaria lived in New York with his wife, Paula, a jewelry designer, and his son Omar, born in 1999. Zakaria, who positioned himself with moderate Republicans or conservative Democrats, aimed to become an American citizen, a move he saw as central to truly integrating himself into the nation's politics. He aspired to work with a presidential campaign and, eventually perhaps, in the White House. Zakaria was close with many people surrounding President George W. Bush. Condoleeza Rice, Bush's chief foreign policy adviser, aptly summed up Zakaria's expertise by saying Zakaria was "intelligent about just about every area of the world." ◆

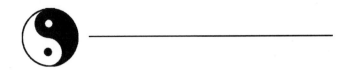

1829

Chang and Eng Bunker begin touring the United States and England as oddities.

1848

Gold is discovered in the state of California and Chinese immigrants begin to arrive there along with immigrants from many other groups.

1850

California adopts a "Foreign Miner's Tax", and concentrates enforcement of the law on Chinese miners.

1858

The state of California passes legislation barring the entry of Chinese and "Mongolians" into the state.

1860

Japan sends a group of diplomats to the United States.

1865

Central Pacific Railroad Co. begins recruiting Chinese immigrants for work on the transcontinental railroad project.

1868

The governments of the United States and China sign the Burlingame-Seward Treaty, which recognizes the rights of citizens of each nation to emigrate.

1870

California passes a law prohibiting the importation of Chinese and Japanese women for prostitution.

1872

The California Civil Procedure Code is changed to allow court testimony by people of Chinese descent.

1878

The U.S. Supreme Court rules in *In re Ah Yup* that Chinese are not eligible to become naturalized United States citizens.

1879

A U.S. district court delcares unconstitutional a California state law that requires the removal of all Chinese outside incorporated towns and cities.

1880

The United States and China sign a treaty that gives the U.S. the ability to limit but not prohibit Chinese immigration.

The California Civil Code prohibits licenses to be issued for marriages between Caucasians and "Mongolians, Negroes, mulattoes, and persons of mixed blood."

1886

The U.S. Supreme Court states that a law that has an unequal impact among different groups is unconstitutional in *Yick Wo v. Hopkins*.

1894

A U.S. circuit court rules that Japanese are not eligible for naturalized United States citizenship in *In re Saito*.

1898

The U.S. Supreme Court rules in *Lem Moon Sing v. U.S.* that individuals of Chinese descent born in the United States may not be stripped of their citizenship.

The United States annexes Hawaii and the Philippines.

1907

The United States and Japan reach an agreement in which the Japanese government ceases issuing passports to workers who wish to emigrate to the United States.

1913

The state of California passes a law known as the Alien Land Law, which prohibits "aliens ineligible to citizenship" from buying or leasing land for more than three years.

1917

The United States commits troops to World War I.

1918

Military servicemen of Asian heritage who served in World War I for the United States receive naturalization rights.

1922

The United States Supreme Court declares that Japanese are ineligible for naturalized citizenship in *Takao Ozawa v. U.S.*

1923

Asian Indians are ruled to be ineligible for naturalized American citizenship in *U.S. v. Bhagat Singh Thind.*

1929

Anna May Wong stars in the motion picture *Picadilly* and makes her stage debut in *Circle of Chalk.*

1934

The Tydings-McDuffie Act outlines the plan for Philippine independence and reduces immigration of Filipinos to the United States to 50 per year.

1941

Japan attacks the U.S. Navy at Pearl Harbor, Hawaii, on December 7, igniting U.S. participation in World War II.

Over 2,000 Japanese community leaders in the Pacific Coast states and Hawaii are interned in camps administered by the U.S. Department of Justice.

1942

President Franklin Roosevelt signs Executive Order 9066, which authorizes the designation of military areas within the United States "from which any and all persons may be excluded."

The United States Congress passes legislation imposing sanctions on those who disobey the implementation and execution of Roosevelt's executive order.

1943

Carlos Bulosan writes "Freedom From Want" for the *Saturday Evening Post*.

Congress repeals all Chinese exclusion laws and grants naturalization rights to Chinese within the United States.

1947

An amendment to the War Brides Act-adopted in 1945-permits Chinese American war veterans to bring their wives to the United States.

1949

About 5,000 Chinese scholars living in the United States are granted status as refugees when China becomes a communist nation.

1952

Sammy Lee becomes the first male Olympic athlete to win two consecutive gold medals in platform diving.

Congress passes the McCarran-Walter Act which includes a clause granting U.S. naturalization rights and a small immigration quota to Japanese.

1956

Chen Ning Yang shares the Nobel Prize for physics with his collaborator in recognition for their work on the conservation of parity law.

Toshiko Akiyohsi becomes the first Japanese person to win a scholarship to the Berklee School of Music in Boston.

Chien-Shiung Wu conducts research in beta decay that would lead to a Nobel Prize for her colleagues on the project.

1957

Tsung Dao Lee wins the Nobel Prize for physics.

Sessue Hayakawa is nominated for an Academy Award for his work in *The Bridge On the River Kwai*.

1959

Hiram Fong is elected to serve in the United States Senate representing the new state of Hawaii.

1962

Minoru Yamasaki's architectual firm is hired to design the World Trade Center.

Daniel Inouye is elected to represent Hawaii in the United States Senate.

1965

Patsy Mink of Hawaii begins serving as a member of the United States House of Representatives.

Congress abolishes "national origins" as a basis for allocating immigration quotas.

1968

Har Gobind Khorana shares the Nobel Prize for medicine.

1969

Yoko Ono marries singer/songwriter John Lennon.

1970

Le Ly Hayslip escapes from Vietnam and arrives in the United States.

1974

George R. Ariyoshi is the first person of Japanese descent to be elected governor of Hawaii.

1975

Over 130,000 refugees come to the United States to escape Communist regimes in Vietnam, Laos, and Cambodia.

Lawrence Yep wins the Newbery Honor Award for *Dragonflies*.

1976

President Gerald Ford rescinds Executive Order 9066, which had remained in place since Franklin Roosevelt issued the order in 1942.

1977

Cartoonist Lynda Barry creates "Ernie Pook's Comeek."

1978

Robert Matsui is elected to the United States House of Representatives.

Television journalist Ken Kashiwahara is named bureau chief for ABC News in San Francisco.

The Japanese American Citizens League adopts an official position calling for redress and reparations for the internment of Japanese Americans during World War II.

1979

Photographer Dith Pran escapes from his native Cambodia and the Khmer Rouge.

Maxine Kingston's *The Woman Warrior* is named one of the top ten nonfiction works of the decade by *Time* magazine.

1980

A design by architectual student Maya Lin is selected to become the Vietnam Veterans Memorial in Washington, D.C.

1981

The Minister of Culture of the People's Republic of China invites Dong Kingman to showcase an exhibition in China.

Congress establishes the Commission on Wartime Relocation and Internment of Civilians, which holds hearings across the nation. The commission concludes that the internment was a "grave injustice" resulting from "race prejudice, war hysteria, and a failure of political leadership."

1983

Subrahmanyan Chandra wins the Nobel Prize.

David Chu founds the clothing company Nautica.

1984

Yo Yo Ma wins his first Grammy Award.

Pat Morita garners an Oscar nomination for his role in *The Karate Kid*.

1986

Yuan Tesh Lee wins the Nobel Prize for chemistry.

1987

Dinesh D'Souza is hired as a policy expert in the Reagan administration.

1988

David Henry Hwang achieves his greatest success as a playwright with *M. Butterfly*, which is based on the famous opera *Madam Butterfly*.

B.D. Wong stars in *M. Butterfly* and earns various accolades and awards for his performance.

1989

President George Bush signs a bill that provides for the payment of $20,000 to every surviving Japanese American internee from World War II.

Shirley Geok-lin Lim wins the National Book Award for *The Forbidden Stitch*.

The United States reaches an agreement with the government of Vietnam in which political prisoners held in Vietnam will permitted to emigrate to the U.S.

Michael Chang wins the French Open tennis championship.

1990

Flossie Wong-Staal is named chair of AIDS research at the University of California, San Diego.

Daniel Akaka is elected to represent Hawaii in the United States Senate.

1991

Bapsi Sidwha's *Cracking India* gains recognition from *The New York Times* as one of the year's notable books.

Gish Jen publishes her first novel *Typical American*.

1992

Sarah Chang becomes the youngest artist to ever receive the prestigious Avery Fisher Career Grant.

1993

Jason Scott Lee plays the lead role in *Dragon: The Bruce Lee Story*.

Russell Wong plays an abusive spouse in *The Joy Luck Club*.

Connie Chung shares the anchor desk with Dan Rather on the CBS *Evening News*.

1994

Benjamin Cayetano becomes governor of Hawaii, the first person of Filipino heritage to hold the post.

Martin Yan wins the James Beard Award for Best Cooking Television Show.

1995

Sun-Yung Chang wins the Ruth Lyttle Satter Prize in Mathematics.

1996

David Ho is named Man of the Year by *Time* magazine.

Gary Locke is elected governor of Washington state.

Fred Lau is sworn in as the chief of police in San Francisco, California.

Amy Chow wins a silver medal at the Olympic Games for her individual performance on the parallel bars.

Deepak Chopra founds the Center for Well Being in La Jolla, California.

1997

Steven Chu wins the Nobel Prize for physics.

The Rape of Nanking by Iris Chang is published to critical acclaim.

Bill Lann Lee is named acting Assistant Attorney General for Civil Rights in the U.S. Justice Department.

Tiger Woods wins The Masters, his first major professional golf championship victory; he is the youngest Masters champion in history.

Jerry Yang is ranked 32nd on the *Forbes* technology listings.

1998

Sabeer Bhatia sells his Hotmail company to the Microsoft corporation for over 2.5 million shares of Microsoft.

David Wu is elected to the U.S. House of Representatives from the 1st district of Oregon.

Joan Chen directs her first feature film, *Xiu Xiu, The Sent-Down Girl.*

Rep. Jay Kim is sentenced to various fines and penalties after pleading guilty to multiple misdemeanors for taking illegal campaign contributions.

Michelle Kwan wins a silver medal in figure skating at the Winter Olympic Games in Nagano, Japan.

1999

Ha Jin wins the National Book Award for *Waiting.*

Lisa Ling becomes a co-host on the ABC daytime talk show *The View.*

2000

Jhumpa Lahiri wins the Pulitzer Prize for fiction, the first time a person of South Asian origin wins the individual award.

President Bill Clinton names Norman Mineta Secretary of Commerce and becomes the first Asian-American member of the Cabinet.

Fareed Zakaria is named editor of *Newsweek* magazine's international edition.

2001

Mineta is named Secretary of Transportation by President George W. Bush.

Ang Lee accepts the Academy Award for Best Foreign Film for *Crouching Tiger, Hidden Dragon.*

Tiger Woods wins his second Masters championship and becomes the first golfer in history to hold each of the major professional championships simultaneously.

The following authors contributed the new articles for **Macmillan Profiles:** *Asian American Portraits:*

Mary J. Carvlin
Nancy Gratton
Jill Hamilton
William Kaufman
Matthew May
Eleanor Stanford
Jeff Turner

Photo Credits

Photographs appearing in *Asian American Portraits* are from the following sources:

Akaka, Daniel (page 4): Daniel Akaka
Akiyoshi, Toshiko (page 7): Jack Vartoogian
Ariyoshi, George R. (page 9): George Ariyoshi
Barry, Lynda (page 13): AP/Wide World
Bulosan, Carlos (page 18): Filipino American National Historical Society
Carrere, Tia (page 25): Kobal Collection
Cayetano, Benjamin J. (page 28): Benjamin Cayetano
Chandrasekhar, Subrahmanyan (page 31): AP/Wide World
Chang, Michael (page 37): Corbis
Chang, Sun-Young Alice (page 41): Mathematisches Forschungsinstitut Oberwolfach
Chen, Joan (page 48): Archive Photos, Inc.
Chiao, Leroy (page 54): U.S. National Aeronautics and Space Administration
Chopra, Deepak (page 59): AP/Wide World
Chow, Amy (page 62): AP/Wide World
Chu, Steven (page 67): Stanford University Press News Service
Chung, Connie (page 70): AP/Wide World
Curry, Ann (page 75): The Gamma Liaison Network
Fong, Hiram F. (page 84): AP/Wide World
Ho, David (page 97): David Ho
Howe, James Wong (page 102): Kobal Collection
Hwang, David Henry (page 106): AP/Wide World
Inouye, Daniel (page 113): AP/Wide World
Ito, Lance (page 116): AP/Wide World
Jin, Ha (page 122): AP/Wide World

Kashiwahara, Ken (page 127): Ken Kashiwahara
Khorana, Har Gobind (page 130): AP/Wide World
Kingston, Maxine Hong (page 141)
Kwan, Michelle (page 145): AP/Wide World
Lau, Fred H. (page 151): AP/Wide World
Lee, Brandon (page 158): AP/Wide World
Lee, Bruce (page 162): Corbis
Lee, Samuel (page 172): AP/Wide World
Lee, Tsung Dao (page 175): Library of Congress
Lee, Wen Ho (page 178): AP/Wide World
Locke, Gary (page 194): Gary Locke
Ma, Yo Yo (page 197): AP/Wide World
Matsui, Robert (page 200): AP/Wide World
Mehta, Zubin (page 206): Corbis
Mink, Patsy (page 224): Patsy Mink
Morita, Pat (page 227): AP/Wide World
Mukherjee, Bharatu (page 233): Kobal Collection
Ono, Yoko (page 254): Corbis
Ozawa, Seiji (page 258): Library of Congress
Paik, Nam June (page 262): AP/Wide World
Pei, I.M. (Page 265): Corbis
Pran, Dith (page 268): Corbis
Shinseki, Eric (page 281): Public Domain
Takaki, Ronald (page 300): Ronald Takaki
Takei, George (page 303): Corbis
Trinh, Eugene Huu (page 315): U.S. National Aeronautics and Space Administration
Wang, An (page 322): Corbis
Wang, Vera (page 330): Vera Wang
Wong-Staal, Flossie (page 342): Flossie Wong-Staal
Woods, Eldrick "Tiger" (page 344): PGA Tour, Inc.
Yamaguchi, Kristi (page 351): Corbis
Yang, Chen Ning (page 357): Library of Congress

Additional
Resources

GENERAL SOURCES

BOOKS

Bloom, Harold, ed. *Asian-American Writers*. Chelsea House, 1998.

Chang, Gordon H. *Asian Americans and Politics: Perspectives, Experiences, Prospects*. Stanford University Press, 2001.

Chiu, Christina, and Ronald Takakai. *Lives of Notable Asian Americans: Literature and Education*. Chelsea House, 1995 [young adult].

Choi, Helen, and Phd Rhee. *The Korean-American Experience: A Detailed Analysis of How Well Korean-Americans Adjust to Life in the United States*. Vantage Press, 1995.

De Tran, Andrew Lam, and Hai Dai Nguyen, eds. *Once upon a Dream . . . : The Vietnamese-American Experience*. Andrews McMeel Publishing, 1995.

Eng, Alvin, ed. *Tokens?: The NYC Asian American Experience on Stage*. Temple University Press, 2000.

Fong, Timothy P. *The Contemporary Asian American Experience: Beyond the Model Minority*. Prentice Hall, 1998.

Fong, Timothy P., and Larry H. Shinagawa, eds. *Asian Americans: Experiences and Perspectives*. Prentice Hall, 1999.

Faderman, Lillian, and Ghia Xiong. *I Begin My Life All Over: The Hmong and the American Immigrant Experience*. Beacon Press, 1999.

Gan, Geraldine, and Ronald Takakai. *Lives of Notable Asian Americans: Arts, Entertainment, Sports*. Chelsea House, 1995 [young adult].

Kim, Hyung-chang, et al., eds. *Distinguished Asian-Americans: A Biographical Dictionary*. Greenwood Press, 1999.

Marvis, Barbara J. *Contemporary American Success Stories: Famous People of Asian Ancestry*. Mitchell Lane Multicultural Biography Series, 1994- [series; young adult].

Morey, Janet Nomura, and Wendy Dunn. *Famous Asian Americans*. Cobblehill, 1992.

Rutledge, Paul James. *The Vietnamese Experience in America*. Indiana University Press, 1992.

Takakai, Ronald. *From the Land of Morning Calm: The Koreans in America*. Chelsea House, 1994.

Takakai, Ronald. *India in the West: South Asians in America*. Chelsea House, 1994.

Takakai, Ronald, and Angelo Ragazza. *Lives of Notable Asian Americans: Business, Politics, and Science*. Chelsea House, 1995 [young adult].

Wu, Dana Ying-Hui. *The Chinese-American Experience*. Millbrook Press, 1993.

Yung, Judy. *Chinese Women of America: A Pictorial History*. University of Washington Press, 1993.

Zia, Helen. *Asian American Dreams: The Emergence of an American People*. Farrar Straus & Giroux, 2000.

Zia, Helen, Susan B. Gall, and Geoge Takei, eds. *Notable Asian Americans*. Gale Group, 1995.

VIDEORECORDINGS

Another America, National Asian American Telecommunications Association, 1996.

The Asianization of America, Films for the Humanities, 1993.

Filipino Americans: Discovering Their Past for the Future, Moon Rae Production & National Video Profiles, Inc., for the Filipino American National Historical Society, 1994.

From Hollywood to Hanoi, Indochina Film Arts Foundation, 1994.

I'm on a Mission from Buddha, KQED San Francisco, 1991.

The Joy Luck Club, Hollywood Pictures, 1993.

Knowing Her Place, Women Make Movies Productions, 1990.

Mixed Blood, National Asian American Telecommunications Association, 1992.

New Hmong Life in America, Worthwhile Films, 1989.

Picturing Oriental Girls: A (Re)Educational Videotape, National Asian American Telecommunications Association, 1992.

The Polynesians, KCSM TV60 New Americans Series, 1994.

Rebuilding the Temple: Cambodians in America, Direct Cinema Ltd., 1991.

Relocations, National Asian American Telecommunications Association, 1991.

Renee Tajima Reads Asian Images in American Film, Paper Tiger Television, 1984.

Shopping for Fangs, Margin Home Video, 1998.

Slaying the Dragon, National Asian American Telecommunications Association, 1988.

Something Strong Within, Japanese American National Museum, 1995.

Tapestry: Asian Women in America, Third World Newsreel, 1991.

Vietnamese Refugees in America, Barr Films, 1986.

When East Meets East, Kalli Paakkspuu [Canada, independent], 1997.

WEBSITES

Asian American History, http://americanhistory.about.com/homework/americanhistory/cs/asianamerhistory/

Asian American Internet Sites, http://latino.sscnet.ucla.edu/Asian.links.html

Asian American Net, http://www.asianamerican.net/

Asian American Resources, http://www.dartmouth.edu/˜hist32/Books/Topic.htm

Asian Americans in the Humanities, http://www.ithaca.edu/library/htmls/humasia.html

Asian Americans in the United States and Hawaii [list of videorecordings], http://www.sinclair.hawaii.edu/HTMLpages/lists/Asian_Americans.html

AsianConnections, http://www.asianconnections.com/

Asian Pacific American Community Server, http://eramen.net/

Chinese American Political Association, http://www.capa-news.org/capa/

Goldsea, http://goldsea.com/

Hmong People in the U.S., http://www.jefflindsay.com/Hmong_tragedy.html

Hmong Web Pages, http://stthomas.edu/˜www/s/slee1/hmong_web_pages.html

Internet Resources on Asian Americans, http://newton.uor.edu/Departments&Programs/AsianStudiesDept/asianam.html

Immigration and Naturalization Service Statistics, http://www.ins.usdoj.gov/graphics/aboutins/statistics/index.htm

Japanese-American Network, http://janet.org/

Korean-American WWW sites, http://www.duke.edu/˜myhan/s-kawww.html

San Francisco Chinatown: Information and Resources, http://www.sfchinatown.com/

Voices From the Gaps, http://voices.cla.umn.edu/

AKAKA, DANIEL K.

Kiyosaki, Wayne S., and Daniel K. Akaka. *A Spy in Their Midst : The World War II Struggle of a Japanese-American Hero*. Madison Books, 1995.

Senator Daniel Akaka, Democrat from Hawaii, http://www.senate.gov/~akaka/

Schwartz, Maralee. "Rep. Akaka named to fill Senate seat from Hawaii." *Washington Post*, April 29, 1990.

AKIYOSHI, TOSHIKO

Hentoff, Nat. "Toshiko Akiyoshi: triple outside." *The Progressive*, July 1981.

Jazz is My Native Language. Rhapsody Films, 1989.

Jazz Profiles: Toshiko Akiyoshi,
http://www.npr.org/programs/jazzprofiles/takiyoshi.html

Rothbart, Peter. Toshiko Akiyoshi. *Down Beat*, Aug. 1980

Toshiko Akiyoshi: Jazz Orchestra: Strive for Jive. View Video, 1997.

ARIYOSHI, GEORGE R.

Ariyoshi, George R. *With Obligation to All*. University of Hawaii Press, 1997.

"Ariyoshi, George, R(yoichi)." *Current Biography*, Jan. 1985.

Borreca, Richard. "Renewed popularity for George Ariyoshi." Honolulu Star Bulletin, July 23, 1997.

"Statehood gave us our politcal voice." (Interview with George R. Ariyoshi) *U.S. News & World Report*, Aug 27, 1984.

BARRY, LYNDA

Barry, Lynda. *Cruddy*. Scribner, 2000.

"Barry, Lynda." *Current Biography*, Nov. 1994.

Barry, Lynda. *The Greatest of Marlys*. Sasquatch Books, 2000.

Blair Interview: Lynda Barry: Funk Queen USA,
http://www.blairmag.com/blair5/lynda/questions.html

Hempel, Amy. "Laugh Lines." *New York Times Magazine*, Nov. 27, 1988.

Hubbard, Kim. "In Lynda Barry's world, poodles are tough and the weasels drink daiquiries." *People Weekly*, March 30, 1987.

BHATIA, SABEER

"The Hotmail Hero." *Business Asia*, Aug. 2000.

Interview - Sabeer Bhatia, http://www.aandm.com/Interviews/SabeerBhatia.htm

Rediff on the Net, Infotech: An Interview with Sabeer Bhatia, founder and CEO of Hotmail, http://www.rediff.com/computer/1998/aug/28bhatia.htm

"A Typhoon of Venture Capital?" *Business Week*, Jan. 31, 2000.

BULOSAN, CARLOS

Bulosan, Carlos. *America Is in the Heart: A Personal History*. University of Washington Press, 2000 [first published 1946].

"Bulosan, Carlos, 1913-1956." In *Benet's Reader's Encyclopedia of American Literature*, HarperCollins, 1991, p. 134.

Bulosan, Carlos, and E. San Juan, ed. *The Cry and the Dedication*. Temple University Press, 1995.

Bulosan, Carlos, and E. San Juan, ed. *On Becoming Filipino: Selected Writings of Carlos Bulosan*. Temple University Press, 1995.

Carlos Bulosan, Biography and Analysis, http://www.stanford.edu/~jsangria/bulosan/

Evangelista, Susan. *Carlos Bulosan and His Poetry: A Biography and Anthology.* University of Washington Press, 1985.

Guyotte, Ronald L. "Generation gap: Filipinos, Filipino Americans and Americans, here and there, then and now." *Journal of American Ethnic History,* Fall 1997.

Morantte, P.C. *Remembering Carlos Bulosan: His Heart Affair with America.* New Day Publishers, 1984.

BUNKER, CHANG AND ENG

Hale, James W. *An Historical Account of the Siamese Twin Brothers, From Actual Observations.* Elliot and Palmer, 1831.

Hunter, Kay. *Duet for a Lifetime: The Story of the Original Siamese Twins.* Coward-McCann, 1964.

Strauss, Darin. *Chang and Eng.* E. P. Dutton, 2000.

Wallace, Irving, and Amy Wallace. *The Two: A Biography: The Story of The Original Siamese Twins.* Simon & Schuster, 1978.

CARRERE, TIA

Mulloy, Peggy. "Tia Carrere: rising sun's rising star." *Interview,* Aug. 1993.

Scarred City, Vidmark/Trimark, 1999.

Schneller, Johanna. "Tia Time." *GQ - Gentlemen's Quarterly,* Aug. 1993.

Tia Carerre Biography, Pictures and Career Highlights, http://www.moviestarpages.com/tia_carrere/

Wayne's World, Paramount Studio, 1992.

CAYETANO, BENJAMIN

Benjamin Cayetano on the Issues, http://www.issues2000.org/Benjamin_Cayetano.htm

Governor Benjamin J. Cayetano, http://gov.state.hi.us/

Janofsky, Michael. "Shift in politics and economics seen for Hawaii." *New York Times,* Aug. 24, 1998.

"Maui's mayor to challenge Cayetano in governor's race." *New York Times,* Sept. 21, 1998.

CHANDRASEKHAR, SUBRAHMANYAN

Autobiography of S. Chandraskehar, http://www.nobel.se/physics/laureates/1983/chandrasekhar-autobio.html

Chandrasekhar, Subrahmanyan. *Truth and Beauty: Aesthetics and Motivations in Science.* University of Chicago Press, 1991.

Kameshwar, C. Wali. *Chandra: A Biography of S. Chandrasekhar.* University of Chicago Press, 1992.

CHANG, IRIS

Chang, Iris. *The Rape of Nanking: The Forgotten Holocaust of World War I*. Penguin, 1998.

Chang, Iris. *Thread of the Silkworm*. Basic Books, 1996.

Online Newshour: Gergen Dialogs: Iris Chang, http://www.pbs.org/newshour /gergen/february98/chang_2-20.html

Ringle, Ken. "The forgotten holocaust." *Washington Post*, Dec. 11, 1997.

Will, George F. "Breaking a sinister silence." *Washington Post*, Feb. 19, 1998.

CHANG, MICHAEL

"Chang, Michael." *Current Biography*, July 1997.

Dell, Pamela. *Michael Chang: Tennis Champion*. Childrens Press, 1992 [juvenile].

Ditchfield, Christin. *Sports Great Michael Chang*. Enslow Publishers, 1999 [juvenile].

Noonan, Tim. "Chang is a smash on and off court in Asia." *Asian Wall Street Journal Weekly*, Apr. 29, 1996.

The Official Michael Chang Website, http://www.mchang.com/intro.html

CHANG, SARAH

Sarah Chang Biography, http://www.ugcs.caltech.edu/~levy/Sarah.html

Caplan, Jeremy. "A Violin Prodigy Sees the World." *Newsweek International*, Aug 9, 1999.

Chang, Sarah, violin. *Simply Sarah: Sarah Chang Plays Popular Encores*. EMD/EMI Classics, 1997 [audio CD].

Chang, Sarah, violin. *Sweet Sorrow* [Chang performs music of Vivaldi, Gluck, Brahms, and others]. EMD/EMI Classics, 1999 [audio CD].

Stryker, Mark. "Stern and Chang: The prodigy and the maestro." *Knight-Ridder Tribune News Service*, May 13, 2000.

Tommasini, Anthony. "Avery Fisher prize goes to women for the first time." *New York Times*, May 5, 1999.

CHANG, SUN-YUNG (ALICE)

Profiles of Women in Mathematics: Sun-Yung Alice Chang, http://www.awm-math.org/noetherbrochure/Chang01.html

Sun-Yung Alice Chang, http://www-groups.dcs.st-andrews.ac.uk/~history /Mathematicians/Chang.html

Sun-Yung Alice Chang Home Page [includes list of published work], http://www.math.princeton.edu/~chang/

CHAO, ELAINE L.

Biography of Elaine Chao, U.S. Secretary of Labor, http://www3.itu.int /MISSIONS/US/BIOS/Chao%20Elaine.htm

Harrison, Joan. "Elaine Chao." *Directors & Boards*, Spring 1999.

The Honorable Elaine L. Chao, United States Secretary of Labor, http://www.dol.gov/dol/_sec/public/aboutosec/chao.htm

Swoboda, Frank. "Chao Sees Her Role As Agent of Change; Labor Secretary Sets Broad Agenda To Examine Basic Workplace Laws." *Washington Post*, March 20, 2001.

CHAWLA, KALPANA

"Astronauts fumbled satellite release." *Atlanta-Journal Constitution*, April 16, 1998.

Biographical Data: Kalpana Chawla, Ph.D., http://www.jsc.nasa.gov/Bios/htmlbios/chawla.html

Kalpana Chawla becomes the first Indian woman in space, http://www.rediff.com/news/nov/20kalp.htm

CHEN, JOAN

"Groundbreaking actor-director Chen comfortable charting her own path." *Seattle Post-Intelligencer*, Aug. 24, 2000.

Joan Chen: From China to Hollywood, http://www.cnn.com/SHOWBIZ/Movies/9906/02/joan.chen/

The Last Emperor. Artisan Entertainment, 1987 [video release, 1999].

Lidz, Franz. "Joan Chen." *Interview*, Aug. 2000.

Marvis, Barbara J. *Contemporary American Success Stories: Famous People of Asian Ancestry*. Mitchell Lane, 1994.

Mooney, Joshua. "Director Chen grew up with film." *Dallas Morning News*, Aug 22, 2000.

CHEN, JOIE

Alum Joie Chen brings lessons home to Medill, http://www.medill.northwestern.edu/inside/jchen.html

CNN Anchors & Reporters: Joie Chen, http://www.cnn.com/CNN /anchors_reporters/chen.joie.html

Interview with CNN's Joie Chen, http://www.journalismjobs.com/interview_chen.cfm

CHIAO, LEROY

Astronaut Bio: Leroy Chiao, http://www.jsc.nasa.gov/Bios/htmlbios/chiao.html

Berthelsen, John. "Flying high: first Chinese-American astronaut is set to blast off into space next month." *Far Eastern Economic Review*, June 30, 1994.

Carreau, Mark. "Space station coming together; Astronauts prepare outpost for delivery of power module." *Houston Chronicle*, Oct. 18, 2000.

CHO, MARGARET

Bardin, Brantly. "Cho & tell." *The Advocate*, Feb 1, 2000.

"Cho, Margaret." *Current Biography*, Oct. 2000.

Cho, Margaret. *I'm the One That I Want.* Ballantine Books, 2001.

Cho, Margaret, et al. *The Comedians of the Year.* Uproar Entertainment, 1999 [audio cassette].

Leff, Lisa. "For Margaret Cho, an 'all American' arrival." *Washington Post*, Sept. 11, 1994.

The Official Margaret Cho Website, http://www.margaretcho.com/

CHOPRA, DEEPAK

"Chopra, Deepak" *Current Biography*, Oct. 1995.

Chopra, Deepak. *How to Know God: The Soul's Journey into the Mystery of Mysteries.* Harmony Books, 2000.

Deepak Chopra: The Seven Spiritual Laws of Success. Unapix, 1995.

Deepak Chopra Box Set, Unapix, 1998.

FriedMan, Max. "A tide that cannot be stopped: Deepak Chopra's mind-body medicine is a hit with the masses." *Vegetarian Times*, July 1994.

Nacson, Leon, ed. *A Deepak Chopra Companion: Illuminations on Health and Human Consciousness.* Three Rivers Press, 1999.

The Offical Deepak Chopra Website, http://www.chopra.com/

CHOW, AMY

Clarey, Christopher. "Chow tries to balance everything in life." *New York Times*, July 14, 1996.

CNNSI.com - Olympic Sports: Dawes, Chow going back to Olympics, http://sportsillustrated.cnn.com/olympics/news/2000/08/20/gymtrials_day4_ap/

DeArmond, Mike. "Chow isn't burdened by Atlanta memories." *Detroit Free Press*, Sept. 16, 2000.

Kleinbaum, Nancy C., Amy Chow, et al. *Magnificent Seven: The Authorized Story of American Gold.* Bantam Doubleday Dell, 1996 [young adult].

Naversen, Laurel. "7 ups and downs." *Women's Sports and Fitness*, Jan 2000.

USA Gymnastics Official Biography: Amy Chow, http://www.usa-gymnastics.org/athletes/bios/c/achow.html

CHU, DAVID

Fashion Page: David Chu interview, http://www.fashionz.co.uk/DChu/interview2/

Gault, Ylonda. "At Nautica, lots to Chu on; founder prudently expands brand name." *Crain's New York Business*, Dec. 16, 1996.

Mckinney, Melonee. "For Spring '99, David Chu's NST line is a street-inspired take on sports." *Daily News Record*, Oct. 5, 1998.

CHU, STEVEN

Autobiography of Steven Chu, http://www.nobel.se/physics/laureates/1997/chu-autobio.html

Galnz, James. "Master of molecule manipulation works on the wild side." *New York Times*, June 30, 1998.

Levi, Barbara Goss. "Work on atom trapping and cooling gets a warm reception in Stockholm." *Physics Today*, Dec. 1997.

Steven Chu Home Page [includes list of published work], http://www.stanford.edu/group/chugroup/steve.html

Wailoo, Keith. "Interview with physics professor Steven Chu." *American Scientist*, Jan.-Feb. 1998.

CHUNG, CONNIE

Connie Chung Biography, http://abcnews.go.com/onair/wnt/html_files/chungc.html

"Chung, Connie." *Current Biography*, July 1989.

Hickey, Mary C. "This is her life." *Ladies Home Journal*, Oct 1993.

Malone, Mary. *Connie Chung, A Broadcast Journalist*. Enslow Publishers, 1992.

Marvis, Barbara J. *Contemporary American Success Stories: Famous People of Asian Ancestry: Pat Suzuki; Minoru Yamasaki; An Wang; Conni E Chung; Carlos Bulosan*. Mitchell Lane, 1993.

Wallace, Carol. "D.C. newsman Maury Povich anchors NBC's Connie Chung after a longtime cross-country romance." *People Weekly*, June 10, 1985.

CHUNG, EUGENE

Eugene Chung Career Highlights, http://sports.nfl.com/2000/playerhighlights?id=413

Eugene Chung Statistics, http://cbs.sportsline.com/u/football/nfl/players/3251.htm

Sheridan, Phil. "Eagles Sign Three, Including Chung." *Philadelphia Inquirer*, March 16, 2000.

CURRY, ANN

"Ann Curry" [The 50 Most Beautiful People]. *People Weekly*, May 11, 1998.

Interview with Ann Curry, http://www.abcflash.com/template/special/special2.html

Levine, Daniel. "My first job." *Reader's Digest*, March 2000.

OnAir Bios - Ann Curry, http://www.msnbc.com/onair/bios/a_curry.asp

Robins, J. Max. "How Curry delivered septuplet scoop." *TV Guide*, Dec. 13, 1997.

"Super Sub." *People Weekly*, Oct. 12, 1998.

D'SOUZA, DINESH

D'Souza, Dinesh. *The End of Racism: Principles for a Multiracial Society*. Free Press, 1996.

D'Souza, Dinesh. *The Virtue of Prosperity: Finding Values In An Age Of Techno-Affluence*. Free Press, 2000.

Goode, Stephen. "D'Souza Finds Virture in Modern Prosperity." *Insight on the News*, Dec. 18, 2000.

Hart, Ron. "Rising Young Stars." *Conservative Digest*, Jan.-Feb. 1989.

Loury, Glenn C. "Blind ignorance: Dinesh D'Souza has learned nothing with the reissue of 'The End of Racism'." *Emerge*, Dec 1996.

Online NewsHour Forum: Authors' Corner: Dinesh D'Souza, http://www.pbs.org/newshour/authors_corner/july-dec97/dsouza_12-19.html

Woodson, Robert L., Sr. "The end of racism? Hardly." *New York Times*, Sept. 23, 1995.

FONG, HIRAM LEONG

Chou, Michaelyn P. *The Education of a Senator: Hiram L. Fong 1906-1954*. Ph.D. dissertation, University of Hawaii, 1980

Fong, Hiram Leong - A-to-Z Geography - DiscoverySchool.com, http://school.discovery.com/homeworkhelp/worldbook/atozgeography/f/203130.html

Fong, Hiram Leong, 1906- Biographical Information, http://bioguide.congress.gov/scripts/biodisplay.pl?index=F000245

"Hall of Fame." *Hawaii Business*, Jan. 1995.

Jokiel, Lucy. "The House of Fong." *Hawaii Business*, June 1988.

Oakley, Doug. "Former senator showcases garden." *Travel Weekly*, Sept. 25, 2000.

United States Congress. Senate. *Tributes to the Honorable Hiram L. Fong*. U.S. Government Printing Office, 1977.

GEOK-LIN-LIM, SHIRLEY

Geok-lin-Lim, Shirley. *Among the White Moon Faces: An Asian-American Memoir of Homelands*. Feminist Press, 1996.

Geok-lin-Lim, Shirley. *What the Fortune Teller Didn't Say*. University of Mexico Press, 1998.

Shirley Geok-lin-Lim Overview, http://landow.stg.brown.edu/post/singapore/literature/s.lim/s.limov.html

Voices from the Gaps: Shirley Geok-lin-Lim, Biography-Criticism, http://voices.cla.umn.edu/authors/shirleylim.html

HATTORI, JAMES

CNN Anchors & Reporters - James Hattori, http://www.cnn.com/CNN/anchors_reporters/hattori.james.html

CNN Newscaster Speaks About Diversity in Journalism, http://www.studentadvantage.lycos.com/lycos/article/0,4683,c2-i0-t0-a30763,00.html

"James Hattori becomes one of the few Asian anchormen in U.S. television." *Asian Week*, May 17-23, 1996.

HAYAKAWA, SESSUE

The Bridge on the River Kwai, Columbia Tri-Star, 1957.

The Cheat, Timeless Video, Inc., 1997 [film made in 1915].

Hayakawa, Sessue. *The Bandit Prince* [novel]. Macaulay, 1926.

Hayakawa, Sessue. *Zen Showed Me the Way* [autobiography]. Bobbs-Merrill, 1960.

Sessue Hayakawa, http://www.mdle.com/ClassicFilms/FeaturedStar/perfor69.htm

Sessue Hayakawa Filmography,
http://us.imdb.com/M/person-exact?Hayakawa%2C%20Sessue

HAYSLIP, LE LY

Babcock, Martha K. "A Vietnam menoir." *People Weekly*, Dec. 18, 1989.

Hayslip, Le Ly. *When Heaven and Earth Changed Places: A Vietnamese Woman's Journey from War to Peace*. Doubleday, 1993.

Heaven and Earth, Warner Studios, 1993.

Voices From the Gaps: Le Ly Hayslip, http://voices.cla.umn.edu/authors
/LeLyHayslip.html

HO, DAVID

David Ho Lab [includes list of published works], http://www.rockefeller.edu
/labheads/ho/ho.html

Dr. David Ho: Turning the Tide Against AIDS (Time Man of the Year),
http://www.time.com/time/special/moy/ho/

Gideonse, Ted. "Checking in with David Ho." *Rolling Stone*, April 29, 1999.

"Ho, David D." *Current Biography*, June 1997.

Wilkinson, Alec. "Please Leave David Ho Alone." *Esquire*, March 1999.

HOWE, JAMES WONG

Eyman, Scott. *Five American Cinematographers: Interviews with Karl Strauss, Joseph Ruttenberg, James Wong Howe, Linwood Dunn, and William H. Clothier*. Scarecrow Press, 1987.

James Wong Howe, http://us.imdb.com/M/person-exact?Howe%2C+James+Wong

James Wong Howe, http://www.mdle.com/ClassicFilms/BTC/camra5.htm

Parrish, Robert. "Lights! Camera! Stirfry!" *American Film*, April 1986.

Rainsberger, Todd. *James Wong Howe, Cinematographer*. A. S. Barnes, 1981.

HWANG, DAVID HENRY

David Henry Hwang, http://dolphin.upenn.edu/~mosaic/spring94/page19.html

"Hwang, David Henry." *Current Biography*, May 1989.

Hwang, David Henry. *FOB and Other Plays*. Plume, 1990.

Street, Douglas. *David Henry Hwang*. Boise State University, 1989.

"With four successful plays to his credit, David Henry Hwang is scaling the great wall of fame." *People Weekly*, Jan 9, 1984.

IHA, JAMES

"James Iha." *Rolling Stone*, 1998 [interview].

James Iha Biography, http://www.smashing-pumpkins.net/bios/jamesbio.htm

Iha, James. *Let It Come Down*. EMD/Virgin, 1998 [audio CD].

RollingStone.com - James Iha Main Page, http://www.rollingstone.com/artists/default.asp?oid=3810

INOUYE, DANIEL

Goodsell, Jane. *Daniel Inouye*. Crowell, 1977.

"Inouye, Daniel." *Current Biography*, Sept. 1987.

Inouye, Daniel, and Lee H. Hamilton. *Iran-Contra Affair with the Minority View*. Times Books, 1988.

Senator Daniel Inouye - Hawaii Democrat, http://www.senate.gov/~inouye/

"Senator Daniel K. Inouye." *The Officer*, Dec. 2000.

ITO, LANCE

Gleick, Elizabeth, et al. "Order in the court." *People Weekly*, Aug. 15, 1994.

Hayes, Elizabeth. "Now Out of Limelight, Lance Ito Gets Back to Business." *Los Angeles Business Journal*, Feb. 7, 2000

Lance Ito - Biography, http://www.law.umkc.edu/faculty/projects/ftrials/Simpson/Ito.htm

Tharp, Mike. "Ito's fairness doctrine: how his parents' World War II internment shaped his life in the law." *U.S. News & World Report*, Oct. 31, 1994.

Toobin, Jeffrey. "Ito and the truth school." *New Yorker*, March 27, 1995.

JEN, GISH

Jen, Gish. *Mona in the Promised Land*. Alfred A. Knopf, 1996.

Jen, Gish. *Typical American*. Houghton Mifflin, 1991.

Powell's Book Interviews: Gish Jen, http://www.powells.com/authors/jen.html

Roxe, Hillary. "Asian Balancing Act: Gish Jen mends conflicting aspects of immigrant culture with candor, humor and poignancy." *Time International*, Aug. 9, 1999.

Smith, Wendy. "Gish Jen: 'The Book that Hormones Wrote.'" *Publishers Weekly*, June 7, 1999.

Voices From the Gaps: Gish Jen, http://voices.cla.umn.edu/authors/gishjen.html

JIN, HA

Emory Magazine, Spring 1998: Ha Jin, http://www.emory.edu/EMORY_MAGAZINE/spring98/hajin.html

Garner, Dwight. "Ha Jin's cultural revolution." *New York Times Magazine*, Feb. 6, 2000

Jin, Ha. *Waiting*. Pantheon Books, 1999.

Jin, Ha. *Wreckage*. Hanging Loose Press, 2001.

Powell's Book Interviews: Ha Jin, http://www.powells.com/authors/jin.html

Simon, Linda. "Love Among the Revolutionaries - Chinese expatriate Ha Jin writes of love, freedom, and repression in his native land." *World and I*, May 2000.

KASHIWAHARA, KEN

Carman, John. "ABC News Pulling Plug On S.F. Bureau." *San Francisco Chronicle*, April 9, 1998.

"An eyewitness and relative recounts Benigno Aquino's fatal journey home to Manila." *People Weekly*, Sept. 5, 1983.

Ken Kashiwahara, http://abcnews.go.com/onair/wnt/html_files/kashiwak.html

KHORANA, HAR GOBIND

Biography of Har Gobind Khorana, http://www.nobel.se/medicine/laureates/1968/khorana-bio.html

H. Gorind Khorana [includes listing of published works], http://web.mit.edu/biology/www/Ar/khorana.html

KHOSLA, VINOD

Fetters, Dave. "Top 10 Most Influential People: No. 10 —Vinod Khosla." *Network Computing*, Oct. 2, 2000.

Holson, Laura M. "A capitalist venturing in the world of computers and religion." *New York Times*, Jan 3, 2000.

Lashinsky, Adam. "Sand Hill Road's Networking Guru Plugs Us In: Vinod Khosla on Cisco, Redback, Juniper, and more." *Fortune*, Aug. 14, 2000.

Starting Up in High Gear: An Interview with Venture Capitalist Vinod Khosla, http://www.hbsp.harvard.edu/products/hbr/julaug00/R00403.html

Thurm, Scott. "The quiet man who put sizzle in the Cisco deal." *Wall Street Journal*, Aug. 27, 1999.

KIM, JAY

Asianweek: News: Jay Kim Back in the Running, http://www.asianweek.com/1999_12_16/news_jaykim.html

"Congressman sentenced for taking illegal funds." *New York Times*,

Eilpern, Juliet. "Days in the life of Jay Kim in the U.S. House of Correction." *Washington Post*, May 22, 1998.

Interview with Congressman Jay Kim, http://hcs.harvard.edu/~yisei/backissues/summer_97/kim.html

KINGMAN, DONG

Artist Index Page: Kingman, Dong Moy Chu,
http://askart.com/artist/K/dong_moy_chu_kingman.asp

Dong Kingman on the Internet,
http://www.artcyclopedia.com/artists/kingman_dong.html

Kingman, Dong. *Portraits of Cities*. M. James Fine Art, 1997.

Kingman, Dong, and Helena Kuo Kingman. *Dong Kingman's Watercolors*. Watson-Guptil Publications, 1980.

"Watercolor king." *New Orleans*, Feb. 1981.

KINGSTON, MAXINE HONG

"Kingston, Maxine Hong." *Current Biography*, March 1990.

Kingston, Maxine Hong. *China Men*. Vintage Books, 1989.

Kingston, Maxine Hong. *The Woman Warrior: Memoirs of a Girlhood Among Ghosts*. Econo-Clad Books, 1999 [young adult].

Martin, Tera, ed. *Conversations with Maxine Hong Kingston*. University Press of Mississippi, 1998.

Simmons, Diane. *Maxine Hong Kingston*. Twayne, 1999.

Skandera-Rombley, Laura E., ed. *Critical Essays on Maxine Hong Kingston*. G. K. Hall, 1998.

Voices From the Gaps: Maxine Hong Kingston,
http://voices.cla.umn.edu/authors/MaxineHongKingston.html

KUSAMA, KARYN

Baker, Aaron. "A New Combination: Women and the Boxing Film." *Cineaste*, Fall 2000.

Girlfight, Columbia Tri-Star, 2000.

Interview with Karyn Kusama,
http://www.popmatters.com/film/interviews/kusama-karyn.html

Tannen, Mary. "The Rookie." *Harper's Bazaar*, July 2000.

KWAN, MICHELLE

Lovitt, Chip. *Skating for the Gold: Michelle Kwan & Tara Lipinski*. Archway, 1997 [young adult].

Park, Alice. "Amazing Grace." *Time*, Feb. 9, 1998.

Starr, Mark. "Michelle's Next Turn: Skating's princess tries to hold on to her crown." *Newsweek*, March 26, 2001.

U.S. Figure Skating Online: Athlete Profile - Michelle Kwan,
http://www.usfsa.org/athletes/teama/kwanmich.html

Winner, Barry. *Michelle Kwan: Star Figure Skater*. Enslow Publishers, 2001.

KYUATOR, ABIKO

Abiko Kyuator in *Distinguished Asian-Americans: A Biographical Dictionary*, pp.4-5, Greenwood Press, 1999.

Ichioka, Yuji. "Kengakudan: The Origin of Nisei Study Tours of Japan." *California History*, Vol. 73, No.1 California Historial Society; 1994; also available at http://www.calhist.org/frost1/quarterly-text/v73-1/keng.html

Motoyoshi, Michelle. *The Japanese in California.* Toucan Valley Publications, 1999 [young adult].

LAHIRI, JHUMPHA

Flynn, Gillian. "Passage To India: First-time author Jhumpa Lahiri nabs a Pulitzer." *Entertainment Weekly*, April 28, 2000.

Hajari, Nisid. "The Promising Land: Indian-American Jhumpa Lahiri's heralded debut only partly lives up to its advance hype." *Time International*, Sept. 13, 1999.

Lahiri, Jhumpha. *Interpreter of Maladies: Stories of Bengal, Boston, and Beyond.* South Asia Books, 1999.

Jhumpha Lahiri, interview by Gaiutra Bahadur, http://www.cpcn.com /articles/091699/feat.20q.shtml

Sawnet Bio: Jhumpa Lahiri, http://www.umiacs.umd.edu/users/sawweb/sawnet/books/jhumpa_lahiri.html

Shapiro, Laura. "India Calling: The diaspora's new star." *Newsweek*, July 19, 1999.

LAU, FRED H.

Lau, Fred H. "The Chief's Message." SFPD Spring 1998 Newsletter, http://www.ci.sf.ca.us/police/newsletters/98spring/sfpdnl31.htm

Lau, Fred H. "Role of Business in Crime Fighting." *San Francisco Chronicle*, May 22, 1996.

San Francisco's Civic Conference Participants - Fred H. Lau, http://206.14.7.53/nsf/civconparticipants.html

LEE, ANG

Gordon, Devin. "It's the Year of the Dragon: With 'Crouching Tiger, Hidden Dragon,' director Ang Lee takes the leap of his career." *Newsweek*, Dec. 4, 2000

The Ice Storm, Twentieth Century Fox, 1997.

"Lee, Ang." *Current Biography*, March 1997.

Lee, Ang. *Eat Drink Man Woman/The Wedding Banquet/Two Films.* Overlook Press, 1994.

The Mr. Showbiz Interview: Ang Lee, http://mrshowbiz.go.com/celebrities /interviews/572_1.html

Rich, B. Ruby. "Gleaners Over Gladiators." *The Nation*, Apr. 9, 2001.

Wang, Huiling, et al. *Crouching Tiger, Hidden Dragon: A Portrait of Ang Lee's Epic Film.* Newmarket Press, 2001.

LEE, BILL LANN

"Bill Lann Lee." *Washington Post*, March 25, 1999 [editorial].

Catanzaro, Michael. "Bill Lann Lee's big victory." *American Spectator*, June 2000.

Kelly, Michael. "Bill Lann Lee: upholder of the loophole?" *Washington Post*, Nov. 13, 1997.

Speeches and Testimony of Senior Members of the Civil Rights Division, http://www.usdoj.gov:80/crt/speeches/

LEE, BRANDON

Baiss, Bridget. *The Crow: The Story Behind the Film*. Oliver Books, 2000.

The Crow, Dimension Home Video, 1994.

Dyson, Cindy. *Brandon Lee (They Died Too Young)*, Chelsea House, 2001.

Harris, Mark, et al. "The brief life and unnecessary death of Brandon Lee." *Entertainment Weekly*, April 16, 1993.

Hoffman, Charles. *Bruce Lee, Brandon Lee, and the Dragon's Curse*. Randon House, 1995.

LEE, BRUCE

Chunovic, Louis, and Linda Lee Cadwell. *Bruce Lee: The Tao of the Dragon Warrior*. St. Martin's Press, 1996.

Dragon: The Bruce Lee Story, Universal Studios, 1993.

Heroic Bloodshed - Bruce Lee Biography, http://www.heroic.addr.com/bruce2.htm

Little, John, ed. *Bruce Lee: Artist of Life*. Charles E. Tuttle, 1999.

Little, John, ed. *Words of the Dragon: Interviews 1958-1973*. Charles E. Tuttle, 1997.

Miller, Davis. *The Tao of Bruce Lee: A Martial Arts Memoir*. Crown, 2000.

LEE, CHANG-RAE

Anisfield-Wolf Book Awards - 2000 Winners: Chang-Rae Lee, http://www.anisfield-wolf.org/lee.htm

Garner, Dwight. "Adopted Voice." *New York Times Book Review*, Sept. 5, 1999.

Lee, Chang-Rae. *A Gesture Life*. Riverhead Books, 1999.

Lee, Chang-Rae. *Native Speaker*. Riverhead Books, 1995.

LEE, JASON SCOTT

Dragon: The Bruce Lee Story, Universal Studios, 1993.

Internet Movie Database: Jason Scott Lee, http://us.imdb.com/M/person-exact?Lee,%20Jason%20Scott

Jason Scott Lee Biography, http://web.singnet.com.sg/~shade/insight4.htm

Krause, Eliza Bergman. "They call him Bruce?" *Premiere*, May 1993.

Tale of the Mummy, Disney Studios, 1999.

LEE, MARY PAIK

Lee, Mary Paik. *Quiet Odyssey: A Pioneer Korean Woman in America.* University of Washington Press, 1990.

Leonard, Karen. "Quiet Odyssey: A Pioneer Korean Woman in America." *Journal of American Ethnic History,* Winter 1993.

Western Women's Autobiographies Database: Mary Paik Lee, http://www.library.csi.cuny.edu/dept/history/lavender/389/pace.html

LEE, SAMMY

Bingham, Walter. "Swimming & diving - pathways to the Olympics." *Sports Illustrated,* Aug 1, 1988.

Dr. Sammy Lee, Olympic Gold Medalist, http://headingeast.vconline.org/sammy.html

Lee, Sammy. *Diving.* Athenium, 1978.

Wampler, Molly Frick. *Not Without Honor: The Story of Sammy Lee.* John Daniel & Company, 1987.

LEE, TSUNG DAO

Biography of T. D. Lee, http://www.nobel.se/physics/laureates/1957/lee-bio.html

Physics Webnet - Tsung Dao Lee, http://www.physicsweb.net/scientist/TDLee.html

Villamil, Kara. "An east-west physicist." *World and I,* May 1998.

LEE, WEN HO

Pincus, Walter. "Interrogation of Lee Raises New Questions, Sources Say." *Washington Post,* Feb. 4, 2001.

Purdy, Matthew, and James Sterngold. "The making of a suspect: the case of Wen Ho Lee." *New York Times,* Feb 4, 2001.

Purdy, Matthew, and James Sterngold. "The prosecution unravels: the case of Wen Ho Lee." *New York Times,* Feb 5, 2001.

Scheer, Robert. "No Defense: How the New York Times Convicted Wen Ho Lee." *The Nation,* Oct 23, 2000.

Wen Ho Lee Home Page, http://wenholee.org/

LEE, YUAN TSEH

Baum, Julain. "Reactive agent: Nobel laureate returns home to stir up a sleepy institution." *Far Eastern Economic Review,* April 6, 1995.

Biography of Yuan Tseh Lee, http://www.nobel.se/chemistry/laureates/1986/lee-bio.html

Normile, Dennis. "Academy Head Touted For Top Political Post." *Science,* March 24, 2000.

"Science and Technology for the 21st Century"; speech by Dr. Yan Tseh Lee, http://www.australia.org.tw/oztech/html/opening/DR%20LEE.htm

LIN, MAYA

Branch, Mark Alden. "Maya Lin: after the wall." *Progressive Architecture*, Aug. 1994.

"Lin, Maya." *Current Biography*, Apr. 1993.

Malone, Mary. *Maya Lin: Architect and Artist*. Enslow Publishers, Inc., 1995 [young adult].

Maya Lin: A Strong Clear Vision. Tapeworm Studio, 1995.

Maya Lin: Notes, Pictures, Online Resources, http://music.acu.edu/www/iawm/pages/lin/lin.html

Maya Lin on the Internet, http://www.artcyclopedia.com/artists/lin_maya.html

LING, LISA

Asia in America - Lisa Ling, http://www.asiainamerica.net/people/lisa.htm

Hirano, Steve. "Media dar-ling" *Transpacific*, June 1994.

Goldsea Asian American Personalities: Lisa Ling, http://goldsea.com/Personalities/Linglisa/linglisa.html

Poniewozik, James. "The View At The Top." *Time*, May 22, 2000.

LIU, LUCY

Charlie's Angels, Columbia/Tristar Studios, 2000.

Krulik, Nancy E., and Nola Thacker. *Angels: The Inside Scoop on the Stars of Charile's Angels*. Alladin Paperbacks, 1997 [young adult].

Mr. Showbiz Celebrities: Lucy Liu Profile, http://mrshowbiz.go.com/celebrities/people/lucyliu/index.html

Ryan, James. "Lucy on the loose." *GQ - Gentlemen's Quarterly*, Nov. 1999.

Weeks, Janet. "Once, twice, three times an angel." *TV Guide*, Oct. 28, 2000.

LOCKE, GARY

Donahue, Bill, et al. "American tale: Washington Governor Gary Locke explores his roots in Jilong, China." *People Weekly*, Nov. 24, 1997.

Egan, Timothy. "When to campaign with color; an Asian-American told his story to whites and won. For black politicians, it's a riskier strategy." *New York Times*, June 20, 2000.

Governor Gary Locke's Home Page, http://www.governor.wa.gov/

Interview with Gary Locke, http://www.waceo.com/archive/oct00/1000-CoverStory-1.html

"Washington State Governor Makes a Splash on Radio, TV Air Waves." *Knight-Ridder/Tribune Business News*, March 25, 2001

MA, YO YO

Blum, David. "A process larger than oneself." *New Yorker*, May 1, 1989.

Blum, David. *Quintet: Five Journeys Toward Musical Fulfillment*. Cornell University Press, 1999.

Handy, Bruce, and Daniel S. Levy. "Yo Yo Ma's suite life." *Time*, March 23, 1998.

Ma, Marina, and John A. Rallo. *My Son, Yo-Yo: A Biography of the Early Years of Yo-Yo Ma*. University of Michigan Press, 1995.

Yo Yo Ma Official Home Page, http://www.yo-yoma.com/

MATSUI, ROBERT

Aaronson, Susan, William Roth, and Robert Matsui, *Trade and the American Dream: A Social History of Postwar Trade Policy*. University Press of Kentucky, 1966.

AsianWeek.com: Feature: Viewpoints: Robert Matsui, http://www.asianweek.com/2000_08_10/feature_viewpt4_matsui.html

Congressman Robert T. Matsui - Calif. 5th District - Home Page, http://www.house.gov/matsui/

"Matsui, Robert T." *Current Biography*, Oct. 1994.

Vita, Matthew. "On Hill, Clinton Turns To Calif. Free-Trader; Matsui Has Key Role on China Legislation." *Washington Post*, April 5, 2000.

MATSUNAGA, SPARK

Matsunaga, Spark. *Rulemakers of the House*. University of Illinois Press, 1976.

Matsunaga, Spark. *The Mars Project: Journeys Beyond the Cold War*. Hill and Wang, 1986.

"Spark M. Matsunaga." *Washington Post*, April 18, 1990 [Editorial].

Spark Matsunaga (1916-1990) Biographical Information, http://bioguide.congress.gov/scripts/biodisplay.pl?index=M000250

MEHTA, ZUBIN

Bookspan, Martin, and Ross Yockey. *Zubin: The Zubin Mehta Story*. Harper & Row, 1978.

Brelis, Dean, and Alma Claiborne. "A quarrel forgiven, maestro Zubin Mehta finds his heart again in a sentimental passage to India." *People Weekly*, Oct. 8, 1984.

Davis, Peter D. "Mehta faces the music." *New York*, Jan 14, 1985.

Sony Classical Artist: Zubin Mehta, http://www.sonyclassical.com/artists/mehta_bio.htm

Zubin Mehta in Rehearsal, Image Entertainment, 1996 [DVD].

MERCHANT, ISMAEL

Long, Robert Emmert. *The Films of Merchant Ivory*. Harry N. Abrams, 1997.

Merchant of Dreams, National Centre for South Asian Studies, 1997.

Merchant, Ismael. *Hullabaloo in Old Jeypore: The Making of The Deceivers*. Viking, 1998.

Meer, Amena. "Ismael Merchant." *Interview*, April 1994.

MIDORI (GOTO)

McLellan, Joseph. "A prodigy grows up; Midori, reaching children with her music." *Washington Post*, Feb. 5, 1993.

"Midori." *Current Biography*, June 1990.

Midori, Live at Carnegie Hall. Sony Classics, 1992 [released on both VHS and audio CD].

Midori Plays Mozart Sinfonia Concertante, Sony Classics, 2001 [audio CD].

Official Midori Home Page, http://www.sonyclassical.com/artists/midori

Schwartz, K. Robert. Glissando: the violinist Midori had sailed through Juilliard and Carnegie Hall by the time she was 18. Now she's practicing the passage to adulthood. *New York Times Magazine*, March 24, 1991.

MIN, ANCHEE

Mesic, Penelope. "Freedom Writer." *Chicago*, Jan. 1994.

Min, Anchee. *Becoming Madame Mao*. Houghton Mifflin, 2000.

Min, Anchee. *Katherine*. Riverhead Books, 1995.

Powell's Book Interviews - Anchee Min, http://www.powells.com/authors/min.html

Questions and Answers with Anchee Min, http://carolinanavy.com/navy/creativewriting/sking/ancheemin/quest.html

MINETA, NORMAN

"A nod to Democrats and Asian-Americans: Transportation nominee Norman Mineta is a party stalwart, though pro- business." *Christian Science Monitor*, Jan 4, 2001.

Norman Y. Mineta, http://www.dot.gov/affairs/mineta.htm

Profile: Norman Mineta, http://abcnews.go.com/sections/politics/DailyNews/profile_mineta.html

Sanchez, Humberto. "DOT's Mineta Has an Agenda, But Now Comes the Hard Part." *The Bond Buyer*, Jan 29, 2001.

Schindehette, Susan. "The wounds of war; a California Congressman recalls the trauma of World War II internment." *People Weekly*, Dec. 14, 1987.

MING, JENNY

"A savvy captain for Old Navy." *Business Week*, Nov. 8, 1999.

Getting to Know Jenny Ming from Old Navy, http://www.mhhe.com/business/busadmin/nickels_6_ub/graphics/nickels6ub/common/ch_01.pdf

"Old Navy's Skipper: Jenny Ming heads Gap Inc.owned Old Navy Clothing Co." *Business Week*, Jan 10, 2000.

MINK, PATSY

Davidson, Sue. *A Heart in Politics: Jeannette Rankin and Patsy T. Mink*. Seal Press, 1994 [young adult].

Mayer, Caroline E. "Getting personal on product liability; two lawmakers' opposing views stem form their own painful experiences." *Washington Post*, March 7, 1995.

Mink, Patsy Takemoto (1927-), http://bioguide.congress.gov/scripts/biodisplay .pl?index=M000797

Website of Representative Patsy T. Mink, http://www.house.gov/mink

MORITA, PAT

Kenny, Glenn. "He's got sage presence: movie martial arts master Pat Morita." *Entertainment Weekly*, Dec. 22, 1995.

The Next Karate Kid. Columbia/Tristar Studios, 1994.

Noriyuki Pat Morita: In the Footsteps of a Sensei, http://www.furyu.com/archives /issue6/Morita.html

Pat Morita Biography, http://us.imdb.com/Bio?Morita,+Pat

MOW, WILLIAM

Bugle Boy, Founded by RPI Alumnus William Mow, Files for Bankrupcy, http://www.rcnj.org/alumni_news/2001/02/02/2042228.shtml

Spevak, Rachel. "Mow to acquire Nesi's stock in Bugle Boy Industries." *Daily News Record*, Aug 29, 1995.

William C. Mow 1995 Distinguished Engineering Alumni - Purdue University, http://www.ecn.purdue.edu/ECN/DEA/1995/William_C_W_Mow

William Mow '63 Entrepreneur of Rensselaer, http://scte.mgmt.rpi.edu /entrepreneurs/mow.html

MUKHERJEE, BHARATI

Alam, Fakrul. *Bharati Mukherjee*. Twayne, 1995.

Mukherjee, Bharati. *Holder of the World*. Alfred A. Knopf, 1993.

Mukherjee, Bharati. *Jasmine*. Grove Weidenfeld, 1989.

Steinberg, Sybil. "Bharati Mukherjee; a series of novels and short stories reflect her own experiences as a clear-eyed but affectionate immigrant in American society." *Publishers Weekly*, August 25, 1989.

Voices From the Gaps: Bharati Mukherjee, http://voices.cla.umn.edu/authors /bharatimukherjee.html

NATORI, JOSIE

Fragrance Foundation - Josie Natori, http://fragrance.org/FTforum_josie.html

Goodman, Wendy. "Paris ensemble; lingerie designer Josie Natori teams up with Jacques Grange to decorate her grand pied-a-tierre on the rue Francois-1er." *House & Garden*, Sept. 1990.

"Josie Natori: queen of the night(gown)." *Cosmopolitan*, Dec. 1991.

Willen, Janet L. "Fashioning a Business." *Nation's Business*, Feb. 1995.

Woman to Watch: Women.com Interview Josie Natori, http://www.women.com /career/natori.html?a42

NGOR, HAING

Biography for Haing S. Ngor, http://us.imdb.com/Bio?Ngor,+Haing+S

Hewitt, Bill. "Journey's End." *People Weekly*, March 11, 1996.

The Killing Fields, Warner Studios, 1984.

Ngor, Haing, with Roger Warner. *A Cambodian Odyssey*. Macmillan, 1987.

Wilkinson, Alec. "The good doctor: remembering an evening with Dr. Haing S. Ngor." *New Yorker*, March 11, 1996.

NGUYEN, DUSTIN

About Dustin, http://H.T.Ioki.tripod.com/Dustin/About_Dustin.htm

Dustin Nguyen Filmography, http://us.imdb.com/Name?Nguyen,+Dustin

No Escape, No Return, Pm Entertainment, 1993.

Siegler, Bonnie. "Lean—But Not So Mean—Fighting Maching." *American Fitness*, Jan 2000.

Vespa, Mary. "A survivor of the fall of Saigon, 21 Jump Street's Dustin Nguyen re-lives the ordeal on TV." *People Weekly*, April 25, 1988.

NOGUCHI, ISAMU

Hakutani, Yoshinobu. "Father and son: a conversation with Isamu Noguchi." *Journal of Modern Literature*, Summer 1990.

Hunter, Sam, et al. *Isamu Noguchi*. University of Washington Press, 2000.

Isamu Noguchi, Public Media, Inc., 1990.

Isamu Noguchi on the Internet, http://www.artcyclopedia.com/artists/noguchi_isamu.html

Kornbluth, Jesse. "Noguchi does it his way: the sculptor's new museum." *New York*, May 20, 1985.

Maeda, Robert J. "Isamu Noguchi: 5-7-A, Poston, Arizona." *Amerasia Journal*, Spring 1994.

Tracy, Robert. *Spaces of the Mind: Isamu Noguchi's Dance Design*. Limelight Editions, 2001.

ONIZUKA, ELLISON S.

Anderson, Jack, and Dale Van Atta. "Ellison Onizuka's dream." *Washington Post*, Feb. 9, 1986.

Astronaut Bio: Ellison Onizuka, http://www.jsc.nasa.gov/Bios/htmlbios/onizuka.html

Bartlett, Tony. "Kona's Space Center museum dedicated to Challenger astronaut." *Travel Weekly*, May 25, 1992.

Ellison S. Onizuka, Mission Specialist/Challenger STS, 51-L,http://www.challenger.org/cc/cc_body_51onizuka.htm

ONO, YOKO

Cott, Jonathan, ed. *The Ballad of John and Yoko*. Doubleday, 1982.

Interview with Yoko One, http://www.best.com/~abbeyrd/yoko.htm

Kimmelman, Michael. "Yoko Ono: painter, sculptor, musician, muse." *New York Times*, Oct. 27, 2000.

Ono, Yoko. *Grapefruit: A Book of Instructions and Drawings*. Simon & Schuster, 2000.

Ono, Yoko. *Instruction Paintings*. Weatherhill, 1995.

Ono, Yoko, et al. *Y E S Yoko Ono*. Harry N. Abrams, 2000.

Onoweb, http://www.metatronpress.com/onoweb/

OZAWA, SEIJI

"Seiji Ozawa." *Current Biography*, July 1998.

Seiji Ozawa: Russian Night, View Video, 1996.

Smedvig, Caroline, ed. *Seiji: An Intimate Portrait of Seiji Ozawa, Music Director of the Boston Symphony Orchestra*. Houghton Mifflin, 1998.

Sony Classical Artist: Ozawa, Seiji, http://www.sonyclassical.com/artists/ozawa/

Tan, Sheri. *Seiji Ozawa*.

PAIK, NAM JUNE

Denison, D. C. "Video's art guru." *New York Times Magazine*, April 25, 1982.

Hanhardt, John G., et al. *The Worlds of Nam June Paik*. Harry N. Abrams, 2000.

Joselit, David. "Planet Paik." *Art in America*, June 2000.

Nam June Paik on the Internet, http://www.artcyclopedia.com/artists/paik_nam_june.html

Paik, Nam June. *Fluxus/Video*. Verlag der Buchhandlung Walther Konig, 2000.

PEI, I.M.

Forgey, Benjamin. "Just one look is all it took." *Washington Post*, Aug. 27, 1995.

I.M. Pei: First Person Singular, PBS Home Video, 1997.

I.M. Pei - Great Buildings Online, http://www.greatbuildings.com/architects/I._M._Pei.html

"Pei, Ieoh Ming." *Current Biography*, March 1990.

Von Boehm, Gerald. *Conversations With I.M. Pei: Light Is the Key*. Prestel USA, 2000.

Wiseman, Carter. *I.M. Pei: A Profile in American Architecture*. Harry N. Abrams, 2001.

PRAN, DITH

Bachman, S.L. "Holocaust survivor on a crusade to remember, avenge deaths of 1 million Cambodians in Khmer Rouge." *Knight-Ridder/Tribune News Service*, Feb 15, 1994.

Dith Pran's Biography, http://www.dithpran.org/dithbio.htm

Pran, Dith, et al. *Children of Cambodia's Killing Fields: Memoirs by Survivors.* Yale University Press, 1997.

Schanberg, Sidney H. *The death and life of Dith Pran.* Penguin, 1985.

SAIKI, PATRICIA

Brown, Warren. "Senate confirms Saiki as SBA's new administrator." *Washington Post*, March 25, 1991.

Saiki, Patricia Fukuda, 1930- , http://bioguide.congress.gov/scripts/biodisplay .pl?index=S000014

Saddler, Jeanne. "SBA's Saiki grapples with agency's high-profile ills; already, new chief is credited with boosting morale at the 'rat hole.'" *Wall Street Journal*, May 13, 1991.

Wood, Bill. "Why CEOs don't run for governor." *Hawaii Business*, Oct. 1997.

Wood, Donna B. "GOP has rare shot in Hawaii governor race." *Christian Science Monitor*, Sept. 23, 1994.

SAUND, DALIP SINGH

Congressman Saund - The First Native of Asia, http://www.la-indiacenter.com/page10.htm

Marvis, Barbara J. *Contemporary American Success Stories: Famous People of Asian Ancestry: Dalip Singh Saund; Patsy T. Mink; Daniel Ken Inouye; Yoshiko Uchida; Haing ngo.* Mitchell Lane, 1993.

Saund, Dalip Singh. *Congressman From India.* Dutton, 1960.

Saund, Dalip Singh. *My Mother India.* Pacific Coast Khalsa Diwan, 1930.

Saund, Dalip Singh, 1899-1973, http://bioguide.congress.gov/scripts/biodisplay .pl?index=S000075

SHENG, BRIGHT

Bright Sheng - Biography, http://www.schirmer.com/composers/sheng_bio.html

Bright Sheng: Flute Moon/China Dreams/Postcards. Bis, 2000 [audio CD].

Cameron, Lindsay. "At home in two worlds." *New York Times*, Feb. 16, 1997.

Hanson, Henry. "Lyric composer pens terror of life in China." *Chicago*, Jan. 1991.

The Song of Majnun, Delos, 1997 [audio CD].

SIDWHA, BAPSI

Dhawan, R.K, and Novy Kapadi, eds. *Novels of Bapsi Sidwha*. South Asia Books, 1997.

Homepage of Bapsi Sidwha, http://hometown.aol.com/bsidhwa

Sidwha, Bapsi. *An American Brat*. Milkweed, 1993.

Sidwha, Bapsi. *The Bride*. St. Martins Press, 1983.

Sidwha, Bapsi. *Cracking India: A Novel*. Milkweed Editions, 1992.

SHINSEKI, ERIC

Biography - Chief of Staff Shinseki, http://www.army.mil/csa/bio.htm

Frontline Interview: General Eric K. Shinseki, http://www.pbs.org/wgbh/pages /frontline/shows/future/interviews/shinseki.html

"New chiefs are chosen for Army and Marines." *New York Times*, April 22, 1999.

Ricks, Thomas E. "For today's Army, suffering an identity crisis, choice of new chief assumes larger significance." *Wall Street Journal*, March 3, 1999.

SHYAMALAN, M. NIGHT

Interview with M. Night Shyamalan, http://www.creativescreenwriting.com /interviews/Shyamalian10,09,99.html

Lerangis, Peter, and M. Night Shyamalan. *The Sixth Sense*. March 2000 [young adult].

M. Night Shyamalan, http://us.imdb.com/Name?Shyamalan,+M.+Night

Patel, Roxanne. "Day for Night." *Philadelphia Magazine*, March 1998.

The Sixth Sense. Walt Disney Home Video, 1999.

Sunshine Linda, and M. Night Shyamalan, eds. *Stuart Little: The Movie and the Moviemakers, The Illustrated Story Behind the Amazing Film*. Newmarket Press, 2000.

SUGIERA, KANEMATSU

Kanematsu Sugiera in *Dictionary of American Biography*, Supplement 10, pp. 768–770. Charles Scribner's Sons, 1995.

Moss, Ralph. *The Cancer Industry*. Equinox Press, 1996.

Remembering Dr. Sugiera, http://www.ralphmoss.com/sugiura.html

SUI, ANNA

Anna Sui offical website, http://www.annasui.com/

Sitbon, Martine. "Oui, Sui!" *Interview*, May 1999.

Spindler, Amy M. "Behind the seams." *New York Times Magazine*, Nov. 14, 1999.

"Sui, Anna." *Current Biography*, July 1993.

Vogue Biography - Anna Sui, http://www.vogue.co.uk/content/ie4/295/356575-0-1-1.html

TABUCHI, SHOJI

Goldsea Asian American Persoanlities - Shoji Tabuchi, http://goldsea.com/Personalities/Tabuchi/tabuchi4.html

Graham, Ellen. "Word-of-mouth creates an idol; without benefit of TV, fiddler Shoji Tabuchi is a star in Missouri." *Wall Street Journal*, June 1, 1999.

Shoji Tabuchi official website, http://www.shoji.com/

TAKAKI, RONALD

A conversation with Ronald Takaki, http://www.ascd.org/readingroom/edlead/9904/exthalford.html

An interview with Ronald Takaki, http://dolphin.upenn.edu/~mosaic/spring95/page16.html

McDowell, Edwin. "Return of the native." *New York Times Magazine*, Nov. 6, 1983.

Mooney, Carolyn J. "A 'stranger from a different shore' recounts the little-known history of Asian Americans." *Chronicle of Higher Education*, Oct. 11, 1989.

Takaki, Ronald. *Double Victory: A Multicultural History of America in World War II*. Little, Brown and Co., 2000.

Takaki, Ronald. *Iron Cages: Race and Culture in 19th-Century America*. Alfred A. Knopf, 1989.

TAKEI, GEORGE

George Takei official website, http://www.georgetakei.com/

Graf, L. A. *Star Trek: Envoy (A Captain Sulu Adventure)*. Simon & Schuster, 1995 [audio cassette]; 1999 [audio CD].

Hersh, Amy. "Author, actors of 'The Wash' on role models, roadblocks & Sulu." *Back Stage*, Nov. 2, 1990.

Takei, George. *To the Stars: The Autobiography of George Takei, Star Trek's Mr. Sulu*. Pocket Books, 1994.

TAN, AMY

An Interview with Amy Tan, http://dolphin.upenn.edu/~mosaic/fall94/page15.html

Bloom, Harold, ed. *Amy Tan*. Chelsea House, 2000.

"Tan, Amy." *Current Biography*, Feb. 1992.

Tan, Amy. *The Bonesetter's Daughter*. Putnam, 2001.

Tan, Amy. *The Joy Luck Club*. Putnam, 1989.

Voices From the Gaps: Amy Tan, http://voices.cla.umn.edu/authors/AmyTan.html

TIEN, CHANG-LIN

Chang-Lin Tien Biography,
http://www.glue.umd.edu/afs/glue.umd.edu/home/enme/faculty/balab/pub
/lectures/1997-98/lecture3.html

Tien, Chang-Lin, ed. *Annual Review of Heat Transfer*. Begell House, 1990- [series].

James, Mary. "UC Berkeley's Chang-Lin Tien: he's got to tell thousands of A students they aren't good enough." *California*, Jan. 1991.

Shao, Maria. "He's seen our future, and. . . ." *World Monitor: The Christian Science Monitor Monthly*, July 1992.

TING, SAMUEL CHAO CHUNG

Autobiography of Samuel Chao Chung Ting, http://www.nobel.se/physics
/laureates/1976/ting-autobio.html

Samuel Chao Chung Ting in *Distinguished Asian-Americans: A Biographical Dictionary*, pp. 341-342. Greenwood Press, 1999.

Sawyer, Kathy. "A physicist finds space station has a certain magnetic pull; 'Dark Matter' hunt shows scorn giving way to research." *Washington Post*, Dec 30, 2000.

Schecter, Bruce. "The once and future Ting." *Omni*, July 1981.

TRINH, EUGENE HUU-CHAU

Eugene H. Trinh Professional History and Education,
http://www.eng.yale.edu/news/dist_lecturer/trinh.htm

Payload Specialist Bio: Eugene H. Trinh, http://www.jsc.nasa.gov/Bios/PS/trinh.html

"Vietnamese named to mission." *New York Times*, March 4, 1991.

TSUI, DANIEL C.

Browne, Malcolm W. "5 quantum theorists share 2 Nobel prizes in sciences." *New York Times*, Oct. 14, 1998.

Daniel C. Tsui Biography [includes list of published works], http://www.ee
.princeton.edu/bios/tsuibio.html

Nobel Prize in Physics, Co-Awarded to Researcher Professor Daniel Tsui,
http://www.poem.princeton.edu/news/cui/cui.html

Quan, Margaret. "Nobel prize in physics goes to 3 Bell Labs scientists." *Electronic Engineering Times*, Oct. 19, 1998.

WANG, AN

Berney, Karen. "An Wang: getting to the essentials." *Nation's Business*, Dec. 1987.

Connolly, James. "An Wang says entrepreneurial road has become tougher: reflects on triumphs, errors of 35-year career." *Computerworld*, Nov. 3, 1986.

"An interview with Dr. Wang." *Patty Seybold's Office Systems Report*, May 5, 1986.

Marvis, Barbara J. *Contemporary American Success Stories: Famous People of Asian Ancestry: Pat Suzuki; Minoru Yamasaki; An Wang; Conni E Chung; Carlos Bulosan.* Mitchell Lane, 1993.

"Wang, An." *Current Biography*, Jan. 1987.

WANG, CHARLES

Computer Associates - Press Center - Executive Bios - Charles B. Wang, http://www.cai.com/press/bios/cbw_bio.htm

Eastwood, Allison. "CA's straight-talking CEO: a profile of Charles Wang." *Computing Canada*, Aug. 4, 1992.

Goldsea 100, No 1: Charles Wang, http://goldsea.com/Profiles/100/wangcharles.html

Royal, Weld. "The Global Marketer." *Sales & Marketing Management*, May 1999.

Wang, Charles B. *Techno Vision: An Executive's Survival Guide to Understanding and Managing Information.* McGraw-Hill, 1994 [revised 1997].

WANG, GARRETT

First Garrett Wang Fansite, http://www.osprey.net/~kira/gbio.html

"Garrett Wang" [50 Most Beautiful People]. *People Weekly*, May 12, 1997.

Garrett Wang Online, http://ensignkim310.tripod.com/

Hundred Percent, I Can Make It Myself Productions, 1997.

Ivory Tower, Vanguard Films, 1997.

WANG, VERA

AsianWeek: Main Feature: Vera Wang Bringing Style to the Bay, http://www.asianweek.com/2000_05_18/feature_verawang.html

Sporkin, Elizabeth M. "Wedding belle: when the glitterati get the urge to merge, they flock to bridal expert Vera Wang." *People Weekly*, July 8, 1991.

Strongwater, Peter. "The bride wore Wang." *Interview*, Dec. 1990.

Vera Wang offical website, http://www.verawang.com/

Wang, Vera. "Nostalgia." *Vogue*, March 2001.

Witchel, Alex. "Vera Wang." *New York Times Magazine*, June 19, 1994.

WANG, WAYNE

Chinese Box, Vidmark/Trimark Studio, 1998.

Lu, Alvin. "Invisible cities: Wayne Wang." *Film Comment*, July-Aug. 1998.

Mark, Diane, ed., and Wayne Wang. *Chan Is Missing: A Film.* Bamboo Ridge Press, 1984.

Reichl, Ruth. "Chan is Missing but Wayne Wang is back; with a new wife and a new movie." *San Francisco*, Oct. 1983.

"Wayne Wang Interview." *Literature Film Quarterly*, Vol. XXII, 1994.

WONG, ANNA MAY

Anna May Wong Profile,
http://www.mdle.com/ClassicFilms/FeaturedStar/star49.htm

Okrent, Neil. "Right place, Wong time: why Hollywood's first Asian star, Anna May Wong, died a thousand movie deaths." *Los Angeles Magazine*, May 1990.

Shanghai Express, Universal Studios, 1932 [VHS release 1993].

The Thief of Bagdad (1924), Image Entertainment, 1985 [VHS]; 1998 [DVD].

WONG, B. D.

B.D. Wong Filmography, http://us.imdb.com/Name?Wong, +B.D.

Mulan, Disney Studios, 1998.

Online Directory of Asian Pacific American Artists: B. D. Wong, http://www.public.asu.edu/~dejesus/210entries/bdwong/bdwong.htm

Raymond, Gerard. "B.D. Wong." *Premiere*, Dec. 1991.

Stiff, Ellen. "The metamorphosis of B.D. Wong." *GQ - Gentlemen's Quarterly*, May 1989.

WONG, RUSSELL

Darling, Cary. "Russell Wong brings another view of Asian-American life to weekly TV." *Knight/Ridder News Service*, Jan 13, 1995.

Official Russell Wong Web Site, http://www.russellwong.com/

Romeo Must Die, Warner Studios, 2000.

Sengupta, Somini. "Charlie Chan, retooled for the 90's." *New York Times*, Jan 5, 1997.

Yoo, Paula. "No more Mr. White Guy." *People Weekly*, Feb. 24, 1997.

WONG-STAAL, FLOSSIE

Alvarez, Emilio, and Anne Crystal Angeles. "Science Superstar." *National Geographic World*, June 1993.

Coghlan, Andy. "Controlled Infection." *New Scientist*, June 17, 2000.

Fikes, Bradley J. "In fight against AIDS, she tries to win one for humanity: first to decipher the HIV virus, Flossie Wong-Staal remains a vital asset to San Diego's scientific research community." *San Diego Business Journal*, June 15, 1992.

Flossie Wong-Staal,
http://www-biology.ucsd.edu/shadow/sa/newbrochure/wong-staal.html

Gallo, Robert C., and Flossie Wong-Staal. *Retrovirus Biology and Human Disease.* Marcel Dekker, 1989.

WOODS, TIGER

Feinstein, John. *The First Coming: Tiger Woods: Master or Martyr?* Ballantine Books, 1998.

Rosaforte, Tim. *Raising the Bar: The Championship Years of Tiger Woods*. St. Martin's Press, 2000.

Strege, John. *Tiger: A Biography of Tiger Woods*. Broadway Books, 1998.

Tiger Woods - The Heart of a Champion, Goldhill Home Media, 2000.

Tiger Woods Official Golf Website, http://www.tigerwoods.com

Woods, Earl. *Training a Tiger: A Father's Account of How to Raise a Winner in Both Golf and Life*. Harpercollins, 1997.

"Woods, Tiger." *Current Biography*, Nov. 1997.

WU, CHEIN-SHIUNG

Chien-Shiung Wu 1912-1997, http://www.physics.ucla.edu/~;cwp/Phase2/Wu,_Chien_Shiung@841234567.html

Dicke, William. "Chien-Shiung Wu, 84, dies; top experimental physicist." *New York Times*, Feb. 18, 1997.

Dr. Chien-Shiung Wu, http://www.nstm.gov.tw/nobel/evip/evip_wujs.htm

Wu, Chien-Shiung, and S.A. Moszkowski. *Beta Decay*. Interscience Publishers, 1966.

WU, DAVID

Barnett, Jeff, and Jim Manning. "U.S. Lawmaker Votes against China Trade Status despite Impact on Nike." *Knight-Ridder/Tribune Business News*, July 29, 1999.

Nichols, John. "The Nation Dozen." *The Nation*, Oct. 30, 2000.

Office of Congressman David Wu, Oregon, http://www.house.gov/w

YAMAGUCHI, KRISTI

"A skating sprite with a towering talent, Kristi Yamaguchi wants to ice the world title." *People Weekly*, March 20, 1989.

Kristi Yamaguchi: Triumph On Ice. Andrews McMeel Publishing, 2000.

Kristi Yamaguchi Web Page, http://www.polaris.net/˜shanhew/

"Yamaguchi, Kristi." *Current Biography*, June 1992.

Yamaguchi, Kristi, et al. *Figure Skating for Dummies*. Hungry Minds, Inc. 1997.

YAMASAKI, MINORU

Doumato, Lamia. *Minoru Yamasaki*. Vance Bibliographies, 1986.

Marvis, Barbara J. *Contemporary American Success Stories : Famous People of Asian Ancestry: Pat Suzuki; Minoru Yamasaki; An Wang; Conni E Chung; Carlos Bulosan*. Mitchell Lane, 1993.

Oral History Interview with Minoru Yamasaki, http://artarchives.si.edu/oralhist/yamasa59.htm

Yamasaki, Minoru. *A Life in Architecture*. Weatherhill, 1979.

YAN, MARTIN

Martin Yan Interview,
http://www.globalgourmet.com/food/egg/egg0296/yan0296.html

McGurn, William. "American TV chef brings his wok to Asia." *Far Eastern Economic Review*, Nov. 25, 1993.

Yan Can Cook Official Website, http://www.asianconnections.com/yancancook/

Yan, Martin. *Martin Yan's Feast: The Best of Yan Can Cook*. Kqed, 1998.

Yan, Martin. *Martin Yan's Invitation to Chinese Cooking*. Bay Books, 2000.

Yan, Martin. *The Well-Seasoned Wok*. Fine Communications, 1998.

YANG, CHEN NING.

Biography of Chen Ning Yan,
http://www.nobel.se/physics/laureates/1957/yang-bio.html

Chen Ning Yang Home Page, http://www.physics.sunysb.edu/~yang/

"President Awards National Medals of Science." *Physics Today*, July 1986.

YANG, JERRY

Deutschmann, Alan. "Yahoo's secret weapon." *GQ - Gentlemen's Quarterly*, Oct. 1999.

Goodell, Jeff. "Jerry Yang." *Rolling Stone*, March 30, 2000.

Sherman, Joseph. *Jerry Yang and David Filo: Chief Yahoos of Yahoo*. Twenty First Century Books, 2001 [young adult].

"Yang, Jerry." *Current Biography*, Oct. 1997.

YEP, LAWRENCE

Yep, Lawrence. *The Mark Twain Murders*. Four Winds Press, 1982.

Yep, Lawrence. *Seademons*. Perennial, 1979.

Yep, Lawrence. *Tiger Woman*. Bridgewater Books, 1995.

Yep, Lawrence - Educational Paperback Association,
http://www.edupaperback.org/authorbios/Yep_Laurence.html

Yep Page, http://www.scils.rutgers.edu/special/kay/yep.html

ZAKARIA, FAREED

Bumiller, Elisabeth. "At 34, worldly-wise and on his way up." *New York Times*, Sept. 24, 1999.

Fareed Zakaria Profile, http://www.saja.org/zakaria.html

Hoge, James F., Jr., and Fareed Zakaria, eds. *The American Encounter: The United States and the Making of the Modern World: Essays from 75 Years of Foreign Affairs*. Basic Books, 1997.

Zakaria, Fareed. *From Wealth to Power: The Unusual Origins of America's World Role*. Princeton University Press, 1998.

Zakaria, Fareed. "Will Asia Turn Against the West?" *New York Times*, July 10, 1998.

acidity amount of acid in a particular object or thing.

acquiesce submit or agree.

acumen skill.

aegis sponsorship.

aesthetic having a particular sensitivity and affection for a particular art.

affirmative action government policy of reserving a set number of positions in the workplace, schools, or other areas for minorities.

adjunct professor a member of a university faculty who is not a full-time or tenured professor.

adjutant staff officer in the military who assists a commanding officer.

Agent Orange an herbicide used widely in the Vietnam War to clear foiliage; contains dioxin as a contaminant.

allegory expressing generalizations or truths of human experience through symbolic fictional figures.

alma mater a school, college, or university which one has attended or graduated.

apartheid an official policy of segregation and inequality against non-European groups in South Africa.

apostle believer and advocate.

atheist individual who does not believe in the existence of God.

auspices kindly patronage and support.

avant garde a group of intelligentsia that develops new concepts in art or literature.

Ayurvedic medicine the ancient Indian doctrine of physical and mental well-being are interrelated; ayurvedic is a Sanskrit word meaning "life science."

bacteriology the study of bacteria.

Bard nickname for William Shakespeare; a writer of heroic, epic verse.

bilingual the ability to speak two language fluently.

binary something made of two parts or things.

bohemian person living an unconventional lifestyle, usually in a community of like-minded people.

bourgeois relating to or characterization of the middle social class.

Brahmin a Hindu of the highest social state.

briefs documents submitted by attorneys to a court of law explaining and arguing their side of a particular case before that court.

Bronze Star a United States military medal awarded for heroic or meritorious service to the nation not involving aerial flights.

Buddhist individual practicing the religion of Buddhism, a religion of central and eastern Asia derived from the teachings of Gautama Buddha; the central tenent is that suffering is inherent in life, and that one is relieved from suffering by moral and mental self-purification.

bureaucracy the organization of non-elected government workers and officials.

burgeoning growing.

Cantonese the dialect of Chinese spoken in and around Canton.

chemotherapy the use of chemical agents in treating a serious physical or mental illness.

cerebral edema an abnormal accumulation of serous fluid in the brain.

cholera any of a range of diseases in humans and domestic animals usually characterized by severe gastrointestinal problems.

Christianity the religion derived from the teachings of Jesus Christ, based on the Holy Bible of scriptures.

clique a group of people with particular commonalities who regularly associate with one another.

communist an advocate or supporter of communism, a system in theory in which property and goods are owned collectively and distributed equally.

concubine a woman living with a man to whom she is not legally married.

Congregationalist member of a body of Protestant churches deriving from the 17th century English Independents, supporting local autonomy of churches.

conjoined brought together so as to meet, touch, or overlap.

constituency group of people to whom an elected official is beholden.

coolie an unskilled laborer or porter, usually in or from the Far East and hired for low wages.

contemporary modern.

convalescing recuperating; recovering from an injury or illness.

cum laude graduating from an educational institution with distinction.

derisive mocking; taunting.

dissidence disagreement; dissent.

Distinguished Service Cross U.S. Army medal awarded for extraordinary heroism during action against an armed enemy.

Distinguished Service Medal United States military medal awarded for exceptional service to the nation during war.

dojo a training school for various martial arts.

doughty marked by fearless resolution.

draconian cruel measures.

dragooned to force or attempt to force; to coerce.

dramatis personae characters in a play or production.

eastern bloc nations group of eastern European nations under Soviet rule during the Cold War such as East Germany, Poland, and Czechoslovakia.

eclectic encompassing a variety of categories into one entity.

egalitarianism belief in human equality with respect to social, economic, and political rights.

elope to secretly run away with the intention of marrying, usually without parental consent.

emcee master of ceremonies at a performance or event.

emeritus holding an honorary title in retirement.

eminent premier.

endocrinology the science dealing with the endocrine glands.

entreaty plea; urgent request.

entreprenuer individual who manages, organizes, and assumes the risk of a business or enterprise venture.

enzyme any of numerous complex proteins produced by living cells and catalyze specific bio-chemical reactions at body temperatures.

epithets disparaging or insulting words or phrases.

equipoise state of balance; equilibrium.

espionage the practice of spying to obtain information about plans and activities, especially of foreign and/or enemy governments and nations.

ethereal unworldy; spiritual.

ethos the moral sentiment or characteristics that set a group or individual apart.

etudes pieces of music used for the practice of technique.

evocation imaginative re-creation.

exitentialist an adherent of exitentialism, a philosophical movement that embraces various doctrines but centers on the individual existence in the unfathomable universe and the plight of individuals who must act without truly knowing what is right and wrong.

extra vehicular activity work space shuttle astronauts perform in space outside of the shuttle, such as a spacewalk.

fealty fidelity; obligation.

feigning faking; impersonating.

fiber optics a branch of physics based on the transfer of light through transparent fibers of glass or plastic.

fledgling one that is new or inexperienced to a particular subject or craft.

fluid dynamics a branch of engineering concerned with the study of aerodynamics, the forces on an object moving through the air.

fluid mechanics the study of the motion of liquid or gas fluids and the physics upon that motion.

freelancer an independent agent available for hire and not affiliated with or bound by a single entity.

funerary associated with burial.

furlough limited release from an organized institution or group.

Gaelic of or relating to the language of and speech of the Celts in Ireland, the Isle of Man, and the Scottish Highlands.

genre style or category of form and content.

Grammy annual award given in various categories for excellence in the music recording industry.

guerrilla one who engages in irregular warfare tactics, especially as a member of an independent unit.

gypsy an individual who lives somewhat of a nomadic life.

hemophiliacs an individual afflicted with hemophilia, a blood defect in males marked by delayed blood clotting and difficulty controlling hemorrhages.

hieroglyph character in a system of writing depicted in pictures or codes.

holistic concerned with wholes or complete systems instead of analysis of parts.

immunology the science of the causes of immunity and immunity repsonses.

inchoate partly in existence.

indentured bound to perform a particular service for a fixed amount of time.

indicted state of standing formally accused of an offense by a judicial process known as a grand jury.

injunction official court order commanding an individual or entity to cease a particular act.

insidious subtle.

ion a charged atom that has either gained or lost electrons.

Islam religious faith of Muslims that includes belief in Allah as the sole deity and Muhammad as his prophet.

isotopes any of two or more species atoms of a chemical element with the same position on the periodic table and atomic number, and virtually the same chemical behavior, though with differing atomic mass and physical properties.

issei first generation Japanese immigrant to the United States.

jam improvisational playing by musicians who may not be familiar with one another.

japes mocking or humorous statements.

jazz American muscial form derived from ragtime and blues; marked by syncopated rhythms and ensemble playing, improvisation, and deliberate changes of pitch and timbre.

Jesuit member of a Roman Catholic society founded by St. Ignatius Loyola in 1534; devoted to educational and missionary work.

judo a marital art developed from jujitsu that emphasizes quick movement and leverage against an opponent.

jujitsu an art of fighting without weapons using holds, throws, and paralyzing blows to disable or subdue an opponent.

juris doctorate title conferred upon graduates of law school.

kendo a Japanese sport of fencing with bamboo swords.

Khmer the official language of Cambodia.

kimono a traditional Japanese long robe with wide sleeves and worn with a broad sash.

kitschy appealing to somewhat lowbrow or popular taste in poor quality.

Legion of Merit United States military medal awarded for exceptionally meritorious conduct in the performance of outstanding services.

linguistics the study of language.

lowbrow not highly cultivated or cultured.

machine in politics, the organization of a political party usually controlled by one person or group through which strategy is made and patronage given.

magna cum laude graduating from an educational institution with highest distinction.

mah-jongg a game of Chinese origin played by four persons with 144 tiles that are drawn and discarded until one player has a winning hand.

majority leader individual elected by colleagues as the leader of the party with the most members among a group of elected representatives of a legislative body.

McCarthyism period of time during the 1950s when U.S. senator Joseph McCarthy of Wisconsin sought to identify and eliminate suspected communists from the United States government, as well as the entertainment industry, and other facets of life.

methotrexate a toxic anticancer drug.

microgravity the condition in outer space; also called zero gravity of weightlessness.

midwifery the art of assisting in childbirth.

milieu setting.

missionaries representatives of a particular religion in a foreign land, seeking to win converts.

moniker label; name given by others.

moratorium a legally authorized period of delay in the performance of a legal obligation or payment of debt.

NAFTA North American Free Trade Agreement; a treaty involving the United States, Mexico, and Canada.

nascent new; just beginning.

nickelodeon movie theater to which admission for a show was five cents.

nisei children of the issei.

novella a story with a pointed and compact plot.

nucleic acids any of various acids composed of a sugar or derivative of a sugar.

obstetrics a branch of medical science dealing with birth.

offensive line line of blockers in American football who help advance the ball by blocking for the quarterback and running backs.

Parsi a descendent of Persian refugees principally settled in Bombay.

patron finanacial supporter.

paucity small quantity.

pedestrian commonplace.

persona non grata Spanish phrase characterizing the least desireable person in a group.

pharmacology the science of drugs.

philanthropic generous; charitable.

pittance a small amount or portion.

plaudits praise.

polymer a mixture of chemical compounds formed by a reaction and consisting of competing structural units.

post traumatic stress syndrome a condition common among veterans of war; recurring nightmares, images, and memories of the brutality and horror of combat.

precocious extremely intelligent or talented at a young age.

probable cause legal phrase signifying a reasonable ground for supposing a criminal charge is well founded.

prodigies unusually precocious and gifted children or young people.

propagandistic description of government-sponsored opinion-shaping methods.

prosody the study of versification.

prospectus a printed proposal describing a potential business enterprise.

protagonist the main character in a story.

Purple Heart United States military medal awarded to individuals wounded or killed in combat during the service of the nation.

purview the range or limit of one's authority to act.

quark a hypothetical particle that carries a fractional electric charge.

rapacity ability to plunder or grasp excessively.

refuge a safe escape or retreat.

repertoire a supply of skills of an individual performer.

routers powerful computers responsible for traffic on the Internet.

rudimentary primitive.

salvos spirited verbal attacks.

Samurai Japanese warrior aristocracy.

Sanskrit an ancient language that is the classic language of India and Hinduism.

sarin an extremely toxic chemical warfare agent.

satire literary work holding human folly to humorous irony or ridicule.

semiconductor any of a class of solids whose electrical conductivity is between that of a conductor and an insulator in being almost as great as that of a metal at high temperatures.

seminal beginning.

Siamese twins congenitally joined twins among man or lower animals.

siphoned drawing something off another source.

sorties missions, usually associated with military affairs.

spectroscopy the production and investigation of a spectra.

Sputnik Soviet satellite launched into orbit around the Earth in 1957, causing alarm among United States officials that the Soviet Union was winning the space race during the Cold War.

summa cum laude graduating from an educational institution with high distinction.

surfactants surface-active substances such as detergent.

synchrotron an apparatus for imparting very high speeds to charged particles by means of combining high-frequency electric fields and low-frequency electric fields.

Tae Kwan Doe Korean martial art resembling karate.

tai chi an ancient Chinese form of meditative movements practiced as exercises.

Tamil Dravidian language of Tamil Nadu state in eastern Ceylon.

TelePrompter a machine used by television personalities and speechmakers; the device unrolls a magnetic script in front of the speaker.

think tank organization of intellectuals who write and propose policy for consideration by lawmakers.

timorous fearful or timid; reluctant to change.

transcend to go beyond the limits or rise above something.

trepidation fears or concerns.

tuberculosis a communicable disease in humans and some vertebrates caused by the tubercle bacillus and characterized by toxic symptoms or allergies in the lungs.

valorous courageous; brave.

vanguard the forefront of a movement or action.

vaudeville a stage performance consisting of acting, singing, and dancing.

veto official rejection of a law passed by a legislature by the executive in a representative democracy.

Viet Cong soldiers in the North Vietnamese armed forces during the Vietnam War.

virologist a scientist studying viruses.

virtuoso superior technical skill in a fine art.

vivacious lively in spirit, conduct, and temper.

voracious enthusiastic; intense.

WTO World Trade Organization.

wanderlust urge to travel frequently without settling in one place for any significant length of time.

white blood cells blood cells without hemoglobin.

Zen a Japanese sect of Buddhism aiming at enlightenment through meditation.

Index